CORNERSTONE
BIBLICAL
COMMENTARY

CORNERSTONE
BIBLICAL
COMMENTARY

Ezra-Nehemiah & Esther

Gary V. Smith

GENERAL EDITOR

Philip W. Comfort

featuring the text of the
NEW LIVING TRANSLATION

TYNDALE HOUSE PUBLISHERS, INC. CAROL STREAM, ILLINOIS

Cornerstone Biblical Commentary, Volume 5b

Visit Tyndale's exciting Web sites at www.newlivingtranslation.com and www.tyndale.com.

Ezra-Nehemiah copyright © 2010 by Gary V. Smith. All rights reserved.

Esther copyright © 2010 by Gary V. Smith. All rights reserved.

Designed by Luke Daab and Timothy R. Botts.

Library of Congress Cataloging-in-Publication Data

Cornerstone biblical commentary.
    p. cm.
    Includes bibliographical references and index.
    ISBN 978-1-4143-2207-0 (hc : alk. paper)
        1. Bible—Commentaries. I. Smith, Gary V.
BS491.3.C67 2006
220.7'7—dc22   2005026928

Printed in the United States of America

16   15   14   13   12   11   10
 7   6   5   4   3   2   1

CONTENTS

VOLUME 5b: EZRA-NEHEMIAH, ESTHER

Gary V. Smith
BA, Wheaton College;
MA, Trinity Evangelical Divinity School;
PhD, Dropsie College;
Professor of Christian Studies, Union University.

GENERAL EDITOR'S PREFACE

The *Cornerstone Biblical Commentary* is based on the second edition of the New Living Translation (2007). Nearly 100 scholars from various church backgrounds and from several countries (United States, Canada, England, and Australia) participated in the creation of the NLT. Many of these same scholars are contributors to this commentary series. All the commentators, whether participants in the NLT or not, believe that the Bible is God's inspired word and have a desire to make God's word clear and accessible to his people.

This Bible commentary is the natural extension of our vision for the New Living Translation, which we believe is both exegetically accurate and idiomatically powerful. The NLT attempts to communicate God's inspired word in a lucid English translation of the original languages so that English readers can understand and appreciate the thought of the original writers. In the same way, the *Cornerstone Biblical Commentary* aims at helping teachers, pastors, students, and laypeople understand every thought contained in the Bible. As such, the commentary focuses first on the words of Scripture, then on the theological truths of Scripture—inasmuch as the words express the truths.

The commentary itself has been structured in such a way as to help readers get at the meaning of Scripture, passage by passage, through the entire Bible. Each Bible book is prefaced by a substantial book introduction that gives general historical background important for understanding. Then the reader is taken through the Bible text, passage by passage, starting with the New Living Translation text printed in full. This is followed by a section called "Notes," wherein the commentator helps the reader understand the Hebrew or Greek behind the English of the NLT, interacts with other scholars on important interpretive issues, and points the reader to significant textual and contextual matters. The "Notes" are followed by the "Commentary," wherein each scholar presents a lucid interpretation of the passage, giving special attention to context and major theological themes.

The commentators represent a wide spectrum of theological positions within the evangelical community. We believe this is good because it reflects the rich variety in Christ's church. All the commentators uphold the authority of God's word and believe it is essential to heed the old adage: "Wholly apply yourself to the Scriptures and apply them wholly to you." May this commentary help you know the truths of Scripture, and may this knowledge help you "grow in your knowledge of God and Jesus our Lord" (2 Pet 1:2, NLT).

PHILIP W. COMFORT
GENERAL EDITOR

ABBREVIATIONS

GENERAL ABBREVIATIONS

b.	Babylonian Gemara	Heb.	Hebrew	NT	New Testament
bar.	baraita	ibid.	*ibidem,* in the same place	OL	Old Latin
c.	*circa,* around, approximately	i.e.	*id est,* the same	OS	Old Syriac
cf.	*confer,* compare	in loc.	*in loco,* in the place cited	OT	Old Testament
ch, chs	chapter, chapters	lit.	literally	p., pp.	page, pages
contra	in contrast to	LXX	Septuagint	pl.	plural
DSS	Dead Sea Scrolls	𝔐	Majority Text	Q	Quelle ("Sayings" as Gospel source)
ed.	edition, editor	*m.*	Mishnah	rev.	revision
e.g.	*exempli gratia,* for example	masc.	masculine	sg.	singular
et al.	*et alli,* and others	mg	margin	*t.*	Tosefta
fem.	feminine	ms	manuscript	TR	Textus Receptus
ff	following (verses, pages)	mss	manuscripts	v., vv.	verse, verses
fl.	flourished	MT	Masoretic Text	vid.	*videtur,* it seems
Gr.	Greek	n.d.	no date	viz.	*videlicet,* namely
		neut.	neuter	vol.	volume
		no.	number	*y.*	Jerusalem Gemara

ABBREVIATIONS FOR BIBLE TRANSLATIONS

ASV	American Standard Version	NCV	New Century Version	NKJV	New King James Version
CEV	Contemporary English Version	NEB	New English Bible	NRSV	New Revised Standard Version
ESV	English Standard Version	NET	The NET Bible	NLT	New Living Translation
GW	God's Word	NIV	New International Version	REB	Revised English Bible
HCSB	Holman Christian Standard Bible	NIrV	New International Reader's Version	RSV	Revised Standard Version
JB	Jerusalem Bible	NJB	New Jerusalem Bible	TEV	Today's English Version
KJV	King James Version	NJPS	New Jewish Publication Society Translation (*Tanakh*)	TLB	The Living Bible
NAB	New American Bible				
NASB	New American Standard Bible				

ABBREVIATIONS FOR DICTIONARIES, LEXICONS, COLLECTIONS OF TEXTS, ORIGINAL LANGUAGE EDITIONS

ABD *Anchor Bible Dictionary* (6 vols., Freedman) [1992]

ANEP *The Ancient Near East in Pictures* (Pritchard) [1965]

ANET *Ancient Near Eastern Texts Relating to the Old Testament* (Pritchard) [1969]

BAGD *Greek-English Lexicon of the New Testament and Other Early Christian Literature,* 2nd ed. (Bauer, Arndt, Gingrich, Danker) [1979]

BDAG *Greek-English Lexicon of the New Testament and Other Early Christian Literature,* 3rd ed. (Bauer, Danker, Arndt, Gingrich) [2000]

BDB *A Hebrew and English Lexicon of the Old Testament* (Brown, Driver, Briggs) [1907]

BDF *A Greek Grammar of the New Testament and Other Early Christian Literature* (Blass, Debrunner, Funk) [1961]

BHS *Biblia Hebraica Stuttgartensia* (Elliger and Rudolph) [1983]

CAD *Assyrian Dictionary of the Oriental Institute of the University of Chicago* [1956]

COS *The Context of Scripture* (3 vols., Hallo and Younger) [1997–2002]

DBI *Dictionary of Biblical Imagery* (Ryken, Wilhoit, Longman) [1998]

DBT *Dictionary of Biblical Theology* (2nd ed., Leon-Dufour) [1972]

DCH *Dictionary of Classical Hebrew* (5 vols., D. Clines) [2000]

DLNTD *Dictionary of the Later New Testament and Its Development* (R. Martin, P. Davids) [1997]

DJD *Discoveries in the Judean Desert* [1955–]

DJG *Dictionary of Jesus and the Gospels* (Green, McKnight, Marshall) [1992]

DOTP *Dictionary of the Old Testament: Pentateuch* (T. Alexander, D.W. Baker) [2003]

DPL *Dictionary of Paul and His Letters* (Hawthorne, Martin, Reid) [1993]

DTIB *Dictionary of Theological Interpretation of the Bible* (Vanhoozer) [2005]

EDNT *Exegetical Dictionary of the New Testament* (3 vols., H. Balz, G. Schneider. ET) [1990–1993]

GKC *Gesenius' Hebrew Grammar* (Gesenius, Kautzsch, trans. Cowley) [1910]

HALOT *The Hebrew and Aramaic Lexicon of the Old Testament* (L. Koehler, W. Baumgartner, J. Stamm; trans. M. Richardson) [1994–1999]

IBD *Illustrated Bible Dictionary* (3 vols., Douglas, Wiseman) [1980]

IDB *The Interpreter's Dictionary of the Bible* (4 vols., Buttrick) [1962]

ISBE *International Standard Bible Encyclopedia* (4 vols., Bromiley) [1979–1988]

KBL *Lexicon in Veteris Testamenti libros* (Koehler, Baumgartner) [1958]

LCL Loeb Classical Library

L&N *Greek-English Lexicon of the New Testament: Based on Semantic Domains* (Louw and Nida) [1989]

LSJ *A Greek-English Lexicon* (9th ed., Liddell, Scott, Jones) [1996]

MM *The Vocabulary of the Greek New Testament* (Moulton and Milligan) [1930; 1997]

NA[26] *Novum Testamentum Graece* (26th ed., Nestle-Aland) [1979]

NA[27] *Novum Testamentum Graece* (27th ed., Nestle-Aland) [1993]

NBD *New Bible Dictionary* (2nd ed., Douglas, Hillyer) [1982]

NIDB *New International Dictionary of the Bible* (Douglas, Tenney) [1987]

NIDBA *New International Dictionary of Biblical Archaeology* (Blaiklock and Harrison) [1983]

NIDNTT *New International Dictionary of New Testament Theology* (4 vols., C. Brown) [1975–1985]

NIDOTTE *New International Dictionary of Old Testament Theology and Exegesis* (5 vols., W. A. VanGemeren) [1997]

PG *Patrologia Graecae* (J. P. Migne) [1857–1886]

PGM *Papyri graecae magicae: Die griechischen Zauberpapyri.* (Preisendanz) [1928]

TBD *Tyndale Bible Dictionary* (Elwell, Comfort) [2001]

TDNT *Theological Dictionary of the New Testament* (10 vols., Kittel, Friedrich; trans. Bromiley) [1964–1976]

TDOT *Theological Dictionary of the Old Testament* (8 vols., Botterweck, Ringgren; trans. Willis, Bromiley, Green) [1974–]

TLNT *Theological Lexicon of the New Testament* (3 vols., C. Spicq) [1994]

TLOT *Theological Lexicon of the Old Testament* (3 vols., E. Jenni) [1997]

TWOT *Theological Wordbook of the Old Testament* (2 vols., Harris, Archer) [1980]

UBS[3] *United Bible Societies' Greek New Testament* (3rd ed., Metzger et al.) [1975]

UBS[4] *United Bible Societies' Greek New Testament* (4th corrected ed., Metzger et al.) [1993]

WH *The New Testament in the Original Greek* (Westcott and Hort) [1882]

ABBREVIATIONS FOR BOOKS OF THE BIBLE

Old Testament

Gen	Genesis	Deut	Deuteronomy	1 Sam	1 Samuel
Exod	Exodus	Josh	Joshua	2 Sam	2 Samuel
Lev	Leviticus	Judg	Judges	1 Kgs	1 Kings
Num	Numbers	Ruth	Ruth	2 Kgs	2 Kings

1 Chr	1 Chronicles	Song	Song of Songs	Obad	Obadiah
2 Chr	2 Chronicles	Isa	Isaiah	Jonah	Jonah
Ezra	Ezra	Jer	Jeremiah	Mic	Micah
Neh	Nehemiah	Lam	Lamentations	Nah	Nahum
Esth	Esther	Ezek	Ezekiel	Hab	Habakkuk
Job	Job	Dan	Daniel	Zeph	Zephaniah
Ps, Pss	Psalm, Psalms	Hos	Hosea	Hag	Haggai
Prov	Proverbs	Joel	Joel	Zech	Zechariah
Eccl	Ecclesiastes	Amos	Amos	Mal	Malachi

New Testament

Matt	Matthew	Eph	Ephesians	Heb	Hebrews
Mark	Mark	Phil	Philippians	Jas	James
Luke	Luke	Col	Colossians	1 Pet	1 Peter
John	John	1 Thess	1 Thessalonians	2 Pet	2 Peter
Acts	Acts	2 Thess	2 Thessalonians	1 John	1 John
Rom	Romans	1 Tim	1 Timothy	2 John	2 John
1 Cor	1 Corinthians	2 Tim	2 Timothy	3 John	3 John
2 Cor	2 Corinthians	Titus	Titus	Jude	Jude
Gal	Galatians	Phlm	Philemon	Rev	Revelation

Deuterocanonical

Bar	Baruch	1–2 Esdr	1–2 Esdras	Ps 151	Psalm 151
Add Dan	Additions to Daniel	Add Esth	Additions to Esther	Sir	Sirach
Pr Azar	Prayer of Azariah	Ep Jer	Epistle of Jeremiah	Tob	Tobit
Bel	Bel and the Dragon	Jdt	Judith	Wis	Wisdom of Solomon
Sg Three	Song of the Three Children	1–2 Macc	1–2 Maccabees		
		3–4 Macc	3–4 Maccabees		
Sus	Susanna	Pr Man	Prayer of Manasseh		

MANUSCRIPTS AND LITERATURE FROM QUMRAN

Initial numerals followed by "Q" indicate particular caves at Qumran. For example, the notation 4Q267 indicates text 267 from cave 4 at Qumran. Further, 1QS 4:9-10 indicates column 4, lines 9-10 of the *Rule of the Community*; and 4Q166 1 ii 2 indicates fragment 1, column ii, line 2 of text 166 from cave 4. More examples of common abbreviations are listed below.

CD	Cairo Geniza copy of the *Damascus Document*	1QIsa[b]	Isaiah copy [b]	4QLam[a]	Lamentations
		1QM	*War Scroll*	11QPs[a]	Psalms
		1QpHab	*Pesher Habakkuk*	11QTemple[a,b]	*Temple Scroll*
1QH	*Thanksgiving Hymns*	1QS	*Rule of the Community*	11QtgJob	*Targum of Job*
1QIsa[a]	Isaiah copy [a]				

IMPORTANT NEW TESTAMENT MANUSCRIPTS

(all dates given are AD; ordinal numbers refer to centuries)

Significant Papyri ($\mathfrak{P}$ = Papyrus)

$\mathfrak{P}$1 Matt 1; early 3rd
$\mathfrak{P}$4+$\mathfrak{P}$64+$\mathfrak{P}$67 Matt 3, 5, 26; Luke 1–6; late 2nd
$\mathfrak{P}$5 John 1, 16, 20; early 3rd
$\mathfrak{P}$13 Heb 2–5, 10–12; early 3rd
$\mathfrak{P}$15+$\mathfrak{P}$16 (probably part of same codex) 1 Cor 7–8, Phil 3–4; late 3rd
$\mathfrak{P}$20 Jas 2–3; 3rd
$\mathfrak{P}$22 John 15–16; mid 3rd
$\mathfrak{P}$23 Jas 1; c. 200
$\mathfrak{P}$27 Rom 8–9; 3rd
$\mathfrak{P}$30 1 Thess 4–5; 2 Thess 1; early 3rd
$\mathfrak{P}$32 Titus 1–2; late 2nd
$\mathfrak{P}$37 Matt 26; late 3rd
$\mathfrak{P}$39 John 8; first half of 3rd
$\mathfrak{P}$40 Rom 1–4, 6, 9; 3rd

𝔓45 Gospels and Acts; early 3rd
𝔓46 Paul's Major Epistles (less Pastorals); late 2nd
𝔓47 Rev 9–17; 3rd
𝔓49+𝔓65 Eph 4–5; 1 Thess 1–2; 3rd
𝔓52 John 18; c. 125
𝔓53 Matt 26, Acts 9–10; middle 3rd

𝔓66 John; late 2nd
𝔓70 Matt 2–3, 11–12, 24; 3rd
𝔓72 1–2 Peter, Jude; c. 300
𝔓74 Acts, General Epistles; 7th
𝔓75 Luke and John; c. 200
𝔓77+𝔓103 (probably part of same codex) Matt 13–14, 23; late 2nd
𝔓87 Philemon; late 2nd

𝔓90 John 18–19; late 2nd
𝔓91 Acts 2–3; 3rd
𝔓92 Eph 1, 2 Thess 1; c. 300
𝔓98 Rev 1:13-20; late 2nd
𝔓100 Jas 3–5; c. 300
𝔓101 Matt 3–4; 3rd
𝔓104 Matt 21; 2nd
𝔓106 John 1; 3rd
𝔓115 Rev 2–3, 5–6, 8–15; 3rd

Significant Uncials

א (Sinaiticus) most of NT; 4th
A (Alexandrinus) most of NT; 5th
B (Vaticanus) most of NT; 4th
C (Ephraemi Rescriptus) most of NT with many lacunae; 5th
D (Bezae) Gospels, Acts; 5th
D (Claromontanus), Paul's Epistles; 6th (different MS than Bezae)
E (Laudianus 35) Acts; 6th
F (Augensis) Paul's Epistles; 9th
G (Boernerianus) Paul's Epistles; 9th

H (Coislinianus) Paul's Epistles; 6th
I (Freerianus or Washington) Paul's Epistles; 5th
L (Regius) Gospels; 8th
P (Porphyrianus) Acts— Revelation; 9th
Q (Guelferbytanus B) Luke, John; 5th
T (Borgianus) Luke, John; 5th
W (Washingtonianus or the Freer Gospels) Gospels; 5th
Z (Dublinensis) Matthew; 6th
037 (Δ; Sangallensis) Gospels; 9th

038 (Θ; Koridethi) Gospels; 9th
040 (Ξ; Zacynthius) Luke; 6th
043 (Φ; Beratinus) Matthew, Mark; 6th
044 (Ψ; Athous Laurae) Gospels, Acts, Paul's Epistles; 9th
048 Acts, Paul's Epistles, General Epistles; 5th
0171 Matt 10, Luke 22; c. 300
0189 Acts 5; c. 200

Significant Minuscules

1 Gospels, Acts, Paul's Epistles; 12th
33 All NT except Rev; 9th
81 Acts, Paul's Epistles, General Epistles; 1044
565 Gospels; 9th
700 Gospels; 11th

1424 (or Family 1424—a group of 29 manuscripts sharing nearly the same text) most of NT; 9th-10th
1739 Acts, Paul's Epistles; 10th
2053 Rev; 13th
2344 Rev; 11th

f¹ (a family of manuscripts including 1, 118, 131, 209) Gospels; 12th-14th
f¹³ (a family of manuscripts including 13, 69, 124, 174, 230, 346, 543, 788, 826, 828, 983, 1689, 1709— known as the Ferrar group) Gospels; 11th-15th

Significant Ancient Versions

SYRIAC (SYR)
syrᶜ (Syriac Curetonian) Gospels; 5th
syrˢ (Syriac Sinaiticus) Gospels; 4th
syrʰ (Syriac Harklensis) Entire NT; 616

OLD LATIN (IT)
itᵃ (Vercellenis) Gospels; 4th
itᵇ (Veronensis) Gospels; 5th
itᵈ (Cantabrigiensis—the Latin text of Bezae) Gospels, Acts, 3 John; 5th
itᵉ (Palantinus) Gospels; 5th
itᵏ (Bobiensis) Matthew, Mark; c. 400

COPTIC (COP)
copᵇᵒ (Boharic—north Egypt)
copᶠᵃʸ (Fayyumic—central Egypt)
copˢᵃ (Sahidic—southern Egypt)

OTHER VERSIONS
arm (Armenian)
eth (Ethiopic)
geo (Georgian)

TRANSLITERATION AND NUMBERING SYSTEM

Note: For words and roots from nonbiblical languages (e.g., Arabic, Ugaritic), only approximate transliterations are given.

HEBREW/ARAMAIC

Consonants

א	aleph	= '	מ, ם	mem	= m
ב, בּ	beth	= b	נ, ן	nun	= n
ג, גּ	gimel	= g	ס	samekh	= s
ד, דּ	daleth	= d	ע	ayin	= '
ה	he	= h	פ, פּ, ף	pe	= p
ו	waw	= w	צ, ץ	tsadhe	= ts
ז	zayin	= z	ק	qoph	= q
ח	heth	= kh	ר	resh	= r
ט	teth	= t	שׁ	shin	= sh
י	yodh	= y	שׂ	sin	= s
כ, כּ, ך	kaph	= k	ת, תּ	taw	= t, *th* (spirant)
ל	lamedh	= l			

Vowels

ַ	patakh	= a		qamets khatuf	= o
ֲ	furtive patakh	= a		holem	= o
ָ	qamets	= a	וֹ	full holem	= o
ָה	final qamets he	= ah		short qibbuts	= u
ֶ	segol	= e		long qibbuts	= u
ֵ	tsere	= e	וּ	shureq	= u
ֵי	tsere yod	= e		khatef patakh	= a
ִ	short hireq	= i		khatef qamets	= o
ִ	long hireq	= i		vocalic shewa	= e
ִי	hireq yod	= i		patakh yodh	= a

GREEK

α	alpha	= a	ι	iota	= i
β	beta	= b	κ	kappa	= k
γ	gamma	= g, n *(before* γ, κ, ξ, χ*)*	λ	lamda	= l
			μ	mu	= m
δ	delta	= d	ν	nu	= n
ε	epsilon	= e	ξ	ksi	= x
ζ	zeta	= z	ο	omicron	= o
η	eta	= ē	π	pi	= p
θ	theta	= th	ρ	rho	= r (ῥ = rh)

σ, ς	*sigma*	= *s*		ψ	*psi*	= *ps*
τ	*tau*	= *t*		ω	*omega*	= *ō*
υ	*upsilon*	= *u*	ʽ		*rough*	= *h (with*
φ	*phi*	= *ph*			*breathing*	*vowel or*
χ	*chi*	= *ch*			*mark*	*diphthong)*

THE TYNDALE-STRONG'S NUMBERING SYSTEM

The Cornerstone Biblical Commentary series uses a word-study numbering system to give both newer and more advanced Bible students alike quicker, more convenient access to helpful original-language tools (e.g., concordances, lexicons, and theological dictionaries). Those who are unfamiliar with the ancient Hebrew, Aramaic, and Greek alphabets can quickly find information on a given word by looking up the appropriate index number. Advanced students will find the system helpful because it allows them to quickly find the lexical form of obscure conjugations and inflections.

There are two main numbering systems used for biblical words today. The one familiar to most people is the Strong's numbering system (made popular by the *Strong's Exhaustive Concordance to the Bible*). Although the original Strong's system is still quite useful, the most up-to-date research has shed new light on the biblical languages and allows for more precision than is found in the original Strong's system. The Cornerstone Biblical Commentary series, therefore, features a newly revised version of the Strong's system, the Tyndale-Strong's numbering system. The Tyndale-Strong's system brings together the familiarity of the Strong's system and the best of modern scholarship. In most cases, the original Strong's numbers are preserved. In places where new research dictates, new or related numbers have been added.[1]

The second major numbering system today is the Goodrick-Kohlenberger system used in a number of study tools published by Zondervan. In order to give students broad access to a number of helpful tools, the Commentary provides index numbers for the Zondervan system as well.

The different index systems are designated as follows:

TG	Tyndale-Strong's Greek number	ZH	Zondervan Hebrew number
ZG	Zondervan Greek number	TA/ZA	Tyndale/Zondervan Aramaic number
TH	Tyndale-Strong's Hebrew number	S	Strong's Aramaic number

So in the example, "love" *agapē* [^{TG}26, ^{ZG}27], the first number is the one to use with Greek tools keyed to the Tyndale-Strong's system, and the second applies to tools that use the Zondervan system.

The indexing of Aramaic terms differs slightly from that of Greek and Hebrew. Strong's original system mixed the Aramaic terms in with the Hebrew, but the Tyndale-Strong's system indexes Aramaic with a new set of numbers starting at 10,000. Since Tyndale's system for Aramaic diverges completely from original Strong's, the original Strong's number is listed separately so that those using tools keyed to Strong's can locate the information. This number is designated with an S, as in the example, "son" *bar* [$^{TA/ZA}$10120, ^{S}1247].

---

1. Generally, one may simply use the original four-digit Strong's number to identify words in tools using Strong's system. If a Tyndale-Strong's number is followed by a capital letter (e.g., ^{TG}1692A), it generally indicates an added subdivision of meaning for the given term. Whenever a Tyndale-Strong's number has a number following a decimal point (e.g., ^{TG}2013.1), it reflects an instance where new research has yielded a separate, new classification of use for a biblical word. Forthcoming tools from Tyndale House Publishers will include these entries, which were not part of the original Strong's system.

Ezra-Nehemiah

GARY V. SMITH

INTRODUCTION TO
Ezra-Nehemiah

EZRA-NEHEMIAH PRESENTS US with a theological record concerning the Hebrew people who, beginning in 538 BC, returned from the Babylonian exile to Jerusalem, rebuilt the Temple (515 BC), rebuilt Jerusalem's wall (445 BC), and continued as a community in Judah. This is not a record of dry ancient events; it is rather a testimony to the fulfillment of God's sovereign plan for his covenant people and his powerful control over every aspect of Israel's history. Many people in Jerusalem wondered if there was any hope for them: Judah had been destroyed by the Babylonians. It was now a small and impotent province in the vast Persian Empire facing opposition to its development by political opponents. Sorrow, joy, and hope filled people's lives as they endured this difficult yet exciting period in the history of Israel. The most important occasions prompted Ezra and Nehemiah to keep "memoirs" of what God was accomplishing among the people during their ministries to reform and restore Jerusalem (458–430 BC). In spite of sinful mistakes of the past, the people would again commit to be separate from the unholy ways of the pagan people around them. God would intervene marvelously on their behalf, even through pagan kings, for the postexilic community was an important continuation of God's chosen people.

AUTHOR

Ezra-Nehemiah does not indicate who wrote it. Some of the earliest traditions in the Babylonian Talmud (*Bava Batra* 15a) state that Ezra wrote 1–2 Chronicles and Ezra-Nehemiah. Josephus's method of counting the biblical books in the Hebrew canon implies that his Scriptures had Ezra-Nehemiah as one undivided book (*Against Apion* 1.38-40). No one can be exactly sure how he divided the 13 books that are not part of the four "divine poems" (Wisdom books and Psalms) or the five books that describe history from "creation to the death of Moses" (the Pentateuch). It is most likely that the 13 books Josephus refers to include five prophetic books (Isaiah, Jeremiah-Lamentations, Ezekiel, Daniel, and the Twelve Minor Prophets) and eight historical books (Joshua, Judges, Ruth, Samuel, Kings, Chronicles, Ezra-Nehemiah, and Esther). Eusebius quoted Melito of Sardis (second century AD) who referred to all the material in Ezra-Nehemiah as the work of Ezra (*Ecclesiastical History* 4.26.14). Since Nehemiah 3:32 was marked as the middle verse of the book, we know that the Masoretic scholars treated Ezra-Nehemiah as one book. In addition, the Septuagint (LXX) treats them as one unified book. Origen (third century AD) mentioned that Ezra-Nehemiah was one book in the Hebrew Bible (Eusebius *Ecclesiastical History* 6.25.2), but he knew of the separation of Ezra and Nehemiah in certain Greek traditions. Jerome divided the text into two books of Ezra in the Vulgate, but the division of the text into two books did not enter into Jewish tradition until the Middle Ages.

This information leads to one conclusion, but it raises an interrelated problem. First, the evidence from the manuscripts and tradition most naturally point to the conclusion that one person wrote/edited both Ezra and Nehemiah, not two people. This person who edited the book used original documents (often called "memoirs") that were written by Ezra (Ezra 7–10; Neh 8–10) and Nehemiah (Neh 1–7, 11–13), plus official government letters (Ezra 4:11-16, 17-22; 5:7-17; 6:2-5, 6-12; 7:12-26) to compose the present book. Often the official letters are presented in their original Aramaic (Ezra 4–6), rather than in a Hebrew translation. Aramaic was the administrative language of the Persian government under which the letters were composed.

For many years commentators supported the idea that the same person wrote both Chronicles and Ezra-Nehemiah (see Fensham 1982:2-4). The support for this theory hinges on four facts:

1. The book of Chronicles ends with the same verses that begin the book of Ezra (cf. 2 Chr 36:22-23 and Ezra 1:1-2).
2. The apocryphal book of 1 Esdras begins with 2 Chronicles 35–36 and continues right into Ezra without a break.
3. These books have common vocabulary and stylistic characteristics.
4. Chronicles and Ezra-Nehemiah have a similar theological perspective.

Those who connect Chronicles and Ezra-Nehemiah usually refer to the editor of this material as "the Chronicler." This theory suggests that he collected the memoirs of Ezra and Nehemiah, several genealogies, and some sources similar to Samuel and Kings, then edited them together into the present books. Some hold the view that this editor distorted the facts by inserting his own theological perspective, while others think he faithfully used his sources (Fensham 1982:2-4).[1]

The theory that there was one author of both Chronicles and Ezra-Nehemiah was seriously undermined when S. Japhet demonstrated 36 significant linguistic and stylistic differences between Chronicles and Ezra-Nehemiah (1968:331-332). R. Braun (1979:52-54) found that the theology of Chronicles had a unique perspective based on a strong concept of retribution (this is mostly absent from Ezra), an inclusive attitude toward foreigners (Ezra and Nehemiah support separation from foreigners), little emphasis on the Exodus tradition (it is stronger in Ezra-Nehemiah), and an emphasis on the Davidic line. Allen (2003:9) found (1) an exilic concept of Israel as exiles in Ezra-Nehemiah (Neh 11:4), in contrast to Chronicles' view of Israel as the 12 tribes (1 Chr 9:3); (2) no royal eschatology in Ezra-Nehemiah, in contrast to Chronicles; (3) a different view of God's wrath on Israel; (4) an emphasis on the Exodus in Ezra-Nehemiah, but an emphasis on David-Solomon in Chronicles; and (5) an omission of Solomon's failures in Chronicles, but an admission of them in Nehemiah 13:26. These differences bear directly on points 3 and 4 given above in support of a single-author view and suggest that the author of Chronicles did *not* write Ezra-Nehemiah.

Though the text does not name an author/editor of Ezra-Nehemiah, Ezra is a possible candidate because he was a skilled scribe and was not as busy with administrative duties as Nehemiah. Favoring this idea, the Ezra sections (commonly called the Ezra Memoirs) in Ezra 7–10 and Nehemiah 8–10 contain detailed lists (Ezra 8:1-14; 10:18-44; Neh 10:1-27), prayers (Ezra 9:6-15; Neh 9:6-37), and several official documents (Ezra 7:12-26; 8:26-27) that have the appearance of first-hand knowledge. In addition, the Nehemiah Memoirs (Neh 1–7; 11–13) and other documents from Nehemiah's work would have likely been available to Ezra. The only serious objection to Ezra's potential authorship is his age. Since the lists of priests and rulers (cf. Ezra 8:1-14; 10:18-44; Neh 10:1-27) extend down to around 405 BC, Ezra must have finished writing the last section of this material when he was quite old (Yamauchi 1988:577). If one assumes he was 40 years old in 458 BC when he came to Jerusalem, he would have been 93 in 405 BC; however, this is not an impossibly old age. Further, if Ezra was 25 when he moved to Jerusalem, then he would have been only 78 in 405 BC. Those who object to this possibility usually suggest that some unknown editor put the memoirs of Ezra and Nehemiah together at a later date.

Since a good deal of evidence seems to point in the direction that Ezra was probably the author/editor of these memoirs, this commentary will assume that Ezra was the person responsible for putting the book of Ezra-Nehemiah together for posterity. It should be noted, however, that the historical value or inspiration of these books does not stand or fall on the basis of this conclusion.

DATE OF WRITING

A key issue in determining the date of Ezra-Nehemiah is the order of Ezra's and Nehemiah's ministries and which kings they served under (Artaxerxes I or Artaxerxes II). Although it appears that Ezra came to Jerusalem in 458 BC (Ezra 7:7), about 13 years before Nehemiah (in 445 BC; Neh 2:1), some biblical scholars think Nehemiah actually began his ministry first.[2] Ezra is placed later by arguing that he served under Artaxerxes II (404–359 BC) rather than Artaxerxes I, or by emending the "seventh" year in Ezra 7:7 (458 BC) to the "thirty-seventh" year (428 BC) of Artaxerxes I. Williamson (1985:xxxix) thinks Ezra's ministry lasted about one year and that the ministries of Ezra and Nehemiah did not overlap. Some of the reasons for suggesting that Nehemiah came before Ezra are as follows:

1. Jerusalem was populated when Ezra came (Ezra 10:1), but few lived there in Nehemiah's day (Neh 7:4; 11:1). Thus, Nehemiah must have been earlier.
2. Nehemiah's list of people in Nehemiah 7 does not include some of the names of the people who came with Ezra (Ezra 8:1-14). This may indicate that Ezra came later.
3. Eliashib was the high priest in the time of Nehemiah (Neh 3:1), but Jehohanan his son was priest in the time of Ezra (Ezra 10:6).
4. Since Ezra gave thanks for the walls of Jerusalem (Ezra 9:9), Nehemiah must have already rebuilt the walls of Jerusalem.
5. Nehemiah's reform (Neh 8–10) would not be needed if Ezra had carried out his reform a few years earlier.
6. Because of political unrest in Egypt and the Persian army's march to Palestine in 458 BC, it seems unlikely that the king would send Ezra at that time.[3]

None of these arguments are conclusive, for the populations of cities rise and fall over a 20-year period for many political and economic reasons (point 1), arguments from silence cannot prove anything (point 2), Jehohanan was a priest but the text does not say he was a priest in Ezra's time (point 3), Ezra's thanksgiving was not for the completed wall around Jerusalem but for God who was a metaphorical wall around "Judah and Jerusalem" (point 4), and carrying out two similar reforms 15 years apart gives plenty of time for people to slide back into the same sins (point 5). Since none of these issues conclusively require Ezra to be put after Nehemiah, it seems best to accept the present canonical ordering as correct. Although every interpretation must recognize that Ezra-Nehemiah has some chapters out of chronological order, the evidence does not support changing the order of Ezra and Nehemiah or their ministries. The author's purpose in writing Ezra-Nehemiah seems to have been dominated more by thematic and theological issues rather than any attempt to reproduce an exact chronological history of the period. This commentary and its discussion of the date of composition for Ezra-Nehemiah are therefore based on the conclusion that Ezra came to Jerusalem first and that his ministry overlapped with Nehemiah's.

The dates of the events mentioned in Ezra include those of Cyrus's decree in the first year of his reign (539/538 BC) in Ezra 1:1-2, the second year of Darius I (520 BC) in Ezra 4:24, and the seventh year of Artaxerxes I (458 BC) in Ezra 7:7. These dates do not cover the complete ministry of Ezra, however, for he appeared again in the midst of Nehemiah's work (Neh 8) and after the complete rebuilding of the city walls in Nehemiah 12:36 (445 BC). Nehemiah's ministry in Jerusalem extended from the twentieth year of Artaxerxes I in Nehemiah 1:1 (445 BC) until around 432 BC (Neh 13:6). Later, after a short time in Persia, Nehemiah returned to Jerusalem, but no precise date is given (Neh 13:7). The date when the author composed these books is unknown, but internal data suggest a date a few years before 400 BC. Those who place Ezra's ministry sometime after Nehemiah (in the time of Artaxerxes II rather than Artaxerxes I) often see a later, unknown redactor editing this material. Such an approach places the writing of the book in the early Hellenistic period, around 300 BC (Williamson 1985:xxxvi).

OCCASION OF WRITING

The things described in Ezra-Nehemiah are not just dry ancient events; instead, they are the fulfillment of God's sovereign plan for his covenant people. They involved real people in disastrous circumstances, where people were killed, as well as in happy situations, where people had the joy of returning to the homeland of their forefathers. Sorrow, joy, and hope filled people's lives as they endured this difficult period in the history of Israel. These occasions prompted Ezra and Nehemiah to keep "memoirs" of what God was accomplishing among the people, which were then used by the author/editor (perhaps Ezra) in his composition of the book. The content of Ezra-Nehemiah can be divided into two historical time periods: (1) events before the time of Ezra and Nehemiah—the Hebrews returned to Jerusalem and rebuilt the Temple (539–516 BC)—and (2) the ministries of Ezra and Nehemiah—the reform and restoration of Jerusalem (458–430 BC). Together,

these two sections span about 120 years of historical events and theological decisions in the life of the nation, but only a few important events are explained from
each era. The first 33 years of the nation's life after its return from exile are traced
in Ezra 1–6, but nothing is said about the next 60 years. Then a few selected events
are recounted from the 28 years when Ezra and Nehemiah were both in Jerusalem
(Ezra 7—Neh 13). Below, historical background will be given for each of the two
periods along with comments on the reasons for its inclusion in Ezra-Nehemiah.

Long before the ministries of Ezra and Nehemiah actually began, the nation of
Judah was captured three times by the Babylonian king Nebuchadnezzar (2 Kgs
25). After Jerusalem was defeated, large groups (cf. 2 Kgs 24:14, 16; 25:11; Jer 39:9;
52:15) of Hebrew people were marched into foreign lands in 605, 597, and finally
in 587/586 BC. The Bible does not say a whole lot about what these people endured
in Babylonian captivity. Jeremiah 29:4-5 suggests they were able to build their own
homes, have a garden, and live a fairly normal life. Ezekiel lived in a Jewish community near the Kebar Canal, probably about 50 miles southeast of Babylon and not
far from the city of Nippur (Ezek 1:1-3). At this place, the Hebrew elders were able
to meet periodically with Ezekiel (Ezek 8:1; 14:1; 20:1), so the people enjoyed some
religious freedom. Some educated Hebrew men were even recruited and trained to
fill high positions in the Babylonian government. Daniel and his three friends were
able to practice their faith freely most of the time, but there were brief periods of
persecution (Dan 3; 6).

God predicted through the prophet Jeremiah that this captivity would last only
70 years (Jer 25:12; 29:10), so the people were not without some hope during
these dark days of exile. In the first year of Cyrus's reign, the prophet Daniel prayed
for national forgiveness and restoration because he realized that this period of
70 years was about to end (Dan 9:2). Shortly after this, God stirred up the heart
of King Cyrus, and he put out a decree that allowed the exiles to return and build
the Temple in Jerusalem (Ezra 1:1-4). When this happened, many Jewish people
were settled in their homes and were doing well in their businesses in Babylon,
so they chose not to return to the ruined city of Jerusalem. Little is known about
the people who stayed in Babylon, but the books of Ezra and Nehemiah describe
what God did among those exiled people of Judah who left Babylon and returned
to Jerusalem. God fulfilled his promises and prepared the way for them to restore
Jerusalem and the worship of God at the Temple.

Ezra 1:1 dates the beginning of these events to the first year of the reign of Cyrus
king of Persia (538 BC), less than a year after Babylon was defeated on October 29,
539 BC. According to documents from the time of Nabonidus (ANET 306, 562-563)
and the Cyrus Cylinder (ANET 315-316), Nabonidus, the last king of Babylon, and
his son Belshazzar (Dan 5) were not popular rulers because they rejected the religion and priests of the god Marduk and favored the worship of the moon god Sin
at the temples in Ur and Haran. According to these documents, Cyrus, the powerful
ruler over the Medes and Persians, attacked and quickly defeated Babylon without
much of a fight (ANET 306, 315-316). Once in charge, Cyrus allowed all the different ethnic groups exiled in Babylon to go back to their homelands. Sheshbazzar was
the leader of about 50,000 Hebrew people (Ezra 1:8; 2:64-65). Thus the Hebrews
returned to Jerusalem and built the Temple during the years 539–516 BC.

It is difficult to estimate the exact number of people who were in the Babylonian exile at this time. E. Yamauchi (1988:567-568) lists a number of scholarly guesses, but they range from 50,000 to 235,000. Yamauchi thinks that 150,000 is about right; thus, only one-third of those in exile went back to Jerusalem in response to Cyrus's decree (Ezra 1:8; 2:64-65; 5:14). Once in Jerusalem, these people built an altar and worshiped God (Ezra 3:3). Then they began to repair the foundations of the Temple itself (Ezra 3:7-10). When the leaders of the Hebrews refused to let the people of the land (foreigners whom Esarhaddon had deported there—see Ezra 4:2) help them rebuild the Temple, the local residents started trouble and told the Persians that the Hebrews were going to rebel against the king (Ezra 4:1-23). This caused the work on the Temple to stop for over 15 years, until the second year of Darius I (reigned 522–486 BC; see Ezra 4:24). Although this frustrating delay tried the patience of many, God used the prophets Haggai and Zechariah to challenge the people to finish rebuilding the Temple.

The beginning of Darius's reign was filled with conflict, so the attempt to restart the construction of the Temple was filled with problems. Cambyses (530–522 BC), the king before Darius I, was fighting a war in Egypt when news came that someone had taken over the government of Persia while he was away from the capital. Cambyses decided to return to his capital and retake his throne, but mysteriously died on his way home. The Greek historian Herodotus reported that Cambyses was accidentally cut with his own sword and died of the severe injuries, but this may be a cover-up for a more sinister plot of assassination (*Histories* 3.64). Darius I then rose to power but had to deal with a series of revolts for the first year and a half of his reign (Hoglund 1992:24). Once order was established, Darius I set out to establish a system of satraps over large areas of the country, governors over regional provinces, and military commanders to keep order in the vast Persian Empire. This reorganization brought new stability to the diverse Persian kingdom.[4] Under this system, Tattenai was the satrap over the province west of the Euphrates River (Ezra 5:3), and Sheshbazzar was the local governor in Yehud (Judah).

After these revolts were put down, the people of Judah appealed for permission to begin rebuilding the Temple in Jerusalem as Cyrus had decreed many years earlier. Officials under Darius I found Cyrus's original document in the archives of the Persian fortress at Ecbatana (Ezra 6:1-5). It gave the Jewish people permission to rebuild the Temple. With the discovery of this official document, Darius I not only allowed the people of Judah to build the Temple in Jerusalem unhindered by their enemies, but he actually offered to pay the full cost of building the Temple from royal taxes (Ezra 6:7-8). In four years the Temple was completed (516/515 BC; see Ezra 6:15). This illustrates the Persians' tolerance (and even promotion) of different religious beliefs outside their own Zoroastrian belief in the god Ahura Mazda (see Boyce 1982).

Although the exact date when Ezra wrote of these historical events is unknown, a central part of his political and religious reform movement was based on reminding his audience about their historical and religious roots. He wanted his audience to see the hand of God at work in their lives and to encourage them to separate themselves from the pagan people they were marrying; the story of their ancestors' efforts to build the Temple and their willingness to separate themselves from their pagan neighbors provided an inspiring example of such attitudes and actions for his listeners. As the author/editor, Ezra wrote about these historical events to teach the wayward Jews, who had lost their sense of community and dedication to God, that God required them to live according to his covenant stipulations in the Torah. Ezra's method of editing provides a theological emphasis on separation from pagans in chapter 9 and explains why he chose to preface news about his own spiritual reform with information about the nation's earlier commitment to be separate from the half-pagan people of the land (Ezra 4:1-5).

The next group of materials written in Ezra-Nehemiah describes the period of reform and restoration under Ezra and Nehemiah that occurred during the reign of Artaxerxes I (464–424 BC). Early in his reign, Artaxerxes I struggled to keep control of the distant ends of his empire in Greece and especially in Egypt. These instabilities encouraged the king to entrust Ezra and Nehemiah with the difficult task of establishing a secure and stable society in the neighboring province of Yehud so that the Egyptian troubles would not spread elsewhere in the empire. Ezra the scribe was made responsible for obtaining funds for his work from the treasurer of the province west of the Euphrates River (Ezra 7:21) and was given the power to exempt Temple workers and priests from state taxation (Ezra 7:24), appoint judges for the courts (Ezra 7:25), teach people the laws of the land, and severely punish those who refused to follow those laws (Ezra 7:26). When Ezra found out that many of the leaders and priests had intermarried with pagan people from surrounding nations, he prayed for forgiveness and helped the people institute a lifestyle that was consistent with the law of God (Ezra 9:1–10:44).

Later, when Nehemiah arrived in the twentieth year of Artaxerxes I (445 BC; see Neh 1:1; 2:1), the ruined walls of Jerusalem were rebuilt in 52 days (Neh 3–6). More theological reform continued when Ezra read God's law to the people and promoted the reestablishment of the Festival of Shelters (Neh 8–10). After Nehemiah organized and repopulated the city of Jerusalem (Neh 11–12), he returned to the Persian capital in Susa to give a report to the king concerning his accomplishments (Neh 13:6). Later, he returned to Jerusalem and carried out additional reforms (Neh 13:6-30). In 12:22 Nehemiah mentions "Darius the Persian," which probably means Darius II (423–404 BC), but it is difficult to know how long Nehemiah's ministry lasted.

The occasion for writing the Ezra Memoirs in Ezra 7–10, plus the entire record of Nehemiah's ministry, is tied to the nature of the ministries of these men. Ezra clearly stated that his purpose in life as a Levitical scribe was "to study and obey the Law of the LORD and to teach those decrees and regulations to the people" (Ezra 7:10). Nehemiah's purpose was to rebuild the walls of Jerusalem so that the disgrace of the nation could be removed and God's name would again be honored (Neh 1:3; 2:3). In order to accomplish these goals, both men needed to address critical problems in the Jewish community. The memoirs of Ezra and Nehemiah were written during their service to justify their actions, to encourage people to support their reforms and building projects, and to motivate the people to maintain the social and religious standards of covenant life the community had agreed to. In addition, the Nehemiah Memoirs (Neh 1–7; 11–13) show how God continued to restore the vitality of his people in spite of repeated failures to separate themselves as a holy people.

In summary, this book is a testimony of what God did through the ministry of Ezra and Nehemiah. It served to (1) make future generations aware of the sinful mistakes of the past; (2) motivate people to be separate from the unholy ways of the pagan people around them; (3) illustrate the marvelous ways God sovereignly intervened on their behalf, even through pagan kings; (4) draw people back to the teaching of the word of God in the Torah; (5) reinforce the importance of the people's vows of devotion to God and the bold decisions of earlier generations to be separate; (6) testify to the concrete results the people achieved because there was unity and community dedication to mutually important tasks; and (7) show the postexilic community that they were an important continuation of God's chosen people. Hopefully the new generation of spiritual and political leaders would continue in the path established by Ezra and Nehemiah.

AUDIENCE
Ezra and Nehemiah addressed Persian kings (Neh 2) and their political enemies in Yehud (Ezra 4:1-4; 5:1-17; Neh 4:1-4; 6:1-14; 13:4-9), but most of the time these leaders were encouraging, organizing, or confronting the Jewish people who settled in Jerusalem. God directed both Ezra and Nehemiah to lead a group of people back to Jerusalem and to carry out political, social, and religious reforms among those living in Jerusalem. Apathy, greed, disorganization, compromise, unholy marriage relationships, and ignorance of the word of God characterized these people. When the people did not have strong leaders to challenge them to live holy lives that would honor God, some syncretized their faith with the pagan cultures around them. They needed to confess their sins, follow God's law, and boldly step forward to do the will of God.

When the whole book was completed, at some undefined date a few years after the active ministry of Ezra and Nehemiah, it was probably addressed to an audience of Jewish people in Judah who were struggling with how to remain faithful Jews while living in close proximity to foreign people. This required them to decide how to deal with mixed marriages and conduct proper worship, following the requirements of the Torah. Initially this might have included some of the same people or the children of the people Nehemiah addressed in Nehemiah 13:6-31.

CANONICITY AND TEXTUAL HISTORY
There never was much doubt about the canonicity of Ezra-Nehemiah, but the presence of apocryphal books called Esdras in the Old Greek (LXX) and the Latin Vulgate have created confusion concerning what exactly was to be included in the Canon. The confusion is caused because of apocryphal works assigned to Ezra (Esdras A and D). The chart below shows the relationships and overlapping material in these three traditions.[5]

LXX	VULGATE	ENGLISH
Esdras A	Esdras III	1 Esdras (in the Apocrypha)
Esdras B	Esdras I	Ezra
Esdras C	Esdras II	Nehemiah
Esdras D	Esdras IV	2 Esdras (cf. *4 Ezra* or *Ezra Apocalypse* [= 2 Esdras 3–14])

The title "Esdras" is the Greek rendering of Ezra. We do not know why Esdras D/ Esdras IV includes such diverse apocalyptic material. These apocryphal books were included in the Septuagint (LXX) and the Vulgate but were never included in the Hebrew canon. Throughout the Middle Ages, the Catholic tradition held Esdras III and Esdras IV in an intermediate position between canonical and spurious books, but the Council of Trent (AD 1546) relegated them to noncanonical status. As mentioned in the discussion under "Author," Ezra-Nehemiah was known in the early Hebrew manuscripts as one canonical book called Ezra. The oldest Greek manuscripts (codices Vaticanus, Sinaiticus, and Alexandrinus) also treat these as one canonical book. For some unknown reason, Ezra-Nehemiah was omitted from the canon of the Syrian Church.

The Hebrew and Aramaic text of Ezra-Nehemiah is well preserved, with only a few difficult textual problems (see the notes after each portion of text). The Hebrew has some unique syntactical constructions and vocabulary that mark it as a postexilic book (see Fensham 1982:22-23 for examples). In addition to the Persian names for the Persian monarchs, there are 14 or 15 Persian words that are employed over 40 times (mostly in the Aramaic documents written by Persian officials).[6] The official government documents included in Ezra 4:8–6:18 and 7:12-26 are written in Imperial Aramaic, the original language of these letters. The Dead Sea Scrolls include three fragments of Ezra-Nehemiah (Ezra 4:2-6 in Hebrew; 4:9-11 and 5:17–6:5 in Aramaic) that follow the Masoretic tradition quite closely (Blenkinsopp 1988:70-72).

LITERARY STYLE

The literary style of Ezra-Nehemiah is complex because the book contains letters that were not written by Ezra (see Ezra 4–6), draws from the memoirs of Nehemiah (Neh 1-7, 11–13), and includes several lists of people (see Ezra 2; 8; 10; Neh 7; 10–12). The author's use of quoted documents indicates a concern for authentic information and detailed accuracy, as well as a belief in the importance of each person (their names are meticulously recorded for posterity). If the author was Ezra, he no doubt based some of this information on his own personal involvement with Nehemiah's work during these years. The detailed lists of names were likely copied from Nehemiah's official reports to the Persian king Artaxerxes (Williamson 1985:xxvi). Such close dependence on written sources has inevitably influenced the style of these passages, although it is almost impossible to determine what words or phrases belong to the author of this book and which belong to the sources that were quoted. Some find a stylistic preference for a chiastic arrangement of verses and larger segments in these chapters (Throntveit 1992:6). Common structural sequencing of events within similar narratives also illustrates the author's style of creating parallel panels. This can be illustrated in a chart of Nehemiah 7–10 (Throntveit 1992:7).

	7:73b–8:12	8:13–18	9:1–10:39
A. Time	7:73b	8:13a	9:1a
B. People gather	8:1-2	8:13b	9:1b-2
C. Law read	8:3-6	8:13c	9:3
D. Call for action	8:7-11	8:14-15	9:4-37
E. People's response	8:12	8:16-18	9:38-10:39

Stylistic parallelism is also evident in the author's repetition of key ideas. Talmon (1976:322) notes how the author liked to insert a digression from the main point and then return to the main idea by repeating a key clause used just before the digression in a slightly different form. He gives four examples:

1. Ezra 4:5 is interrupted by the digression in 4:6-24a, and then the narrative is continued in 4:24b with the phrase "King Darius of Persia."
2. Ezra 6:16-22 is interrupted by the digression in 6:19-22a, and then the reference to "joy" is continued in 6:22b.
3. Ezra 2:1-70 is interrupted by the digression in 2:2-69, a long list of names, and then the progression of the story continues in 2:70 with the priests and Levites who returned setting up the altar to God.
4. Nehemiah 7:4–11:1 is interrupted by the digression that talks about the reform movement of Ezra in 7:73b–10:39, and then the story continues in 11:1 with what the people in 7:73a did next.

The careful presentation of the character of each main actor within the plot of the narratives is used to develop tension and the resolution of the problems faced by Ezra and Nehemiah. The brief notifications that some of the main characters offered a short prayer to God (e.g., Neh 1:5-11; 2:4b; 4:4-5, 9; 5:19; 6:9b, 14; 13:14, 22, 29, 31) form a significant stylistic and theological emphasis the author comes back to again and again.

Structure. Ezra 1–6 makes up the first major literary unit of Ezra-Nehemiah. These chapters form a separate section because they refer to historical events that occurred about 60 years before Ezra came to Jerusalem. They extend from Cyrus's decree to allow the Jews to return to Jerusalem in 538 BC to the completion of the Temple in 516 BC. These chapters set the theological stage for what happened in the time of Ezra-Nehemiah and are literarily connected to material later in the story (see the similar lists of returnees in Ezra 2 and Neh 7:6-73). Each section repeats the thematic pattern of (1) returning to Jerusalem, (2) facing opposition to God's work, and (3) the resolution of the problem by God's sovereign hand on a spiritual leader. This pattern is present in Ezra 1–6 when the people of the land oppose the building of the Temple and is repeated in Ezra 7–10 when Ezra returns to find people intermarried with foreigners. It also occurs again in Nehemiah 1–7 when Nehemiah comes to build the walls and in Nehemiah 13 when Nehemiah comes back to Jerusalem a second time. The contrast between these stories is that sometimes the opposition is from outside the Jewish nation, while at other times the problem arises because of the unfaithfulness of the covenant people themselves.

The end of Ezra 1–6 is marked by the successful resolution of the purpose of the first return (the building of the Temple) and is linguistically marked by the end of a section using the Aramaic language (Ezra 4:8–6:18). The themes in the first major subsection (Ezra 1–2) focus on the return of the exiles from Persia to Jerusalem. Opposition to the work of rebuilding the Temple is not present in this initial section. The focus is on God's stirring up Cyrus and moving some exiles to return (Ezra 1:1-5; 2:1-35) and on the provision of clergy, money, and utensils that would be needed to restart worship at the Temple (Ezra 1:6-11; 2:36-54, 68-70). The narrative ends with the people settled in their homes (Ezra 2:70), having enough resources to begin working on the Temple (Ezra 2:68-69).

The key theme in Ezra 3–4 is opposition to rebuilding the Temple and the walls of Jerusalem. The high hopes of restoring the kingdom of Judah with all its glory and its sacred religious institutions were not realized without considerable effort. The main stumbling block was the neighboring people who lived in the land. They saw this new group of Jews as a threat to their political and economic authority. They used Jerusalem's past rebellious history as a means to portray their actions in Yehud as an attempt at political freedom, and thus persuaded the Persians to counteract the Jews' ambition to attain religious separatism. This delayed the people's dream of setting up the Temple and restoring the city of Jerusalem. The enemies of the Jewish people were opposing two of the most important principles that defined this community of believers. They opposed the Jewish insistence on purity (Ezra 4:1-5) and their plan to resettle in the land God gave them (Ezra 4:12-16). Without purity and separation from pagan religious forces, their identity as the people of God would disappear. Without resettlement on their land, they could never live on the covenant inheritance God had given them.

Ezra 5–6 is centered on the sovereign plan of God (Ezra 5:5), explained by the prophets Haggai and Zechariah. They brought renewed hope to those who wanted to finish rebuilding the Temple (Ezra 5:1-2). Haggai's messages were about the people getting their priorities focused on glorifying God (Hag 1:8) and being holy (Hag 2:10-19), while Zechariah called the people to repentance (Zech 1:1-5). The content of their prophetic messages is not included in Ezra, but their impact motivated the Jewish leaders to overcome the political and spiritual roadblocks interfering with the completion of the Temple. The surprising Persian approval of the Temple rebuilding project, plus the removal of all opposition to it (Ezra 6:6-12), was an astonishing work of divine intervention. This led to a return of joy and the worship of God (as in Ezra 3) at the regular Jewish festivals (Ezra 6:16-22). All of this happened because "their God was watching over them" (Ezra 5:5) and because "the LORD had caused the king of Assyria to be favorable to them, so that he helped them" (Ezra 6:22). With God's help, all things were possible.

Ezra 7–10 begins the second half of the book by introducing the work of Ezra. The first section (Ezra 7-8) emphasizes God's sovereign hand of grace working in the hearts of pagan kings on behalf of God's people (Ezra 7:6, 9, 28; 8:18, 23, 31) and his provision of a safe trip back to Jerusalem without any military escort. The priest Ezra, who dedicated his life to studying, doing, and teaching the law of Moses (Ezra 7:1-10), guided the community through his teaching. This law provided instruction concerning what the people should do in what might today be called the secular and the religious realms. In this return to Jerusalem, Ezra brought additional priests and Levites to serve in God's Temple, as well as an enormous monetary gift to honor God at the Temple.

The final chapters of Ezra (Ezra 9-10) deal with the theme of separating the people from paganism so that they would be a holy people to God (cf. Ezra 4:1-5). Through prayer and confession, Ezra guided the people to rededicate themselves to God and divorce those spouses that refused to worship Israel's God.

When the story picks up with Nehemiah's memoirs (445 BC), the first section focuses on the problem of rebuilding the walls of Jerusalem (Neh 1:1-7:73a). After Nehemiah heard of the disgraceful situation in Jerusalem, he lamented, confessed their sins, and interceded for about four months (Neh 1:1-11). One day, the king granted all of Nehemiah's requests and sent him to rebuild Jerusalem's walls. Soon after arriving, Nehemiah made a secret inspection of the walls and then persuaded the people of Jerusalem to join him in removing this great disgrace from Jerusalem (Neh 2:16-18). Although there was some local objection to his plan to rebuild (Neh 2:19-20), most of the Jewish people accepted a small assignment to rebuild a short section of the wall (Neh 3:1-32). The enemies of Nehemiah mocked the quality of the work on the wall and in their fury made plans to attack the city (Neh 4:1-12). In response, Nehemiah prayed for God to confound his enemies (Neh 4:1-5, 9), placed additional guards in key locations (Neh 4:13), armed his workers (Neh 4:16-18, 23), and motivated the people to trust completely in the power of God (Neh 4:14-15). In the final days before the wall was finished (Neh 6:15-16), Sanballat, Tobiah, and Geshem tried a couple more schemes to destroy Nehemiah's reputation and stop the work on the wall, but each time Nehemiah saw through their evil plans and depended on God for his help (Neh 6:1-14).

The second section deals with the theme of bringing covenantal renewal to the people (Neh 7:73b-10:39). Standing in front of a great assembly, Ezra read the law of God from the books of Moses in Hebrew, while numerous priests translated and explained it in Aramaic (Neh 7:73b-8:8). The people repented with weeping (Neh 8:9-12) and then joined together in a great celebration of the Feast of Shelters (or Booths; Neh 8:13-18). Two weeks later at another great assembly, the people wept and confessed their sins and promised to separate themselves from sin (Neh 9:1-4). After a long prayer confessing God's faithfulness and compassion and their own rebellion and sinfulness (Neh 9:5-38), a large group of people signed their names to a sealed document (Neh 10:1-27) and promised to obey God's word, to not marry pagan spouses, to pay the annual Temple tax, and to support the priests by bringing the firstfruits of their harvest to the Temple (Neh 10:28-39).

The final section deals with Nehemiah's efforts to resettle and organize Jerusalem after the walls were built (Neh 11:1-13:3) and his confrontation of the people's sins when he returned again to Jerusalem after a period of service in Susa (Neh 13:4-31). Since Jerusalem was thinly populated, Nehemiah enlisted a tenth of the people from the countryside to settle in Jerusalem (Neh 11:1-36); then they dedicated the walls of Jerusalem with a celebration that included sacrificing and choral singing to thank God for his power and faithfulness to them (Neh 12:27-43). In spite of clear instruction from God's word, when Nehemiah returned to Jerusalem after a brief stay in Susa, he found that the people were no longer living according to God's instructions (e.g., in Neh 13:17 the people violated Exod 20:9-11). They let an inappropriate person live in the Temple complex, so Nehemiah literally threw him out (Neh 13:6-9). They were no longer bringing tithes to support the priests, so Nehemiah confronted them and got them to start doing what they were supposed to do (Neh 13:10-14). Some of the people of Jerusalem were working on the Sabbath, and others were buying and selling on the Sabbath, so Nehemiah stopped these practices in order to make the Sabbath a holy day to God (Neh 13:15-22). Finally, he found some people had gone back to the practice of marrying pagans, so he attacked this problem once again (Neh 13:23-31). In all these things Nehemiah boldly rooted out sin and prayed to God for protection and blessing (Neh 13:14, 22, 29, 31).

MAJOR THEMES

Ezra-Nehemiah is not just a historical document about the restoration of God's people in Jerusalem after the Babylonian exile. It was written with theological themes and purposes in mind, so the reason for including certain narratives and the method of presenting the stories came with an underlying theological edge. God was communicating a theological message to transform the thinking of the listeners and readers (including us). Those themes that are overtly and repeatedly highlighted throughout these narratives create the main theological emphasis.

The Sovereign Rule of God over All. The broadest and most pervasive theme that the author of Ezra-Nehemiah emphasized was God's powerful control over every aspect of Israel's history. Because of the past destruction of Judah by the Babylonians, its small and impotent status in the vast Persian Empire, and the opposition to its development by political opponents, many people in Jerusalem wondered if there was any hope for them. Did God care, and would he help them? Were they still his special covenant people? Would they ever be able to rebuild Jerusalem with walls and a Temple so they could get back to some sort of normal life again? Would God intervene in their history and have compassion on his people? Ezra and Nehemiah knew these were questions their audiences were asking, so they peppered their speeches, teaching, and writing with phrases that reassured their listeners and readers that God was sovereignly working out his will for them in marvelous ways.

God's rule of his people was prominently illustrated in his providential control over foreign nations and kings. The very first verses of Ezra refer to God's powerful stirring of Cyrus's heart. God directed Cyrus's thinking so that the king gave the people of Judah permission to return to their land and build a Temple to their God in Jerusalem (Ezra 1:1-4). This was consistent with Persian government policy to send all the people the Babylonians had exiled back to their original land and allow each group to rebuild its local temples. The Persians expected that the gracious way they dealt with these nations would cause them to pay their taxes and be loyal to Persia. But this did not all happen just because of Persian policy; it was God's sovereign plan to return the people after the Exile. This was announced through the prophet Jeremiah long before the rise of King Cyrus (Jer 29:10). God promised that the return to Jerusalem would happen after a 70-year captivity. In fact, the prophet Isaiah even announced that the name of the king who would help the Hebrews rebuild Jerusalem was Cyrus (Isa 44:28–45:1). God knew how he would work out all these details over 150 years before they happened.

God's sovereignty is visible in the actions of later Persian rulers as well. When Darius I found Cyrus's original decree at Ecbatana (Ezra 6:1-2) and intervened on behalf of the Jews in Jerusalem, decreeing that no one was to stop the building of the Temple and that the full cost would be paid out of the provincial taxes (Ezra 6:6-12), it was a fulfillment of the divine promise that God made through Haggai: "The treasures of all the nations will be brought to this Temple" (Hag 2:7-8). After the Temple was finished, the people celebrated that Passover and rejoiced because "the LORD had caused the king of Assyria to be favorable to them, so that he helped them to rebuild the Temple of God" (Ezra 6:22). (The "king of Assyria" is another title for Darius I, for he was king of Media, Persia, Babylon, Assyria, and many other territories.)

Some years after this, when Ezra wanted to come to Jerusalem, the Persian king Artaxerxes I "gave him everything he asked for, because the gracious hand of the LORD his God was on him" (Ezra 7:6). God even influenced Artaxerxes I to decree that Ezra should instruct people in the law of God and offer sacrifices to God. The king's letter instructed the treasurer of the province beyond the Euphrates River to "be careful to provide whatever the God of heaven demands for his Temple" (Ezra 7:23). Ezra responded to these words with, "Praise the LORD, the God of our ancestors, who made the king want to beautify the Temple of the LORD in Jerusalem!" (Ezra 7:27). When Ezra began the long and dangerous trip back to Jerusalem, he did not ask the king for a military escort to protect the people from enemies along the way because he believed that "God's hand of protection is on all who worship him" (Ezra 8:22). Upon arriving at Jerusalem, Ezra gave testimony to the fact that "the gracious hand of our God protected us and saved us from enemies and bandits along the way" (Ezra 8:31).

Nehemiah also realized that Artaxerxes I granted his request to go to Jerusalem to rebuild its walls because "the gracious hand of God" was on him (Neh 2:8). Later, when Tobiah, Sanballat, and Geshem tried to stop the work of God on the walls, Nehemiah prayed for God to fight for the Jews and protect them (Neh 4:4, 9, 20; 6:14), so God frustrated their evil plans (Neh 4:15). In the great prayer for God's compassion, God is seen as the one who gave the people their land (Neh 9:8), defeated the Egyptians (Neh 9:9-11), helped them conquer Sihon and Og (Neh 9:22), and later brought enemies to conquer Israel when they fell into sin (Neh 9:28).

God was recognized as sovereign in creating heaven and earth, in making the land and the seas, in giving life to animals, people, and even the angels in heaven (Neh

9:6). Ezra and Nehemiah did not take credit for their accomplishments, nor did they assume that they could have accomplished what they did through their own wisdom or leadership abilities. Their lives demonstrated this, and they frequently confessed that their source of strength was the sovereign power of God. From the theological perspective of the author of Ezra-Nehemiah, nothing was done without God's help.

God's sovereign power is not limited to his power over the earth or over the pagan kings; he also rules over his own people. He sovereignly "stirred the hearts of the priests and Levites and the leaders of the tribes of Judah and Benjamin" so that they would be willing to return to rebuild the Temple in Jerusalem (Ezra 1:5). Once the people returned and began to worship God, they praised God because "He is so good! His faithful love for Israel endures forever!" (Ezra 3:11). After around 15 frustrating years of making no progress on the Temple, God sovereignly sent Haggai and Zechariah to challenge the people to finish the building. The political authorities tried but failed to stop this effort because "God was watching over them" (Ezra 5:5) and controlling what would happen. The Hebrews in Jerusalem realized that it was God's anger over their sin that had caused them to go into exile in the first place (Ezra 5:12), not the strength of any human army. They also realized that God "helped them to rebuild the Temple of God" (Ezra 6:22); it was not just their own hard work. When Ezra was permitted to leave for Jerusalem, he praised God "for demonstrating such unfailing love to me" (Ezra 7:28). On his trip to Jerusalem, Ezra reported his request that "God would take care of us" (Ezra 8:21-23), a prayer that was dependent on his confidence that God would rule over their lives according to his plan. Ezra confessed that the people's sin of intermarrying with pagans polluted the holy seed (Ezra 9:2). He confessed that the nation's then peaceful situation was due to God's grace, for "God has brightened our eyes and granted us some relief from our slavery" (Ezra 9:8). The divine ruler did not abandon them but had given them a "protective wall in Judah and Jerusalem" (Ezra 9:9), a metaphor that means God was watching over and protecting the people. Ezra believed that God was the one who controlled the blessings of the land and of children (Ezra 9:12) and would justly remove those blessings if the people were to fall into sin (Ezra 9:13-15). When the people admitted their sin, they turned to do what God demanded (Ezra 10:11). This was an act of submission to the rule of God.

Nehemiah's prayers have a similar theological basis in God's powerful blessings and cursings (Neh 1:8-9). These principles partially explain how God rules over his people. At times God is freely gracious and sovereignly gives his servants surprising success when they pray (Neh 1:11; 2:8). When his servant Nehemiah had the difficult task of rebuilding the walls, God put a plan in his heart (Neh 2:12), and he encouraged the people to follow that plan. When some opposed this plan, Nehemiah claimed that "the God of heaven will help us succeed" (Neh 2:20). When opposition arose, Nehemiah encouraged people with the reminder, "Remember the Lord, who is great and glorious, and fight for your brothers, your sons, your daughters, your wives, and your homes!" (Neh 4:14). When there was internal conflict because the rich Jews were charging the poor ones high interest rates, Nehemiah threatened them by stating that God had the power to shake them from their homes if they did not stop what they were doing (Neh 5:13). Nehemiah knew that the completion of the walls of Jerusalem in 52 days was not accomplished because he had so many skilled workers; it was completed with God's help. Even Nehemiah's enemies came to realize this (Neh 6:16). God's rule is even credited with giving Nehemiah the idea to register the people (Neh 7:5). Nothing happens outside the plan of God, and nothing can defeat God's determined will to restore his people.

The foundational belief that God rules over everything gave Ezra, as well as the community of believers with him, the everyday courage and practical faith to step outside their comfort zone and walk those 800 miles to Jerusalem, to not request government troops to guard them on their long journey to Jerusalem, to say no to compromising their faith with unbelievers, and to say yes to the difficult decision to maintain a holy people by divorcing those spouses who did not worship God alone. This conviction about God's rule enabled these people to interpret what God was doing in the hearts of pagan kings and their local adversaries. Because God could sovereignly control their situation, these leaders prayed repeatedly for God to intervene, and they depended on God's will in the Torah for guidance. Because God had the power to bless or curse, the leaders led the people in revivals that would remove the threat of divine punishment. Because "the hand of God was upon" these leaders, God did great things through them.

Separation from Impurity and Dedication to Worshiping God. One of the main motivations for returning to Jerusalem was to set up the altar, rebuild the Temple, restore proper worship of God, and have the people present themselves as a holy people before God. Surprisingly, King Cyrus also saw this as the basic rationale for allowing the people of Judah to return (Ezra 1:3-4). In response to Cyrus's decree, God stirred up the hearts of people to go back to Jerusalem expressly to "rebuild this Temple of the LORD, the God of Israel, who lives in Jerusalem" (Ezra 1:3). The goal was not to set up a new kingdom, establish the old borders of Israel, or rebuild the armies of Judah. This reestablishment of proper worship involved the return of the sacred gold vessels that Nebuchadnezzar had taken from the Temple when Jerusalem was destroyed (Ezra 1:7-11; Dan 1:1-2), plus installing priests, singers, and Temple servants to conduct this worship (Ezra 2:40-54). The theological importance of worship was symbolized by the community's quick move, under the leadership of the high priest Jeshua (Ezra 3:2), to rebuild "the altar of the God of Israel" so they could sacrifice burnt offerings on it and celebrate the "Festival of Shelters," sometimes called the Feast of Tabernacles or Booths (Ezra 3:4). This led to the process of beginning to rebuild the Temple in the second year after their return to Jerusalem and an emotional dedication of the foundations of the Temple (Ezra 3:7-12). But this joy and progress was short-lived because the work was stopped almost immediately when the people refused to compromise the purity of their faith (Ezra 4:1-4). They determined to separate themselves from the people who had been brought to the area by the Assyrian king Esarhaddon, even though their neighbors claimed to worship the same God (Ezra 4:2). Having this help would have enabled the Hebrews to quickly finish the difficult task of building the Temple, but Zerubbabel and Jeshua said, "You may have no part in this work. We alone will build the Temple for the LORD, the God of Israel" (Ezra 4:3), thereby indicating that purity of worship was an even higher priority than peace or quickly completing the rebuilding of the Temple. About 15 years later, when Haggai and Zechariah appeared, the focus went back to building the Temple (Ezra 5:1-2). The official letters in Ezra 5 and 6 are all about reestablishing God's worship at the Temple, and this crisis ends with Darius I ordering that the worship of God should continue (Ezra 6:6-12). Once the Temple was completed, there was great joy at its dedication and at the Passover feast (Ezra 6:16-22).

The importance of the Temple and purity of worship in Ezra 1–6 provides the backdrop for the rest of Ezra-Nehemiah, for in the following years the people struggled to maintain the pure worship of God. Ezra himself was a priest from the line of Aaron (Ezra 7:1-5), so he had a strong interest in Temple worship. When he returned with additional exiles, he brought with him offerings from the Persian king and the Jewish people who stayed in Babylon. In response, Ezra praised God for moving the pagan Persian king to want "to beautify the Temple of the LORD in Jerusalem" (Ezra 7:27). Just before leaving Persia, the returnees fasted and worshiped God (Ezra 8:21-23) and set the priests apart as holy to the Lord so they could transport back to Jerusalem the gold and silver given to God (Ezra 8:28). When these new returnees got to Jerusalem, they immediately sacrificed burnt offerings to the Lord (Ezra 8:35-36). But things in Jerusalem were not all rosy, for Ezra learned that some priests and leaders had intermarried with foreigners and had polluted the holy race by following detestable pagan practices (Ezra 9:1-2). Ezra was enraged because the people failed to separate themselves from impurity. This led to a revival when the people separated themselves from the people of the land (Ezra 10:11).

Although Nehemiah's memoirs (Neh 1–7; 11–13) deal more with building the walls of Jerusalem, his writings begin with him worshiping God and confessing the nation's sins (Neh 1:4-11) and show in general how God continued to restore the vitality of his people in spite of their repeated failures to separate themselves as a holy people. Immediately after the walls were finished, Nehemiah appointed gatekeepers, singers, and Levites to return the city to normal operations (Neh 7:1-3). The book of Nehemiah also describes an undated revival led by Ezra and the worship of God in the courtyards of the Temple on the Festival of Shelters (also called Tabernacles or Booths; see Neh 8). A couple weeks after this, while the people were fasting and worshiping God, additional people confessed their sins and determined to separate themselves from all foreign influences in order to maintain the purity of the nation (Neh 9:1-4). In the great prayer of confession in Nehemiah 9, the people were reminded of their failure to worship God when they turned in worship to the golden calf (Neh 9:17-18). And they were reminded of how they did not separate themselves from the Canaanites in the Promised Land (Neh 9:26-31). Nehemiah recorded the names of a group of people who promised to keep the purity of their faith by tithing to provide for the work at the Temple, keeping the Sabbath, and not intermarrying with the pagan people (Neh 10:30-39). The final section of Nehemiah's memoirs describes the settlement of the "holy city" (Neh 11:1), highlighting the roles of the priests and Levites (Neh 11:10-20). The dedication of the walls of Jerusalem was another opportunity to worship God and joyously celebrate what God had done for the people (Neh 12:27-43). Nehemiah also set up a system of supplying for the needs of the Temple priests (Neh 12:44-47) and did everything he could to keep Eliashib the priest from compromising with Tobiah (Neh 13:1-8). When Nehemiah returned to Jerusalem after a brief stay in Persia, he again encouraged the people to separate themselves from impure worship by stopping traders from profaning the Sabbath and stopping people from intermarrying with pagans (Neh 13:15-31). Throughout this material, the desire to worship God in purity was a major motivating factor.

Faithfulness to the Law in the Covenant Community. Ezra and Nehemiah's religious, social, and economic reforms were heavily dependent on reestablishing the law of Moses (the Torah) as the guide to appropriate behavior for the people in Jerusalem. Twenty-eight times Ezra, Nehemiah, or a Persian king refer to the laws of Moses to legitimate what they are saying. Artaxerxes promoted the behavioral instructions concerning God's will for the people in Jerusalem and gave Ezra full authority to govern all the people in Yehud (Judah) based on these laws (Ezra 7:25-26). Ezra was a scribe who was well versed in the law because he dedicated himself to the study and teaching of the law (Ezra 7:6, 10, 12, 21). The law included instructions on how to offer sacrifices and provide for the needs of the Temple (Ezra 3:2; Neh 10:34-36; 12:44). Earlier traditions in the law of Moses (see Deut 7:1-4) forbade intermarriage with pagans, and Ezra relied on this principle to legitimate his call for the people to separate themselves from impurity and preserve the holy seed (Ezra 10:3; Neh 10:29-30). And although Nehemiah makes no explicit mention of the law of God, it is obvious that Nehemiah knew the Mosaic traditions about not charging interest on loans to Jewish brothers (Neh 5; see Exod 22:25; Lev 25:36) and the laws against working on the Sabbath (Neh 13:15-22; see Exod 20:8-11; 34:21). Ezra and Nehemiah insisted the community would only remain a unified covenant people as long as the people were faithful to what God had instructed in the Torah.

Public worship involved reading the law aloud and interpreting or translating it into terms that the people could understand and apply (Neh 8:1, 3, 8). This divine revelation brought weeping, confession, and enlightenment concerning what God desired of his people (Neh 8:9, 13, 18; 9:3). The people realized that they were ignorant of what God wanted, had rebelled against his will, and needed to repent (Neh 9:14, 26, 29, 34).

Prayer. Ezra and Nehemiah were men of prayer, and their example is a powerful reminder of what God wants of all spiritual leaders. Ezra's long prayer in Ezra 9 is a model of humility, confession, and intercession for God's grace. Once he heard about the sinful intermarriage with pagans, he was immediately struck by the unfaithfulness of the people. He did not rise up and curse them or preach a sermon against their evil ways. Instead, he recognized God's great grace to them in bringing them out of Babylonian captivity and allowing them to rebuild the Temple. He contrasted this with the people's ignorance of God's laws, which resulted in unfaithfulness to the covenant. All he could do was confess these sins. His confession and humble weeping was heard by many of the people in Judah, and they were convicted of their sins, confessed their sins, and turned from their wicked ways so that they could avoid the fierce anger of God (Ezra 10:1-15). In this case, prayer was the means of restoring the people's relationship with God. Earlier,

Ezra had fasted and prayed earnestly for God's protection on the long journey from Babylon to Jerusalem, but not much of that prayer was recorded (Ezra 8:21-23).

Another long intercessory prayer is found in Nehemiah 1, after the king's cup-bearer heard that the walls of Jerusalem were in ruins. This prayer was accompanied by intense emotions, mourning, fasting, and weeping. Nehemiah first recognized God's faithful love and grace to his people, and then he confessed the people's sins. At the end of his intercession, Nehemiah requested that God would grant him success in talking with King Artaxerxes about the problems in Jerusalem.

Elsewhere Nehemiah offered short prayers for help. Sometimes the narrative only mentions "a prayer to the God of heaven" (Neh 2:4); other times we hear an imprecatory request for God to stop the enemies who are interfering with the work on the wall (Neh 4:4-5). Elsewhere Nehemiah just called out to God to remember him and bless his work (Neh 5:19; 6:14; 13:14, 22, 29, 31). These prayers recognized the sovereign power of God to control their lives and the lives of those around them. Some prayers were acts of worship. Some expressed humility and sorrow, while others requested divine help. Frequently Nehemiah noted that God heard his prayer and answered his request. These prayers are an encouragement to all readers to follow the example of Ezra and Nehemiah, for prayer brings God's power to bear on the difficult situations of life.

OUTLINE
The literary organization of Ezra-Nehemiah can be structured around the various sources employed in writing these narratives. D. Howard (1993:278) divides the sources as follows:

1. A historical review (Ezra 1–6)
2. Ezra's memoirs, part 1 (Ezra 7–10)
3. Nehemiah's memoirs, part 1 (Neh 1–7)
4. Ezra's memoirs, part 2 (Neh 8–10)
5. Nehemiah's memoirs, part 2 (Neh 11–13)

This approach helps one understand the sources used in the compositional process but does not explain much about the content or theological themes that are predominant in each section. These sources can help mark out some of the major breaks in a topical outline, but not all commentators choose to make breaks at these places.[7]

   I. The People Return to Jerusalem to Rebuild the Temple (Ezra 1:1–6:22)
     A. God Returns the Exiles to Jerusalem (Ezra 1:1–2:70)
       1. God stirs people to go to Jerusalem to rebuild the Temple (Ezra 1:1-11)
       2. A list of those who returned to Jerusalem (Ezra 2:1-70)
     B. Worshiping God Brings Opposition (Ezra 3:1–4:23)
       1. Restoration of worship (Ezra 3:1-13)
       2. Opposition to the restoration of the Temple (Ezra 4:1-5)
       3. Opposition to the restoration of the walls (Ezra 4:6-23)

C. God Overcomes Opposition to Constructing the Temple
(Ezra 4:24–6:22)
   1. Prophetic encouragement challenges the opposition
   (Ezra 4:24–5:17)
   2. Darius encourages rebuilding the Temple (Ezra 6:1-12)
   3. The joyous celebrations at the completed Temple (Ezra 6:13-22)

II. Ezra Returns to Teach God's Law (Ezra 7:1–10:44)
A. God Brings Ezra to Jerusalem (Ezra 7:1–8:36)
   1. Ezra's divine and royal commission (Ezra 7:1-28a)
   2. God's hand on those who returned to Jerusalem
   (Ezra 7:28b–8:36)
B. Ezra Intercedes Because the Holy Race Was Polluted
(Ezra 9:1–10:44)
   1. Ezra's reaction to unholy marriages (Ezra 9:1-15)
   2. The people separate themselves to the Lord (Ezra 10:1-44)

III. Nehemiah Returns to Build the Walls of Jerusalem (Neh 1:1–7:73a)
A. Nehemiah's Vision to Remove Judah's Disgrace (Neh 1:1–2:20)
   1. Nehemiah asks God to remove Judah's disgrace (Neh 1:1-11)
   2. God causes the king to approve Nehemiah's vision (Neh 2:1-10)
   3. God's grace causes the people to accept Nehemiah's vision
   (Neh 2:11-20)
B. God Overcomes Opposition to Building the Walls (Neh 3:1–7:73a)
   1. The whole community works to rebuild the walls (Neh 3:1-32)
   2. Prayer and hard work overcome outside opposition (Neh 4:1-23)
   3. Confrontation and the fear of God overcome internal opposition
   (Neh 5:1-19)
   4. God helps the people complete the wall in spite of opposition
   (Neh 6:1–7:3)
   5. Nehemiah's census and the census of the first exiles (Neh 7:4-73a)

IV. Ezra's Teaching of the Law of God Brings Covenant Renewal (Neh
7:73b–10:39)
A. The Community Understands God's Word (Neh 7:73b–8:18)
B. The Community Hears God's Word and Prays (Neh 9:1-37)
C. The Community Determines to Obey God's Word (Neh 9:38–10:39)

V. Nehemiah's Organization of the People and His Reforms
(Neh 11:1–13:31)
A. The Resettlement of the People (Neh 11:1-36)
B. A List of Authentic Priests (Neh 12:1-26)
C. The Joyous Dedication of the Walls of Jerusalem (Neh 12:27-43)
D. Organization of Temple Worship (Neh 12:44–13:3)
E. Nehemiah Confronts the People's Sin (Neh 13:4-31)

ENDNOTES
1. Those who are interested in the many theories about the composition of Ezra-Nehemiah from various historical sources should see the discussion in Williamson 1985:xxiii-xxxv or Clines 1984:4-12.
2. For a full treatment of a whole variety of approaches to this problem, see Rowley 1965:137-168.
3. See the listing of 13 arguments to support this case in Clines 1984:17-20.
4. Yamauchi (1990:93-159) has a long and detailed discussion of the Persian documents and monuments that help historians understand the events in this period.
5. This chart follows the illustration in Myers 1965:xxxviii.
6. These include "treasurer" in Ezra 1:8; "basin" in Ezra 1:9; "governor" in Ezra 2:63; "letter" in Ezra 4:7, 18, 23; 5:5; 7:11; "copy" in Ezra 4:11, 23; 5:6; 7:11; "reply, answer" in Ezra 4:17; 5:7, 11; 6:11; "time" in Ezra 5:3; Neh 2:6; "sedition" in Ezra 4:15, 19; "structure" in Ezra 5:3, 9; "officials" in Ezra 5:6; "archives" in Ezra 6:1; "with all diligence" in Ezra 6:12-13; "law" in Ezra 7:12, 25-26; "careful" in Ezra 7:23; "punished by death" in Ezra 7:26.
7. E. Yamauchi (1988:678) made a major break in Neh 13:1 and divided the narrative into Nehemiah's first and second visit to Jerusalem. The outline I propose will help divide the structure of the narratives into meaningful segments and paragraphs.

COMMENTARY ON
Ezra-Nehemiah

◆ I. The People Return to Jerusalem to Rebuild the Temple
(Ezra 1:1–6:22)
A. God Returns the Exiles to Jerusalem (Ezra 1:1–2:70)
1. God stirs people to go to Jerusalem to rebuild the Temple
(Ezra 1:1-11)

In the first year of King Cyrus of Persia,* the LORD fulfilled the prophecy he had given through Jeremiah.* He stirred the heart of Cyrus to put this proclamation in writing and to send it throughout his kingdom:

2"This is what King Cyrus of Persia says: "The LORD, the God of heaven, has given me all the kingdoms of the earth. He has appointed me to build him a Temple at Jerusalem, which is in Judah. 3Any of you who are his people may go to Jerusalem in Judah to rebuild this Temple of the LORD, the God of Israel, who lives in Jerusalem. And may your God be with you! 4Wherever this Jewish remnant is found, let their neighbors contribute toward their expenses by giving them silver and gold, supplies for the journey, and livestock, as well as a voluntary offering for the Temple of God in Jerusalem."

5Then God stirred the hearts of the priests and Levites and the leaders of the tribes of Judah and Benjamin to go to Jerusalem to rebuild the Temple of the LORD. 6And all their neighbors assisted by giving them articles of silver and gold, supplies for the journey, and livestock. They gave them many valuable gifts in addition to all the voluntary offerings.

7King Cyrus himself brought out the articles that King Nebuchadnezzar had taken from the LORD's Temple in Jerusalem and had placed in the temple of his own gods. 8Cyrus directed Mithredath, the treasurer of Persia, to count these items and present them to Sheshbazzar, the leader of the exiles returning to Judah.* 9This is a list of the items that were returned:

gold basins	30
silver basins	1,000
silver incense burners*	29
10 gold bowls	30
silver bowls	410
other items	1,000

11In all, there were 5,400 articles of gold and silver. Sheshbazzar brought all of these along when the exiles went from Babylon to Jerusalem.

1:1a The first year of Cyrus's reign over Babylon was 538 B.C.   1:1b See Jer 25:11-12; 29:10.   1:8 Hebrew *Sheshbazzar, the prince of Judah.*   1:9 The meaning of this Hebrew word is uncertain.

NOTES

1:1 *the LORD fulfilled the prophecy.* Lit., "in order to complete the word of the LORD." The infinitive construct *keloth* [TH3615, ZH3983] (complete, fulfill) indicates purpose. The text does not just assure the reader that God fulfilled his promise through Jeremiah; it makes it clear that God acted with the purpose of completing what he said he would do. This fine distinction highlights God's faithfulness to his foreordained plans. The "word of the LORD" refers to Jeremiah's prophecy of 70 years of exile (Jer 25:11-12; 29:10), as well as to key passages in Isaiah (Coggins 1976:11). The 70 years of exile began in 605 BC when the first groups of Hebrews were brought to Babylon (Dan 1:1-3), and came to an end following Cyrus's decree that allowed the people to return to Jerusalem in 538 BC. If it took around a year for people in exile to get ready to return (to sell their homes and businesses) and then walk the 800 miles back to Jerusalem, then the people should have arrived in Jerusalem no later than 536 BC. See G. Larsson 1967:417-423 and C. F. Whiteley 1954:60-72 for further discussion. Allen (2003:16) points out that there is no evidence that Jews from the northern nation of Israel who were taken captive by the Assyrians in 721 BC returned to Yehud (Judah) at this time.

He stirred the heart of Cyrus. Lit., "The LORD stirred the spirit of Cyrus." The reason for Cyrus's proclamation was God's persuasive movement in his life. The Hebrew word *he'ir* [TH5782, ZH6424] (arouse, stir, move) refers to actions that enliven a person to do something. When the heart is stirred, it is motivated to respond and cannot sit passively. The prophecies about God's stirring up Cyrus's spirit are found in Jer 51:1 (see also Isa 13:17; 45:13; Jer 50:9). Information about the timing of God's fulfillment was derived from Jeremiah's prophecy concerning the 70 years of captivity, but the idea of God's stirring up Cyrus's heart is common to both Isaiah and Jeremiah. Ezra 1:1 and the other references to Cyrus emphasize that this king would not act on his own accord but was stirred or aroused to act by God. Not even the Persian Empire or its powerful king controls the future—God does (for a word study of this key concept of *he'ir*, see NIDOTTE 3.357-360).

1:2 This is what King Cyrus of Persia says. This standard formula for introducing messages in the ancient Near East is found often in the Bible and is sometimes called a "messenger formula."

The LORD, the God of heaven. "God of heaven" (*'elohe hashamayim* [TH430/8064, ZH466/9028]) is a typical title in the postexilic books (17 times in Ezra, Nehemiah, and Daniel) to identify the God of the Hebrews as a high god rather than a local deity connected to a specific city or part of nature. It is quite unexpected that the pagan king Cyrus would use the Hebrew divine name Yahweh (cf. NLT, "LORD"), for even the Hebrews tended not to speak this name for fear of taking God's name in vain. It is possible that Cyrus knew this name because of Daniel (Dan 6). On the other hand, this statement may actually be the author's interpretation of the essence of what Cyrus said; thus, it would not be an exact quote, but would capture the spirit of what Cyrus said from a Hebrew theological perspective.

1:4 let their neighbors contribute toward their expenses. It is unclear if "their neighbors" (lit., "the men of his place") just referred to Jewish neighbors, as the use of *sha'ar* [TH7604, ZH8636] (cf. 1 Chr 13:2; 2 Chr 30:6; 36:20) might suggest (Bickerman 1946:258-260), or if this means that both Jews and Babylonians (Brockington 1969:49) helped the returnees with their financial or travel needs. The suggestion that Babylonians gave assistance proposes an unusual situation in which pagans were helping provide sacrifices for Israel's God. One should not read into this verse a parallel to the Israelites' spoiling the Egyptians as some do (see Blenkinsopp 1988:75; Allen 2003:17; see Exod 3:21-22; 12:35-36). In this case, fellow Hebrews who stayed in Babylon provided financial aid and animals for sacrifices to their Hebrew brothers who returned to Jerusalem. There was no "spoiling" when the Hebrew people left Babylon, God did not defeat the Babylonians with plagues, and there was no second Passover or anything similar to the Red Sea crossing. The only thing that is somewhat similar to the Exodus is that in both cases Hebrew people left a foreign land to return to Israel.

1:5 God stirred the hearts of the priests and Levites and the leaders of the tribes of Judah and Benjamin. God sovereignly moved spiritual leaders (priests and Levites) who were needed to renew worship in Jerusalem, as well as the sociopolitical heads of key family units. Important leaders, who could secure the unified effort of an extended family toward a common goal, headed up the ancestral houses (*ra'sho ha'aboth* [TH7218/1, ZH8031/3], "heads/chief of the fathers"), the basic social unit in the postexilic era. Living on the ancestral land would be difficult at best, so survival in a hostile economic and political setting like Yehud was next to impossible for a single family. These extended family units provided the necessary numbers and skills to form a self-sufficient group, so they would immigrate as a unit. This verse suggests that no members of the other 10 tribes of Israel returned at this point. One of the reasons for this is that they were exiled by Assyria about 140 years before the people of Judah came to Babylon. This verse, however, does not address what happened in other parts of the empire, so one should not argue from its silence that no one from the other tribes returned.

1:6 all their neighbors assisted. Like the admonition in 1:4, this phrase (*kol-sebibothehem* [TH3605/5439, ZH3972/6017], "all those surrounding them") is vague and includes the possibility of both Jewish and Babylonian help (Williamson 1985:16). Some find an Exodus motif behind this statement and try to make this act comparable with the plundering of the Egyptians in Exod 12:35-36, but there is no slavery in this context or plundering of anyone here (contra Breneman 1993:71; Van Wijk-Bos 1998:18, 20). This association with the Exodus reads too much into the text and inserts a parallelism that was not clearly expressed by the writer. Although a comparison of the return of the exiles from Babylon with the Exodus is present in other texts, that association was not clearly made here.

1:7 articles that King Nebuchadnezzar had taken from the LORD's Temple. These "articles" (*keli* [TH3627, ZH3998], "vessels") were the gold and silver basins, incense burners, and bowls used in the sacrificial system at the Temple in Jerusalem (listed in 1:9-11). Nebuchadnezzar may have taken these in the 586 or 605 BC captivities of Judah (see 2 Kgs 25:13-14; Jer 52:17; Dan 1:1-2) and put them in Marduk's temple in Babylon. These were the same vessels that Belshazzar drank from the night Babylon was captured (Dan 5:23). The act of putting the vessels in Marduk's temple symbolized Marduk's power over Israel's God. There is some confusion about whether all the utensils were returned at this time because 7:19 refers to additional utensils being returned to the Temple in 458 BC. Presumably, these new cultic utensils in 7:19 are gifts from the Persian authorities and not part of the original vessels taken from the Temple in Jerusalem by Nebuchadnezzar.

1:8 Mithredath, the treasurer. It is unclear why the "treasurer" (*gizbar* [TH1489, ZH1601], a Persian loan word) would be in charge of these items unless these valuable items of gold and silver were being stored in the treasury instead of in the temple of Marduk.

Sheshbazzar, the leader of the exiles. Lit., "Sheshbazzar, the prince of Judah." Later in 5:14-16 Sheshbazzar is called the appointed "governor" who laid the foundations of the Temple. Other biblical texts state that Zerubbabel was involved with laying the foundation (3:2-10) and was governor (Hag 1:1), but totally ignore Sheshbazzar. One solution to this problem is to hypothesize that these two names refer to the same person. First Esdras 6:18 and Josephus (*Antiquities* 11.13-14) indicate that these were Babylonian and Hebrew names for the same person, similar to Daniel's having a Hebrew and a Babylonian name (Belteshazzar in Dan 1:7). Unfortunately, the Bible never makes this identification, and most commentaries conclude that both names are Babylonian. Some suggest that Sheshbazzar is Jehoiachin's fourth son Shenazzar (1 Chr 3:17-18), who died shortly after arriving back with the exiles (Clines 1984:41). Others believe the title "prince of Judah" was added by a later, ill-informed editor (Williamson 1985:18), while a few link this prince with the one mentioned in Ezek 45:7, 9, 17, 22 (Levenson 1976:57-73). None of these options are as attractive as concluding that Cyrus gave Sheshbazzar official responsibilities for the return from Babylon and that Zerubbabel was a high Jewish official who worked with Sheshbazzar and took over his responsibilities when he died. There are no records to indicate when this happened, but it probably took place fairly soon (within two years) after the people returned to Jerusalem. Thus, both were governors (Zerubbabel was later), and both had been involved in laying the foundation of the Temple.

1:9-10 *basins . . . incense burners . . . bowls.* It is difficult to identify what these utensils were. The "basin" (*'agartal* [TH105, ZH113]) was some kind of dish, the "incense burner" (*makhalap* [TH4252, ZH4709]) was some kind of pan that was used for burning incense (though the Hebrew text does not say it was silver, it is likely they were made of silver), and the *kepor* [TH3713, ZH4094] was some kind of bowl. They were all used in the Temple to hold blood, incense, or other kinds of offerings.

1:11 *In all, there were 5,400 articles of gold and silver.* The total number of items listed equals 2,499, not 5,400. First Esdras 2:13-15 has a longer list adding up to 5,469, but this does not represent the sum of the items listed. Josephus did not total his list, but his items come to 5,400 (*Antiquities* 11.15). Williamson observed an irregularity in the order of the usual listing of items (object, metal, number) in 1:10 and concluded that a large number has dropped out by a scribal error (1985:5). It was probably not necessary to exhaustively list all the objects given to Sheshbazzar (for example, no knives were included in the list), so it is best to accept the final figure in 1:11 as an approximate, round number of the items returned and to understand the list in 1:9-10 as partial.

COMMENTARY

This narrative describes one of the great miraculous events in the history of Israel. This return to Jerusalem was not accompanied with plagues, the dividing of the Red Sea, or the defeat of Israel's oppressors, but it was seen as the process that led to the rebirth of the nation in its native land, the Promised Land of Israel. This was not a second "exodus" event (though Isaiah pictured Israel's future in those terms) but a unique "return" to the land by people who were not oppressed in harsh slavery. Although the secular mind might look at these events as a natural outworking of wise political decisions by the Persians and find no miraculous work by God, Ezra 1 emphasizes that God made all this happen when he stirred up the spirit of Cyrus and the hearts of many of the exiles (1:1-2, 5).

It is surprising to have a pagan king claim that the Hebrew God, Yahweh ("the LORD"), moved him to do these things and that this God gave him all the kingdoms of the earth. What is the reader to think of this? Was Cyrus a Jewish convert or did the Jewish author of Ezra put words in his mouth based on his own Hebrew theology? When this decree is compared to the original Aramaic copy of Cyrus's decree in 6:3-5, the content and theology are quite different. Were there two decrees? Some conclude that this proclamation was not Cyrus's actual decree but a Jewish version (Myers 1965:5) or that this was a summary of Cyrus's statement in the Cyrus Cylinder. This clay cylinder reveals that Cyrus "returned to [these] sacred cities on the other side of the Tigris . . . and established for them permanent sanctuaries. I [also] gathered all their [former] inhabitants and returned [to them] their habitations" (ANET 316). Although this contains a similar idea to 1:1-4, the two are different enough to conclude that Cyrus made a separate decree for the Jewish people (and probably for other ethnic or religious groups too). Cyrus was a Zoroastrian who followed the Persian god Ahura Mazda, but he was very tolerant of other religious systems. (See Boyce 1982 for more information on the theology and growth of Zoroastrianism.) For political reasons, when he wrote to the Babylonians, he acknowledged that the Babylonian god Marduk chose him and gave him military victories (ANET 315-316). It appears that Cyrus's proclamation in 1:2-4 was also a politically designed proclamation using conventional terminology (possibly with the help of Jewish officials to get the name of their God right) to gain the support of his Jewish audience. This document had a different purpose from the building permit in 6:3-5; it simply grants permission to return rather than spelling out details such as how big the Temple should be.

Whatever motivations Cyrus had, the fundamental testimony of Scripture is that God acts powerfully to cause people to do his will. This conclusion is based on the evidence that God had developed a plan that he partially revealed to his people many years earlier (Isa 45:1; Jer 29:10). In this predetermined plan, God indicated what he would do (send the people back to rebuild Jerusalem), who would be involved (Cyrus would send Israel home), and when it would happen (in 70 years). Such precision is exceptional, for most prophecies do not include a specific time of fulfillment in years or the names of specific individuals in the future. But in other ways this prophecy is like most other prophecies. In all cases God reveals a portion of his determined will to people so that they will know that they can trust him for their future. He rules over the affairs of men and nations and knows how things will turn out. This foreknowledge is predicated on his ability to control what people will do. If he could not rule over human existence, then uncontrollable forces would eventually interfere with what he planned to accomplish. Ezra 1 assures the reader that God caused pagan kings to fit into his preannounced plans (1:1), caused them to be unusually generous (1:2-4), appointed them to do his will to fulfill his plan (1:2), and revived his people's desire to worship him (1:5). God's sovereign rule explains why things happen as they do.

This implies that everything that happens has theological significance because it is a part of God's plan. Although most people today do not read the newspaper through the lens of God's sovereign plan, God is still actively involved in the details of his master plan for this earth. God has not forgotten what to do next, and he knows the timing for each point in the plan. He will complete that plan by moving people's hearts and minds to do amazing things to accomplish his will. As in the time of Ezra, people need to be ready to act in obedience when God stirs their hearts to follow his plan.

To the Israelites, as well as to God, the continuation of a worshiping community of believers in Jerusalem was of utmost importance. By releasing the precious Temple utensils, Cyrus affirmed the legitimacy of Israel's God and his right to have worship at his own Temple in Judah. Possession of these valuable items created continuity between the ancient past and the new worship activities in Jerusalem. These utensils also gave legitimacy to this new worship. The returnees would worship at the same place using the same Temple utensils as their forefathers.

God had totally rejected the sinful Israelite nation in the past because of their worship of pagan gods. If God's name was to be praised, certain things must be done. The holy God must have a certain kind of altar and a prescribed Temple with appropriate sacrifices offered by pure Levitical priests. The only way for this to happen was for God to establish a new community of believers who knew what would please him from his instructions in the Torah. So God brought his own people back to Jerusalem, not some new group of people. This continuity with the past would assure that the people would return to God's chosen place in Jerusalem (not to some other Temple site), that they would want to rebuild the Temple to worship him (not just rebuild their businesses), and that appropriate priests would use holy utensils to worship God (pagan worship must be excluded). Revival needed to happen among God's own people first if any of this was ever going to take place. Afterwards it would be possible for these people to reach out to others and invite them to observe the wonderful things that God was doing.

This theme of reviving the old community suggests that God will probably work this way in the future. Continuity with the past assures purity and the legitimacy of the new community. Although many look at the Old Testament, the Reformation, or even the old songs and behavioral requirements of their grandparents as outmoded, God connects his present work with his past revelation, his past works of redemption with his future acts of salvation, his past community of believers with his new followers, and his past worship with new ways to praise him. Continuity with the past gives believers the assurance that they are on the right track. The old-time religion is the true faith that is good enough for everyone today, even when it looks or sounds a little different in its modern dress. The same God who guided Israel in the past is in charge of world events today. Our faith does not need to be revised by modern philosophical concepts that destroy the simple truth that we can trust and worship God because he loves us and still rules over everything in our world.

◆ 2. A list of those who returned to Jerusalem (Ezra 2:1-70)

Here is the list of the Jewish exiles of the provinces who returned from their captivity. King Nebuchadnezzar had deported them to Babylon, but now they returned to Jerusalem and the other towns in Judah where they originally lived. 2Their leaders were Zerubbabel, Jeshua, Nehemiah, Seraiah, Reelaiah, Mordecai, Bilshan, Mispar, Bigvai, Rehum, and Baanah.

This is the number of the men of Israel who returned from exile:

3 The family of Parosh 2,172
4 The family of Shephatiah 372
5 The family of Arah............................. 775
6 The family of Pahath-moab
    (descendants of Jeshua
    and Joab)....................................2,812
7 The family of Elam............................1,254
8 The family of Zattu............................ 945

9 The family of Zaccai........................... 760
10 The family of Bani 642
11 The family of Bebai 623
12 The family of Azgad 1,222
13 The family of Adonikam................... 666
14 The family of Bigvai 2,056
15 The family of Adin.............................. 454
16 The family of Ater (descendants
    of Hezekiah)......................................98
17 The family of Bezai............................ 323
18 The family of Jorah............................. 112
19 The family of Hashum 223
20 The family of Gibbar............................95
21 The people of Bethlehem................. 123
22 The people of Netophah.....................56
23 The people of Anathoth 128
24 The people of Beth-azmaveth*..........42
25 The people of Kiriath-jearim,*
    Kephirah, and Beeroth................... 743
26 The people of Ramah and Geba 621

27 The people of Micmash 122
28 The people of Bethel and Ai 223
29 The citizens of Nebo 52
30 The citizens of Magbish 156
31 The citizens of West Elam* 1,254
32 The citizens of Harim 320
33 The citizens of Lod, Hadid,
    and Ono 725
34 The citizens of Jericho 345
35 The citizens of Senaah 3,630

36These are the priests who returned from exile:
    The family of Jedaiah (through the
    line of Jeshua) 973
37 The family of Immer 1,052
38 The family of Pashhur 1,247
39 The family of Harim 1,017

40These are the Levites who returned from exile:
    The families of Jeshua and Kadmiel
    (descendants of Hodaviah) 74
41 The singers of the family of
    Asaph 128
42 The gatekeepers of the families of
    Shallum, Ater, Talmon, Akkub,
    Hatita, and Shobai 139

43The descendants of the following Temple servants returned from exile:
    Ziha, Hasupha, Tabbaoth,
44 Keros, Siaha, Padon,
45 Lebanah, Hagabah, Akkub,
46 Hagab, Shalmai,* Hanan,
47 Giddel, Gahar, Reaiah,
48 Rezin, Nekoda, Gazzam,
49 Uzza, Paseah, Besai,
50 Asnah, Meunim, Nephusim,
51 Bakbuk, Hakupha, Harhur,
52 Bazluth, Mehida, Harsha,
53 Barkos, Sisera, Temah,
54 Neziah, and Hatipha.

55The descendants of these servants of King Solomon returned from exile:
    Sotai, Hassophereth, Peruda,
56 Jaalah, Darkon, Giddel,

57 Shephatiah, Hattil, Pokereth-hazzebaim, and Ami.

58In all, the Temple servants and the descendants of Solomon's servants numbered 392.

59Another group returned at this time from the towns of Tel-melah, Tel-harsha, Kerub, Addan, and Immer. However, they could not prove that they or their families were descendants of Israel. 60This group included the families of Delaiah, Tobiah, and Nekoda—a total of 652 people.

61Three families of priests—Hobaiah, Hakkoz, and Barzillai—also returned. (This Barzillai had married a woman who was a descendant of Barzillai of Gilead, and he had taken her family name.) 62They searched for their names in the genealogical records, but they were not found, so they were disqualified from serving as priests. 63The governor told them not to eat the priests' share of food from the sacrifices until a priest could consult the LORD about the matter by using the Urim and Thummim—the sacred lots.

64So a total of 42,360 people returned to Judah, 65in addition to 7,337 servants and 200 singers, both men and women. 66They took with them 736 horses, 245 mules, 67435 camels, and 6,720 donkeys.

68When they arrived at the Temple of the LORD in Jerusalem, some of the family leaders made voluntary offerings toward the rebuilding of God's Temple on its original site, 69and each leader gave as much as he could. The total of their gifts came to 61,000 gold coins,* 6,250 pounds* of silver, and 100 robes for the priests.

70So the priests, the Levites, the singers, the gatekeepers, the Temple servants, and some of the common people settled in villages near Jerusalem. The rest of the people returned to their own towns throughout Israel.

2:24 As in parallel text at Neh 7:28; Hebrew reads *Azmaveth*.   2:25 As in some Hebrew manuscripts and Greek version (see also Neh 7:29); Hebrew reads *Kiriath-arim*.   2:31 Or *of the other Elam*.   2:46 As in an alternate reading of the Masoretic Text (see also Neh 7:48); the other alternate reads *Shamlai*.   2:69a Hebrew *61,000 darics of gold*, about 1,100 pounds or 500 kilograms in weight.   2:69b Hebrew *5,000 minas* [3,000 kilograms].

NOTES

2:1 Here is the list of the Jewish exiles. The origin of this list and its relationship to an almost identical list in Neh 7 (and 1 Esdr 5:4-46) has confounded interpreters. Although some find the list in Neh 7 to be the source of the material in Ezra 2 (Allen 2003:23), it is equally possible that both used a third document. Since many names are not spelled the same in the Hebrew and since 29 of the 153 numbers are different, the two lists should not be seen as direct copies. Allrik (1954:21-27) gives some possible explanation concerning how an ancient, abbreviated numerical system could have been misunderstood or mis-copied. It is also impossible to identify what exact period of Judah's development this list represents. As the list appears immediately after ch 1, it might be assumed that these were the people who first came to Judah with Sheshbazzar, but his name is not even included among the list of leaders in 2:2 (instead, Zerubbabel is the leader), and many people had already settled in their towns (cf. 2:1, 70). The list was drawn from a town list, a family list, and a priestly list, which were put together sometime when Zerubbabel was the governor. It must be a list of people living in Yehud and not simply those who originally returned (some had died). The list was a summary of those who should be considered part of the true community of Israel. Once the list was made, government officials could have used the list for many different purposes. Nehemiah 7:5 refers to this list as a "genealogical record" (lit., "book of genealogies"), but it is clearly different from the genealogies in 1 Chr 1-9. This list shows that there was continuity with the past, for each family returned to resettle in its original town and presumably on its own eternal land inheritance.

the provinces. This refers to the area where the Jewish people lived after they returned to their homes. This would include the newly established province or administrative district of Yehud where Zerubbabel was the governor and maybe a neighboring province where a few people lived. The exact geographic boundaries of Yehud are still somewhat unclear. Ezra 2:21-35 identifies people by the places where they lived, but interpreters do not universally regard the cities Lod, Hadid, and Ono as being within the borders of the Persian province of Yehud. For this reason, some commentaries and translations (including NLT) refer to the plural "provinces" where the people settled (the Hebrew noun is singular). Fensham (1975:795-797) indicates that the Aramaic word for province could refer to a large satrapy or a smaller division (the province or state) of a satrapy.

2:2 Their leaders were Zerubbabel, Jeshua, Nehemiah . . . Mordecai . . . Bigvai. Shesh-bazzar was no longer the leader of the people; instead, Zerubbabel was in charge. Jeshua is the high priest mentioned in Hag 1:1 (see 5:2), though there his name is spelled Joshua. The rest of the list consists of lesser-known men whose names are identical with those of other biblical characters. In other words, the Nehemiah in this verse is *not* the later gover-nor who rebuilt the walls. This Mordecai is not the man mentioned in the book of Esther. Bigvai is a Persian name, but this is not the same person (Bagoas/Bagohi) who became gov-ernor of Yehud after Nehemiah (Cowley 1923:30.1 and 32.1). The inclusion of this Persian name indicates either that influential Jewish people took Persian names or that Persians were converted to faith in God.

2:3-20 The family of. Lit., "sons of." The first list connects people to an important patriar-chal figure. Some of these names have been found in secular documents of that time during excavations in Persia (Fensham 1982:51).

2:21-35 the people of. Lit., "the sons of" (*bene* [TH1121, ZH1201]), or in a few verses, "the men of" (*'anshe* [TH376, ZH408]; 2:22, 23, 27, 28). The second list of people associates them with towns that were primarily north of Jerusalem in Benjamin. Other towns, like Bethlehem, were south, Jericho was east, and Lod was west in the Sharon plain. Williamson (1985:34) thinks these were the towns the exiles were from, not the towns where people settled when they returned, but 2:1 specifically mentions that these exiles "returned" (*wayyashubu* [TH7725, ZH8740]) to their towns (lit., "each to his town"). Some of these places are well-known in the history of Israel, while others are obscure ("Kiriath-arim" in 2:25 is Kiriath-jearim; for others, see Clines 1984:47-53).

2:36-42 *priests . . . Levites*. Although David originally established 24 families of priests (1 Chr 24) to take care of the Temple, only four families are listed among those that returned to Yehud (more came with Ezra in 458 BC; 8:2-3). These and the additional families were included in other priestly lists in 1 Chr 9:10-13; 24:7-18; Neh 10:1 8; 11:10-14; 12:1-7.

2:43-58 *Temple servants . . . servants of King Solomon*. Based on 8:20, it appears that the Temple servants assisted the Levites. These servants (*nethinim* [TH5411, ZH5987], from the root *nathan* [TH5414, ZH5989], meaning "to give, devote, dedicate") were probably Gibeonites (Josh 9:23-27; 1 Chr 9:35-44) or war captives (Num 31:30-47). (See Haran 1961:159-169 regarding various opinions on who the Nethinim were.) They did mundane but essential tasks like carrying water, cutting wood, and sweeping the floors. Since the servants of Solomon were included in the same total in 2:58, most assume they also assisted with some tasks related to the daily functioning of the Temple (see also Neh 7:60; 11:3). Their names suggest that they were Canaanite captives (Myers 1965:19) who may have cared for Temple herds (Pokereth-hazzebaim [2:57] means "gazelle-keeper") or kept track of the inventory of tithes brought to the Temple storehouses (Hassophereth [2:55] means "scribe").

2:62 *they were disqualified from serving as priests*. The genealogical records in 1 Chr 1-9 demonstrate the care taken to preserve the genealogical history of each family. First Chronicles 9:1 indicates that all the people listed themselves in the genealogical records, and Nehemiah continued this tradition in Neh 7:5. Those who "could not prove that they or their families were descendants of Israel" (2:59) or who had lost their family records (2:62) were welcomed into the community of Israel but were disqualified from Temple service, even if they claimed priestly origins. The idea of being "disqualified" comes from the root *ga'al* [TH1351, ZH1458] (to defile, pollute, desecrate); thus, they were excluded from serving until this question about their defilement could be clarified.

2:63 *The governor*. To avoid the danger of bringing uncleanness into the Temple, a "governor" (2:63, *tirshatha'* [TH8660, ZH9579]; cf. Hoglund 1992:75-80), probably Sheshbazzar or Zerubbabel, temporarily excluded these people from eating "the priests' share of food," (*miqqodesh haqqadashim* [TH6944, ZH7731], "from the most holy things"; see Lev 7:21-36) until it could be determined if they were of priestly descent.

until a priest could consult the LORD about the matter by using the Urim and Thummim. The Urim and Thummim were small objects that the high priest used to determine the will of God in certain instances (Exod 28:30; Num 27:21; 1 Sam 23:9-12). The details of this method of determining God's will are hidden in mystery. Urim may mean "curses" and Thummim "goodness," so these objects may have indicated that something was good or bad. See E. Lipinski 1970:495-496, which cites an Assyrian text in which an Assyrian god answers a question based on the choice of a "desirable" or "undesirable" die. In the present case of Ezra-Nehemiah, the record never reports what the Urim and Thummim indicated about these families. If 8:33 and Neh 3:4 are connected (and they likely are), one discovers that Hakkoz's grandson Meremoth was functioning as an accepted priest in later years (see 2:61).

2:64 *total of 42,360 people returned to Judah*. This total does not match the sum of all the individual numbers (29,818) nor the sum of 31,089 in Neh 7 (but Nehemiah also gives 42,360 as the total). Some suggest that the difference is due to the exclusion of women from the smaller figure (Allen 2003:26), but this would be far too few women for the number of men. Another suggestion is to hypothesize that minor children were included in the total but not included in the individual listing. First Esdras 5:41 claims that the 42,360 total includes only those over 12 years old, suggesting that the difference between 42,360 and 29,818 (i.e., 12,542 people) could refer to those under 12 years of age.

2:65 in addition to 7,337 servants and 200 singers. The inclusion of such a large group of servants (the ratio to singers is 6 to 1) suggests that there was a fairly large number of wealthy Israelites who could afford the luxury of having servants. These singers are not listed among the Temple singers in 2:41 because they were secular singers who were employed by the wealthy (Williamson 1985:38).

2:68-70 the family leaders made voluntary offerings toward the rebuilding of God's Temple on its original site. The final verses (2:68-70) were not part of the genealogical records but were added to complete the statistical information about those coming to rebuild the Temple. Similar to the original building of the Tabernacle (Exod 25:2-7; 35:4-9), the Temple (1 Chr 29:1-9), and the renovation under Joash (2 Kgs 12), donations were given to finance the project (3:7). These funds supplemented the financial assistance given by Cyrus (6:4) and the contributions of those who stayed in Babylon (1:4-6; see note on 1:4). While Ezra said that "some of the family leaders made voluntary offerings" (lit., "gave freewill offerings"), Neh 7:70-72 indicates that some of the family leaders, the governor, and the rest of the people contributed to this project. That the text says "some" gave is not negative—it does not say "only some" gave or say anything negative about those who did not give. This is not a judgmental statement concerning those who could not contribute large sums (McConville 1985:17), for each gave "as much as he could" (2:69). Some families were quite wealthy, while others had no extra money to contribute. Although Ezra's and Nehemiah's numbers (which total these gifts) are not identical, the amount given was enormous on either account.

2:69 gold coins . . . silver. The "gold coins" were Persian *zahab darkemonim* [TH2091/1871, ZH2298/2007] (gold drachmas), not the later Greek drachma, while the "silver" refers to the Babylonian *kesep manim* [TH3701/4488, ZH4084/4949] ("silver mina" coins). Later, Darius I began minting the "daric" (the Persian word *dari* means "gold"). The daric coin was 98 percent pure gold, about three-fourths of an inch in diameter, and equivalent to a soldier's monthly pay (Yamauchi 1988:620). The "mina" was equal to 60 shekels, so this was a very sizable gift given by some very generous people. R. Loewe (1955:141-150) claims a talent was equal to three years' wages.

COMMENTARY

In contrast to Ezra 1, this chapter does not talk about what God did or how he led the people from Babylon. This narrative gives the results of God's moving in the hearts of the people in 1:5. It gives the names of the people who responded to God's call to go rebuild the Temple in Jerusalem. No mention is made of their faith, obedience, perseverance, dedication, or suffering; the only thing that is important at this juncture is that these people and their families returned to Jerusalem. Forever their names will be known as the people who made possible the reestablishment of the Jewish community in Jerusalem. This kind of listing is somewhat similar to the list of the charter members of every church and organization. These were the people who stuck their necks out and courageously did what others were afraid to do. They should not be forgotten by later generations. Surely God will not forget them. This reminds one of God's great books that contain a list of the names and deeds of every person (Dan 7:10; Rev 20:12). That list and Ezra's list indicate that each person is important in God's eyes and each person's deeds are significant.

The list is significant in that it records the names of the people who took the responsibility to be leaders (2:2), what family units set out together, what priestly and Levitical families were motivated to restart the sacred worship at the altar, and which upper- and lower-income (the servants) people were included in the "community of Israel." This list of forefathers was a testimony to God's many years of grace to those families (Holmgren 1987:16). These genealogies protected the purity of the nation by excluding others who did not come from a Hebrew family background. Requiring all the people to identify themselves by their family genealogy ensured separation from the impurity that might come from non-Jewish people. This meant that only legitimate priests would perform priestly responsibilities, that proper Temple singers would fulfill those roles, and that menial Temple servants would function according to their appointed tasks. Although being on the list as one of the founding fathers could lead to pride, the greater danger in later generations was the assumption that one's chosen status was based more on hereditary connections (see Rom 9:6; Phil 3:3-8) rather than one's spiritual relationship with God (Breneman 1993:83). Although being a person of Jewish descent was significant, and having parents that are members of a local church is good, God looks beyond these external factors to a person's heart. These people were stirred up in their hearts so much that they followed God's guidance.

The frequent listing of priests in postexilic books shows the importance of identifying the authentic priests who could legitimately carry out the priestly duties at the Temple. No one in this list claimed to be from the line of Aaron, but the prophet Haggai stated that Jeshua was the high priest in his day (Hag 1:1). Curiously, the Levitical numbers are very low (2:40-42). Later, Ezra found that no Levites volunteered to return with him (8:15); so he enlisted some leaders in exile to persuade Iddo from Casiphia to send some Levites. They convinced only 38 Levites to join Ezra. Why was this so? Some speculate that this was because they would get no inheritance in the land of Israel (see Josh 13:33). Others speculate that they were not interested in going to Jerusalem because their social status was downgraded during the exilic period, because they were already well employed in secular jobs in exile, or because there were very few Levites still alive (Clines 1984:54).

Singers and gatekeepers also had important roles (see 1 Chr 9:17-29; 15:16-24) in the Temple, and additional people from these groups came back with Ezra (7:7). The singers played instruments and sang for Temple services (1 Chr 25; Pss 73–83), while the gatekeepers (Neh 11:19; 12:25) administered the Temple storehouse (1 Chr 9:26-27) and secured the purity of the Temple by regulating who entered its gates (2 Chr 23:19).

The section begins and ends (2:1, 70) with a statement about the people settling the land. Corresponding to the initial comment in 2:1, the final verse of the chapter returns to the idea that people settled in their towns. The author was resuming his narrative where he left off in 2:1. One might think of this as an insignificant point that does not need to be repeated, but the possession of the land was of central theological importance to the Jewish people. This was the land God gave them, and now, by the grace of God, they were inheriting this great covenant gift once again.

The process of returning and settling in the land was part of the theology of the land, an idea included in the promises to Abram (Gen 12:1-3, 7), the exodus from Egypt (Exod 3:8), the conquest and inheritance of land by each tribe under Joshua (Josh 1:2-6; 13:1–19:51), the Davidic promise (2 Sam 7:8-10), and the prophetic eschatological promises (Amos 9:11-15). (See Brueggemann 1977 for an outline of land theology.) This was God's land (Lev 25:23), which he gave to his people as an eternal inheritance, so coming back to live in the land was fulfilling the divine plan. Settling in the land also enabled the people to offer sacrifices again at the one place God had chosen for his name to dwell (cf. Deut 12). It opened up the possibility of rebuilding the Temple and restoring the worship of God as it was originally designed. It was part of God's plan before the Exile to bring a remnant of his people back to the land. Their journey was not just a geographical one—it was a theological move to restore the people of God in the land of God for the purpose of worshiping God. This was an enormously important step for the Kingdom of God.

The people's commitment to this plan is displayed by their actions: They returned and gave generous financial gifts in support of rebuilding the Temple (2:68-69). It appears from the size of the gifts that the people were not just giving their tithe; they were freely giving from their resources far more than anything that was required. This response suggests that the community of Israel was united together in their commitment to the new opportunity to impact the future and the new situation in Jerusalem (McConville 1985:17). These people must have believed that if they would take seriously the new opportunities to serve God in this new land and fully support the challenge to rebuild the Temple, God could do great things through them.

This is the challenge that every new generation of believers faces, especially those who are trying to start a new work for God in a new place. They will ask, How can God use us to make a significant impact on this world? They must commit themselves to do what others fear to do. They must stand out in a hostile, sinful world as the community of believers who dare to raise up a new standard for God. They must commit themselves to unity and purity and work together to see God bless their efforts. The generous giving of one's money and oneself is also usually a key ingredient that accompanies the fulfillment of God's work even today.

◆   B. Worshiping God Brings Opposition (Ezra 3:1–4:23)
      1. Restoration of worship (Ezra 3:1-13)

In early autumn,* when the Israelites had settled in their towns, all the people assembled in Jerusalem with a unified purpose. ²Then Jeshua son of Jehozadak* joined his fellow priests and Zerubbabel son of Shealtiel with his family in rebuilding the altar of the God of Israel. They wanted to sacrifice burnt offerings on it, as instructed in the Law of Moses, the man of God. ³Even though the people were afraid of the local residents, they rebuilt the altar at its old site. Then they began to sacrifice burnt offerings on the altar to the LORD each morning and evening.

⁴They celebrated the Festival of Shelters as prescribed in the Law, sacrificing the number of burnt offerings specified for each day of the festival. ⁵They also offered the regular burnt offerings and the offerings required for the new moon

celebrations and the annual festivals as prescribed by the LORD. The people also gave voluntary offerings to the LORD. ⁶Fifteen days before the Festival of Shelters began,* the priests had begun to sacrifice burnt offerings to the LORD. This was even before they had started to lay the foundation of the LORD's Temple.

⁷Then the people hired masons and carpenters and bought cedar logs from the people of Tyre and Sidon, paying them with food, wine, and olive oil. The logs were brought down from the Lebanon mountains and floated along the coast of the Mediterranean Sea* to Joppa, for King Cyrus had given permission for this.

⁸The construction of the Temple of God began in midspring,* during the second year after they arrived in Jerusalem. The work force was made up of everyone who had returned from exile, including Zerubbabel son of Shealtiel, Jeshua son of Jehozadak and his fellow priests, and all the Levites. The Levites who were twenty years old or older were put in charge of rebuilding the LORD's Temple. ⁹The workers at the Temple of God were supervised by Jeshua

with his sons and relatives, and Kadmiel and his sons, all descendants of Hodaviah.* They were helped in this task by the Levites of the family of Henadad.

¹⁰When the builders completed the foundation of the LORD's Temple, the priests put on their robes and took their places to blow their trumpets. And the Levites, descendants of Asaph, clashed their cymbals to praise the LORD, just as King David had prescribed. ¹¹With praise and thanks, they sang this song to the LORD:

"He is so good!
   His faithful love for Israel endures
      forever!"

Then all the people gave a great shout, praising the LORD because the foundation of the LORD's Temple had been laid.

¹²But many of the older priests, Levites, and other leaders who had seen the first Temple wept aloud when they saw the new Temple's foundation. The others, however, were shouting for joy. ¹³The joyful shouting and weeping mingled together in a loud noise that could be heard far in the distance.

3:1 Hebrew *In the seventh month.* The year is not specified, so it may have been during Cyrus's first year (538 B.C.) or second year (537 B.C.). The seventh month of the ancient Hebrew lunar calendar occurred within the months of September/October 538 B.C. and October/November 537 B.C.   **3:2** Hebrew *Jozadak,* a variant spelling of Jehozadak; also in 3:8.   **3:6** Hebrew *On the first day of the seventh month.* This day in the ancient Hebrew lunar calendar occurred in September or October. The Festival of Shelters began on the fifteenth day of the seventh month.   **3:7** Hebrew *the sea.*   **3:8** Hebrew *in the second month.* This month in the ancient Hebrew lunar calendar occurred within the months of April and May 536 B.C.   **3:9** Hebrew *sons of Judah* (i.e., *bene Yehudah*). *Bene* might also be read here as the proper name Binnui; *Yehudah* is probably another name for Hodaviah. Compare 2:40; Neh 7:43; 1 Esdras 5:58.

NOTES

3:1 *In early autumn.* Lit., "In the seventh month." See NLT mg.

with a unified purpose. Lit., "as one man" (*ke'ish 'ekhad* [TH3509.1/376/259, ZH3869/408/285]). The unity of the nation (Batten 1913:107) was very important at this time, for they were few in number and were living in a hostile environment (3:3; 4:1-5).

3:2 *Jeshua son of Jehozadak joined his fellow priests and Zerubbabel son of Shealtiel with his family in rebuilding the altar.* These two important people and their families took a leadership position in reestablishing worship. Jeshua was listed first because this was a religious activity, not a political event. Later, Jeshua is called the high priest and Zerubbabel is identified as the governor (Neh 12:1; Hag 1:1, 12, 14; 2:2, 4), but in Ezra these titles are not used (2:2; 3:2; 4:3; 5:2). This purposely de-emphasizes the official roles these men had (we do not know when the titles and official roles started). This may indicate that several people in these families, and not just the leaders, motivated people to action (Japhet 1968:84). Jehozadak, Jeshua's father, was the high priest when Jerusalem was destroyed in 587–586 BC (1 Chr 6:14-15).

as instructed in the Law of Moses. The people knew they needed to sacrifice on the right kind of altar (built of uncut stones), built in the right place (the original site God chose), with proper sacrifices (unblemished animals), offered by divinely appointed priests (Levitical priests) because they were using the instructions in the law of Moses as their guide. Some commentators believe this rebuilding of a new altar required them to demolish a makeshift altar that was built after the Babylonians destroyed the Temple (see Jer 41:5, in which a grain offering is brought after the fall of Jerusalem [Jer 39:1-8]; this perhaps involved a makeshift altar; cf. Myers 1965:26-27; Jones 1963:12-31) because it was defiled by heathen worship (Clines 1984:65). Nothing is said in the text about destroying an existing altar, so any opinion in support of this interpretation is rather speculative. The Jewish people put a high priority on purity of worship, so if there was an impure altar, it would not be used. A strict adherence to the law of Moses characterized the lifestyle of the returnees.

3:3 *afraid of the local residents.* Lit., "in fear of the people of the land." Nickolson (1965:59-66) asserts that the text "people of the land" refers to different groups in differ-ent texts. Sometimes it refers to poor people (2 Kgs 25:12; Jer 39:10), but here it means the people of Samaria who were living in the land before the Jewish people returned from exile. This fear of the local Ammonites, Moabites, Edomites, and Samarians could be due to the small number of the Jewish immigrants at Jerusalem, who had no military force to protect them from intruders. It would be easy to become intimidated by threats of attack. This new altar was exclusively Jewish, so the neighboring people could not use it (Fensham 1982:59). This exclusivity probably angered some of their non-Jewish neighbors.

each morning and evening. This refers to the daily sacrifices of a lamb plus flour, wine, and oil (Exod 29:38-42; Num 28:3-8), which signified the people's dedication of that day to God.

3:4 *Festival of Shelters.* This was the joyous celebration (also known as the Feast of Tab-ernacles; Exod 23:14-16; Lev 23:33-43; Deut 16:13-16), which commemorated the time when the people lived in tents during their 40-year journey from Egypt to the Promised Land. "Shelters" (*sukkoth* [TH5521, ZH6109]) refers to the huts or tents the people lived in. On each day of this festival, the people offered specific sacrifices of worship and dedication to God (Num 29:12-38). No doubt the people realized some similarities between their own return to the land and their forefathers' wilderness journey to the land, but no explicit comparison is made in the text. This feast was combined with praise to God and joy over the fall harvest, so many freewill offerings (3:5) were presented at this time. In light of this great feast and other earlier celebrations (1 Kgs 8), it is strange to have Nehemiah say that the Festival of Shelters in his day was unlike any other since the time of Joshua (Neh 8:17). Apparently, the joy and enthusiasm in Nehemiah's day was even greater than the joy described here in Ezra 3.

3:6 *before they had started to lay the foundation of the LORD's Temple.* This temporal marker requires the events in 3:1-6 to be put at an early date, shortly after the people's return, not 18 years later at 520 BC. The people joyfully celebrated the event even though they had not begun to work on the Temple building itself, perhaps concluding that some worship was better than none. The verb *yussad* [TH3245, ZH3569], which is translated "lay the foundation," can be used of any act of repairing or rebuilding and should not be tied only to the original setting of the foundation stones (Gelston 1966:232-235). The founda-tion of the old Temple was most likely underground but still in place, but probably some foundation stones were broken and needed replacing, or some had moved over the 70 years of exile and needed to be put back in place. This statement does not suggest that this was a totally new foundation that was started in another place. They used the old foundation, but repaired it.

3:7 *King Cyrus had given permission for this.* The difficult word *rishyon* [TH7558, ZH8397] (permission) is found only here in the OT, so it is difficult to know exactly what it means. However, "permission" does not refer to a "grant" of money from Cyrus to pay for these things (6:4), nor to Cyrus's general letter that granted the people "permission" or authority to build this Temple (Myers 1965:27). This permission is related to getting supplies from the king's forest in Lebanon.

3:8 *midspring.* Lit., "the second month." This was the logical time (April/May) to begin building a large construction project because the spring harvest of barley was over and the dry season was starting. Thus, the builders had already completed their agricultural responsibilities related to the harvest and did not have to contend with mud when moving lumber and stones. Solomon also began his building of the Temple in the second month of the year (1 Kgs 6:1). The rebuilding of the Temple began in the second year after arriving at Jerusalem, so the altar must have been constructed in the first year. One reason for the delay was that it would take some time for the people to get settled in their homes and several months to cut and then transport timber from Lebanon to Jerusalem.

The Levites who were twenty years old or older were put in charge of rebuilding the LORD's Temple. During the construction of this holy building, it was appropriate that the Levites (Jeshua and Kadmiel) be in charge of the work. Although Zerubbabel the governor was involved, he and Jeshua delegated responsibility for the specific tasks of rebuilding to all the Levites. In order to find enough Levites to direct the work (Allen 2003:34-35), the age of eligible priests was lowered to include all those over age 20 (age 20 was the limit in 1 Chr 23:27, but Num 8:24 used 25, and Num 4:3 used 30 for the beginning of priestly duties). Supervision by the Levites ensured that the work was done according to Mosaic requirements and was ritually correct (Fensham 1982:64).

3:10 *When the builders completed the foundation.* The author gave minor attention to the initial reconstruction details and instead put major emphasis on the joyous celebration of the people. In continuity with the past, the priests wore the proper attire, the Levitical singers (2:41) blew their trumpets and clashed cymbals, and the people praised and thanked God. All this happened just as in the golden age before the Exile: The people followed Davidic traditions and patterns set in earlier Temple celebrations when David brought the Ark to Jerusalem and when Solomon dedicated the Temple in Jerusalem (1 Chr 15–16; 2 Chr 5; 7).

3:11 *With praise and thanks, they sang this song to the LORD.* Lit., "They responded (*wayya'anu* [TH6030A, ZH6702]) with praise and gave thanks to the LORD." Two types of songs (praise and thanksgiving) were sung after the initial instrumental musical presentation, possibly as antiphonal responses.

COMMENTARY

The first section (3:1-6) describes the returnees' initial community worship of God at Jerusalem, which occurred in the seventh month, the month of Tishri (September/October). In this one month, Rosh Hashanah (New Year's Day; see Lev 23:23-25), Yom Kippur (the Day of Atonement; see Lev 16; 23:27), and Succoth (the Festival of Tabernacles or Shelters; see Lev 23:34-36) are all celebrated. Yamauchi (1988:621) proposes that this celebration occurred only a few months after their arrival in Jerusalem, though the text does not indicate in what year it occurred. Other commentators prefer to date these events about 17 years later (around 520 BC) because the people could not have settled in their towns (3:1) so quickly (it would take years for them to rebuild their homes) and because 4:24–5:2 and Haggai 1:1 place the activity of Zerubbabel and Jeshua (3:2) in the second year of Darius, 520 BC (Williamson 1985:43-44). This latter approach views 4:4-5 as a "summary notation" that recapitulates what was said in 3:1-6 (Talmon 1976:322), and it dates the whole episode to the time of Darius I, not Cyrus. This approach is based on the "repetitive resumption" of the story in 4:24, which is clearly dated to the time of Darius I. Although most recognize the value of these literary characteristics (the "summary notation" and "repetitive resumption"), their main purpose was to make literary-theological connections, rather than to serve as temporal markers. Thus, the building in Cyrus's day in 3:1–4:5 was tied thematically and theologically (not chronologically, as an identical event) to events in the time of Darius I in 4:24.

The Jews' desire to worship God at their own altar in Jerusalem brought the people together. With 50,000 people on hand, it is clear that they did not agree on everything, but all minor issues of disagreement were quickly put in the background so they could accomplish the main reason for returning to Jerusalem. Arguments and division would hinder their ability to bring glory to God, while a unified desire to worship God would promote unity and the accomplishment of their deepest spiritual desire.

Before the workers could build the walls of the Temple, they needed to make repairs to the foundation of the building. The Temple was destroyed in the Babylonian conquest, but it is unlikely that the Babylonians went to the effort of digging down and removing the large foundation stones of the Temple. Earthquakes, freezing water, tree roots, and falling stones may have broken a few foundation stones that needed to be replaced, leveled, or straightened.

Ezra 3:7 tells us that "the people hired masons and carpenters and bought cedar logs from the people of Tyre and Sidon." There are parallels between the building of this Temple and Solomon's building of the first Temple (1 Chr 22:1-5; 2 Chr 2:7-16). Both used tall and strong cedars from Lebanon, hired foreigners to do some of the work, brought the logs in through the natural Mediterranean seaport of Joppa, and paid these workers with gold and common agricultural commodities that were grown in Palestine. While it is unlikely that there was a direct literary connection between these two building accounts (i.e., Ezra was not copying this text from Chronicles), historical necessity (e.g., Lebanon was the only place one could find tall cedars) and the author's desire to create continuity with the past (and thus legitimacy) resulted in similarities between the two construction accounts.

Ezra 3:8 indicates that "the work force was made up of everyone who had returned." The author repeatedly recorded the strong unity and enthusiasm of those involved in the project of rebuilding. Jeshua and Zerubbabel are not named as the leaders of the community in this passage, but by listing only these two men, the author implicitly ranked them as people who were committed to the task of getting the work done. The text does not say exactly what everyone did, only that everyone worked. It was important that everyone be involved in some way to support this community project. Some lifted stones, some transported wood from Joppa, some baked food for the workers to eat, and some organized the people into work teams. This large rebuilding effort could not be finished if everyone did not pitch in and help or if there was a spirit of disunity or laziness among the people.

Ezra 3:10-12 relates the emotional response of the people to the rebuilding of the foundation of the Temple. Although they had only completed the initial phase of laying the foundation, they were excited. Their emotional outburst recognizing the goodness of God (Millard 1966:115-117), as well as his steadfast covenant love (*khesed* [TH2617, ZH2876]; see further Sakenfeld 1978 on the meaning of *khesed*), did not concentrate on all the work they had yet to do to complete the Temple, but on what God had already accomplished through them.

The emotional outburst gave way to singing. The people may have sung hymns like Psalms 100, 106, or 107, or the repetitive Psalm 136 that focuses on God's everlasting covenant love. The people gave loud shouts of jubilation, showing their gladness and appreciation for God's grace. This was a great and monumental day for the people of God. They had seen God's hand at work and were anxiously looking forward with great anticipation to completing the rest of the Temple building.

The emotional outburst also gave way to weeping. The text does not explicitly state the reason why some of the older generation that remembered Solomon's magnificent Temple wept. Were these people overcome with immense joy at seeing the rebuilding of Solomon's Temple, or were these tears of sorrow because this building would never match the glory and splendor of what they remembered from the past? Some commentators have interpreted this weeping based on later comments in Haggai 2:3. Haggai mentioned the complaints of the older people about the lack of glory in this new Temple (about 16 years later, when the Temple was actually finished), and many have read that same attitude back into this passage in Ezra (McConville 1985:210; Myers 1965:29). It seems better to see these as separate events, for Haggai 2:3 does not mention any weeping and Ezra mentions no negative comparative attitudes by the older people. There was no opposition by the older generation to rebuilding the Temple at this early date, so it is best to conclude that the tears in Ezra 3 are tears of joy. Finally God was giving them the unbelievable joy of seeing the Temple in the process of being rebuilt. Their joy was probably similar to the joyful tears of the Israelis who finally reached the Wailing Wall in the war for Jerusalem in 1967 (Yamauchi 1988:625).

The theological significance of being settled in the land and rebuilding the altar and Temple on their original sites was enormous. This was the place where Abraham offered Isaac (Gen 22:2; 2 Chr 3:1); it was the only place in the world where the Jews could offer legitimate sacrifices for atonement of sin. This Temple was the one place on earth where the worshiper could come into the presence of God. God's name and reputation rested on this place. The Psalms tell of the people's longing to have the wonderful opportunity of participating in the worship in these courts (Pss 26:8; 84:1-2; 100:4-5). Of course, the importance of this event was heightened by the fact that many of these people had never worshiped here in all their lives. They left Babylon so they could help rebuild the altar and the Temple; this was one of their greatest dreams come true. The meaning drawn from participating in the first burnt offering in their lifetimes, the joy of celebrating their first Festival of Shelters, and the thrill of hearing the trumpets and Levitical choir at their first Temple event would be overwhelming. Surely God was good to them; he deserved thanks for his steadfast covenantal love to such a rebellious people. The loud shouting, praise, and weeping only reaffirmed the emotionally charged atmosphere of the situation. This was the kind of spirited worship that pleases God, and it should characterize all worship by God's people today.

In the midst of this description of Israel's worship, another important theological theme is demonstrated—the theme of unity. From the outset we see the unity of the people who "assembled in Jerusalem with a unified purpose" to worship God (3:1). After all those years in exile with all kinds of pagan influences that could have led people astray, these people managed to proclaim their solidarity by singing God's praise together (Throntveit 1992:22). Their unity was demonstrated in a very practical way because "the work force was made up of everyone who had returned" (3:8), not just people from one tribe or one city. This was not the time for people to argue about who would do what job, what hymns or choruses should be sung, or who should sit where. Everyone was overjoyed to be there worshiping their great God.

Unity was partially based on the consistent care taken to preserve the continuity between what Jewish people had done over the past centuries and what the people were doing at this time. The altar and Temple were placed where their grandparents used to stand (3:3, 6), and everything was to be done exactly "as instructed in the Law of Moses" (3:2, 4) or "as King David had prescribed" (3:10). The right stones were used for the altar, the right procedures were carried out for the Festival of Shelters, the right people sang the Temple songs, and the right people oversaw the construction. Care was taken to avoid mistakes that might cause disunity. As mentioned above, the weeping in 3:12 was not a note of discord in the ranks but a natural emotional response to God's love and the thrill of what was happening. Unity was also enhanced because everyone had one thing in mind: the desire to praise and thank God for his abundant goodness and his steadfast covenant love for them (3:10-11). These sacrifices, feasts, and the worship at the dedication of the Temple were all based on God's character of grace toward his undeserving people. These people did not deserve what they were enjoying, and they were quick to turn their words of praise and glory toward God.

A rather minor emphasis in the text is the presence of good leaders. It is mentioned that the sons of Asaph led in the singing (3:10), the Levites Jeshua and Kadmiel and their families provided oversight for the Temple rebuilding (3:9), and Jeshua and Zerubbabel gave oversight to the construction of the altar (3:2). But very little is made of these servant leaders. Leaders earn their stripes when they lead in difficult times, not when everything is going great. Servant leaders were needed, and many served effectively, but God was the one the people glorified and praised. This building was not the accomplishment of one leader; it was God's work of grace.

◆   ## 2. Opposition to the restoration of the Temple (Ezra 4:1-5)

The enemies of Judah and Benjamin heard that the exiles were rebuilding a Temple to the LORD, the God of Israel. ²So they approached Zerubbabel and the other leaders and said, "Let us build with you, for we worship your God just as you do. We have sacrificed to him ever since King Esarhaddon of Assyria brought us here."

³But Zerubbabel, Jeshua, and the other leaders of Israel replied, "You may have no part in this work. We alone will build the Temple for the LORD, the God of Israel, just as King Cyrus of Persia commanded us."

⁴Then the local residents tried to discourage and frighten the people of Judah to keep them from their work. ⁵They bribed agents to work against them and to frustrate their plans. This went on during the entire reign of King Cyrus of Persia and lasted until King Darius of Persia took the throne.*

4:5 Darius reigned 521–486 B.C.

NOTES

4:1 *The enemies of Judah and Benjamin.* These people were the people of Samaria (not the Samaritans as Josephus suggests in *Antiquities* 11.84). They were moved to Samaria by the Assyrians (4:2) and seemed to combine the worship of God with that of pagan gods.

the exiles were rebuilding a Temple. Some maintain that this event did not take place early in Cyrus's reign, two years after the returnees first came to Jerusalem; instead, they place this opposition 16 years later, in the time of Haggai and Zechariah, during the reign of Darius I, around 520 BC (Williamson 1985:43). Since 3:8-11 places the initial work on the Temple in the second year after the people returned, it is more natural to place the events of 4:1-5 shortly after the dedication of the foundations, not 15 years later.

4:2 *We have sacrificed to him.* The consonants of MT read "we have not sacrificed," which makes no sense if the neighbors wanted to build the Temple with the Hebrews. The Qere reading of MT and the Old Greek and Vulgate indicate that *lo'* [TH3808, ZH4202] (not) should be spelled as a preposition with a third-person sg. suffix *lo* [TH3807.1/2050.2, ZH4200/2257] (to him). This understanding ("we have sacrificed *to him*") makes much better sense.

4:3 *You may have no part in this work.* Lit., "It is not for you and for us." The response to the seemingly friendly suggestion of cooperation in 4:2 was a rather strong "No, thank you." There were two rationales for this decision: (1) In contrast to their neighbors' claim, the Jewish leaders believed that they did not worship the same God. Thus, there was no basis for cooperation. (2) A literal interpretation of the decree of Cyrus indicated that authorization to rebuild the Temple was granted only to the Jews who returned from Babylon. Both points naturally lead to the conclusion that Israel's neighbors could not be allowed to join in the rebuilding project. It is interesting that some of these Samarian people in 6:21 separated themselves from the impurities of their past religious beliefs and were welcomed to join in worship with the Jewish people (Allen 2003:37).

4:4 *local residents tried to discourage and frighten the people of Judah.* The local residents included, but were not limited to, those who wanted to help rebuild the Temple. They were offended by the Jewish leaders' rebuff of their offer of cooperation and set out to frustrate and intimidate them. (*Umebalahim* [TH1089, ZH1164], "to deter," is found only here in the Bible, so some prefer *umebahalim* [TH926, ZH987], "to frighten," which is found in the Qere. Either word makes sense in this context, and the meanings are not that different. The Kethiv of MT is a more difficult reading, though it is easy to see how a writing mistake—the He and the Lamedh are in a different order in the two texts—may have created this unusual form that is not found elsewhere in the Hebrew Bible.) We do not know exactly what these enemies did to discourage and frighten people. They probably threatened to physically harm them, which forced some people to turn their attention to their own safety rather than the rebuilding project. The hostile environment could have affected travel, economics, and law and order. Their enemies probably told lies about what the Jewish people were up to, thus causing people who had a positive relationship with the Jewish returnees to distrust them.

4:5 *They bribed agents to work against them.* One of the ways the enemies discouraged the Jewish populace was by influencing the decisions of different Persian politicians. By bribing Persian officials on the provincial and national level, permission to cut and haul wood could be delayed, Persian financial assistance could be cut off for a time, and an atmosphere of distrust and suspicion could develop. This slowed the work to a complete standstill and put the whole reconstruction project on hold for 16 years, from 536 until 520 BC, when Darius I was king (see Hag 1:1).

COMMENTARY

Verses 1 and 2 deal with opposition during the time of Cyrus around 536 BC. The text does not immediately define the enemies of Yehud by their ethnic background or their political loyalties, but in 4:2 these people identify themselves as the exiles King Esarhaddon of Assyria resettled in the northern nation of Israel. After Israel was defeated in 721 BC and exiled out of the land (2 Kgs 17:24-40), the Assyrian king Sargon II transported people from Babylon, Cuthah, Avva, Hamath, and Sepharvaim to Israel to take their place. (Millard [1976:1-14] demonstrates that the names of these towns in Hebrew are very similar to their original names in Akkadian.) Because these people did not worship the true God of Israel, God sent lions to destroy many of them (2 Kgs 17:26). Consequently, the Assyrian king sent a few Israelite priests back to Bethel to teach these foreign people to worship Israel's God. Although these people did know about Israel's God, they did not stop offering sacrifices to their own pagan gods. There is no other biblical information on this second group of people that Esarhaddon (681–669 BC) brought to this territory. He did have a military campaign in the area, so it is possible that he settled people in Palestine at that time (ANET 290). Isaiah 7:8 refers to a significant event in Israel about 65 years later (around 670 BC), which fits within the reign of Esarhaddon. Isaiah was focusing on Israel's judgment and did not predict exiles moving into the land that had been the northern kingdom of Israel. It appears that this new group, which included a few Israelite priests, followed the pattern of worshiping their own gods as well as Israel's God. The grandchildren of these people probably became the Samaritans of later history (John 4; Josephus *Antiquities* 11.19).

These people claimed to worship the same God the Israelites worshiped, but they did not say that they exclusively worshiped Israel's God. Missing from their description of their worship was any claim to have done all that was prescribed in the law of Moses; this was a contrast to the returnees (3:2, 4-5; cf. 3:10). One can assume that these enemies had hidden political motives behind this offer to help the Jewish returnees rebuild the Temple. Although helping in this project would have cost these neighbors money and many hours of labor, it would have given them some control over what happened there and a means of influencing political decisions in the future (Blenkinsopp 1988:107). But these ulterior political motives were masked by the attention focused on theological things.

The returnees decided not to let the enemies of Judah and Benjamin help them in the rebuilding project. There was clear religious conviction and political unity on this decision. The politician Zerubbabel did not decide what to do on his own without considering the implications of this decision on the community. Instead, he gathered all the community leaders together so that they could consider their options and benefit from the wisdom of all the members of the group. They wisely chose purity of worship over financial aid, temporal expediency, or even peace with their neighbors. They decided that they were willing to suffer persecution for the sake of maintaining the purity of their faith.

The reader should not view the Jewish population in Jerusalem as presenting lame excuses that hid a political agenda or some sort of racial prejudice. Religious purity was highly prized by those who returned to Jerusalem; they repeatedly did things exactly as instructed in their Scriptures and according to the permission given by Cyrus (3:2, 4, 7, 10). They knew that the Exile had been caused by syncretism with baalism and other pagan practices, and they did not want to repeat those mistakes again. Rejecting all other gods and worshiping only the God of Abraham, Isaac, and Jacob was the defining characteristic of these people. If they gave up on this key point, they would not survive as the people of God. Of course, any religious cooperation with non-Jewish neighbors could also have had political consequences. If they made political decisions outside the parameters defined by Cyrus, they might jeopardize the generosity the Persians had already shown.

The theological significance of the decision not to cooperate with the people of the land was monumental. It set a standard for purity of worship and separation from the world that Ezra could raise as a standard to the people of his day, for in Ezra's time people were cooperating and intermarrying with pagans (9:1-3). This decision pitted moral compromise and expediency against maintaining high theological standards and suffering persecution. Standing up for what is true and right is often a matter of making tough calls on issues that are somewhat gray. Someone could make the argument that the people of the land truly did worship the God of Israel, gave the traditional sacrifices, and were open to helping the Jews do something that would bring honor to God. Would it not be better to include these people and then persuade them to reform some of their inappropriate behavior later? If they excluded these people immediately, how could they ever hope to reach out and influence them for good? But it would not make any sense to conclude that the Jews could never talk to unbelievers, sell or buy from an unbeliever, go to an unbelieving doctor, or permit an unbeliever to attend a worship service (cf. Deut 16; 2 Chr 30:25). So today, conversions require people to have personal relationships with unbelievers, to be salt and light in the midst of darkness, to offer a way of hope to those who are seeking a better way. Radical separation into a monastery or a fortress church does nothing to spread the Good News about God's way of forgiveness and blessing.

Nevertheless, the radical choice of maintaining a holy separation from the worship of other gods was and is a fundamental dividing marker between those who love God with all their hearts and those who do not. All people must answer the question: Whom do we serve? Is God the supreme Lord and master of my life? Although some will speak the name of Jesus and know all about the Gospel parables and the exodus from Egypt, knowledge about the Bible is not what God requires. God will not share his glory with any other gods or persons, so absolute dedication to the glorification of God must motivate behavior and put a limit on cooperation. There is no wiggle room when it comes to a person's commitment to God. People are either for God or against him. Those who are for him love him with all their hearts and minds and obey his commandments (John 14:15). Jesus also warned that the world would hate us because it hated him (John 15:18). Persecution is not something a true believer can avoid. Thus, people must choose: Will we say no to the world that hates God and be persecuted, or will we compromise our faith and enjoy peace with those who hate God?

This stance does not exclude evangelism or require seclusion into a separatist community. It requires total dedication to the process of drawing other people into the community of those who truly worship God. Friendship with unbelievers is not excluded but required by the nature of everyday life. Nevertheless, friendship and care for unbelievers is drastically different from accepting their theological beliefs and behavioral standards as one's own. When believers let friendships with unbelievers influence them toward unchristian behavior, those who are mature in the faith should be doing everything possible to transform their minds (Rom 12:1-2). Having clear convictions about the truth should motivate believers to reach out to win others to trust in God.

◆   ## 3. Opposition to the restoration of the walls (Ezra 4:6-23)

⁶Years later when Xerxes* began his reign, the enemies of Judah wrote a letter of accusation against the people of Judah and Jerusalem.

⁷Even later, during the reign of King Artaxerxes of Persia,* the enemies of Judah, led by Bishlam, Mithredath, and Tabeel, sent a letter to Artaxerxes in the Aramaic language, and it was translated for the king.

⁸*Rehum the governor and Shimshai the court secretary wrote the letter, telling King Artaxerxes about the situation in Jerusalem. ⁹They greeted the king for all their colleagues—the judges and local leaders, the people of Tarpel, the Persians, the Babylonians, and the people of Erech and Susa (that is, Elam). ¹⁰They also sent greetings from the rest of the people whom the great and noble Ashurbanipal* had deported and relocated in Samaria and throughout the neighboring lands of the province west of the Euphrates River.* ¹¹This is a copy of their letter:

"To King Artaxerxes, from your loyal subjects in the province west of the Euphrates River.

¹²"The king should know that the Jews who came here to Jerusalem from Babylon are rebuilding this rebellious and evil city. They have already laid the foundation and will soon finish its walls. ¹³And the king should know that if this city is rebuilt and its walls are completed, it will be much to your disadvantage, for the Jews will then refuse to pay their tribute, customs, and tolls to you.

¹⁴"Since we are your loyal subjects* and do not want to see the king dishonored in this way, we have sent

the king this information. [15]We suggest that a search be made in your ancestors' records, where you will discover what a rebellious city this has been in the past. In fact, it was destroyed because of its long and troublesome history of revolt against the kings and countries who controlled it. [16]We declare to the king that if this city is rebuilt and its walls are completed, the province west of the Euphrates River will be lost to you."

[17]Then King Artaxerxes sent this reply:

"To Rehum the governor, Shimshai the court secretary, and their colleagues living in Samaria and throughout the province west of the Euphrates River. Greetings.

[18]"The letter you sent has been translated and read to me. [19]I ordered a search of the records and have found that Jerusalem has indeed been a hotbed of insurrection against many kings. In fact, rebellion and revolt are normal there! [20]Powerful kings have ruled over Jerusalem and the entire province west of the Euphrates River, receiving tribute, customs, and tolls. [21]Therefore, issue orders to have these men stop their work. That city must not be rebuilt except at my express command. [22]Be diligent, and don't neglect this matter, for we must not permit the situation to harm the king's interests."

[23]When this letter from King Artaxerxes was read to Rehum, Shimshai, and their colleagues, they hurried to Jerusalem. Then, with a show of strength, they forced the Jews to stop building.

4:6 Hebrew *Ahasuerus*, another name for Xerxes. He reigned 486–465 B.C.   4:7 Artaxerxes reigned 465–424 B.C.   4:8 The original text of 4:8–6:18 is in Aramaic.   4:10a Aramaic *Osnappar*, another name for Ashurbanipal.   4:10b Aramaic *the province beyond the river;* also in 4:11, 16, 17, 20.   4:14 Aramaic *Since we eat the salt of the palace.*

NOTES

4:7 later, during the reign of King Artaxerxes of Persia. The opposition to Jewish reconstruction continued during parts of Artaxerxes' reign (465–424 BC), but the exact years are unknown. The text does not coordinate these events with the life of Ezra, who was sent in the seventh year of Artaxerxes (7:6-7), or with the life of Nehemiah, who was commissioned to go to Jerusalem in the twentieth year of Artaxerxes (Neh 2:1). Since Artaxerxes was bothered by Egyptian revolts, plus attacks by the Greeks, he probably listened seriously when his provincial officials warned him that some people were planning to revolt in Jerusalem. It was a wise move to keep a lid on all suspicious activity until all portions of the kingdom were securely under his control.

sent a letter to Artaxerxes in the Aramaic language. Aramaic (*'aramith* [TH762, ZH811]) was the common diplomatic language of Palestine at that time. Since 4:8-23 are in the Aramaic language, it would appear that the author of this book had actual copies of these letters and was summarizing or quoting from them. The verse refers to Aramaic twice (lit., "It was written in Aramaic and translated Aramaic"). The second reference to Aramaic seems unnecessary, but it may be a marker indicating where the Aramaic section starts (immediately after that word), and was not an intended part of the verse (Clines 1984:77). Some translations suggest that the second reference to Aramaic indicates that the letter was translated "from" Aramaic, that it relates to the Aramaic type of script (Williamson 1985:61; Allen 2003:41), or that it was a bilingual text with a section translating the Aramaic into Persian for the sake of the Persian king (Blenkinsopp 1988:112).

4:8 Rehum the governor and Shimshai the court secretary wrote the letter. The role of Rehum is not totally clear. He seems to be a local official who was sympathetic to the complaints of Bishlam, Mithredath, and Tabeel. Some think he was a high-ranking government administrator (*be'el-te'em* [TA/ZA10116/10302, S1169/2942], "the master of a decree"), but not the governor (Williamson 1985:61). Apparently, one of Rehum's responsibilities was to correspond with higher officials in Susa so that they would be informed about the political conditions within the province. The court secretary Shimshai was a skilled scribe who had the ability to write and translate messages in different languages. Oppenheim (1965:253) emphasizes the importance of the scribe because he (even more than the speaker of the message) determined how a message would be expressed and how it would be heard by the Persian king. Clines suggests that 4:8 contains the information on the outside of the letter, based on similarities with other Aramaic papyri letters (Clines 1984:78; Allen 2003:41).

Since 4:8 is in Aramaic, it might appear that it is part of the letter. But the verse ends with *kenema'* [TA/ZA10358, S3660] (as follows, omitted in NLT), which should come just before the beginning of the letter. Nevertheless, it is quite clear that the actual quotation of the Aramaic letter does not actually begin until 4:11. Consequently, 4:8-10 appears to be an Aramaic summary of the opening section of the letter, with the word-for-word quotation beginning in 4:11.

4:9 all their colleagues. Lit., "the rest of their companions." This list lets the reader know what people were standing behind the accusations made in this letter. An impressive list of key people (politicians, judges, leaders) from various nations—Tarpel, which may be the city of Tripoli on the coast of Phoenicia about 50 miles north of Beirut (according to Yamauchi 1988:633; but Allen 2003:41 rejects the identification with Tripoli), Persia, Babylon, Erech, Susa, and Assyria—supported the case that these accusations were well known to all and not just the prejudiced opinion of one small group that might have a grudge against the Jews. Such widespread agreement on the accusations against the people in Jerusalem would cause the Persian king to think that this was a serious problem that must be addressed. The enemies of the Jewish people knew how to work the political system to make things sound very bad in order to get what they wanted.

4:10 Ashurbanipal. Lit., "Osnappar," a variant of the same name. This odd spelling came about through regular linguistic changes to Persian words (e.g., final "l" becomes an "r") when they were used in Aramaic. The name refers to the Assyrian king Ashurbanipal (668–627 BC). Verse 2 refers to the people Esarhaddon exiled to this area, but there is no other biblical data about Ashurbanipal exiling people into this area. In 648 BC Ashurbanipal fought against Babylon, so it is possible that the Babylonians who were defeated and captured at this time were brought to Samaria and the surrounding countryside.

4:11 To King Artaxerxes, from your loyal subjects in the province west of the Euphrates River. Lit., "To Artaxerxes the King, your servants, the men from Beyond the River: And now." This is the salutation of the letter, and it follows the normal form of Persian letters. This strongly supports the idea that Ezra was quoting the actual letter.

province west of the Euphrates River. Lit., "the land across the river." Rainey (1969:51-78) identifies the territory west of the Euphrates River (the fifth Persian satrapy) as including Syria, Lebanon, Moab, Edom, Phoenicia, and Israelite territory.

4:12 Jews . . . are rebuilding this rebellious and evil city. This refers to the Jewish people who came to Jerusalem in the reign of Cyrus with Sheshbazzar (chs 1–2) as well as to those who came with Ezra in the seventh year of Artaxerxes (chs 7–8). The reason for these accusations and the relationship between this building of the walls and Nehemiah's later efforts are not clear, but a possible chronology is (1) Jerusalem was being rebuilt before Nehemiah entered the picture, sometime around 450 BC; (2) Megabyzus started a revolt in Egypt around 448 BC, and Persia stopped the revolt; (3) this letter of objection was sent by

Rehum to stop the reconstruction of the city; (4) some of Jerusalem's walls were destroyed to prevent the people of Jerusalem from revolting like the Egyptians did; (5) Nehemiah was sent to stabilize the situation and rebuild the walls in 445 BC (see Blenkinsopp 1988:113-114). The building of the walls in this verse does not refer to Nehemiah's later work, so one has to assume that this building took place at an earlier date. Unfortunately, this passage does not supply a date, but the above hypothetical reconstruction of events provides a plausible dating of this chapter.

The letter writers' description of Jerusalem as "rebellious and evil" reveals his prejudiced point of view. The fear about the completion of the walls is an exaggeration, especially since the Jewish people had only finished the foundation. The Aramaic verb for "laid the foundations" (*yakhitu* [TA/ZA10253, S2338]) is uncertain, but likely refers to the lower layers of blocks or the broad subfoundations of the large stone wall (Fensham 1982:74).

4:13 *it will be much to your disadvantage, for the Jews will then refuse to pay their tribute, customs, and tolls to you.* The letter writers claimed to be standing up for the king and probably hoped to gain some advantage through this. There was a good deal of political fearmongering in their words, for the Jews were not strong enough to withhold taxes, and even if they did, it would not amount to much money. The "tribute" (*mindah* [TA/ZA10402, S4061], or *middah* in 4:20) was a fixed annual tax, the "custom" (*belo* [TA/ZA10107, S1093]) was probably a duty on goods sold or purchased (a sales tax), and the "toll" (*halak* [TA/ZA10208, S1983]), which comes from the word "go, walk" could be a charge for travel on roads (Yamauchi 1988:631). "Much to your disadvantage" involves the translation of the Aramaic word *'appethom* [TA/ZA10063/A, S674], which some interpret to mean "the storehouse/treasury" (Fensham 1982:74); thus, one could translate the phrase "the treasury of the king will suffer loss." Better is the translation "in the end," which gives the meaning "eventually the king will incur damage."

4:14 *Since we are your loyal subjects.* Lit., "Since all of us have salted the salt of the palace." This appears to be a metaphor that refers to taking an oath of allegiance to the king or to being obligated because they have enjoyed the hospitality of the king (Kidner 1979:52). Leviticus 2:13 and 2 Chr 13:5 (cf. NLT mg) also refer to salt playing a part in the ratification of a covenant obligation between two parties. While tattling on their neighbors, they are patting themselves on the back again, professing their undying loyalty.

4:18 *has been translated.* The word *meparash* [TA/ZA10597, S6568] is sometimes literally rendered "read separately," but it means that they "translated" the Aramaic (Yamauchi 1988:633), or "clearly" gave the meaning of the letter to the king. All of these imply that the letter had to be translated into the Persian language for it to be clearly understood by the king (Blenkinsopp 1988:115). Another interpretation of the word suggests that this letter was read "verbatim, in full" and not just in a summary fashion (Williamson 1985:53, 56; Allen 2003:42). See comments on Neh 8:8.

4:19 *In fact, rebellion and revolt are normal there!* Lit., "Rebellion and sedition happened in it." The ancient Assyrian and Babylonian records may have included the account of Hezekiah's revolt against Assyria in 701 BC (Isa 36–39), or the revolts against Babylon in 598–597 BC by Jehoiakim and 588–587 BC by Zedekiah. Unfortunately, the king did not notice that there had been no revolts in Judah for the past 130 years because Assyria was not an international power at that time and Israel was not a vassal at that point. This raises questions about the basis and objectivity of the king's decision, for it seems to be based on a limited amount of information and not the full history of Israel. Was it a political move made out of fear, or a reasoned response based on factual information about the behavior of the people who now lived in Judah?

4:20 *Powerful kings have ruled over Jerusalem and the entire province.* It is unlikely that Solomon would be mentioned in these sources because Israel was not a threat or a near neighbor; instead, these records would have mentioned Jeroboam II, Uzziah, or Hezekiah, though none of these actually ruled over the whole province beyond the Euphrates. Maybe the Persian king also read about the kings in Syria, Moab, Ashdod, Tyre, and Edom, who controlled independent states in the province west of the Euphrates River.

COMMENTARY

Like the preceding section, this one (4:6-23) deals with opposition to Jewish attempts to build the Temple and the walls of Jerusalem. There are no direct statements that these opponents of the Jews hated the God of the people in Jerusalem, but their behavior demonstrated the wisdom of the people's decision to build the Temple without help from their neighbors (4:3). The acts of the neighbors around Jerusalem demonstrated a hatred for God's Holy City and his chosen people that led them to do everything possible to prevent God's people from having personal security from danger and enjoying the worship of God. These would-be friends ended up working against the construction of the Temple (4:1-5) and arguing against the political independence of Israel, becoming the enemies of God. The "people of the land" (often called Samaritans, but see note on 4:1) feared that if the Israelites excluded them from being involved with Jewish affairs in Jerusalem (the building of the Temple), they would soon lose control of Jerusalem and its surrounding cities. Thus they would have less power and fewer financial and labor resources to accomplish their own plans.

Ezra 4:6-23 consists of parenthetical remarks about later opposition against Jewish attempts to reestablish the nation long after the time of Cyrus and Darius I. These verses are out of chronological order since after this parenthesis (4:6-23) the account returns to the time of Darius I. This indicates that Ezra was following a thematic arrangement of his material rather than a chronological system. Josephus was confused by this ordering of events (*Antiquities* 11.21-30), so he identified the name Ahasuerus (cf. 4:6, NLT mg) with Cambyses, Cyrus's son, but nothing is said here or in any other text about any opposition to Jewish rebuilding in the days of King Cambyses (530-522 BC). This section deals with opposition to rebuilding the city and walls of Jerusalem, an issue that arose long after the Temple was completed. Verse 6 mentions written opposition to the Jewish people in Xerxes' reign (486-465 BC). These complaints could be related to the revolts taking place in Egypt at that time (Blenkinsopp 1988:111). These false accusations against the Jewish people by the local inhabitants probably encouraged the Persians to distrust the returned exiles, lest they revolt like the Egyptians and cause more trouble for the Persian king.

Since the king had a vast empire, it was impossible for him to know what was happening unless he had people in each province who were honestly reporting what was going on in that area. This required an elaborate group of people who would function as the "eyes and ears" of the king. (Xenophon, in *Cyropaedia* 8.2.10-12, describes this system of Persian spies.) Of course, the problem was that the king sometimes didn't know who to believe or how to separate the facts from prejudiced interpretation of the facts. In this case, the letter writers' political ambitions and religious hatred caused them to give the king advice that was only partially based on the facts.

Notice that the letter's writers identified themselves as "loyal subjects" of the king, implying that they were trustworthy and were only interested in serving the king. Although there is nothing in the letter to suggest that these men were disloyal to the king, the content of the letter suggests that their interpretation of the events happening in Jerusalem was not a fair or unprejudiced appraisal of what was actually going on in the city.

The writers asked that "a search be made in your ancestors' records" (4:15). To discover past revolts in Jerusalem, the king would have to have access to Assyrian and Babylonian annals. In the third century BC, Berossus used the Babylonian Chronicles that covered from around 800 BC to 350 BC (Drews 1975:39-55). So it seems that the Persians would have had access to this information as well. This whole course of argumentation about the rebelliousness of the Jews assumes that the Jewish people never would change and would always be rebellious. It falsely compared what a once powerful nation did many years ago when Babylon ruled it with what a small nation with no army might do in the future while under Persian rule.

Then the writers made the bald statement, "If this city is rebuilt . . . the province west of the Euphrates River will be lost to you" (4:16). Their vastly exaggerated conclusion claimed that building the walls around this one city would cause the loss of a whole province. Rehum was playing on the Persians' fears because of past revolts in Egypt and the heavy expenses the Persians incurred in fighting against the Greeks. He was suggesting that the Persians needed to draw a line in the sand and stop the Jews right now, or the empire would be lost. This was pure manipulation of the facts, crying wolf when there was no threat at all. If Herodotus is correct, the Fifth Satrapy paid only about 2 percent of the taxes for the royal treasury's annual income (Baron 1952:162), so the potential loss of income from the small city of Jerusalem was not going to have much of an impact on Persia's royal treasury.

The letter that came in response shows the king's strong desire to control what was going on in the provinces near Egypt and demonstrates that he feared the Egyptian revolt might spread into the area of Yehud. We have no knowledge that this kind of micromanagement of affairs in Judah was characteristic of Persian rule in other provinces, though official permissions were always necessary to build new structures (see Neh 2). This provision maintained the king's unlimited authority, but it also provided a way around the local officials who might oppose the Jews. Though the work must stop now and could not start again without the king's orders, Nehemiah's work a few years later was based on the king's express permission.

When Rehum, Shimshai, and their colleagues got the letter, "they hurried to Jerusalem. Then, with a show of strength, they forced the Jews to stop building" (4:23). One assumes that a military force made the Jews stop (see 1 Esdr 2:30). Some hypothesize a destruction of those parts of Jerusalem's walls that were rebuilt at this time, an action that would keep the Jews from benefiting from their alleged illegal action. If this is what happened, this would probably be the destruction that Nehemiah heard about from Hanani in Nehemiah 1:3 (Kidner 1979:52-53; Blenkinsopp 1988:115). If this is correct, Rehum and his colleagues greatly overstepped their authority, for there was no indication in the Persian king's reply that they had permission to dismantle the walls of Jerusalem. This comment ends the parenthetical remarks about opposition during the time of Artaxerxes I.

What we learn from this section is that opposition to God's people, God's holy place, and the worship of God takes many forms. Persecution can involve threatening God's people to discourage them (4:4) or slyly influencing political authorities to frustrate believers so that some will eventually stop following God's divine plan (4:5). Persecution often happens when those who hate God's work gather their friends together to make a concerted effort to oppose what God is doing (4:7-9). This oppression can involve false statements or exaggerated claims that paint believers with false generalizations or raise unfounded fears (4:13-16). Those who persecute believers may be motivated by the desire for greater political power or any number of prideful or revengeful attitudes. Believers throughout the ages have faced opposition like this, and the Bible indicates that those who put their faith in Christ will continue to face the hatred of the world (John 15:18-19; 17:14-17). Jesus encouraged his followers by telling them that those who suffered persecution would be blessed (Matt 5:10), while Peter encouraged his readers to expect persecution, for Christ also suffered for things he did not do (1 Pet 3:13-18).

God will sometimes allow persecution to succeed in stopping his glorification for a time when the people of God have not lived honorable lives before their neighbors. For example, Jerusalem was destroyed because the people of God were sinful. Although the Hebrews did not praise God for destroying the city, eventually some learned through this experience, repented, and turned back to glorifying God. The length of these times of persecution are in God's hands, but believers should expect opposition again and again if they refuse to follow God. Sometimes persecution tests what people are really made of and forces people to face mistakes in their past. The opposition against God's people was partially based on past rebellions against foreign overlords; thus, a negative testimony negatively influenced those living in the "province west of the Euphrates River" as well as those in Persia. These past sins caught up with the people in Jerusalem and supported the hateful attitude of those around them.

In addition, the sharp way in which their neighbors were rebuffed (4:3) turned potential friends into enemies. Why didn't the leaders respond with a conditional or qualified yes? They could have said, "You may help us if you turn away from all other gods and worship only the God we worship here in Jerusalem." This seems to be the approach of the Jews later in 6:21, but not here. Were the Jewish people motivated by political fear that the Samarian people of the land might try to dictate what could go on in Jerusalem, or was this just a positive act of religious separation? Ultimately, we do not know what was in their hearts, but it appears that the Jewish people were not without past sins, and these impacted the way their neighbors dealt with them.

Living in a fallen, sinful world requires God's people to choose how to relate to other sinful people. They can act like sinful people and join them, or they can choose to be separate from them. Throughout the nation's past history, many Israelites acted sinfully, like their neighbors, and this resulted in rebellions, wars, and the exile of the nation. When the people would choose to be separate from their neighbors, as in the reforms of Hezekiah and Josiah, they were always faced with the question of how separate they would be. God required that his people "be holy because I . . . am holy" (Lev 19:2); thus, the Torah described a variety of things the people should and should not do, because they were to be different from other nations. These relate to appropriate worship practices (Lev 20:22-27), sexuality (Lev 18), economics (Lev 19:9-19, 33-37), and politics (Deut 17:14-20). Compromising on these sacred principles would defile the land and the holy kingdom of priests. This would destroy the people's covenant relationship with God and lead to their destruction.

But separation is never complete, unless a person is secluded in a monastery, and seclusion from others is not the focus of biblical holiness. Separation must be based on values and beliefs that are inconsistent with the way sinful people live. If there is no difference in beliefs, separation does not accomplish anything. It only isolates people from their neighbors and lessens their ability to witness to them. Jesus did separate himself for times of prayer, but most of the time he mixed freely with sinful people throughout his ministry. Thus, physical separation is not nearly as significant as moral and theological separation from sin. Although this text does not explain the rationale of the Jewish people at this time, 2 Kings 17:24-40 suggests that Zerubbabel and Jeshua's decision to separate from the people in the land was based on a central theological difference between the Jews who worshiped only one God and their neighbors who mixed the worship of this God with other gods. These leaders knew that these theological differences would have a serious effect on Jewish worship practices if the two groups became too close.

A theological problem arises in this story in that God allowed these sinful enemies to successfully persecute those who faithfully followed God in Jerusalem. Why did God not defeat these enemies and cause the Persians to see through their lies and trumped-up charges? The Jewish people had no desire to rebel and were not a threat to the vast Persian Empire. Why did God not help the Persians see through the political motivations of these provincial officials so the Temple and the walls could be rebuilt right away? Was God not still in control of these nations? Are God's people just hopeless pawns in the hands of their enemies? Where was God's sovereign control of the nations that was so evident in Ezra 1?

Although we cannot always know why God does what he does, it may be that God was testing his people to see if they would compromise their faith or choose to be a separate people totally dedicated to him. Of course, when we read the whole story, we see that this opposition was only a brief interlude before God sovereignly worked to cause the Persians to approve the original plan to build the Temple (Ezra 5–6). Consequently, we should conclude that some of our questions about what God is doing in our lives are shortsighted and impatient reactions to brief setbacks that God will rectify in the near future. On the other hand, we realize that if it were not for opposition and persecution by sinful people, God would have no way of demonstrating his powerful ability to control the affairs of this world and demonstrate his love for his people. The Bible never leads us to expect that there will be no opposition to or persecution of believers; it promises only that God will be with us through those difficult days and that his kingdom will be established at the end of time.

◆   **C. God Overcomes Opposition to Constructing the Temple
        (Ezra 4:24–6:22)**
        **1. Prophetic encouragement challenges the opposition
            (Ezra 4:24–5:17)**

²⁴So the work on the Temple of God in Jerusalem had stopped, and it remained at a standstill until the second year of the reign of King Darius of Persia.*

CHAPTER 5

At that time the prophets Haggai and Zechariah son of Iddo prophesied to the Jews in Judah and Jerusalem. They prophesied in the name of the God of Israel who was over them. ²Zerubbabel son of Shealtiel and Jeshua son of Jehozadak* responded by starting again to rebuild the Temple of God in Jerusalem. And the prophets of God were with them and helped them.

³But Tattenai, governor of the province west of the Euphrates River,* and Shethar-bozenai and their colleagues soon arrived in Jerusalem and asked, "Who gave you permission to rebuild this Temple and restore this structure?" ⁴They also asked for the names of all the men working on the Temple. ⁵But because their God was watching over them, the leaders of the Jews were not prevented from building until a report was sent to Darius and he returned his decision.

⁶This is a copy of the letter that Tattenai the governor, Shethar-bozenai, and the other officials of the province west of the Euphrates River sent to King Darius:

⁷"To King Darius. Greetings.

⁸"The king should know that we went to the construction site of the Temple of the great God in the province of Judah. It is being rebuilt with specially prepared stones, and timber is being laid in its walls. The work is going forward with great energy and success.

⁹"We asked the leaders, 'Who gave you permission to rebuild this Temple and restore this structure?' ¹⁰And we demanded their names so that we could tell you who the leaders were.

¹¹"This was their answer: 'We are the servants of the God of heaven and earth, and we are rebuilding the Temple that was built here many years ago by a great king of Israel. ¹²But because our ancestors angered the God of heaven, he abandoned them to King Nebuchadnezzar of Babylon,* who destroyed this Temple and exiled the people to Babylonia. ¹³However, King Cyrus of Babylon,* during the first year of his reign, issued a decree that the Temple of God should be rebuilt. ¹⁴King Cyrus returned the gold and silver cups that Nebuchadnezzar had taken from the Temple of God in Jerusalem and had placed in the temple of Babylon. These cups were taken from that temple and presented to a man named Sheshbazzar, whom King Cyrus appointed as governor of Judah. ¹⁵The king instructed him to return the cups to their place in Jerusalem and to rebuild the Temple of God there on its original site. ¹⁶So this Sheshbazzar came and laid the foundations of the Temple of God in Jerusalem. The people have been working on it ever since, though it is not yet completed.'

¹⁷"Therefore, if it pleases the king, we request that a search be made in the royal archives of Babylon to discover whether King Cyrus ever issued a decree to rebuild God's Temple in Jerusalem. And then let the king send us his decision in this matter."

4:24 The second year of Darius's reign was 520 B.C. The narrative started in 4:1-5 is resumed at verse 24. 5:2 Aramaic *Jozadak*, a variant spelling of Jehozadak. 5:3 Aramaic *the province beyond the river;* also in 5:6. 5:12 Aramaic *Nebuchadnezzar the Chaldean.* 5:13 King Cyrus of Persia is here identified as the king of Babylon because Persia had conquered the Babylonian Empire.

NOTES

4:24 it remained at a standstill until the second year of the reign of King Darius. As noted in NLT mg, the narrative is resumed from 4:5b. The second year of Darius's reign was 520 BC.

5:1 Haggai and Zechariah son of Iddo prophesied. Haggai began prophesying on August 29, 520 BC, the first day of the sixth month, and the people began building the Temple again on September 21, 520 BC, the twenty-fourth day of the sixth month (Hag 1:1, 15). Zechariah began his messages in the eighth month (Zech 1:1), just two months after Haggai. Their messages are recorded in full in the books known as Haggai and Zechariah.

in the name of the God of Israel who was over them. This is yet another brief reminder of how God's words bring about his sovereign plan for his people (McConville 1985:32). This comment noted that part of the prophetic message of encouragement was a reminder that God was with his people (Hag 1:13; 2:5; Zech 4:10) and would enable them to accomplish what he sent them to do. This would happen only through his Spirit's empowerment; it would not be accomplished through their own superior wisdom or might (Zech 4:6-7). God did not give up on them, for he supremely ruled over every aspect of their difficult situation and was working it out through the ministry of his prophets Haggai and Zechariah.

5:3 Tattenai, governor of the province west of the Euphrates River. Tattenai is also named as the governor of the province "Beyond the River" in a Babylonian document: Olmstead (1944:46) refers to a document from 502 BC that listed *Ta-at-tan-ni* as the governor who was under the satrap of *Ebir-nari* "beyond the river." Some think Shethar-bozenai was his "investigator" (Yamauchi 1988:636) or secretary (Clines 1984:85), but there is no way of knowing who else came with them to Jerusalem.

Who gave you permission to rebuild this Temple and restore this structure? The question asked by these officials could be seen as a hostile attack but was not necessarily a provocative challenge against the Jews. It could be simply a request for official documentation from a responsible government official who wanted to make sure that everything was being done according to state requirements and official building codes (Blenkinsopp 1988:120). The meaning of the word "this structure" (*'usharna'* [TA/ZA10082, S846]) is unclear. Tuland (1958:269-275) found this word in an Aramaic papyrus from Egypt with a meaning of either "material" or "equipment." It is found in Elephantine Papyri in contexts where things are being repaired (Williamson 1985:70 gives examples). "This structure" may refer to the wooden framework or scaffolding used to lift stone building blocks into place, or to the wood that was put between every third layer of stone (Allen 2003:46) as 5:8; 6:4; and 1 Kgs 6:36 suggest.

5:4 They also asked. Lit., "We asked" (*'amarna'* [TA/ZA10042, S560]), but this does not make any sense in this contextual setting. All commentators and translations agree that this must be a scribal error for "they asked," as the Old Greek reads.

5:6 This is a copy of the letter. Apparently this was a copy given to the Jewish authorities so they would know what was being requested of the central Persian government. This suggests that Tattenai was not working behind the back of the Jewish leaders and did not have hostile intentions. When archaeologists excavated the Persian capital of Persepolis they found over 2,000 documents from the time of Darius concerning finances within the Persian Empire (Hallock 1969). This indicates that the Persians were meticulous about keeping records and would likely have been able to locate Cyrus's original decree about Jerusalem.

and the other officials. Lit., "and his companions, the inspectors." The word *'aparsekay* [TA/ZA10061, S671] is an Old Persian word for "inspector, investigator" (Myers 1965:42). This translation supports the interpretation that these people were not hostile to what was going on; rather, as inspectors, they were just doing their duty and checking to make sure that the documents produced were not falsified and that everything was being done according to the specifications of the Persian government.

5:8 It is being rebuilt with specially prepared stones, and timber is being laid in its walls. Some interpret the stones to be "huge stones" (NASB; cf. RSV) because the root *gelal* [TA/ZA10146, S1560] means "to roll," which implies that these stones had to be rolled into place. Others think they were "dressed stone, specially prepared," which were smoothed with chisels (Williamson 1985:70). This Temple design followed the pattern of Solomon's Temple (see 1 Kgs 6:36) by putting a layer of wood timbers after every third layer of stone (6:4) to counter the damage strong earthquakes might have on the structure (S. Smith 1941:5-6). Smith's interpretation is better than the view that these timbers refer to rafters (Myers 1965:43) or some sort of wainscoting (Yamauchi 1988:63, 67, based on 1 Kgs 6:15). The reference to a wood layer means that the Temple walls were at least three layers of stone block high at this time (see 6:4; 1 Kgs 6:36), so the people had already made good progress on the reconstruction when this opposition arose.

The work is going forward with great energy and success. The Persian word *'asparna'* [TA/ZA10056, S629] (in full measure, thoroughly) describes more the care and quality of the work than the energy expended by the workers (although great care does require great energy). It was a positive commendation on the progress being made on the Temple. No negative comments or prejudicial statements were made against the Jews in this letter.

5:10 we demanded their names. Lit., "We asked them their names." "Demanded" suggests an adversarial relationship, but these officials seem to be simply doing their job and not overtly opposing those working on this project. They just wanted to be informed and on top of the situation so they would know that everything being done was properly approved. Although the names of the leaders were not included at this point (ch 2 is not this list), apparently the names of the leaders were sent to the king so that everyone would know who was responsible for what was being done and the appropriate people could be held accountable if anything illegal was uncovered.

5:11 a great king of Israel. The great king who originally built this Temple many years ago was Solomon (1 Kgs 5–8), but it is unlikely that the Persians had any records mentioning him. Israel was a rather small country, over 800 miles away from Persia and without any known political relationship to Persia at the time of Solomon. The Jews mentioned this history to show their continuity with the past and to justify their present actions. They were not some new group starting some wild new idea; they were simply continuing the rich traditions of their ancient forefathers.

5:13 King Cyrus of Babylon, during the first year of his reign, issued a decree. We might expect Cyrus to be called the "King of Persia," but he also took the title King of Babylon in some ancient documents (ANET 316). After Cyrus conquered Babylon, it was natural for him to add this prestigious claim to his list of titles. This title also connected him to the deeds of Nebuchadnezzar, who took the Temple utensils from the Jerusalem Temple.

The temporal marker ("during the first year") helped authenticate the decree and caused the Persians to associate it with the general decree in the Cyrus Cylinder that allowed all the exiled people to return to their homelands and build their temples. The claim that it was a "decree" gave them official permission from the king. This idea was not hearsay or a suggestion by a lower-level official, but a decree that carried the signature of the king himself. This was the heart of their defense; everything was legal. Of course, appealing to a decree gave the Persians a means of checking the authenticity of the Jewish leaders' claim. They could look up the various decrees Cyrus issued in his first year and see if he gave permission to rebuild this Temple as the Jewish people were claiming.

5:14 *gold and silver cups . . . presented to a man named Sheshbazzar, whom King Cyrus appointed as governor of Judah.* This verse repeats information found in 1:7-11. The importance of mentioning the gold and silver utensils at this point was to verify the royal decree: Since everyone knew that the Babylonians stripped temples of their valuable objects and took them to Babylon, the presence of these objects in Judah at this time had to be due to a royal decree releasing them. Their presence in Jerusalem was a silent witness to the truthfulness of the claim that Cyrus had decreed that the Jews should go back home and rebuild their Temple in Jerusalem. If there were no decree, the utensils would not be in Jerusalem.

Sheshbazzar's role in 5:14-15 agrees with the information in Ezra 1, although ch 1 does not say he was appointed governor (the Old Greek calls him "the treasurer"). This information raises conflict with statements about Zerubbabel, who is also called the governor (3:2; Hag 1:1; see notes on 1:8 and 5:16).

5:16 *Sheshbazzar came and laid the foundations. . . . The people have been working on it ever since.* This statement does not conflict with the claims that Zerubbabel laid the foundations in 3:8-10 (see also Zech 4:8-10) if both men were involved in the process together (McConville [1985:11] thinks one of these men was a Babylonian and the other a Jewish leader), or if one man started the task and the other finished the initial foundation work. We should not conclude that Sheshbazzar did not lay the foundations (Williamson 1985:79). These verses demand that Sheshbazzar was the governor at one time, but we do not know exactly what Zerubbabel's role was when Sheshbazzar was still in charge. Maybe he was the foreman of the construction project. We do not know why Sheshbazzar was not mentioned in Ezra 3, but arguments from silence do not prove anything one way or the other.

The time that the people worked on the Temple was a relatively short period in 536 BC and then again in 520 BC; one should not interpret the text to say they had been working nonstop on this project for 16 years. Apparently, the author was thinking that "work begun and not completed is work in progress" (Clines 1984:89), or that the present building was a continuation of the earlier work. His point that the present work was just a continuation of the earlier work meant that the earlier authorization covered what the people were now doing (Allen 2003:46).

5:17 *we request that a search be made in the royal archives of Babylon.* This request provided a way of officially proving that the Jews in Jerusalem did receive permission to rebuild the Temple. The Jews' bold request would not have been made if Cyrus never issued such a decree. This means of answering the question demonstrated that the Jewish people believed they were acting in good faith according to the king's wishes and had no intention to rebel against the king's decree. Cyrus's original decree was later found at the royal palace at Ecbatana (6:2) rather than at the royal treasury located in the city of Babylon.

COMMENTARY

In this section the author picks up the story from 4:5b by repeating nearly the same words ("the reign of King Darius of Persia"; 4:24). This does not require or suggest that 4:1-5a happened in the second year of Darius (contrary to Williamson 1985:64). This "resumptive repetition" takes the reader back to where the story left off in 4:5b and helps mark off 4:6-23 as parenthetical topical remarks. This repetitious comment in 4:24 would make little sense if there were not some period of time before Darius when Temple work was stopped. The stop in building progress lasted from approximately 536–520 BC.

But the proclamation of the word of the Lord through the prophets brought a new day in Jerusalem. Haggai began prophesying on August 29, 520 BC, the first day of the sixth month, and the people began building the Temple on September 21, 520 BC, the twenty-fourth day of the sixth month (Hag 1:1, 15). Zechariah began his messages in the eighth month (Zech 1:1), just two months after Haggai. This happened in the second year of Darius I, after he had put down a revolt against his rule. If these prophets had encouraged the people to rebuild the Temple at an earlier time, the Persian authorities would have probably connected the rebuilding project with the rebellion against King Darius I and totally rejected it. Instead, after answering some objections by Tattenai, the people were given permission to complete the Temple construction.

Ezra reported nothing about the economic situation at this time (520 BC) and did not summarize Haggai and Zechariah's messages of rebuke and encouragement. Hints about the political, economic, and religious situation are included in the prophets' messages as they addressed the needs of the people in Judah. One wonders why the governor Zerubbabel and the high priest Jeshua did not lead the people energetically and get the Temple built long before this (Hag 1). Zechariah's visionary words of encouragement to Jeshua (Zech 3) and to Zerubbabel (Zech 4), plus Haggai's words of assurance to Zerubbabel (Hag 2:20-23) suggest that these officials were discouraged and were not giving the people much leadership. They were part of the problem, so Haggai challenged them to set new priorities in his first message (Hag 1). Economically, things were tough for the common people, who depended on agricultural goods, because God had sent a drought on the nation and their crops were poor (Hag 1:6, 9-11). To change the perspective of these discouraged leaders, God provided a new source of vision through the prophets Haggai and Zechariah, and his Spirit stirred up the people to respond in faith and action (Hag 1:12-15).

Ezra 5:2 tells us that "Zerubbabel son of Shealtiel and Jeshua son of Jehozadak responded." It is significant that both Haggai (Hag 1:12) and Ezra credit the leaders with responding and leading the people in the task of rebuilding. If the leaders had not led in faith, if they had not responded to the stirring of the Spirit, it would have been difficult to get the people to act in faith. Haggai 1:12 indicates that God stirred up the hearts of the leaders, as well as the people, to work on rebuilding the Temple.

In all of this, the credit for being able to continue to build was explicitly given to God, not the political astuteness of Zerubbabel or Haggai. Theoretically, Tattenai could have stopped the building immediately for four or five months while the Persians checked their records to see if the people in Jerusalem had been given permission to build, but apparently he believed the claims of the Jews. We are not told if the Jewish leaders showed Tattenai a copy of the permission they originally received from Cyrus, but this might explain his action. If that was the case, Tattenai's letter to Darius I was to check the authenticity of the document. God's providential "eyes" were watching over everything the people said and did so that his plan of rebuilding the Temple would be fulfilled. The Persian "eyes" of Tattenai were not going to interrupt God's work.

Ezra 5:11-17 records the testimony of the Jewish leaders about (1) who they are, (2) their past history, (3) who gave them permission to rebuild the Temple, (4) who was put in charge of the work, (5) what they were told to do, (6) what they have done, and (7) what they would like the Persian king to do to assist them. Apparently, this was included in the letter to the Persian king so that he would hear both sides of the story. The fact that these men allowed the Jewish leaders to state their case directly to the king shows that they were looking for the truth, not trying to give their own slanted opinion to the king.

The Jews who spoke with Tattenai believed that they were servants of the God of heaven and earth. This self-conception implies a humble attitude of devotion and dedication to do the will of their divine master. They did not serve just any God or a pantheon of deities in the ancient Near Eastern world; they were doing the work of the God of heaven and earth. They did not use the title Yahweh or Jehovah, since this personal name would probably not be familiar to the Persians (see note on 1:2). The designation "God of heaven and earth" communicated that the Jewish people worshiped a high God (as did the Persians), not a local deity of a certain place or the god of the grain or rain. Surely the Persians would agree that such an important God should have a Temple in which he could be worshiped.

Rather than assuming a proud and defiant attitude toward the Persians who would read this letter, the Jewish leaders wisely accepted responsibility for past mistakes. The humble honesty of their interpretation of past history is impressive. The Jewish people honestly faced their checkered past and admitted that they were not perfect. The preaching of the prophets and the experience of the Exile taught the people that God punishes those who break his covenant relationship. God abandoned his people when he gave them into the hands of Nebuchadnezzar to defeat the nation, destroy the Temple, and exile the people in 605, 597, and 586 BC (2 Kgs 25). God did all this, but he used Nebuchadnezzar to accomplish his task. The Jews recounted all this in order to explain why they needed to rebuild this ruined Temple.

In summary, this chapter presents a strong contrast with the discouraging situation in Ezra 4 (McConville 1985:32). Negative factors in chapter 4 included opposition by local people, the labeling of the people in Jerusalem as a rebellious lot, a Persian decree against the Jews, and a halt to the rebuilding of the Temple. This all changed in chapter 5, for now work was going forward on the Temple, the Persians did not decree a stop to the work, and the Jews themselves honestly confessed their past failures. No doubt we have a change of attitude by the Jews as well as the Persians in this new setting around 520 BC.

This change came about because God sovereignly worked in the hearts of everyone; and in particular, his word through the prophets changed the hearts of the Jewish people in Jerusalem. As a result, they saw themselves as sinful but dedicated servants of God and developed a new attitude of cooperation and submission to government officials. The broadest theological theme that encompasses and explains everything that takes place on earth is the sovereign work of God. The prophets spoke because God sent them at just this time to deliver his message (5:1). The people's attitude changed because of God's sovereign work of stirring up the hearts of the people to fear and obey God (Hag 1:12-14). The Persians did not stop the work on the Temple because "God was watching over" everything (5:5). God's powerful working in the history of the nations was confessed when the leaders recognized that God's anger caused him to abandon them and let Nebuchadnezzar exile them to Babylon (5:12). In Ezra's eyes, God was the main power directing history (Breneman 1993:108). His anger can bring disaster and destruction, but at other times he marvelously intervenes to allow people to succeed in very surprising ways. God worked with enemies, armies, and his own stubborn, sinful people, and no matter how powerful or sinful these human beings were, he was always in charge of each step along the way.

When things do not go well because of opposition, sinfulness, or the laziness of his people, God can direct history by changing people's attitudes so they repent (Zech 1:1-6), fear God (Hag 1:12), and become his servants (5:11). God empowers people to change their theological perspective toward himself and their enemies by revealing his will through chosen prophets who boldly confront the false ideas that derail godly action (Hag 1). Haggai and Zechariah's prophetic words challenged the status quo and showed the inconsistencies in the people's perverted theological paradigms. When the Spirit anointed God's prophetic word, people's hearts were stirred. The word of God encouraged those who were weak and afraid to act in spite of opposition (Hag 1:14). Without God's words of guidance, correction, and instruction, people tend to wander around in self-pity and hopelessness, not knowing what to do.

Once they have the word of God, people change their view of themselves and others. The Jewish leaders confessed that they had failed their God and that he was just in punishing them (5:11-12). They did not hide their faults and did not blame others for their difficult situation. But they did not see themselves as rebels, but as servants of the living God of heaven and earth (Holmgren 1987:43). As servants, they submitted their will to God's instructions and his plans for their lives. They understood it was their responsibility to construct a Temple for worship of this God of heaven and earth. Their attitude toward their Persian overlords also changed: The people did not view them as the enemy and were not antagonistic or defiant toward them. They saw themselves as cooperative (Williamson 1985:87) and as obedient to the instructions in Cyrus's decree (5:13; cf. Rom 13:1-5), and they wanted the new king, Darius I, to check the government records for this decree that Cyrus gave them. They did not try an end run around anyone or try to pervert the decree to make it say more than it actually said. Tattenai and Darius I were not demonized as the enemies of the people but viewed as the means God would use to grant approval for the rebuilding of the Temple. As long as the people were faithful servants of God and the king, God could work out the political details to finish the Temple according to his own timing.

◆   ## 2. Darius encourages rebuilding the Temple (Ezra 6:1-12)

So King Darius issued orders that a search be made in the Babylonian archives, which were stored in the treasury. 2But it was at the fortress at Ecbatana in the province of Media that a scroll was found. This is what it said:

"Memorandum:
3"In the first year of King Cyrus's reign, a decree was sent out concerning the Temple of God at Jerusalem.

"Let the Temple be rebuilt on the site where Jews used to offer their sacrifices, using the original foundations. Its height will be ninety feet, and its width will be ninety feet.* ⁴Every three layers of specially prepared stones will be topped by a layer of timber. All expenses will be paid by the royal treasury. ⁵Furthermore, the gold and silver cups, which were taken to Babylon by Nebuchadnezzar from the Temple of God in Jerusalem, must be returned to Jerusalem and put back where they belong. Let them be taken back to the Temple of God."

⁶So King Darius sent this message:

"Now therefore, Tattenai, governor of the province west of the Euphrates River,* and Shethar-bozenai, and your colleagues and other officials west of the Euphrates River—stay away from there! ⁷Do not disturb the construction of the Temple of God. Let it be rebuilt on its original site, and do not hinder the governor of Judah and the elders of the Jews in their work.

⁸"Moreover, I hereby decree that you are to help these elders of the Jews as they rebuild this Temple of God. You must pay the full construction costs, without delay, from my taxes collected in the province west of the Euphrates River so that the work will not be interrupted.

⁹"Give the priests in Jerusalem whatever is needed in the way of young bulls, rams, and male lambs for the burnt offerings presented to the God of heaven. And without fail, provide them with as much wheat, salt, wine, and olive oil as they need each day. ¹⁰Then they will be able to offer acceptable sacrifices to the God of heaven and pray for the welfare of the king and his sons.

¹¹"Those who violate this decree in any way will have a beam pulled from their house. Then they will be tied to it and flogged, and their house will be reduced to a pile of rubble.* ¹²May the God who has chosen the city of Jerusalem as the place to honor his name destroy any king or nation that violates this command and destroys this Temple.

"I, Darius, have issued this decree. Let it be obeyed with all diligence."

6:3 Aramaic *Its height will be 60 cubits* [27.6 meters], *and its width will be 60 cubits.* It is commonly held that this verse should be emended to read: "Its height will be 30 cubits [45 feet, or 13.8 meters], its length will be 60 cubits [90 feet, or 27.6 meters], and its width will be 20 cubits [30 feet, or 9.2 meters]"; compare 1 Kgs 6:2. The emendation regarding the width is supported by the Syriac version.   6:6 Aramaic *the province beyond the river;* also in 6:6b, 8, 13.   6:11 Aramaic *a dunghill.*

NOTES

6:1 *in the Babylonian archives, which were stored in the treasury.* Lit., "the house of the scrolls where the treasures were stored there in Babylon." This seems to refer to a separate decree, distinct from that mentioned in 1:2-3, which focuses on giving permission to build a Temple, rather than giving permission to return to Jerusalem. Bickerman (1946:249-275) argues for this point. Two surprising facts confront the interpreter. First, it is odd that Ezra refers to a room for "scrolls" since Persians usually wrote Persian on clay tablets. This may simply represent Ezra's Judean way of thinking, since scrolls, not clay tablets, were the common surface for writing messages in Israel. However, it is possible that there was a separate room for scrolls written in Aramaic that were sent to the central Persian government from the provinces, plus copies of those sent from Babylon to the provinces. R. de Vaux (1972:63-96) reports that Persian officials did use scrolls at times. The Elephantine Papyri support this point. The second surprise is that this scroll room was somehow associated with the treasury of the nation rather than with an area dealing with nonfinancial matters. Since this specific scroll contained information about the government's spending a large amount of money to build the Temple in Jerusalem, it would be natural for the treasury to have the original copy (Clines 1984:90). Archaeological evidence from excavations in Persepolis indicates that the treasury and archival rooms were next to one another (see Schmidt 1939:90).

6:2 at the fortress at Ecbatana . . . a scroll was found. Although the search began in Babylon, the scroll they were looking for was eventually found at the large government fortress at Ecbatana, the former capital of Media (Yamauchi 1976:5-81). According to Xenophon (*Cyropaedia* 8.6.22), Cyrus spent his winters in the warmer climate of Babylon, his springs in Susa, and his summers in the cooler climate of the fortress at Ecbatana. The location of this scroll at Ecbatana suggests that Cyrus originally gave this decree while he was living there in the summer of 538 BC.

6:3 using the original foundations. This phrase is difficult, but "let its foundations be retained" in the NASB may confuse the reader. This decree provided for the rebuilding of a Temple the same size as the first Temple, but no unnecessary expansions beyond its prior footprint are being granted. Thus the people are restoring, realigning, and maybe replacing some of the broken stones in the original foundation of Solomon's Temple.

Its height will be ninety feet, and its width will be ninety feet. These measurements do not match the original foundations of Solomon's Temple (1 Kgs 6:2, 17, 20). The original Temple was 90 feet long, 30 feet wide, and 45 feet high. The absence of a length figure suggests that we have a scribal error that involved the scribe's eye skipping some words (about length) and making a consequent misreading of the height of the Temple (Allen 2003:52-53). Yamauchi (1988:642) thinks the present numbers could be kept as they are if they are understood as the maximum size the Persians would fund, not the required size of the Temple. This solution, however, does not explain why there is no figure given for the length of the building; thus, we can be fairly certain that a copying error occurred in the transmission process.

6:4 Every three layers of specially prepared stones will be topped by a layer of timber. "Specially prepared stones" is literally "rolled stones." Some translate this "large stones" (NIV; cf. NASB, RSV) because large stones need to be rolled into place (see 5:8 and note). "Smoothed/ prepared" is a more likely meaning (Williamson 1985:70). The Aramaic text refers to "new timber," but new timber does not make a good building material because it warps and twists. Most commentators suggest one should drop the ending of *khadath* [TA/ZA10251, ZS2323] (new) to get *khad* [TA/ZA10248, ZS2298] (one): "one layer of timber" (cf. LXX). This makes much better sense and follows the pattern of other Near Eastern temples in and outside of Israel (Thomas 1960:61). It is thought that this row of timber helped these structures endure earthquakes without collapsing. According to 5:8, these details agree with what the Jews were doing.

6:5 the gold and silver cups. It is significant that Cyrus's original decree mentioned these Temple utensils (which included more than "cups"—see 1:9-10), for this explains why these Temple utensils were in Jerusalem with the returnees and demonstrated the truthfulness of the Jews' account as reported in the letter to Darius (5:14-15).

6:6 Now therefore, Tattenai. Verses 1-5 reproduce the key parts of Cyrus's original decree written in 538 BC. Ezra 6:6-12 contains Darius's letter to Tattenai in reply to the letter Tattenai sent to Darius in 5:6-17. There is every reason to believe that the author of Ezra had access to this Aramaic document, although we have no way of knowing if the quotation of it in 6:6-12 includes the whole text. Darius's additional comments in this letter were directed to the king's officials who were in charge of carrying out the king's wishes in the "province beyond the river" (see NLT mg).

stay away from there! This was not a command prohibiting entrance to Jerusalem, as Fensham (1982:89) suggests, or preventing inspection of the building, but rather an instruction prohibiting Tattenai from interfering with the work on the Temple (Williamson

1985:81). Some claim that this is a technical legal phrase meaning "the accusation is rejected" based on similar terminology in the Elephantine Papyri (Fensham 1982:89). Rungren
(1958:209-215) makes this claim based on papyrus documents found in Cowley 1923:16,
18, 22-23. But in this case Tattenai was not making accusations of Jewish wrongdoing; he
was only asking for clarification of the king's wishes (Blenkinsopp 1988:127).

6:7 rebuilt on its original site. It was the common Persian practice to rebuild a Temple
on its original foundation. Some years earlier the Babylonian king Nabonidus also followed this same policy when he authorized the reconstruction of a temple Sargon had
built in Sippar. Ellis (1968:181) refers to an inscription by Nabonidus that says, "I laid
the brick foundation solidly on the foundation that Sargon had made, neither protruding
nor receding an inch."

6:11 Those who violate this decree in any way will have a beam pulled from their house.
Since the nation of Persia was just coming out of a time of rebellion and unrest, Darius
needed to act firmly and establish his authority throughout the realm. His decrees were to
be followed exactly or else. This royal decree contains a series of strong curses on anyone
who might try to oppose the will of the king, even in the slightest manner. These kinds of
penalty clauses were a common part of laws (e.g., the Code of Hammurabi), treaties (e.g.,
the Hittite Treaties), and royal decrees (e.g., the Azitawadda Inscription; see ANET 177-180,
201-202, 653-654). The severity of the punishment might seem extreme or unusual by
modern standards of punishment, but Darius himself recorded on the Behistun Inscription
that he had impaled 3,000 Babylonians when he defeated the city (Kent 1953:127-128).

they will be tied to it and flogged. The NLT translates *zeqip* [TA/ZA10238, S2211] (lifted up)
as "be tied to it," but many think this word indicates that any person who changed this
decree would be "impaled" on the beam taken from his house by being "lifted up" and
having a wooden beam inserted into their chest cavity (Brockington 1969:84; Fensham
1982:90; Yamauchi 1988:644; cf. NIV). Although this interpretation is questioned (Kidner
1979:58; Williamson 1985:72), it is not an unexpected Persian punishment. The loss of
a person's home is similar to the threat Nebuchadnezzar made against the wise men of
Babylon (Dan 2:5; 3:29).

6:12 May the God who has chosen the city of Jerusalem as the place to honor his name.
In addition to Darius's own curse, he also invoked the curse of Israel's God. The theological understanding that God chose a city where his name would be honored seems very
close to Deut 12:11. Although Darius certainly knew that people honored their gods at
temples in special, chosen cities, the presence of this Israelite theological concept seems to
strongly imply that a Jewish scribe or adviser helped Darius compose this part of the decree
(Williamson 1985:83).

COMMENTARY

The two documents in this section—one from Cyrus (6:3-5) and another from
Darius (6:6-12)—guarantee the authorization from the Persian government for the
rebuilding of the Temple. To guarantee the authoritative status and purity of this
Temple, it was important that the returnees rebuild on the exact location of the first
Temple. Retaining the old foundation ensured continuity with the past holy site of
the Temple and also limited the size and cost of the project for the Persians.

    Although it may surprise us that the Persian government was willing to pay the
costs for this Temple, this was probably seen as goodwill to ensure the cooperation and loyalty of the Jewish people. The money did not come directly from the

king's pocket, but indirectly through a distribution of the provincial taxes of the province west of the Euphrates River (6:8). Some question the authenticity of this enthusiastic and unlimited financial support for a Jewish Temple, since Darius was a worshiper of Ahura Mazda, the Zoroastrian high god (see Boyce 1982). But several points argue that Darius did exactly what this text claims: (1) It was in Darius's own self-interest to create a stable and favorable atmosphere in his western provinces after the recent rebellion. This generous act might help do that. (2) Elsewhere, the Persians financially assisted in the reconstruction of other temples. Cowley (1923:30) shows a similar Persian decree permitting the Jewish people in southern Egypt to build a temple. R. de Vaux (1972:92-93) gives other examples of generous Persian support for temple construction and worship in other lands. (3) Darius was only committing the nation to what had already been granted by Cyrus (6:4) and was maintaining the law of the land. (4) Haggai 2:6-8 refers to a future time when God will cause the wealth of all nations to come to Jerusalem to help in the building of the Temple, for ultimately, he owns all the gold and silver in the world. Darius's generous response was probably better than anything the people in Jerusalem could have hoped for, but it only proved that God "is able . . . to accomplish infinitely more than we might ask or think" (Eph 3:20).

Although Darius I could have dismissed Cyrus's earlier statements and taken a new course of action because of the changing political situation, he was faithful to the commitments Cyrus had made, even if they would not make him popular with some of his non-Jewish officials in the province. This verse does not relate this decision to the sovereign work of God, but King Darius's response is attributed to the Lord in 6:22 (Darius is the "king of Assyria"; see note on 6:22). Earlier they were not able to build; now they had permission in writing.

In addition to giving the Jews permission to rebuild and the money to do it, Darius even gave specific commandments about provisions for the priestly duties. The king probably inquired from Jewish officials in Persia about the kind of sacrifices offered to the "God of heaven" so that his decree would not offend anyone. His concern seems to be for the daily sacrifices rather than anything like a "sin offering" or sacrifices for special days.

Ezra 6:10 records Darius's personal hope: "They [the priests] will be able to offer acceptable sacrifices to the God of heaven and pray for the welfare of the king and his sons." This Persian concern for worship and sacrifice at the Temple of a foreign God seems unusual to us, but it was identical to Cyrus's earlier request of the Babylonians in the Cyrus Cylinder: "May all the gods whom I have resettled in their sacred cities ask daily Bel and Nebo for a long life for me" (see ANET 316 and R. de Vaux 1972:73-92 for other examples of this same kind of Persian financial support for non-Zoroastrian worship). Interestingly, Jeremiah instructed the people in exile to pray for their foreign captors: "Work for the peace and prosperity of the city where I sent you into exile. Pray to the LORD for it, for its welfare will determine your welfare" (Jer 29:7). This is consistent with the New Testament exhortation to pray for our political leaders (1 Tim 2:1-2; cf. Rom 13:1-7). These prayers were to be offered when the people presented an "acceptable sacrifice" or "pleasing savor" to God. The terminology is so consistent with earlier sacrificial terminology for the daily sacrifices (Exod 29:18-40; Lev 1:9; 2:12; Num 28) that one must assume that

Darius was assisted in writing this statement by Jewish advisers in Persia (Myers 1965:52). Instead of opposing anything the Jews were doing, Darius seemed to fully support and encourage the people. This does not mean he was a convert or believer in the God in Jerusalem. This was partly good politics and partly a rather inclusive perspective on other religions.

In summary, these two Persian decrees by Cyrus and Darius indicate what the Persians were told about some aspects of the theology of the Jewish people. They knew that the Hebrew God was a high "God of heaven," had a Temple that he chose to place in Jerusalem, and received daily sacrifices to bring honor to his name. They believed this God should have his Temple restored, the proper Temple utensils returned, and acceptable sacrifices reinstated. They also wanted prayers offered on their behalf so that they would receive the favor of this God. They called on the Hebrew God to curse anyone who might fail to follow the king's decree or interfere with the Jewish work to rebuild the Temple. Although these words might sound astonishingly orthodox, as if the king were a true believer in the God of Israel, they probably reflect common Persian political policies toward other religious groups rather than some special affinity toward Israel's God. Nevertheless, the wording of these statements testifies to the fact that faithful Jews had communicated the tenets of their faith to high government officials in a way that gained the respect of the Persians. Jewish people (like Daniel, Ezra, and Nehemiah) were bold enough to tell the Persian rulers about the God of heaven whom they worshiped in Jerusalem. This followed the example of Joseph and Moses, whose witness about God to the Egyptian pharaohs (Gen 41; 47; Exod 7–11) had a role in the salvation of Israel from famine and slavery. This kind of open testimony played an important part in preparing the pagan rulers to follow God's sovereign plan. In a similar manner, the information we share about God may play an important role in the lives of people in minor as well as major positions of authority.

The Scripture thus reminds us that the decisions of Cyrus and Darius were not just wise political judgments, but acts directed by the sovereign power of God (1:1-3; 5:5; 6:22). These decisions of Cyrus and Darius were not made in a vacuum; they came about because key people faithfully sowed the seed and God miraculously produced good fruit. In light of the questions raised by Tattenai, the Persian approval was not a dream come true right out of the blue. As Haggai said, God would soon shake the political world and bring all the gold the people needed to finish the Temple (Hag 2:6-8). God was faithful and fulfilled his promise at this time in order to bring greater glory to this Temple and to his name (6:12; Hag 2:9).

◆   ### 3. The joyous celebrations at the completed Temple (Ezra 6:13-22)

¹³Tattenai, governor of the province west of the Euphrates River, and Shethar-bozenai and their colleagues complied at once with the command of King Darius. ¹⁴So the Jewish elders continued their work, and they were greatly encouraged by the preaching of the prophets Haggai and Zechariah son of Iddo. The Temple was finally finished, as had been commanded by the God of Israel and decreed by Cyrus, Darius, and Artaxerxes, the kings of Persia. ¹⁵The Temple was completed on March 12,* during the sixth year of King Darius's reign.

¹⁶The Temple of God was then dedicated

with great joy by the people of Israel, the priests, the Levites, and the rest of the people who had returned from exile. [17]During the dedication ceremony for the Temple of God, 100 young bulls, 200 rams, and 400 male lambs were sacrificed. And 12 male goats were presented as a sin offering for the twelve tribes of Israel. [18]Then the priests and Levites were divided into their various divisions to serve at the Temple of God in Jerusalem, as prescribed in the Book of Moses.

[19]On April 21* the returned exiles celebrated Passover. [20]The priests and Levites had purified themselves and were cere-monially clean. So they slaughtered the Passover lamb for all the returned exiles, for their fellow priests, and for themselves. [21]The Passover meal was eaten by the people of Israel who had returned from exile and by the others in the land who had turned from their immoral customs to worship the LORD, the God of Israel. [22]Then they celebrated the Festival of Unleavened Bread for seven days. There was great joy throughout the land because the LORD had caused the king of Assyria* to be favorable to them, so that he helped them to rebuild the Temple of God, the God of Israel.

6:15 Aramaic *on the third day of the month Adar,* of the ancient Hebrew lunar calendar. A number of events in Ezra can be cross-checked with dates in surviving Persian records and related accurately to our modern calendar. This day was March 12, 515 B.C.   **6:19** Hebrew *On the fourteenth day of the first month,* of the ancient Hebrew lunar calendar. This day was April 21, 515 B.C.; also see note on 6:15.   **6:22** King Darius of Persia is here identified as the king of Assyria because Persia had conquered the Babylonian Empire, which included the earlier Assyrian Empire.

NOTES

6:13 *complied at once.* This immediate action (in response to the command to "let it be obeyed with all diligence" in 6:12) must have included verbal instructions to prevent any interference and to provide the needed financial support to pay for the work that was being done on the Temple.

6:14 *they were greatly encouraged by the preaching of the prophets Haggai and Zechariah.* Haggai and Zechariah did confront the people about their sins (Zech 1:1-6) and their misplaced priorities (Hag 1:1-11), but here they are remembered because they spoke words of encouragement to the governor Zerubbabel (Hag 2:20-23 and Zech 4), the high priest Jeshua (Zech 3), and the rest of the people. They reminded them of God's promise to be with them (Hag 1:13; 2:4-5), his predictions of blessing and compassion for his people (Hag 2:19; Zech 1:12-13), his promises of new power through God's Spirit (Zech 4:6), and of the joy that would accompany God's setting up his kingdom and dwelling among his people (Zech 2:10-11). These prophets balanced their difficult words of accusation with the joyful words of encouragement.

Artaxerxes. The reference to Artaxerxes (464–424 BC) is surprising in this context, for he did not have anything to do with the building of the Temple. But if a topical rather than chronological interest guided the author, it is appropriate because Artaxerxes, who ruled about 50 years after the Temple was completed, acted favorably toward both Ezra and Nehemiah (7:12-24; Neh 2:1). Artaxerxes thus fits the author's collection of the names of Persian kings who helped the Jews with their building projects.

6:15 *The Temple was completed on March 12.* Lit., "This house was completed on the third day of Adar" (so NLT mg). This building project took only four and a half years to complete (September 21, 520 to March 12, 515 BC), an amazing feat for such a small group of people. (If each family had two children [a small family for those days], the 50,000 people that returned would have only included around 12,500 men to work on this project [plus 12,500 wives and 25,000 children].) With the financial assistance of the Persian government, they were able to hire laborers and complete the work rather quickly. First Esdras 7:5 and Josephus (*Antiquities* 11.104-107) give the twenty-third day of the month as the completion date, not the third day, which some commentaries prefer (Blenkinsopp 1988:129; Williamson 1985:72). It is hard to determine which date is more likely. Blenkinsopp argues for the twenty third day because some think that the third day fell on a Sabbath and the people would not work on the Sabbath. There is no way to prove which conclusion is best. Herod the Great remodeled the Temple shortly before the time of Christ, but the basic structure completed in 515 BC lasted well over 500 years until the Roman army led by Titus destroyed it in AD 70.

6:18 *the priests and Levites were divided . . . as prescribed in the Book of Moses.* The divisions of the priestly and Levitical orders were initially set during the time of Moses (Exod 29; Lev 8; Num 3; 8). Later, these were reorganized during the time of David into 24 groups that would serve one week each (1 Chr 23–27), but Ezra mentions only the instructions in the Mosaic books. This omission of key material regarding a very important topic in the book of Chronicles is another sign that the author of Chronicles did not write Ezra-Nehemiah (Myers 1965:53). With the dedication complete, the author ended his use of the Aramaic language and started to write in Hebrew in 6:19.

6:19 *On April 21.* Lit., "on the fourteenth of the first month," which is the appropriate date for the beginning of the Passover celebration of the Exodus event according to Exod 12:2-6; Lev 23:5-6; Num 9:2-14.

6:20 *The priests and Levites had purified themselves. . . . So they slaughtered the Passover lamb.* The ritual purity (from *taher* [TH2891, ZH3197], "cleanse") of the priests and Levites enabled them to carry out their proper function. They knew about earlier celebrations of the Passover and probably had some oral traditions about the things done when Hezekiah and Josiah celebrated the Passover during their reform movements (see 2 Chr 30:15-17; 35:1-15). At the time of the first Passover (Exod 12), the lambs were killed and eaten by a family in their home, but later this service and the ensuing celebration of the Festival of Unleavened Bread seemed to center around events at the Temple, with the priests and Levites in charge (Fensham 1982:95). The parallel text in 1 Esdr 7:11 adds a phrase before this clause, "not all the returning exiles were purified, but," which may have fallen out of the Hebrew (Allen 2003:54).

6:21 *The Passover meal was eaten by the people of Israel . . . and by the others in the land who had turned from their immoral customs to worship the LORD.* In contrast to the exclusion of non-Israelite people in 4:1-5, the worship and celebration at this Passover included non-Israelite converts from the people who lived in the land of Judah. Hypothetically, this could refer only to Jewish people who were never forced into exile (Breneman 1993:121; Brockington 1969:86), but it seems better to conclude that the author was talking about those who were converts to the Hebrew faith from some pagan religion (Fensham 1982:96). The key to inclusion within the worshiping community was their exclusive commitment to "worship" (*darash* [TH1875, ZH2011], "seek") only the God of Israel and completely separate themselves from the pagan customs of their past. The Jewish people and leaders were not prejudiced against any ethnic or cultural group, and neither is God. People who loved the Lord with all their hearts would be welcomed to the Passover feast (cf. 2 Chr 30:18-20). Even at the first Passover (Exod 12:43-49) some non-Israelites could participate as long as they were circumcised.

6:22 *the Festival of Unleavened Bread for seven days.* This festival started the day after Passover and began a seven-day celebration of joy that reminded the people of God's great deeds in delivering them from the bondage of Egypt (Exod 12:15-20; Lev 23:6-8; 2 Chr 30:21-27).

because the LORD *had caused the king of Assyria to be favorable to them.* In this new celebration of the Festival of Unleavened Bread, the people realized that just as God changed Pharaoh's heart to let the Israelites go out of Egypt, so he had delivered them from the control of their enemies by turning Darius's heart from being an opponent of rebuilding to being a supporter of Temple reconstruction. It is odd to find Darius called the king of Assyria, for the Assyrian empire had been destroyed about 95 years earlier (in 612 BC). Although Darius was the king of Persia, people could refer to kings as ruling over earlier empires they had conquered. The Assyrian King List, for instance, contains Babylonian names (ANET 566), and Herodotus (*Histories* 1.178) referred to Babylon as the capital of Assyria. The Persian kings were the kings of Babylon (5:13; Neh 13:6), and "kings of Assyria" simply referred to the king who ruled over that territory (Neh 9:32).

COMMENTARY

The prophetic words of encouragement by Haggai and Zechariah marked a turning point in the history of the returnees from Babylon. Their theological message challenged the Jewish people to set their priorities on pleasing and glorifying God (Hag 1:8) rather than pleasing themselves. The promise of God's presence with them (Hag 2:4-5) and the assurance that God would help Zerubbabel complete the Temple (Zech 4) motivated the leaders in Judah to move forward even without official Persian permission from Darius I. These prophets reminded the people of the power of God to accomplish his will, and they got the people's minds off the seeming hopelessness of their situation. Indeed, God's work is a work of faith, and believers must act boldly even in the face of opposition. Believers in every era have accomplished the will of God because godly leaders have challenged and inspired them to glorify God and not to be intimidated by the fear of some opposition that stands in their way.

Because of these encouraging prophetic words and because the people acted boldly and "continued their work" (6:14) of building the Temple and because God sovereignly changed the heart of the Persian ruler (6:22), Zechariah's prediction about completing the Temple was fulfilled (6:15; Zech 4:7-9). This work was accomplished because each one encouraged another, the workers did not give up, the people did their work according to what was "commanded by the God of Israel" (6:14), and they did not misuse the authority given by Cyrus or Darius (6:14). These traits of a successful ministry show that God will be faithful in fulfilling his promises if his people are faithful in doing their part. Though no one can predict when God will fulfill his promises, his people are to be faithful before, during, and after they see God's hands bringing fulfillment.

The completion of the Temple was celebrated with a joyful service of dedication (6:16-18). The great joy exhibited at this time reminds the reader of the rejoicing at the dedication of the foundations of this Temple many years earlier (3:8-13) and at the dedication of Solomon's original Temple (1 Kgs 8; 2 Chr 7). The list of people attending the dedication of the Temple includes only Israelites. None of their opponents from Samaria and no Persian officials were included. This was a family affair carried out by the sacred priests and Levites.

The priests offered 12 male goats "as a sin offering for the twelve tribes of Israel" (6:17). The number of animals sacrificed was much less than what the wealthy King

Solomon gave when he dedicated the first Temple (1 Kgs 8:63 lists 22,000 cattle and 120,000 sheep and goats), but the number of people who were to eat those animals was much greater, and the economic conditions of the nation were much more prosperous at that time. The 12 sin offerings represented each one of the 12 tribes of Israel, though it is not clearly stated that people from all of the 12 tribes were at this event. It is interesting that at a later date, Ezra also offered 12 oxen and 12 goats for a sin offering when he came to Jerusalem, even though he was not dedicating anything at that time (8:35). This focus on the 12 tribes demonstrated the leaders' attempt to emphasize the continuity this community had with the original 12 tribes that made up the kingdom of Israel. Sin offerings were used to bring atonement for unintentional sins (Lev 4), to dedicate a priest (Lev 9:1-4), to dedicate the Tabernacle (Num 7:16, 22, 28, 34, 40, 46, 52, 58, 64, 70, 76, 82, 87), and to rededicate the Temple in Hezekiah's time (2 Chr 29:24). These sacrifices were an admission of past failures, but they also symbolized the cleansing of the sacred place to set it apart for God.

The completion of the Temple was not seen as an end in itself. Having a holy place to commune with God distinguished that place from the common or profane environment of this world. But just having a sacred place to go to did not solve all of their problems. To make a real difference, people must use that place to confess their sins, pray for mercy, and fellowship with a holy God. The world will be changed not simply by the "magic" of going to some sacred spot or building but only as people allow the power of a holy God to transform their lives.

The joy of the people was full and exuberant, not only because of what they had finally done, but also because of what they could now do. Once they cleansed the site and dedicated the priests to their appropriate duties, the regular operation of the Temple could begin again. As long as the priestly leaders and the worshiping Israelites followed the instructions "prescribed in the Book of Moses" (6:18), God's name would be glorified through their worship. The great dangers for every past or present place of worship are that the leaders may not be fully dedicated to the spiritual work God has given them, the worship may not follow the instructions in the word of God, and the people may have no joy or awe as they enter the Lord's presence.

The description of the Israelites' celebration of the Passover is surprisingly factual (6:19-22), with little theological description of what people were thinking or saying. One can only imagine the thrill of being there and participating in this great event for the very first time in one's life. The theological emphasis in the chapter falls on the proper ceremonial cleansing of the priests and Levites who slaughtered the Passover lamb and appropriate regulations governing the inclusion of people who had turned away from paganism to worship only the God of Israel. The details of doing things the right way should never be taken for granted or be considered too trivial for our attention. The details of doing things right matter to God, and they should matter to every believer who desires to please God.

Along with the conservative concern to do things exactly as God instructed, however, there was a surprising concern to freely allow any devout outsider the pleasure of witnessing and enjoying the worship of God. This unusual act of inclusion did not contradict the exclusive rejection of foreigners in 4:1-5, for the strangers and foreigners who were fully accepted at this time were committed in their worship of the God of Israel (6:21). The leaders were not allowing non-Jews to bring strange, pagan beliefs and practices into the holy Temple of God. The believers' openness to outsiders was a difficult question faced by the early church in Acts, when uncircumcised Gentiles accepted Christ and were filled with the Spirit (Acts 15). Although all pagan beliefs and rituals were rejected (they were prohibited from eating blood), the people were accepted on the basis of the marvelous work that God had done in their lives (Acts 15:23-29). Openness to people who look and act different from the majority is still a struggle for many churches. New musical tastes, new worship styles, and people who think a little differently are not always welcomed. But if new or different people are fully committed to the worship of God, they are also a part of the body of Christ and should be welcomed.

Finally, this passage teaches that God deserves all the credit for the rebuilding of the Temple and celebration of the festival (see especially 6:22). It was not diplomacy, good luck, political pressure, bribery, or trickery that changed the heart of the Persian king. God sovereignly worked in the king's heart to cause him to turn from a position of not allowing the Jews to build a Temple for God to a position of strongly supporting the building of the Temple in Jerusalem. God brought about this change, and all honor goes to him. If he can change the heart of a pagan king, there is nothing too hard or impossible for God (Gen 18:14; Jer 32:17; Luke 1:37). He can change us and the circumstances that seem so impossible in our lives. He can change our neighbors, the decisions of an obstinate city council, and even the hearts of Supreme Court justices.

◆ **II. Ezra Returns to Teach God's Law (Ezra 7:1-10:44)**
   A. God Brings Ezra to Jerusalem (Ezra 7:1-8:36)
      1. Ezra's divine and royal commission (Ezra 7:1-28a)

Many years later, during the reign of King Artaxerxes of Persia,* there was a man named Ezra. He was the son* of Seraiah, son of Azariah, son of Hilkiah, ²son of Shallum, son of Zadok, son of Ahitub, ³son of Amariah, son of Azariah, son* of Meraioth, ⁴son of Zerahiah, son of Uzzi, son of Bukki, ⁵son of Abishua, son of Phinehas, son of Eleazar, son of Aaron the high priest.* ⁶This Ezra was a scribe who was well versed in the Law of Moses, which the LORD, the God of Israel, had given to the people of Israel. He came up to Jerusalem from Babylon, and the king gave him everything he asked for, because the gracious hand of the LORD his God was on him. ⁷Some of the people of Israel, as well as some of the priests, Levites, singers, gatekeepers, and Temple servants, traveled up to Jerusalem with him in the seventh year of King Artaxerxes' reign.

⁸Ezra arrived in Jerusalem in August* of that year. ⁹He had arranged to leave Babylon on April 8, the first day of the new year,* and he arrived at Jerusalem on August 4,* for the gracious hand of his God was on him. ¹⁰This was because Ezra had determined to study and obey the Law of the LORD and to teach those decrees and regulations to the people of Israel.

¹¹King Artaxerxes had given a copy of the following letter to Ezra, the priest and scribe who studied and taught the commands and decrees of the LORD to Israel:

¹²*"From Artaxerxes, the king of kings, to Ezra the priest, the teacher of the law of the God of heaven. Greetings.

13"I decree that any of the people of Israel in my kingdom, including the priests and Levites, may volunteer to return to Jerusalem with you. 14I and my council of seven hereby instruct you to conduct an inquiry into the situation in Judah and Jerusalem, based on your God's law, which is in your hand. 15We also commission you to take with you silver and gold, which we are freely presenting as an offering to the God of Israel who lives in Jerusalem.

16"Furthermore, you are to take any silver and gold that you may obtain from the province of Babylon, as well as the voluntary offerings of the people and the priests that are presented for the Temple of their God in Jerusalem. 17These donations are to be used specifically for the purchase of bulls, rams, male lambs, and the appropriate grain offerings and liquid offerings, all of which will be offered on the altar of the Temple of your God in Jerusalem. 18Any silver and gold that is left over may be used in whatever way you and your colleagues feel is the will of your God.

19"But as for the cups we are entrusting to you for the service of the Temple of your God, deliver them all to the God of Jerusalem. 20If you need anything else for your God's Temple or for any similar needs, you may take it from the royal treasury.

21"I, Artaxerxes the king, hereby send this decree to all the treasurers in the province west of the Euphrates River*: 'You are to give Ezra, the priest and teacher of the law of the God of heaven, whatever he requests of you. 22You are to give him up to 7,500 pounds* of silver, 500 bushels* of wheat, 550 gallons of wine, 550 gallons of olive oil,* and an unlimited supply of salt. 23Be careful to provide whatever the God of heaven demands for his Temple, for why should we risk bringing God's anger against the realm of the king and his sons? 24I also decree that no priest, Levite, singer, gatekeeper, Temple servant, or other worker in this Temple of God will be required to pay tribute, customs, or tolls of any kind.'

25"And you, Ezra, are to use the wisdom your God has given you to appoint magistrates and judges who know your God's laws to govern all the people in the province west of the Euphrates River. Teach the law to anyone who does not know it. 26Anyone who refuses to obey the law of your God and the law of the king will be punished immediately, either by death, banishment, confiscation of goods, or imprisonment."

27Praise the LORD, the God of our ancestors, who made the king want to beautify the Temple of the LORD in Jerusalem! 28And praise him for demonstrating such unfailing love to me by honoring me before the king, his council, and all his mighty nobles! I felt encouraged because the gracious hand of the LORD my God was on me.

7:1a Artaxerxes reigned 465-424 B.C.   7:1b Or *descendant;* see 1 Chr 6:14.   7:3 Or *descendant;* see 1 Chr 6:6-10.   7:5 Or *the first priest.*   7:8 Hebrew *in the fifth month.* This month in the ancient Hebrew lunar calendar occurred within the months of August and September 458 B.C.   7:9a Hebrew *on the first day of the first month,* of the ancient Hebrew lunar calendar. This day was April 8, 458 B.C.; also see note on 6:15.   7:9b Hebrew *on the first day of the fifth month,* of the ancient Hebrew lunar calendar. This day was August 4, 458 B.C.; also see note on 6:15.   7:12 The original text of 7:12-26 is in Aramaic.   7:21 Aramaic *the province beyond the river;* also in 7:25.   7:22a Aramaic *100 talents* [3,400 kilograms].   7:22b Aramaic *100 cors* [18.2 kiloliters].   7:22c Aramaic *100 baths* [2.1 kiloliters] *of wine, 100 baths of olive oil.*

NOTES

7:1 *Many years later, during the reign of King Artaxerxes of Persia.* The text describes the ministry of Ezra, who came to Jerusalem around 458 BC—the seventh year of Artaxerxes I

(7:7). Although some suggest that this is Artaxerxes II and place Ezra's return to Yehud during 398 BC, I prefer the traditional date (see Williamson 1985:xxxix-xliv or Kidner 1979:146-158 for a full discussion of this problem). See the discussion of the date in the Introduction.

7:1-5 son of . . . Aaron the high priest. The extensive genealogical record of the lineage of Ezra is traced back through Hilkiah (from the time of Josiah in 2 Kgs 22) and Zadok (from the time of Solomon in 1 Kgs 1:8, 32-35; 2:35) to Aaron because it was important to assure everyone in Israel of the legitimate authority of Ezra. This list of 16 ancestors is an abbreviated version, for in 1 Chr 6:3-15, some 23 generations span the time from Aaron to the Exile (Katzenstein 1962:377-384). Based on this information, Seraiah was a great-grandfather and not the actual father of Ezra (he died around 586 BC according to 2 Kgs 25:18-21). This connection with the high priest Aaron did not imply that Ezra was a high priest, but all the space given to Ezra's genealogy implied that this man would be a very important person in the narratives that follow (Eskenazi 1988:63).

7:6 This Ezra was a scribe who was well versed in the Law of Moses. After the parenthetical genealogical details, the author resumptively went back to the information in 7:1 and picked up the story again (Williamson 1985:88). The title "scribe" gives Ezra's social and religious standing in the community; it does not indicate that he held a political position among the Jews (Hoglund 1992:227; Allen 2003:60).

He came up to Jerusalem. Some scholars see a tightly constructed chiastic relationship between the paragraphs in chs 7–8, with the journey to Jerusalem highlighted in the beginning (7:1-10) and at the end (8:31-36) of this section (Throntveit 1992:38).

7:8 Ezra arrived in Jerusalem in August of that year. Lit., "Ezra arrived in Jerusalem in the fifth month of the seventh year of the king." According to this information, it took this fast-moving caravan less than four months to complete the journey. Some question the accuracy of the "seventh year" and change it to "thirty-seventh," thus putting Ezra chronologically after Nehemiah (see the excursus in Blenkinsopp 1988:139-144), but there is no textual evidence to support this change. The August date mentioned in the NLT assumes that the author referred to the "fifth month" of the Jewish religious calendar, which would mean that the travel took place approximately from April to August (see Yamauchi 1988:650).

7:9 He had arranged to leave Babylon on April 8 . . . and he arrived at Jerusalem on August 4. Lit., "He left Babylon on the first of the first month . . . and on the first of the fifth month he came to Jerusalem." According to 8:31 the people did not actually leave Babylon until 11 days after this date. The first of the month was the date they were to assemble to prepare to leave. In those 11 days, Ezra organized the people, searched for some additional Levites, and led the people in a spiritual fast (8:15-30). The journey took 108 days, so they must have traveled about 10 miles per day, though they may not have traveled at all on the Sabbath day. The text says nothing about any connection between the date of their gathering (the first of the first month) and the date of the Exodus (Exod 12:2), but some commentators believe it is very significant that Ezra set the date to gather on the same day the Israelites left Egypt under Moses (McConville 1985:219). But if this was a major point in Ezra's thinking, it seems that he would have commented on this fact in this verse.

the gracious hand of his God was on him. This long journey had gone smoothly and quickly. Ezra knew it was because of God's provision and protection (see also 7:28; 8:18, 22, 31).

7:11 King Artaxerxes had given a copy of the following letter to Ezra. Since 7:12-26 is written in Aramaic, like the earlier Persian letters in ch 4, there is every reason to believe that the text is an accurate copy of portions of Artaxerxes' letter. Some question the

authenticity of this letter because it makes reference to detailed Jewish religious information about priests, Levites, singers, gatekeepers, Temple servants, and various Jewish offerings that the king probably knew little about (see the discussion in Williamson 1985:100-
101). But these factors could be easily explained if the king had a Jewish scribe help him
write this decree (Fensham 1982:103). Already in the present verse, the Hebrew text bor-
rows the Old Persian words *parshegen* [TH6572, ZH7306] (copy) and *nishtewan* [TH5406, ZH5981]
("memorandum" or "letter"; see 4:11, 23), which fits the Persian context and argues for
the authenticity of the letter.

the priest and scribe who studied and taught the commands and decrees of the LORD to
Israel. The repeated identification of Ezra as a priest and teacher of God's law in 7:10-12
raised Ezra's status and legitimized his role in the eyes of the king and those who would
read this decree. He had the respect of the Persian king and had the authority to carry out
the king's wishes.

7:12 *From Artaxerxes . . . to Ezra. . . . Greetings.* The placement of the greeting follows
the regular structure of Persian letters (see 4:17; 5:7). The word translated "Greetings"
(*gemir* [TA/ZA10147, S1585]) means "perfect, complete" and has been interpreted in a variety of
ways. The comparable passages in 1 Esdr 8:9 and in the Syriac have "greetings" and "peace,"
respectively. But *gemir* might be better translated "it is complete," meaning that the king
has made up his mind on this matter (cf. LXX). NJPS translates it "and so forth" based on a
parallel with Rabbinic Hebrew (Allen 2003:61), but also includes a note that the meaning
is uncertain.

the king of kings. Assyrian, Babylonian, and Persian kings commonly used the title "king
of kings" since they were the kings of great empires (Yamauchi 1988:651).

the law of the God of heaven. This phrase refers to the Mosaic law, but the Persian king
used the Persian word for "law" (*datha'* [TA/ZA10186, S1882]) rather than the important
Hebrew word *torah* [TH8451, ZH9368]. This is another clear sign that this was a Persian letter
Ezra was copying, for a Jewish version of this letter would naturally use the Hebrew word
for law at this point.

7:14 *I and my council of seven.* The king and his "council of seven" (see also Esth 1:14)
apparently designed these responsibilities for Ezra based on their discussions with Ezra
and other Jewish leaders. These seven trusted advisers were directly involved with the king's
decisions (Esth 1:14; Xenophon *Anabasis* 1.6.4-5; Herodotus *Histories* 3.71, 83-84) and gave
weight and wisdom to the king's decree.

instruct you to conduct an inquiry into the situation in Judah. The second part of this
decree assigned Ezra to act as the king's official representative (his eyes and ears) to evaluate exactly what was happening in the distant province of Yehud. Possibly the king heard
of some rumors of trouble and wanted Ezra to check things out. The king was not trying to
impose a foreign Persian law on the people in Jerusalem; instead, he wanted Jewish laws
to be followed so that there would be peace and order in this part of his empire. Although
this seems like a very limited role (just investigating things), after Ezra understood the situation, the king gave Ezra permission to enforce the laws of the king and the laws of God
(7:25-26). Ezra 10:16-17 records how Ezra and a group of leading citizens of Jerusalem
investigated and resolved the difficult situation regarding mixed marriages in Jerusalem.
This proves that Ezra was given real power by the king and that he took his responsibility
seriously when he arrived in Jerusalem.

7:15 *take with you silver and gold, which we are freely presenting as an offering to*
the God of Israel. In light of the strong distinction between church and state in modern
cultures, it may seem odd that the government gave so much money (see 7:22-23) for the

Temple offerings. The modern idea of separation would have been wholly unnatural in the ancient world (including Israel and Persia)—to them everything had a religious connection. When compared with official gifts to other religious groups, this generous gift fits the regular Persian pattern (Yamauchi 1988:653). Similar funds were given to a Jewish temple at Elephantine (ANET 492) and to Babylonian and Egyptian temples (R. de Vaux 1972:73-92). These gifts not only caused the Jews to look favorably on the Persians but also encouraged the Jewish people to pray for their Persian rulers (6:9-10). This gift did not mean that the Persian king and his council of seven believed that the God of Israel was the only true God; it simply meant they were wise politicians who respected the different religious beliefs of all the cultures within their empire.

7:16 you are to take any silver and gold . . . as well as the voluntary offerings. One could interpret the first part of the verse to refer to gold and silver donated from non-Jews in Babylon (see 1:4) and the last half to describe Jewish contributions (Clines 1984:103). This statement gave Ezra the right to have a fundraising campaign in Babylon, but 8:25 only mentions gifts from "the king, his council, his officials, and all the people of Israel." These results suggest that they received nothing from any of the common Babylonian people, which is what one would expect.

7:17 These donations are to be used specifically for the purchase of bulls, rams, male lambs, and the appropriate grain offerings and liquid offerings. This gold and silver was not to pay for new construction costs, maintenance expenses, salaries, stock options, or travel expenses for Ezra and his group. It was totally dedicated to the religious function of providing sacrifices at the Temple in Jerusalem. Similar stipulations were put on other Persian gifts to other temples (ANET 491-492). Clearly, the piety of the Jews who worked with the king had impressed him, and he did not want to offend their God in any way. It is amazing how God even worked through pagan kings to bring glory to himself.

7:18 Any silver and gold that is left over may be used in whatever way . . . is the will of your God. At first glance this may look like a blank check to spend lavishly on whatever luxuries one might want, but the use of the king's money on other items was limited to only what was left over (the basic sacrifices listed had to be made), to what could be determined as the will of God (not the will of Ezra or any other person), and implicitly to what Ezra's wisdom and honesty suggested was appropriate. This high level of trust and judgment put a great deal of accountability on those who would spend the king's gold. The inclusion of this statement indicated that the king knew there would be some left over, yet he generously gave that extra amount anyway. His attitude toward giving to God is exemplary and an embarrassment when compared to the miserly approach of the Jewish people who were neglecting the Temple and the priests later in the book of Nehemiah (Neh 10:32-39; 13:10-13).

7:19 as for the cups . . . for the service of the Temple of your God. This reference to Temple cups (*ma'n* [TA/ZA10398, S3984], "utensil, vessel") is surprising, since 1:7-11 indicates that the utensils Nebuchadnezzar took from the Temple were transported back to Jerusalem by Sheshbazzar in 538 BC around 80 years earlier. The utensils mentioned here include 122 valuable items listed in 8:26-27. It is possible that these were vessels overlooked by Cyrus (Kidner 1979:63), or they could be new vessels made in Persia and given as gifts (Brockington 1969:93; Allen 2003:58).

7:20 If you need anything else for your God's Temple . . . you may take it from the royal treasury. At first "anything" seems too generous to be true, but this decree only gave permission to have funds that were necessary, and only those things necessary for the proper functioning of the Temple. Anyone who would ask for additional gold would have to justify the need; it was not freely handed out. In spite of this, one is impressed by the Persians' great generosity. The king's strong trust of Ezra was not expressly stated at this point (it would be embarrassing for Ezra to include this about himself), but certainly that was the foundational basis for this generosity. The king had worked with Ezra and knew he was a responsible and honest man.

7:21 *I, Artaxerxes the king . . . to all the treasurers in the province: . . .'You are to give Ezra . . . whatever he requests of you.'* This statement appears to begin a new and separate decree not addressed to Ezra, but probably carried by Ezra so that he could present it when he needed to get funds from the treasuries of the provinces. Archaeologists found hundreds of travel ration texts while excavating the Persian capital, Persepolis (Yamauchi 1988:653), and therefore some interpreters have concluded that this decree provided for the general travel expenses that Ezra's caravan requested as the group traveled through various towns and provinces on their way back to Jerusalem (Fensham 1982:106). This interpretation narrows the use and availability of the funds indicated by this decree to the daily needs of the travelers (rather than the needs of God's Temple). This idea is supported by the contrast between the focus on the Temple in earlier verses and the lack of any reference to the Temple in 7:21. The main problem with this approach, however, is that 7:23 returns to the discussion of supplying the needs for the Temple in Jerusalem.

7:22 *7,500 pounds of silver, 500 bushels of wheat, 550 gallons of wine, 550 gallons of olive oil, and an unlimited supply of salt.* Lit., "100 talents of silver, 100 cors of grain, 100 baths of wine, and 100 baths of olive oil." A talent weighed about 65 pounds, a cor of grain was just over six bushels, and a bath of oil was about six gallons. These figures all seem very large, and therefore some question their accuracy. Some compare the 100 talents of silver with the 350 talents of tax revenue from the whole province beyond the river (Herodotus *Histories* 3.91) and conclude that a textual error could have corrupted this text (Williamson 1985:103) or that it should read "100 minas of silver," rather than talents (Clines 1984:104). Nevertheless, if this amount was seen as the most Ezra could ask for from the provincial treasurers, rather than the amount he was immediately given, it is less problematic. If this was the intention of this verse, it would be comparable to Darius's provisions for the needs of the people in his decree (6:9).

7:23 *Be careful . . . why should we risk bringing God's anger against the realm of the king.* Darius was very concerned about gaining the favor and blessing of Israel's God and fearful of any divine curse against himself or his kingdom (6:10). Artaxerxes had a similar fear and thus encouraged Ezra to be "careful/faithful" ('*adrazda'* [TA/ZA10012, S149], a Persian loan word) to do what was right, but did not explain how God might show his wrath against the king. If the Persian army was putting down a revolt in Egypt at this time, as some have suggested (Blenkinsopp 1988:150), the king probably wanted God to give the army a successful campaign so that he would not lose part of his empire. The belief that each country's gods controlled the territory within that country was a common theological perspective in the ancient Near East, so it appears that he wanted the gods in every country to act in favor of the Persians (Block 1988:74-96).

7:24 *no priest, Levite, singer, gatekeeper, Temple servant, or other worker in this Temple of God will be required to pay tribute.* The exemption of religious employees from normal forms of taxation was widely practiced. According to Josephus (*Antiquities* 12.3.3 [12.129-144]), Antiochus III (c. 200 BC) gave a similar exemption from taxation to Temple personnel, and Darius himself condemned Gadatas for exacting taxes from workers at a temple for Apollo in Magnesia, Asia Minor (Gadatas Inscription; see Olmstead 1948:156). This was probably one of the benefits that Ezra asked Artaxerxes to extend to the Jewish priests and Levites still in Babylon, so as to encourage some of them to go with him back to Jerusalem.

COMMENTARY

About 60 years of Jewish history is skipped between chapters 6 and 7, omitting any discussion of events from the time of King Xerxes and his wife Esther. The text now describes the ministry of Ezra, who came to Jerusalem around 458 BC—the seventh year of Artaxerxes I (7:7). The first section (7:1-10) introduces the reader to Ezra by describing his family background, his role, his purpose, and the key to his success.

Some scholars have hypothesized that the priest Ezra functioned as a "Secretary of State for Jewish Affairs" (Schams 1998:52-58) because he was given both religious and political responsibilities in Yehud, but this may overstate his role. A "scribe" (*soper* [TH5608A, ZH6221]) was sometimes an important state official (2 Sam 8:17; 1 Kgs 4:3), could serve as a military officer (Jer 52:25), or work as a secretary or amanuensis (4:8; Jer 36:27). Some priestly scribes painstakingly copied manuscripts of the Scriptures (cf. Ps 45:1 [2]), while others taught people what God revealed to his people in the law of Moses (Deut 10:8-9; 33:8-10; Mal 2:6-7). Ezra was "well versed" (*mahir* [TH4106, ZH4542], 7:6)—literally, he was quick or skilled, hence "a professional of the highest order" (Fensham 1982:100). Ezra was a very knowledgeable and effective teacher. He did not teach economics, secular law, or mathematics; he taught the word of God that Moses recorded in the Pentateuch. These covenantal instructions were considered a sacred gift from God to his people.

Ezra was blessed by God in his relationship with the king. Ezra 7:6 says, "The king gave him everything he asked for, because the gracious hand of the LORD his God was on him." The text does not reveal what Ezra asked of the king for his trip to Yehud (Judah). We know that he did not ask the king for soldiers and horsemen to protect the people on this long and dangerous journey back to Jerusalem (8:22). One can probably guess what Ezra requested by analyzing the king's response in 7:11-26. Ezra interpreted the king's overwhelmingly positive response as a direct result of God's sovereign intervention on his behalf. His success was not due to bribery, trickery, political pressure, persuasive argumentation, or personal friendship; it was just the grace of God, nothing else. This is a common theme in 7:9, 28; 8:18, 22, 31; Nehemiah 2:8, 18, and it demonstrates that the author was trying to downplay any "heroic" interpretation of Ezra. He was an important spiritual leader, but it was the sovereign power of God that paved the way for all his accomplishments.

Since Ezra was a priestly scribe concerned about Temple worship, it was natural that he would try to motivate other priests, Levites, singers, gatekeepers, and Temple servants to go up to Jerusalem with him (7:7). These people, who are listed in 8:1-20, amount to about 1,500 men, so the whole group of men, women, and children may have numbered as high as 4,000 or 5,000 (Clines 1984:108). The journey would have taken them up the Euphrates River from Babylon to Syria and then down to Jerusalem, a long trip of over 800 miles.

The text tells us that they made the trip in about four months (see notes on 7:8 and 7:9) because God's gracious hand was on Ezra and because Ezra was a person who "determined to study and obey the Law of the LORD and to teach those decrees and regulations to the people of Israel" (7:10). Ezra's purpose in life was outlined in three goals: (1) to study God's word, (2) to obey what God said, and (3) to teach others the truths that he learned from God's word. This threefold approach to ministry sets a solid model for all those who aspire to serve God. The verb underlying the idea of studying is "to seek, search" (*darash* [TH1875, ZH2011], 7:10). It implies that Ezra spent time searching through the instructions in the Mosaic law books to find out what God had decreed. This first step assures that what one teaches is solidly based on what God has said, not modern cultural norms and customs or some man-made philosophy. The idea of "obeying" is simply the concept of "doing" ('*asah* [TH6213, ZH6913]) what God says one should do. It implies acceptance or internalization of God's truth into a person's beliefs and behavior patterns. This step assures that the teacher is sharing ideas that are vital to the audience's walk with God and not just abstract theoretical ideas that do not relate to real life. "The model teacher in Ezra is a doer. . . . He must *be* what he would have his disciples be" (McConville 1985:47). Finally, the act of teaching others involved Ezra in sharing the theological ideas he learned. This application involved the proclamation of the practical principles imbedded in the stories in Genesis, the commandments in Exodus, the worship instructions in Leviticus, and the call to love God in Deuteronomy. This step enabled Ezra to multiply his ministry through the lives of others as God transformed their thinking through his word. This shows that Ezra was interested in changing people's lives with apt applications drawn from biblical principles. He was not just into gaining esoteric knowledge for himself. Nevertheless, his commitment to study hard suggests that a simple, uneducated, off-the-cuff interpretation was not his ideal.

Artaxerxes had given Ezra a very important letter to take with him. This letter gave Ezra and his companions the official permission they needed to go back to Jerusalem. This document could have functioned almost like a passport as Ezra traveled through various countries on his way back to Judah. This permission to return identified their final destination and the participants involved. The king graciously included anyone from any place who was an Israelite. Ezra was not interested in bringing only people from Judah back to the city of Jerusalem; his theological agenda was to bring back anyone from any of the tribes of Israel. His goal was to resettle the whole people of God in the land of their inheritance. The express reference to priests and Levites shows that Ezra specifically asked that Temple personnel be allowed to return to Jerusalem to help him teach the law of God.

The final section of this letter (7:25-26) describes Ezra's responsibility in establishing law and order around Jerusalem. The Persians had two different courts, one for civil cases and one for state issues; thus, the magistrates served on one and the judges on the other. The king must have had years of experience working with Ezra and recognized that he had a special measure of wisdom from God and a practical ability to find and appoint skilled people to judicial positions of great responsibility. Artaxerxes granted full authority to the judges he appointed and allowed these Jewish judges to make decisions based on Hebrew principles defined in the law of God (see Deut 16–17; 2 Chr 19:1-11), not some foreign concept of right and wrong. Although the king gave Ezra authority to establish judges throughout the province, most conclude that the king was only permitting these judges to settle *Jewish* legal cases in Yehud (Judah). There was no suggestion that he was trying to force non-Jews, like the Samarians or Ammonites, to submit to Jewish laws (Clines 1984:105; Kidner 1979:63). The king's admonition about teaching the Jewish law to those who were not familiar with it presumably means that Ezra was to educate the Jewish people in a common set of established just principles. The king was not encouraging him to go out and proselytize non-Jewish people through this educational process. Thus, Ezra's reform movement concerning intermarriage with unbelievers (Ezra 9–10) should be seen as fulfilling this command because at that time Ezra was attempting to teach people to live according to the principles in God's laws (10:10).

In the final sentence of the letter, Artaxerxes emphasized that the people must obey both the laws of the God of the Jews, as well as the laws of the king of Persia (7:26). The king's laws related to paying taxes, being loyal to the king and his legitimate government officials, serving when called on, and obeying future decrees. The king's generosity to the Jewish people did not mean that he was soft on issues of law and order. Indeed, the decree ends with the harsh words: "Anyone who refuses to obey the law of your God and the law of the king will be punished immediately, either by death, banishment, confiscation of goods, or imprisonment" (7:26). Refusing to obey would bring an immediate and appropriate punishment. Artaxerxes supported various degrees of punishment for different crimes (7:26); some were rather mild if the crime was not serious, while others uprooted people from the community or ended the guilty party's life. Justice was not to be delayed; instead, there was to be an appropriate enforcement of the punishment. This admonition argues against judges "interpreting" laws to their own liking or changing the prescribed punishment; they must follow the punishment guidelines provided in the law. These punishment clauses ended the king's decree and the use of Aramaic in this passage.

The last two verses of chapter 7 record Ezra's praise to God for this decree. It follows the pattern of many hymns and includes (1) an exclamation of praise and (2) the reason for praise. Ezra's first response to the decree is to declare, "Praise the LORD, the God of our ancestors, who made the king want to beautify the Temple" (7:27). The first reason for praise is unexpected, since we do not read about beautification of the Temple elsewhere in Artaxerxes' earlier decree. Thus, one could infer that Ezra used some of the extra money (7:18) to do some Temple restoration (Williamson 1985:105), or that the sacrifices "adorned" the Temple (Isa 60:7; see Fensham 1982:110), or that the word *pa'er* [TH6286, ZH6995] (beautify) was used metaphorically to refer to the "honoring" or "glorification" of the Temple (Yamauchi 1988:656).

Ezra recognized that the unbelievable generosity of the Persian king toward him, the Temple, and the Jewish people was due to a desire that God sovereignly put in his heart. Although the Persians were known for dealing with their vassals in a generous way, they did not have to be this generous; they did not have to give Ezra permission to set up courts that were ruled by the laws of God and the king, and the king did not have to exempt the Temple workers from taxes. Ezra saw a greater truth in what was happening. Ultimately, no person, not even the great king of a large empire, really has complete control over his political decisions—God does. Artaxerxes had some control over religious practices in his nation, but God was the real power that provided religious freedom for his worshipers. Behind the power-hungry facade of rulers who tried to manipulate the scene of human history was the hand of God, guiding, controlling, stirring, and judging. Ezra's praise took all focus off himself and gave full credit to God, where it really belonged.

The final praise to God from Ezra is, "Praise him for demonstrating such unfailing love to me. . . . I felt encouraged because the gracious hand of the LORD my God was on me" (7:28). Literally, this reads, "and who has extended to me unfailing love . . . and I strengthened myself because the hand of the LORD my God was upon me." There is no repeated word for "praise" at the beginning of this verse, just the second reason for praising God. Ezra highlighted God's steadfast covenant love that never failed and the powerful hand of God that strengthened his servants. Although these may seem rather unspectacular, normal reasons for praising God, nothing can be more important or basic than sensing the love and power of God guiding the course of history. Without God's love and power, everything would be impossible. Ezra also drew a connection between God's loving acts on his behalf and the resultant strengthening that occurred in his own life. This humble admission of total dependence on God was a sign of a great leader; Ezra was not deluded by personal accomplishments into thinking that he was anything other than God's chosen instrument. God deserved all the credit, not Ezra.

God willed that Ezra should work together with the pagan Persians and made them willing to assist in the process of establishing God's rule over his people (Williamson 1985:105-106). The Persians did not try to impose any foreign religious beliefs on the Jewish people. The earlier Jews, however, could not work together with the Samarians (as noted in 4:1-6) because although they intended to help the Jewish people build the Temple, there was a real danger that these people would want to worship both the God of Israel and other foreign gods at the Temple. This would have contradicted the law of Moses and would not have led to the glorification of God. This suggests that a supportive government is far less threatening to followers of God than competing ideologies or theologies that distract people from obeying all that God has revealed in his word.

We also learn from this section much regarding what kind of person Ezra was. The biographical information from these memoirs partially explains why Ezra was used of God for this great task. One key was his priestly family background. His lineage from the family of Aaron ensured that he received good training in the law of God, but his priestly credentials did not make him stand out from all the other priests of that day. Even more important than Ezra's priestly background was his commitment to know and live by the divine revelation of God (he was a doer of the word). The testimony of 7:6 shows that Ezra was an outstanding student who searched God's word with a strong dedication to developing exceptional skills in exegesis and application. This gave him credibility; he was a true believer and a dedicated disciple who knew what he was talking about. He did not study the Mosaic law code because he was curious about the ancient traditions of his grandparents. He was not in this occupation because he had to be, because it paid well, or just because his parents pushed him into it. After all, not all men in the priestly line did what Ezra chose to do—he could have rebelled and worshiped Baal, he could have become a farmer and refused priestly roles, he could have copied manuscripts instead of focusing on teaching. Ezra stands out as a follower of God who was serious about what God has said. He was so convinced of the truthfulness and practicality of this divine revelation that he dedicated his life to teaching others about it. Ezra did not keep his life's purpose a secret, for the king and his council knew him as "the teacher of the law of the God of heaven" (7:12, 21). The king trusted Ezra with an important government appointment, a large amount of money, and the freedom to do whatever was needed. This demonstrates that Artaxerxes had firsthand knowledge of this man's wisdom and honesty (7:25). Finally, Ezra was a humble person who gave God credit for what was accomplished (7:6, 9, 27); he was not a proud person who saw his role as the key to everything that was going to happen in Jerusalem.

One cannot overemphasize the importance of the "law of God" or the "Law of Moses" to Ezra's life and mission. Ezra's worldview was shaped by this revelation that had come from God as a gift to his covenant people. It identified what it meant to be a Jewish person, what was involved in following a holy God, and what should be avoided in order to be separate from sin. The law was not something new that Ezra devised and introduced (Throntveit 1992:43); it was those stories and regulations Moses received long ago. Thus, Ezra was not trying to create a new paradigm that was more practical or culturally relevant for returnees after the Babylonian exile. He was calling people back to the foundational truths that God had revealed centuries earlier. This is the law "which is in your hand" (7:14), not some unknown or mysterious secret; it is the will of God (7:18) that regulated life in the Temple, in the family, and in the courts (7:25). The revelation of God in this law served as the standard for Ezra's investigation of life in Yehud (7:14), and the teaching of the laws of God would be the cure to reordering life in Jerusalem (7:25). Those who refused to obey God's law were dealt with severely (7:26) but appropriately and justly. Although this emphasis may appear excessively focused on obedience and devoid of freedom of expression, there never was a better way than God's way of doing things. As long as Ezra avoided a legalistic formula of doing works to earn God's approval and blessing, there was nothing wrong with instructing people in God's words of revelation. They provided the covenant people with instructions on how to live holy and just lives so that they could maintain their covenant relationship with God and enjoy worshiping him in the Temple. God's word is a light to the traveler's path (Ps 119:105), a guide to keep people from sin (Ps 119:9-11), and a source of revival (Ps 119:40). It was a privilege to have copies of the words of God to read. This precious, life-giving resource should be something a believer loves and meditates on every day (Ps 119:97).

◆ ### 2. God's hand on those who returned to Jerusalem (Ezra 7:28b–8:36)

And I gathered some of the leaders of Israel to return with me to Jerusalem.

CHAPTER 8

Here is a list of the family leaders and the genealogies of those who came with me from Babylon during the reign of King Artaxerxes:

² From the family of Phinehas: Gershom. From the family of Ithamar: Daniel.

From the family of David: Hattush, ³a descendant of Shecaniah.

From the family of Parosh: Zechariah and 150 other men were registered.

⁴ From the family of Pahath-moab: Eliehoenai son of Zerahiah and 200 other men.

⁵ From the family of Zattu*: Shecaniah son of Jahaziel and 300 other men.

⁶ From the family of Adin: Ebed son of Jonathan and 50 other men.

⁷ From the family of Elam: Jeshaiah son of Athaliah and 70 other men.

⁸ From the family of Shephatiah: Zebadiah son of Michael and 80 other men.

⁹ From the family of Joab: Obadiah son of Jehiel and 218 other men.

¹⁰ From the family of Bani*: Shelomith son of Josiphiah and 160 other men.

¹¹ From the family of Bebai: Zechariah son of Bebai and 28 other men.

¹² From the family of Azgad: Johanan son of Hakkatan and 110 other men.

¹³ From the family of Adonikam, who came later*: Eliphelet, Jeuel, Shemaiah, and 60 other men.

¹⁴ From the family of Bigvai: Uthai, Zaccur,* and 70 other men.

¹⁵ I assembled the exiles at the Ahava Canal, and we camped there for three days while I went over the lists of the people and the priests who had arrived. I found that not one Levite had volunteered to come along. ¹⁶ So I sent for Eliezer, Ariel, Shemaiah, Elnathan, Jarib, Elnathan, Nathan, Zechariah, and Meshullam, who were leaders of the people. I also sent for Joiarib and Elnathan, who were men of discernment. ¹⁷ I sent them to Iddo, the leader of the Levites at Casiphia, to ask him and his relatives and the Temple servants to send us ministers for the Temple of God at Jerusalem.

¹⁸ Since the gracious hand of our God was on us, they sent us a man named Sherebiah, along with eighteen of his sons and brothers. He was a very astute man and a descendant of Mahli, who was a descendant of Levi son of Israel.* ¹⁹ They also sent Hashabiah, together with Jeshaiah from the descendants of Merari, and twenty of his sons and brothers, ²⁰ and 220 Temple servants. The Temple servants were assistants to the Levites—a group of Temple workers first instituted by King David and his officials. They were all listed by name.

²¹ And there by the Ahava Canal, I gave orders for all of us to fast and humble ourselves before our God. We prayed that he would give us a safe journey and protect us, our children, and our goods as we traveled. ²² For I was ashamed to ask the king for soldiers and horsemen* to accompany us and protect us from enemies along the way. After all, we had told the king, "Our God's hand of protection is on all who worship him, but his fierce anger rages against those who abandon him." ²³ So we fasted and earnestly prayed that our God would take care of us, and he heard our prayer.

²⁴ I appointed twelve leaders of the priests—Sherebiah, Hashabiah, and ten other priests—²⁵ to be in charge of transporting the silver, the gold, the gold bowls, and the other items that the king, his council, his officials, and all the people of Israel had presented for the Temple of God. ²⁶ I weighed the treasure as I gave it to them and found the totals to be as follows:

24 tons* of silver,
7,500 pounds* of silver articles,
7,500 pounds of gold,
²⁷ 20 gold bowls, equal in value to
1,000 gold coins,*
2 fine articles of polished bronze,
as precious as gold.

²⁸ And I said to these priests, "You and these treasures have been set apart as holy to the LORD. This silver and gold is a voluntary offering to the LORD, the God of our ancestors. ²⁹ Guard these treasures well until you present them to the leading priests, the Levites, and the leaders of Israel, who will weigh them at the storerooms of the LORD's Temple in Jerusalem." ³⁰ So the priests and the Levites accepted the task of transporting these treasures of silver and gold to the Temple of our God in Jerusalem.

³¹ We broke camp at the Ahava Canal on April 19* and started off to Jerusalem. And the gracious hand of our God protected us and saved us from enemies and bandits along the way. ³² So we arrived safely in Jerusalem, where we rested for three days.

³³ On the fourth day after our arrival,

the silver, gold, and other valuables were weighed at the Temple of our God and entrusted to Meremoth son of Uriah the priest and to Eleazar son of Phinehas, along with Jozabad son of Jeshua and Noadiah son of Binnui—both of whom were Levites. 34Everything was accounted for by number and weight, and the total weight was officially recorded.

35Then the exiles who had come out of captivity sacrificed burnt offerings to the God of Israel. They presented twelve bulls for all the people of Israel, as well as ninety-six rams and seventy-seven male lambs. They also offered twelve male goats as a sin offering. All this was given as a burnt offering to the LORD. 36The king's decrees were delivered to his highest officers and the governors of the province west of the Euphrates River,* who then cooperated by supporting the people and the Temple of God.

8:5 As in some Greek manuscripts (see also 1 Esdras 8:32); Hebrew lacks *Zattu.*   8:10 As in some Greek manuscripts (see also 1 Esdras 8:36); Hebrew lacks *Bani.*   8:13 Or *who were the last of his family.*   8:14 As in Greek and Syriac versions and an alternate reading of the Masoretic Text; the other alternate reads *Zabbud.*   8:18 *Israel* is the name that God gave to Jacob.   8:22 Or *charioteers.*   8:26a Hebrew *650 talents* [22 metric tons].   8:26b Hebrew *100 talents* [3,400 kilograms]; also in 8:26c.   8:27 Hebrew *1,000 darics,* about 19 pounds or 8.6 kilograms in weight.   8:31 Hebrew *on the twelfth day of the first month,* of the ancient Hebrew lunar calendar. This day was April 19, 458 B.C.; also see note on 6:15.   8:36 Hebrew *the province beyond the river.*

NOTES

7:28b ***And I gathered.*** Although it is possible to place the paragraph division with the chapter division at 8:1, it makes more sense to see 7:28b as the beginning of the next section. Ezra's words of thanksgiving to God seem to end at 7:28a; 7:28b contains no words of praise but turns to the material ahead in ch 8 by introducing the list in 8:1-14 as those he gathered together.

8:1 ***a list of the family leaders and the genealogies.*** This phrase begins a parenthetical listing (8:1-14) of families that returned with Ezra. The "assembling" of people in 8:15 resumes the narrative by picking up the idea of "gathering" the people in 7:28b. Most believe this is an authentic list (Blenkinsopp 1988:161; Fensham 1982:111), even though it includes only 15 families. Ezra lists 1,514 people, some of whom are mentioned in ch 2. This overlap does not mean this list was copied from ch 2, for it would be natural for people in the same family to want to go to Jerusalem to be with their relatives there. The total group going with Ezra to Jerusalem may have been as large as 5,000 people when one adds women and children.

8:2 ***From the family of Phinehas . . . family of Ithamar.*** The priestly families were listed first, showing Ezra's concern to bring new Temple personnel with him. Eleazar and Ithamar were Aaron's sons, and Phinehas was Ithamar's son (Exod 6:25). The number of the men from these families (cf. the numbers in 8:3-14) was evidently lost in the transmission of the text.

Hattush. Descended from the line of King David, this man was a prince (1 Chr 3:21-22), but he did not have a royal role in these narratives.

8:13 ***who came later.*** Lit., "last." The significance of this word is puzzling. It could be someone's name, or it may indicate that the "last" members of this family had now returned to Jerusalem (Williamson 1985:108).

8:15 ***I assembled the exiles at the Ahava Canal.*** The new section (8:15-36) picks up the narrative where it was interrupted (7:28) by the lists of people in 8:1-14. Ezra began his staging preparations by the Ahava Canal (its location is unknown; Ezekiel was by the Kebar Canal in Ezek 1:1) somewhere outside of Babylon. Names were listed, the caravan was organized, and final preparations were made.

8:16 *leaders of the people . . . men of discernment.* Ezra employed the skills of a few of the known leaders and wise men and sent them to enlist some Levites from Casiphia, a town where Levites lived. These "wise men" (*mebinim* [TH995, ZH1067]) could be "intelligent" men (Clines 1981:110) or "teachers, interpreters" (Fensham 1982:113), based on Neh 8:8-9.

8:17 *Iddo, the leader of the Levites at Casiphia.* Lit., "Iddo, the leader at Casiphia the place." Some think Iddo was both the leader and a teacher at a Levitical school, hypothesizing an exilic temple or synagogue at Casiphia, with "the place" (*maqom* [TH4725, ZH5226]) referring to the place of the temple in Casiphia—per Deut 12 and Jer 7 (Brockington 1969:100; Blenkinsopp 1988:165-166). But this interpretation puts too much weight on interpreting the word "place" as a sacred place of worship. Although the Jewish people surely had places of worship and schools for theological training in Babylon, there is nothing in this text to prove exactly what existed at Casiphia. Some identify Iddo (cf. Neh 12:16) as the (grand)father of the prophet Zechariah (Ezra 5:1; Zech 1:1), but there is no way to prove this.

to ask him. This paraphrases the literal "I put in their mouths the words to say," which pictures Ezra guiding these leaders with advice on how to persuade Iddo and his relatives to bring Levitical servants who would be willing to return with them to Jerusalem so that they could serve God at the Temple.

8:18-20 *Since the gracious hand of our God was on us.* Ezra and the local leaders were the means of recruiting (1) Sherebiah and his 18 sons and brothers, (2) Hashabiah and Jeshaiah and 20 sons and brothers, plus (3) 220 Temple servants—but God deserved the full credit for leading these people to return with Ezra to Jerusalem. Ezra was amazed that God would move so many to return with them at such short notice.

a very astute man. Sherebiah's "astuteness" or practical wisdom may explain why he is mentioned several times in important roles in Ezra-Nehemiah (8:24; Neh 8:7; 9:4-5; 10:12; 12:8, 24).

8:23 *he heard our prayer.* This phrase could be translated and interpreted as if it was Ezra's conclusion after the journey was over—similar to 8:31 (Clines 1984:112). But since it is placed here at the beginning of the journey, it probably refers to some assurance that Ezra received from God before the journey began. The text does not explain how God communicated this sense of assurance to Ezra.

8:24-30 This section records the official arrangements for transporting all the holy gifts for the Temple and precious gold from Persia. Before the people could leave, someone had to be put in charge of the king's generous provisions. Ezra delegated responsibility to trusted, holy men. Two interpretations are possible: (1) Sherebiah, Hashabiah, and the 10 others were the 12 men Ezra appointed; or the more likely view, (2) Ezra appointed 12 priests, plus Sherebiah, Hashabiah, and 10 others. This latter approach would make the first group of priests responsible for handling the sacred objects, while the latter group, who were technically Levites (8:18-19), were responsible for transporting or carrying them. (According to Num 4, Levites were responsible for carrying holy things during the wilderness journey.) This also means there would have been more people to guard the sacred objects when the caravan was stopped for the night.

8:26-27 *I weighed the treasure . . . 24 tons of silver, 7,500 pounds of silver articles, 7,500 pounds of gold.* The amount of gold and silver was enormous. Twenty-four tons (lit., "650 talents") of silver was equal to the annual income of between 100,000 and 500,000 men (Clines 1984:113), so it is not surprising that Clines suggests that the original text probably had the smaller "minas" of gold and silver rather than "talents." (A mina was perhaps 1/60 of a talent). Others explain the large amount as a mixture of hyperbole or exaggeration, plus scribal error (Blenkinsopp 1988:169; Williamson 1985:119). William-son (1985:114) repoints this noun to a dual form and gets "of two talents." But it might be best to leave the amount blank and unknown. The text of "7,500 pounds of silver articles" is problematic. Lit., the text refers to "100 vessels of silver, worth talents," but does not say how many talents. It is unlikely that the 100 in the verse refers to talents. Both in terms of weight and value, this was an incredible amount for Ezra to transport to Jerusalem. Would the Persians have given this much and then sent Ezra off without a royal escort to protect the king's investment from robbers? There is no way of knowing for sure, but the Masoretic tradition describes a huge financial gift.

8:28-29 *You and these treasures have been set apart as holy to the LORD. . . . Guard these treasures well.* Ezra charged the priests with the solemn responsibility of guarding this treasure horde. The charge was theologically based on the fact that this gold and silver belonged to God; it was a freewill offering to him. Not an ounce should be lost because it was holy, totally set apart, and consecrated to God. It was appropriate that the holy priest should take charge of what belonged to God, and it was important that the whole congregation of returnees respect the theological role of the priests. This would be a heavy responsibility, but one that involved no compensation for the priests or Levites. The goal of using this money to further the worship of God at Jerusalem justified their efforts and sacrifice.

8:30 *So the priests and the Levites accepted the task.* Ezra was not a dictator but a man who led and challenged his followers with rational decisions based on traditional roles in the books of Moses. His followers willingly accepted this responsibility, making adherence to the law of Moses their own purpose. It was not just a burdensome job they had to do, but a means of serving God so that his name would be glorified through their efforts.

8:31 *the gracious hand of our God protected us and saved us from enemies.* The toil and struggle of this long, four-month journey faded into the background after they finally reached Jerusalem. We know nothing about the various trials and tribulations along the way; all we know is that God protected them. They may have actually been attacked, as the verb "save" (*natsal* [TH5337, ZH5911]) can imply, or God may have protected them from being attacked.

8:32 *we rested for three days.* After the long journey was over, they rested three days, similar to Nehemiah's rest upon arrival (Neh 2:11). Some hypothesize that this was due to an arrival on a Friday; thus they waited until after the Sabbath to deliver the silver and gold to the Temple (Fensham 1982:120, who follows A. Jaubert). Of course, some of the three days would have involved greeting old friends and relatives as well as finding places for the 5,000 new immigrants to live. In addition, it would take some time for the priests at the Temple to empty and prepare secure rooms to store all the silver and gold they were receiving from the Persian king.

8:33 *Meremoth . . . Eleazar . . . Jozabad . . . Noadiah.* Two priests and two Levites in Jerusalem received this large gift. Although the Hakkoz family originally lost its genealogical records (2:61-63), the responsibility of Meremoth, son of Uriah, son of Hakkoz in this narrative assumes that they found their genealogy or that another priest consulted God and discovered they really were priests. Later Meremoth helped build the walls of Jerusalem (Neh 3:4, 21). The Levite Jozabad is still listed as an official at the Temple in the time of Nehemiah (Neh 11:16; 12:8).

8:35 *They presented twelve bulls for all the people of Israel. . . . They also offered twelve male goats as a sin offering.* This verse introduces a third-person narrative (in contrast to first person used in 8:15-34), but that does not imply that someone other than the author added this material as some assume (e.g., Blenkinsopp 1988:172). Brockington (1969:89) thinks these words were added as an editorial note; Myers (1965:72) sees these as editorial notes by the Chronicler who compiled Ezra and Nehemiah's memoirs.

8:36 *The king's decrees were delivered to his highest officers and the governors . . . who then cooperated.* Ezra fulfilled his duty to pass on the king's decree (probably 7:21-24) to government officials that lived throughout the province near Judah. The NLT properly refers to these leaders as the "highest officers" (*'akhashdarpan* [TH323, ZH346]) in the province, though elsewhere this term referred to the official over a satrapy. The king's messages affected all levels of government control, from the provincial level of the Fifth Satrapy to the governors of smaller states within the Fifth Satrapy. These officials did what the royal decree said and supported the Jewish people, but we do not know if this was done willingly or grudgingly.

COMMENTARY

Although the list of names in 8:1-14 may seem rather pedantic and boring, it was theologically essential to know who was going to return to Jerusalem and what their genealogical background was. An emphasis was placed on being the people of Israel and especially on having legitimate priests and Levites serving in the Temple. Unfortunately, no Levites were found among the returnees, and only a few had returned earlier with Sheshbazzar (2:40). We do not know why they did not want to go back to Jerusalem or why Ezra thought it necessary to have some Levites. Being a priest himself, Ezra was probably concerned that Temple worship continue. He may have known about a shortage of Levites in Jerusalem, or he may have recruited Levites to ensure that he would be able to offer the sacrifices the king was giving. In any event, the whole group was held up 11 days while key leaders persuaded about 40 Levites and 220 Temple servants to go with them. These details show how important it was to have the right spiritual leaders serving the community in order for God to be glorified at the Temple. Having mature, capable, spiritual people leading worship should be the ideal of every group of believers.

Ezra emphasized that all the details of the trip worked out for the returnees because the sovereign hand of a gracious God was blessing their efforts (8:18). This central theological idea was not just pious jargon to Ezra; it was the guiding force that motivated his willingness to travel to Yehud without a military guard. Ezra knew that their safety through several provinces would involve traveling through desolate areas where they would be at the mercy of the local inhabitants. Robbers might attack and kill people, officials might refuse to give permission to continue through their territory, farmers might not have grain to sell them, the weather could be unusually difficult, and crossing rivers and mountains could be dangerous. The wagons could break down, people could get seriously sick, some might get discouraged and want to settle down on some attractive piece of land along the way, or others might rebel against Ezra's leadership. With about 5,000 people traveling together for over 800 miles, there would be plenty of opportunities for external problems as well as internal disunity. Ezra encouraged the travelers to fast and humble themselves before God. This would motivate them to depend on God for safety and protection from evil, to humbly put the good of the group above their own wishes, and to daily look to God for his blessing. Ezra was teaching his followers that this move back to Jerusalem was going to be an act of faith, not a Caribbean cruise with the finest accommodations, slick entertainment, and the best in safety precautions.

Ezra and his friends had already talked to the king and bragged about God's power and care for his people (lit., "the hand of our God brings good upon those who seek him"; 8:22). So he would have looked rather foolish and two-faced if he had asked the king for military protection on their trip to Jerusalem. They believed and claimed that God would protect them on the journey. Now they had to put this theoretical belief into practice. Ezra's fast challenged the people to have a consistency between their faith claims and their action. Failure was pictured in terms of God's anger, not the attacks of some enemy along the way. Failure would come if God's people abandoned their walk of faith and forsook God—"It is impossible to please God without faith" (Heb 11:6). (Later, Nehemiah would have an armed escort [Neh 2:9], but the circumstances were very different. He was a governor and political appointee of the king on a political mission [Fensham 1982:117]. There is no indication that Nehemiah asked for the king's troops or any implication that Nehemiah did not have faith in God.)

The long journey to Jerusalem was important, but the text does not give much attention to any trials during the journey, and only a few verses deal with the people's worship of God at the journey's end in Jerusalem. Instead, a great deal of space is spent describing the enormous gift of gold and silver for God from the Persian king and his seven councillors. It is amazing how God was able to provide for the needs of his people and for worship at the Temple in unexpected ways.

Within this narrative, the text emphasizes Ezra and the priests' responsibility to deal honestly with financial matters. It is obvious that Ezra had proven his honesty to the king before this trip; therefore, the king had no trouble trusting him with this huge amount of gold. Part of the reason why the king trusted Ezra was that both Ezra and the king saw this money as a gift to God, to glorify the God of Israel. Since Ezra was intent on treating the gold and silver as sacred, there was no danger of losing any of this vast treasure. He required that it be handled and carried by sacred people and checked at the Temple to make sure not one ounce was missing (8:24-34; cf. Num 4).

Ezra was very wise. He wanted to do everything openly so that everyone would know that meticulous care was being given to doing the will of the king. Ezra, the family leaders, the priests, and the Levites were not involved in order to get rich off the king's generosity, and they did not want people falsely accusing them of skimming gold for themselves. This careful accounting also would have discouraged anyone who went on the trip with them from trying to steal any of the gold. Everyone knew there would be a counting at the end of the trip to see if all the gold and silver were accounted for. Indeed, great care was taken in weighing and counting everything. The results of this final inventory showed that everything was in order down to the very pound; so a final document recording these facts was prepared. These results show the faithfulness of Ezra and the priests who were given responsibility for the silver and gold. Riches or a handsome reward did not motivate them; they were serving God. They were strongly committed to being responsible servants of the king and deeply committed to bringing glory to God through these generous gifts.

The principles that Ezra lived by could apply broadly to many areas of life. If people believe life is sacred, they will treat people as God's sacred trust, requiring care and honest treatment. When something loses its sacred character, people kill, steal, and abuse what is common and not valued. The key is to understand how God values things and people so that we will value what is important in his eyes. This narrative indicates that money is one of the things that matters to God; so it should be treated as God's sacred money. There is no place for waste or carelessness, for the glorification of God is tied up with the way people use his money. Ezra's open handling of money and his belief that all this gold belonged to God are two perspectives that are needed by the leaders of every organization that desires to glorify God.

When the people arrived at Jerusalem, the king's gold was used to buy animals to present sin and burnt offerings to God for the 12 tribes of Israel (8:35). This demonstrates that Ezra did offer sacrifices as the king commanded, and thus Ezra fulfilled his duty (7:17). The priests offered burnt offerings and sin offerings for forgiveness of sins and as a symbol of the people's deep love for and dedication to God. Ezra does not provide an explanation for why they chose to sacrifice 96 rams and 77 lambs. The 12 bulls and goats represented the 12 tribes of Israel that made up the exilic community (see 7:17), though there is no indication that people from all 12 tribes were present. These offerings ritually cleansed the people so that they could enjoy the worship of God at the Temple.

We see that the returnees' first priority was to establish a right relationship to God by confessing their sins and rededicating themselves to God. There was a deep, internal heart desire to worship God; they were not participating in sacrificial services just to please the Persian king. Yes, it was important that everything be done as the Persian king wished and according to the instructions of God in the law of Moses, but the thrill of one's very first worship experience at the holy Temple in Jerusalem far outweighed any thought of satisfying the demands of the king.

◆　　**B. Ezra Intercedes Because the Holy Race Was Polluted (Ezra 9:1-10:44)**

　　　1. Ezra's reaction to unholy marriages (Ezra 9:1-15)

When these things had been done, the Jewish leaders came to me and said, "Many of the people of Israel, and even some of the priests and Levites, have not kept themselves separate from the other peoples living in the land. They have taken up the detestable practices of the Canaanites, Hittites, Perizzites, Jebusites, Ammonites, Moabites, Egyptians, and Amorites. ²For the men of Israel have married women from these people and have taken them as wives for their sons. So the holy race has become polluted by these mixed marriages. Worse yet, the leaders and officials have led the way in this outrage."

³When I heard this, I tore my cloak and my shirt, pulled hair from my head and beard, and sat down utterly shocked. ⁴Then all who trembled at the words of the God of Israel came and sat with me because of this outrage committed by the returned exiles. And I sat there utterly appalled until the time of the evening sacrifice.

⁵At the time of the sacrifice, I stood up from where I had sat in mourning with my clothes torn. I fell to my knees and lifted my hands to the LORD my God. ⁶I prayed,

"O my God, I am utterly ashamed; I blush to lift up my face to you. For our sins are piled higher than our heads, and our guilt has reached to the heavens. ⁷From the days of our ancestors until now, we have been steeped in sin. That is why we and our kings and our priests have been at the mercy of the pagan kings of the land. We have been killed, captured, robbed, and disgraced, just as we are today.

⁸"But now we have been given a brief moment of grace, for the LORD our God has allowed a few of us to survive as a remnant. He has given us security in this holy place. Our God has brightened our eyes and granted us some relief from our slavery. ⁹For we were slaves, but in his unfailing love our God did not abandon us in our slavery. Instead, he caused the kings of Persia to treat us favorably. He revived us so we could rebuild the Temple of our God and repair its ruins. He has given us a protective wall in Judah and Jerusalem.

¹⁰"And now, O our God, what can we say after all of this? For once again we have abandoned your commands! ¹¹Your servants the prophets warned us when they said, 'The land you are entering to possess is totally defiled by the detestable practices of the people living there. From one end to the other, the land is filled with corruption. ¹²Don't let your daughters marry their sons! Don't take their daughters as wives for your sons. Don't ever promote the peace and prosperity of those nations. If you follow these instructions, you will be strong and will enjoy the good things the land produces, and you will leave this prosperity to your children forever.'

¹³"Now we are being punished because of our wickedness and our great guilt. But we have actually been punished far less than we deserve, for you, our God, have allowed some of us to survive as a remnant. ¹⁴But even so, we are again breaking your commands and intermarrying with people who do these detestable things. Won't your anger be enough to destroy us, so that even this little remnant no longer survives? ¹⁵O LORD, God of Israel, you are just. We come before you in our guilt as nothing but an escaped remnant, though in such a condition none of us can stand in your presence."

NOTES

9:1 *have not kept themselves separate from the other peoples living in the land.* One would expect that the events of 9:1 took place immediately after those of 8:36, but 10:9 indicates that chs 9-10 took place just before December 19, about four months after Ezra's arrival on August 4 (7:9). What was Ezra doing all that time, and why was he not aware of this intermarriage problem much earlier? Some commentators suggest that Ezra's reading of the law on October 8 (Neh 8:1-3) was the catalyst for the reform in chs 9-10 and that Nehemiah 8-10 should chronologically fit just before Ezra 9:1 (Blenkinsopp 1988:174; Williamson 1985:127, 283). On this interpretation, the statement "When these things had been done" (9:1) refers to the completion of the reading of the law and the celebration of the feast in Nehemiah 8-10. The reading of the law would then explain how the listeners knew that Moses condemned intermarriage with foreigners who served other gods.

This reconstruction of events is unlikely because it leaves unexplained why Ezra was so shocked about these marriages. Why was there a need for Ezra's reform on December 19 (Ezra 9-10) if the issue of intermarriage had already been dealt with in October (Neh 8-10)? Instead, I would suggest that it took several months for Ezra to settle in the new returnees from Babylon, appoint and teach new judges (7:25), and travel to deliver the king's messages to the various government officials in the surrounding provinces (8:36). Thus, Ezra was probably out of town for at least a couple months on official government business. It is possible that Ezra had already begun teaching the people in Jerusalem some portions of the law before he left to visit the surrounding governors, but that issues of intermarriage did not come up immediately. When this issue was eventually raised, leaders came to Ezra (9:1) and informed him that many people, including priests and Levites, were not following the Mosaic regulations. Such a situation would probably not have existed if Ezra had had a reform a month and a half earlier, in October.

9:3 When I heard this, I tore my cloak and my shirt, pulled hair from my head and beard, and sat down utterly shocked. Ezra's reaction was astonishment, mixed with deep personal grief. This was not just an emotional act to impress people; Ezra was outraged at this irresponsible act of sin and its potential repercussions. He instinctively reacted by tearing his outer robe, pulling his hair out, and collapsing in a heap. This was a typical cultural response to astonishing news such as hearing of the death of a close relative (see Gen 37:34; 2 Sam 13:19; 2 Kgs 22:11; Job 1:20; 2:12; see Jastrow 1900:23-39). Those who try to insert Neh 8–10 before Ezra 9 have trouble with Ezra's shocked response. Williamson (1985:132) claims Ezra was not surprised; it was just "stylized or symbolic" action. Blenkinsopp (1988:177) calls Ezra "almost absurdly intemperate."

9:4 I sat there utterly appalled. The repetition of words of "trembling," "shocked," "appalled," and "outrage" demonstrate that Ezra and his followers were totally baffled and amazed beyond belief at this callous, sinful behavior by the leaders and priests. The emotional response was strong, and it resulted in a trembling desire to seek God's help. How could these acts of unfaithfulness have happened?

9:5 At the time of the sacrifice . . . I fell to my knees. The evening sacrifice was around 3:00 p.m. (*m. Pesahim* 5:1), but there is no indication how long Ezra wept before the beginning of the evening sacrifice.

where I had sat in mourning. Lit., "my mortification" (*ta'anith* [TH8589, ZH9504]. Symbolizing his humility, mortification, and the earnestness of his prayer, Ezra knelt while lifting up his hands to God in supplication (Exod 9:29; Isa 1:15). He prayed for God's help because he could not "fix" the problem; instead, he trusted God to hear, answer, and sovereignly overrule in this situation.

9:8 we have been given a brief moment of grace. "A brief moment" contrasts with the long years of oppression and rule by foreign kings in 9:7.

He has given us security. The word "security" (*yathed* [TH3489, ZH3845]) means lit., "nail, tent peg." Clines (1984:123) and Williamson (1985:135) see the rebuilt Temple as that security or nail that firmly established the people in the land.

brightened our eyes. Lit., "made our eyes shine." These small glimmers of hope were set in stark contrast to the death, robbery, and disgrace that repeatedly came from sin. The grace that caused "a few . . . to survive as a remnant" stood in sharp contrast with the many forefathers, kings, priests, and people who sinned and were oppressed by foreign kings in 9:7. All the good things were attributed to God's work of grace to the undeserving people of 9:7. There was no doubt about it; God was good to his people, in spite of their sinful past.

9:9 in his unfailing love our God did not abandon us. . . . He has given us a protective wall in Judah. Sinful people deserve God's judgment, but God did not abandon his people as they deserved. Instead, in his *khesed* [TH2617, ZH2876] ("unfailing love" or "steadfast covenant love"), God sovereignly (1) directed Cyrus and Darius to "revive" the Jewish nation (ch 1; 6:1-2, 6-7), (2) stirred up the returnees to rebuild the Temple (6:13-18; Hag 1), and (3) provided divine protection for the returnees (6:6-12). The word for "protective wall" (*gader* [TH1447, ZH1555]) referred to a low fence that was built around fields (Allen 2003:78) comparable to the wall around the vineyard in Isa 5:5, and does not refer to Nehemiah's wall around the small city of Jerusalem (Rowley 1965:147-151). Here it symbolically refers to God's protection around the whole nation, not just the city of Jerusalem.

9:11 *Your servants the prophets.* It may appear somewhat strange for Ezra to attribute this warning to "your servants the prophets" when the quotation is a combination of Lev 18:27-30, Deut 7:1, 3, and various other texts (Clines 1984:124), but the prophets also told the people not to mix with those who worshiped Baal. It is evident that Ezra classified Moses as one of the prophets (cf. Deut 18:15; 34:10; Hos 12:13).

9:13-14 *we are again breaking your commands. . . . Won't your anger be enough to destroy us?* Ezra's prayer lamented the future of the nation. God brought a remnant back to Jerusalem, but if things did not change, he would have to destroy this remnant because the people were committing the same sins again. Ezra 9:14 has two questions that were rhetorically addressed to those listening to this prayer. The first, "We are again breaking your commands and intermarrying. . . ?" is translated as a statement in NLT. The second is, "Won't your anger be enough to destroy us?" The answers the listeners would give are obvious: No, it made no sense to make the same mistake again by marrying pagans, and yes, God would be angry enough to destroy the nation because of it. Notice that Ezra had not yet asked for forgiveness; his focus was on getting the people to see the seriousness of their sin. He had to get them to see their sins as a terrible affront to the holiness of God and as a threat to their continued existence as a people. True confession must come first. People can come to God to receive mercy and forgiveness only after they realize that God hates sin and will punish them for their sins. Some may try to seek his mercy without confessing their sins first, but their petition will not be heard or answered while sin blocks their relationship to God (Isa 59:1-2).

9:15 *you are just. We come before you in our guilt as nothing.* Ezra did not sugarcoat the situation; he did what every sinner must do: He admitted guilt and recognized that divine justice was due. None of the sinful people deserved "to stand before God," a legal phrase that meant that no one deserved to be acquitted by a holy God (Clines 1984:125). When Ezra said that God is just, he did not mean that God was granting them "salvation" (based on texts like Isa 46:13; 51:5). It would be inappropriate to include that meaning here (contra Breneman 1993:155), for Ezra was focusing on God's just punishment of their sins. Ezra recognized their unworthiness; they did not deserve any grace from God.

COMMENTARY

This chapter describes how one man dealt with a sin that was discovered within the community of believers. Many of the Jews had married pagans, contrary to the law. The requirement to keep "themselves separate from the other peoples living in the land" came from passages such as Deuteronomy 7:1-4. This prohibition was not racially or ethnically motivated, for Abram married Hagar the Egyptian (Gen 16:3), Moses married an Ethiopian (Num 12:1), and Boaz married the Moabite Ruth (Ruth 4). This prohibition was theologically based, because God knew that pagan spouses would lead the people away from him to worship other gods (Deut 7:4). Since Israel was a holy people, they were to separate themselves from the detestable worship practices of pagans (Exod 19:6; Lev 18:24-30). The list of people the Israelites had intermarried with is similar to the lists of native people in Canaan found in Genesis 15:19-21; Deuteronomy 7:1; 23:3-6; this list in 9:1 includes Moabites and Egyptians in order to fit the social situation during the postexilic era (see Neh 13:23-26; Blenkinsopp 1988:175).

Since God called his covenant people to be holy (Exod 19:6), he expected them to reject the abominable beliefs and customs of their neighbors (Lev 19:2-4; 20:6-8, 22-26; Deut 7:6). This pollution of the holy "seed" (*zera'* [TH2233, ZH2446]; 9:2) through intermarriage would defile the holiness of the community by mixing godly with ungodly people, holy with unholy behavior (Ps 106:35). These marriages were part of a pluralistic tendency to accept foreign religious beliefs; but if this process continued, it would soon destroy the unique identity of Israel as a holy people set apart to God. If a few lower-class individuals in the distant hills made this mistake, it might not be so shocking, but when leaders and priests were engaged in this outrageous behavior (*ma'al* [TH4604, ZH5086], "unfaithfulness"; 9:2), it would inevitably have an impact on the whole nation. Spiritual leaders should be held to a higher standard, but these leaders were behaving worse than most common Israelites.

Ezra's strong negative reaction to this sin suggests that he thought God would deal very seriously with the people and might destroy the nation for this sin. Ezra's lamenting response also got the attention of those around him and demonstrated to them that he was very upset by this news. Ezra 9:4 says that "all who trembled at the words of the God of Israel came and sat" with Ezra. It was important that Ezra not be alone in his opposition to this sin. There is no indication of the size of this group of like-minded individuals who strictly interpreted and followed the law of Moses (10:3). Their reporting this problem to Ezra shows they opposed this trend of intermarriage, but they did not have the political or religious stature to change the way some Jewish leaders were acting. Ezra solidified this group's opposition to this unfaithfulness, and his boldness empowered them to take a stand against the broad-minded acceptance of the intermarriage practices of other Jews. Their united public opposition did not directly address the offending parties, but the sincerity of their sorrow and the compassion of their prayers touched the hearts of those who listened. They took the problem to God first, instead of gossiping to their friends about the sins of others.

Ezra's prayer of confession and intercession fills the rest of this chapter (9:5-15). Surprisingly, there was no direct request for forgiveness. Ezra identified with the plight of the community; he was one of them, and their judgment would be his judgment. This is a reminder that as a community we are responsible for one another; we are not just individuals who can do our own thing (Breneman 1993:152). Ezra did not talk about what "they" did, but about "our" guilt and shame. Although Ezra was innocent of any sin, he, like Moses (Exod 32), Jeremiah (Jer 14:19-22), and Daniel (Dan 9:4-19), confessed the sins of the nation and looked to God for mercy. The structure of the prayer includes a lament for past failures (9:6-7), a recognition of God's past grace (9:8-9), a confession of ignoring what God said (9:10-12), and a recognition of unworthiness (9:13-15). The prayer was indirectly aimed at causing the sinful people, who were listening to Ezra pray, to turn from their sinful ways and repent (see 10:1-2; Blenkinsopp 1988:181).

The prayer focused on shame and the pain of guilt first, because people must begin to see themselves as sinners deserving God's judgment before they can truly repent and seek forgiveness. There was no attempt by Ezra to pass blame on others, society, or circumstances, just an honest admission that "we" have sinned. They were caught doing something God despised, so there was some embarrassment in coming to God. But that was their only hope. Ezra blushed from shame because these sins were not hidden at all; they were fully known to God in heaven. Ezra was also ashamed because there were so many sins. Admitting guilt and accepting the shame of doing wrong are painful steps, but they are helpful if they motivate people to turn from evil and confess their sins to God. Although not all sins should be confessed so publicly, public sins that affect a large group of people need to be dealt with publicly before that group.

Ezra's theological interpretation of the nation's history was characterized by two acts: (1) their persistent bent to sin and (2) their consequent punishment by other nations (9:7). At this point, Ezra did not say God judged them, but that is implied in the rest of the prayer. His purpose at the beginning of the prayer was to remind himself and his listeners that throughout their history (lit., "since the days of our fathers until this day"), iniquity, infidelity, and guilt had happened again and again. Ezra saw this sinful pattern being passed down from generation to generation: We ourselves, our kings, and our priests have followed the sins of our fathers (9:7). Everyone, even the leaders, was part of the problem—even those who tolerated others who did these shameful things (Clines 1984:120). There was no excuse for such repeated sinfulness, and there was no doubt about why the people were killed, oppressed, ruled, disgraced, and exiled by foreign kings. Ezra seemed to be saying that it just did not make any sense for them to destroy themselves like this again and again. Although unstated, the obvious question is, "Will this disgrace ever end?"

In light of the facts, the Jewish people had absolutely no excuses. As Ezra confessed, he wanted his listeners to admit their wrong and to see their action as another in a long series of failures to pay attention to what God said. God's covenant agreement was clear then, as it is today (1 Cor 7:39; 2 Cor 6:14). They were not to intermarry with the people groups living in the land or promote their peace and prosperity. The reason for this was that these people were impure because of their detestable pagan ritual and immorality, and the land was filled with corruption (lit., "uncleanness"). The advantages of keeping God's covenant would be that Israel would "be strong" (tekhezqu [TH2388, ZH2616]), enjoy the fruit of the land, and be able to leave the land to their children as an everlasting inheritance (9:12). This potential was not realized because the people rebelled against God's instructions, were defeated by other nations, and lost their own land (9:5-7). God had graciously brought them back to their land after the Exile, and the people were beginning to commit the same sins as their parents. As Ezra said, there was no excuse for such idiotic behavior. The people knew what the problem was, and they knew what the punishment would be, so why go down this road to destruction again?

In summary, this chapter describes how one man dealt with a sin that was discovered within the community of believers. Once he knew it was there, he did not rationalize it away, ignore it, make excuses for it, try to redefine it as something that was not that bad, sweep it under the rug, or claim that it was someone else's problem. Ezra knew sin must not be ignored, but squarely and honestly faced. The consequences of sin for the individual and the community must be fully understood and owned. Only a fool would ignore a cancer that would soon bring death. Tolerating sin, especially among leadership, only condemns the community to destruction and permits people to redefine sin for themselves. People need to know what God has said about sin, and they need to understand why God calls certain acts sin. Sin is rebellion against God's words, impurity that defiles the holy people of God, and unfaithfulness or wickedness that is characterized by despicable moral and ritual behavior. Sometimes sin is not intentional, but other times people make decisions that are a rejection of the warnings of Scripture or the admonitions of a fellow believer (9:11). Of course, some sins are more dangerous because they lead down a slippery slope into more and more unfaithfulness to God. Marriage to an unbeliever is one such example, because if a believer marries an unbeliever, there will be a continual negative influence on the believer. Over time the temptation to accept what is wrong will be very strong. The holy state of marriage is defiled and complete unity is impossible when one partner is not committed to God.

When sin is encountered, it should drive people to their knees in prayer and lamentation. If the sinner does not acknowledge something as sin, then spiritual people who tremble at the words of God (9:4) need to confess the offender's sins and intercede for God's grace. The intercessor needs to see these sins as "our sins," not "his sins," because God will deal with the community as a whole—both the praying and the offending brother. How can God bless the praying brother if he allows his offending brother to continue in his sin unchallenged? Once the sin is known, the first step is to confess it to God, not to attack the errant brother. Our hatred of sin should embarrass us and shock us so much that we are ashamed and appalled that it exists in our midst. This astonishment will partly arise because it is so unreasonable and treasonous to reject God after he has been so gracious to us (9:8-9). It makes no sense to be enjoying God's blessings, enlightenment, love, protection, and deliverance and then ignore all that God has asked us to do. When such unfaithfulness to God becomes apparent, it must be openly admitted, and its dire consequences must be recognized (9:5-7).

Although we may deserve the wrath of God's justice because of our guilt (9:8, 15), sometimes God deals with us graciously, not as we deserve (9:13). After a brief period of past punishment, God may allow us to prosper and protect us. When such things happen, a return to our old sinful ways is inexcusable. When a nation has all of God's glorious promises open before it, how could these same people turn their backs on God again?

Finally, this chapter suggests that our prayers may do as much, if not more, to reach and transform another believer as our nagging and accusing. We must be broken by sin and not proudly condemn the other person. Nevertheless, we cannot ignore or condone sin; it must be called sin and confessed. Once the house of God is pure, it will be a shining light to the grace of God. God's unfailing love and grace bring hope, but sin brings death and hopelessness.

◆   2. The people separate themselves to the Lord (Ezra 10:1-44)

While Ezra prayed and made this confession, weeping and lying face down on the ground in front of the Temple of God, a very large crowd of people from Israel—men, women, and children—gathered and wept bitterly with him. ²Then Shecaniah son of Jehiel, a descendant of Elam, said to Ezra, "We have been unfaithful to our God, for we have married these pagan women of the land. But in spite of this there is hope for Israel. ³Let us now make a covenant with our God to divorce our pagan wives and to send them away with their children. We will follow the advice given by you and by the others who respect the commands of our God. Let it be done according to the Law of God. ⁴Get up, for it is your duty to tell us how to proceed in setting things straight. We are behind you, so be strong and take action."

⁵So Ezra stood up and demanded that the leaders of the priests and the Levites and all the people of Israel swear that they would do as Shecaniah had said. And they all swore a solemn oath. ⁶Then Ezra left the front of the Temple of God and went to the room of Jehohanan son of Eliashib. He spent the night* there without eating or drinking anything. He was still in mourning because of the unfaithfulness of the returned exiles.

⁷Then a proclamation was made throughout Judah and Jerusalem that all the exiles should come to Jerusalem. ⁸Those who failed to come within three days would, if the leaders and elders so decided, forfeit all their property and be expelled from the assembly of the exiles.

⁹Within three days, all the people of Judah and Benjamin had gathered in Jerusalem. This took place on December 19,* and all the people were sitting in the square before the Temple of God. They were trembling both because of the seriousness of the matter and because it was raining. ¹⁰Then Ezra the priest stood and said to them: "You have committed a terrible sin. By marrying pagan women, you have increased Israel's guilt. ¹¹So now confess your sin to the LORD, the God of your ancestors, and do what he demands. Separate yourselves from the people of the land and from these pagan women."

¹²Then the whole assembly raised their voices and answered, "Yes, you are right; we must do as you say!" ¹³Then they added, "This isn't something that can be done in a day or two, for many of us are involved in this extremely sinful affair. And this is the rainy season, so we cannot stay out here much longer. ¹⁴Let our leaders act on behalf of us all. Let everyone who has a pagan wife come at a scheduled time, accompanied by the leaders and judges of his city, so that the fierce anger of our God concerning this affair may be turned away from us."

¹⁵Only Jonathan son of Asahel and Jahzeiah son of Tikvah opposed this course of action, and they were supported by Meshullam and Shabbethai the Levite.

¹⁶So this was the plan they followed. Ezra selected leaders to represent their families, designating each of the representatives by name. On December 29,* the leaders sat down to investigate the matter. ¹⁷By March 27, the first day of the new year,* they had finished dealing with all the men who had married pagan wives.

¹⁸These are the priests who had married pagan wives:
From the family of Jeshua son of Jehozadak* and his brothers: Maaseiah, Eliezer, Jarib, and Gedaliah. ¹⁹They vowed to divorce their wives, and they each acknowledged their guilt by offering a ram as a guilt offering.
²⁰From the family of Immer: Hanani and Zebadiah.
²¹From the family of Harim: Maaseiah, Elijah, Shemaiah, Jehiel, and Uzziah.
²²From the family of Pashhur: Elioenai, Maaseiah, Ishmael, Nethanel, Jozabad, and Elasah.

23 These are the Levites who were guilty: Jozabad, Shimei, Kelaiah (also called Kelita), Pethahiah, Judah, and Eliezer.

24 This is the singer who was guilty: Eliashib.

These are the gatekeepers who were guilty: Shallum, Telem, and Uri.

25 These are the other people of Israel who were guilty:

From the family of Parosh: Ramiah, Izziah, Malkijah, Mijamin, Eleazar, Hashabiah,* and Benaiah.

26 From the family of Elam: Mattaniah, Zechariah, Jehiel, Abdi, Jeremoth, and Elijah.

27 From the family of Zattu: Elioenai, Eliashib, Mattaniah, Jeremoth, Zabad, and Aziza.

28 From the family of Bebai: Jehohanan, Hananiah, Zabbai, and Athlai.

29 From the family of Bani: Meshullam, Malluch, Adaiah, Jashub, Sheal, and Jeremoth.

30 From the family of Pahath-moab: Adna, Kelal, Benaiah, Maaseiah, Mattaniah, Bezalel, Binnui, and Manasseh.

31 From the family of Harim: Eliezer, Ishijah, Malkijah, Shemalah, Shimeon, 32 Benjamin, Malluch, and Shemariah.

33 From the family of Hashum: Mattenai, Mattattah, Zabad, Eliphelet, Jeremai, Manasseh, and Shimei.

34 From the family of Bani: Maadai, Amram, Uel, 35 Benaiah, Bedeiah, Keluhi, 36 Vaniah, Meremoth, Eliashib, 37 Mattaniah, Mattenai, and Jaasu.

38 From the family of Binnui*: Shimei, 39 Shelemiah, Nathan, Adaiah, 40 Macnadebai, Shashai, Sharai, 41 Azarel, Shelemiah, Shemariah, 42 Shallum, Amariah, and Joseph.

43 From the family of Nebo: Jeiel, Mattithiah, Zabad, Zebina, Jaddai, Joel, and Benaiah.

44 Each of these men had a pagan wife, and some even had children by these wives.*

10:6 As in parallel text at 1 Esdras 9:2; Hebrew reads *He went.*   10:9 Hebrew *on the twentieth day of the ninth month,* of the ancient Hebrew lunar calendar. This day was December 19, 458 B.C.; also see note on 6:15.   10:16 Hebrew *On the first day of the tenth month,* of the ancient Hebrew lunar calendar. This day was December 29, 458 B.C.; also see note on 6:15.   10:17 Hebrew *By the first day of the first month,* of the ancient Hebrew lunar calendar. This day was March 27, 457 B.C.; also see note on 6:15.   10:18 Hebrew *Jozadak,* a variant spelling of Jehozadak.   10:25 As in parallel text at 1 Esdras 9:26; Hebrew reads *Malkijah.*   10:37-38 As in Greek version; Hebrew reads *Jaasu, 38Bani, Binnui.*   10:44 Or *and they sent them away with their children.* The meaning of the Hebrew is uncertain.

NOTES

10:1 *a very large crowd . . . wept bitterly with him.* Ezra 10 was written in the third person, unlike 9:3-15, which was in the first person. Although some question whether this material came from the Ezra Memoirs, such shifts are not uncommon (see 7:1-10; 8:35-36, or even the Cyrus Cylinder). This rhetorical shift causes the reader to look at things from a different perspective (Eskenazi 1988:127-135) and gets the attention onto what the people did instead of what "I" (that is, Ezra) did.

10:2 *Shecaniah.* The man Shecaniah could be a leader among the people, or maybe just the first person brave enough to publicly admit that Ezra was right.

We have been unfaithful to our God, for we have married these pagan women. Shecaniah's confession acknowledged that they were "unfaithful" (*ma'al* [TH4603, ZH5085], also in 9:4) by breaking the covenant and marrying (*nosheb* [TH3427, ZH3782]; lit., "dwelling with") foreign wives who did not believe in Israel's God.

10:3 *Let us now make a covenant with our God to divorce our pagan wives and to send them away with their children.* This is a call for action to address the issue of sin. This sin should not lead to the destruction of the nation if the people would confess it and turn from it. The question was, what must they do to correct the situation? This covenant could be looked at as a renewal of their covenant relationship with God (Fensham 1982:134), or more likely, a pledge or binding agreement with one another to a specific plan of action related to acceptable marriages (Williamson 1985:143, 150; Blenkinsopp 1988:188). The plan was, literally, "to cause all the foreign wives to go out" (*lehotsi'* [TH3318, ZH3655]), which is not the usual word for "divorce" (*shalakh* [TH7971, ZH8938]) but is a word that does mean divorce in Deut 24:2.

the advice given by you and by the others who respect the commands of our God. Lit., "the advice of my lord and those who tremble at (*kharedim* [TH2730, ZH3007]) God's commandments" (see 9:4). Their pure lives, commitment to God's word, and mournful concern for the community legitimated their point of view to the rest of those who gathered to hear Ezra pray. There is some question concerning who "my lord" refers to. The MT has "my Lord" (a pl. of respect or majesty), which usually refers to God, but most translations and commentaries (Allen 2003:82) conclude that this is a respectful way of referring to their "lord" Ezra because (1) God usually tells people what to do, rather than giving advice; (2) in this section God is referred to as "our God" (10:2b, 3a, 3b); (3) God is mentioned later at the end of the verse; and (4) 1 Esdras and the Old Greek both make this refer to Ezra (Williamson 1985:143).

Ezra 9 does not record when Ezra or his fellow mourners recommended this solution to the problem, but it does not appear to be an idea that Shecaniah thought up by himself. Divorce was allowed (Deut 24:1-4; cf. 22:19, 29) in cases where some "shameful thing" was discovered about the wife, so apparently they thought of the deeds and beliefs of these pagan wives as shameful. Highest value was given to obeying God's instruction; its requirements could not be minimized or skirted for any reason.

10:4 *it is your duty to tell us how to proceed in setting things straight. We are behind you.* The people recognized Ezra as an authority on God's law and knew that he would know best what to do.

10:6 *Jehohanan son of Eliashib.* This reference has caused some to conclude that Ezra came after Nehemiah, rather than before him, because Neh 3:1 has Eliashib as the high priest during Nehemiah's era, from 445–433 BC. In addition, the Elephantine Papyri indicate that a man named Johanan was the high priest in 410 BC (Cowley 1923:143-144). This evidence is not as strong as it first appears, for Jehohanan is not said to be the high priest in 10:6, so there is no way to positively connect Jehohanan with Johanan (Kidner 1979:153-155). Since this evidence is inconclusive, it is preferable to maintain the traditional view that Ezra served before Nehemiah.

10:7 *that all the exiles should come to Jerusalem.* Ezra was not the sole author of the proclamation, but along with the leaders of the community he called the people together. Now the demand was that "all" come to Jerusalem, but realistically it was impossible for all the shepherds and farmers to just leave their animals with no one to care for them. Many animals might die, and some might be stolen or run away. Thus, representatives from every family were called so that the community as a whole could confess their sins together and decide what to do about the pagan marriages.

10:9 *This took place on December 19. . . . They were trembling both because of the seriousness of the matter and because it was raining.* The community gathered at the Temple in Jerusalem on December 19 (lit., "the twentieth day of the ninth month"), a season when it is often cold and raining in Palestine. In spite of bad weather, they came because of the "seriousness of the matter." Their inner emotional response of trembling demonstrated that people knew why they were called together and realized the devastating impact this decision would have on friends and families in their local communities. Those who married pagans were especially fearful because social and religious pressure would be put on them to conform to the will of the community.

10:10-11 *You have committed a terrible sin. . . . So now confess your sin. . . . Separate yourselves from the people of the land.* This brief summary of Ezra's admonition identified the nature of their sin (*ma'al* [TH4603, ZH5085], "unfaithfulness") and called for them to "confess" (*tenu todah* [TH8426, ZH9343]; lit., "give thanks, praise") to God. Like the sinful Achan (Josh 7:19), who was instructed to give glory to God, Ezra called upon the people to get right with God and confess their thanks to their just and holy God. This confession of praise and thanksgiving must be accompanied by separation from ungodliness. This hard message was not compromised or shaded to make it more appealing or popular. Each family must decide if it would side with God and thank him or side with the people of the land and their gods. Although marrying a pagan had become socially acceptable in some circles among the people of Judah, everyone now knew how Ezra viewed this sin. Now they would have to decide if they also thought of this as a sin.

10:12 *Then the whole assembly raised their voices and answered, "Yes, you are right."* With almost 100 percent agreement (but see 10:15), they took Ezra's challenge that they separate themselves from these unfaithful acts. No doubt there were some discussions and questions (Williamson 1985:155), but the overwhelming social approval of this basic solution subverted most opposition.

10:13 *this is the rainy season, so we cannot stay out here much longer.* The practical problems of the cold and rain, plus the time it would take to carry out the implications of this decision, caused the group to propose a logical procedure of implementation. There was no need to act unwisely, hastily, or without great care for all involved. Some of the cases might be problematic and would need a fair bit of deliberation to decide what should be done. Witnesses might need to be called, and evidence of pagan worship by some wives might need to be substantiated. Rules and proper procedures carried out by respected leaders in a logical manner would ensure that this difficult task was done rightly.

10:15 *opposed this course of action.* Only four people opposed (lit., "stood against"; *'amedu 'al* [TH5975/5921, ZH6641/6584]) what happened, but it is unclear if they opposed the plan as too lax (Clines 1984:130; Williamson 1985:157) or opposed making people divorce their wives (Breneman 1993:161). If Meshullam came to Jerusalem with Ezra (8:16), it is unlikely that he had already married a foreign wife or that he would oppose Ezra's leadership. Thus, it appears that the opposition was probably by a right-wing minority that thought some part of the plan was too lax.

10:16-17 *Ezra selected leaders. . . . By March 27 . . . they had finished.* The Hebrew text of 10:16 is difficult to understand. The verb is a passive pl. (*wayyibbadelu* [TH914, ZH976], "they were selected"), not an active sg. (though the parallel text in 1 Esdr 9:16 has "he selected"). This suggests that Ezra did not do the choosing, but the people chose Ezra and the family leaders to serve on this commission.

On December 29, the leaders sat down to investigate the matter. A scribal error created "to Darius" (*ledaryosh* [TH1867A, ZH2004]) instead of the more likely reading "to investigate" (*lidrosh* [TH1875, ZH2011]; Williamson 1984:144). It could have been an investigation of whether some were not forced to divorce, or how they were handling the financial support for the divorced wives and their children. Over 100 men divorced their wives (10:10-44), so we know that this commission worked slowly, case by case, a few cases each day over a three-month period (and they probably did not deal with cases on the Sabbath). This seems like a low number of mixed marriages for the number of returnees and for all the

furor Ezra caused (9:1-7). It is possible that many wives converted when they were faced
with the threat of divorce, that the problem was not as widespread as Ezra was led to
believe at first, or that the list is incomplete (it may not list the people who were investigated and not asked to divorce).

10:18-44 *These are the priests . . . the Levites . . . the singer . . . the gatekeepers . . .*
the other people. The commission recorded the names of all the men who had to divorce
their wives and listed them by family, with the Temple personnel leading the list. Twenty-
seven were from the families of Temple personnel, and 83 were from other families. Each
acknowledged his guilt, pledged to divorce his wife, and sacrificed a guilt offering (Lev
5:14-19), since this was an unintentional act of breaking the law. The record lists only those
who divorced their wives; it does not say if any people refused to come to have their situation examined, if any husbands were divorced, or if any refused to follow the recommenda-
tions of this commission. Although Ezra's effort to preserve the holy people of God appears
to be very successful from this text, one must take into consideration the presence of this
same problem only a few years later during Nehemiah's ministry (Neh 9–10). One wonders
if these later cases had been missed by Ezra, if people knowingly and stubbornly refused
to obey God's instructions, or if this is simply a case of the community standards of holiness being quickly eroded by compromise with the enticing things of the world. Rudolph
(1949:97) thinks the list is incomplete (listing only the leaders) because a full listing of all
the people would be embarrassing. Although this is possible, there is no basis for suggesting that the list contains only the leaders.

COMMENTARY
Ezra 10:1-9 summarizes how the people responded to Ezra's mourning and
confession of sin; thus, it continues the narrative of 9:3-4. His tears not only made
people wonder what was wrong, but his lamentation "proved infectious" (Fensham
1982:133) to the large gathering of men, women, and children. They spontaneously
"wept bitterly" (lit., "wept with much weeping"), not because of Ezra's stern sermon
of condemnation but because of Ezra's evident godliness and commitment to see
the transformation of God's people (McConville 1985:69). By listening to Ezra's
prayer of confession, others came under conviction and recognized their guilt.

The first to do so was Shecaniah, who was a member of the family of Elam and
who most likely came with the first group of returnees (2:7) rather than with the
second group that came with Ezra (8:7). Shecaniah knew the seriousness of the
problem, for his relatives and his own father Jehiel were among those who confessed that they had married foreign women (10:26). But in spite of the seriousness
of the problem, Shecaniah believed there was a possibility of hope for the guilty
community if they would make some drastic changes in their behavior. This demonstrates that Ezra did not present a hopeless situation that made people give up
and conclude they were too sinful for God to forgive them. Ezra's confession noted
that in the past God had forgiven the people and blessed them after they confessed
their sins; therefore, it was logical to believe there was hope for God's grace again,
if they would truly confess their sins now.

The moment of truth and real leadership had arrived for Ezra. It was time to take
a difficult but courageous step of obedience that might be controversial and divisive.
Ezra had probably never encountered a similar situation while living in Persia, but
now the expert on interpreting the law of God had to decide how the community

should proceed in implementing God's will in this practical matter. The problem was that there is no explicit information in the law about how to proceed in such a situation. So Ezra needed to firmly but sensitively construct a process that would be true to God's ideals and acceptable to his audience. Ezra had to act while the people were under conviction and willing to cooperate with him.

Ezra had heard one man's confession of guilt, but he did not know how many others felt this way. This change of heart happened very quickly, so Ezra's plan was to initially determine if the spiritual leaders among the priests, Levites, and people supported Shecaniah's proposal. Because of the seriousness of this proposal, Ezra had these leaders swear by an oath that they favored this solution to the problem (10:5). He did not want halfhearted support or uninformed, fuzzy thinking floating around when the public ceremony was conducted. The oath the people made was a promissory statement about future action that was ensured by a curse for non-compliance. (See Blank 1950:73-95 and examples of oaths in 2 Sam 3:35 and Ruth 1:17.) Thankfully, everyone there swore this oath, so Ezra knew he had community support, represented by this large crowd of people, to move ahead.

Ezra immediately withdrew from this meeting and spent the night in prayer and fasting in a nearby Temple chamber (10:6). Total fasts (no food or water) were rare (Exod 34:28; Jonah 3:7), and this one probably expresses the seriousness of Ezra's mourning for the nation's "unfaithfulness" (ma'al [TH4603, ZH5085], as in 9:4; 10:2) and the depth of his intercession for the people who would have to decide if their wives were more important than God. Although it might appear from the preceding agreement that the battle was already won, Ezra knew that some wives would oppose this action and that many husbands did not want to lose the wife they loved or their children.

Ezra 10:8 tells us that "those who failed to come within three days would, if the leaders and elders so decided, forfeit all their property and be expelled from the assembly." The three days gave time for the messengers to travel throughout the territory and for people to respond and get to Jerusalem. The penalty for non-compliance was severe but was within the power the Persian king granted to Ezra and the judges he appointed (7:26). The punishment was not automatic, however, or administered without grace, for at their discretion, the leaders of the community could grant exceptions in cases of sickness, old age, or other extenuating circumstances. "Forfeit all their property" literally refers to the property being "devoted" to God, "put under the ban" by destroying it or giving it to the Temple treasury. Being "expelled from the assembly" excluded a person from owning property, worshiping at the Temple, and having an influence among friends and neighbors. These strong punishments for noncompliance showed how serious the matter was in the eyes of the leaders of the community.

A specific group of leaders was chosen to investigate and decide each case. This commission arranged a time when they would hear what each family had to say; then they verified this information, and if necessary, arranged divorce terms in consultation with the local leaders and judges in each village. The issues that the judges decided are not defined. Likely, the judges would need to discover the true lineage of various wives, judge if each foreign woman was still worshiping pagan gods, and arrange for proper financial support for divorced wives and children. Although this was a terrible experience for the husbands, the wives, and the children, the spiritual motivation for these difficult actions was to remove the wrath of God caused by the people's unfaithfulness. This kind of "discipline" was what kept the people of God a holy people, separated unto God.

When leaders bend the rules and do not challenge sinful people to repent and change, the instructions in God's word are not followed, and an opportunity to restore a brother is missed. If sin becomes acceptable behavior for a few, it will tend to spread to the rest of a community. When this happens, that community ceases to be the holy people of God, and God's judgment is not far off.

The marital problems and subsequent divorces were difficult issues to deal with from both theological and practical points of view. In order to survive and prosper in Judah, the returnees naturally drifted into social, business, and political relationships with people from other nations who worshiped other gods. Being without good biblical exposition of the laws of Moses from people like Ezra, relationships with neighboring peoples developed from a stage of fear, to respect, to appreciation, to full acceptance. Soon it became common practice to intermarry with these neighbors, particularly if one's social or financial situation could be measurably improved through intermarriage with an upper-class family.

The problem with this trend was that it introduced people who did not worship the God of Judah into the very fabric of Jewish families. This was contrary to God's earlier covenant instructions (Deut 7:1-5) and threatened to defile the holy nation that was supposed to be separated from the pagan customs (9:1-2). The problem was defined by earlier tradition in the Mosaic laws, so there was not much theological debate about what God really wanted. It was plain for everyone to see: They were not to marry pagans. Although God's word does not speak to every modern issue as clearly as this one (for example, the problems of genetic engineering and cloning), it is very clear on many issues. The known will of God on clear issues allows the believer to create appropriate theological doctrines and principles of conduct for those areas that are less clear.

Although God's will was clear, the solution to this problem was not clearly defined. What should be done if someone did marry a foreigner? Who would judge the case, and what should be the penalty? Since the political and religious leaders were also intermarrying with pagan women, there was a real danger that the identity of God's people was going to dramatically change if reform was not introduced quickly. Israel could not function as God's elect nation that would bless the rest of the world if it lost its connection to God. Something radical has to be done anytime believers make sinful behavior normative. Change, repentance, and transformation must be attempted.

Ezra perceived the seriousness of the problem and proposed a solution (9:3-15; 10:3). He did not impose this solution on the populace, but through his intercession and weeping, this single dedicated man impressed on many the seriousness of the problem (10:1). But how does one right a wrong that will seriously affect so many families? Families, children's lives, and sacred marriages were involved. Was it excessive to suggest that the foreign wives should be divorced? Was it too radical to put faithfulness to God above family solidarity and marriage vows? What human person is able to judge who should be divorced and whose word people should trust?

Ezra wisely worked with the community of repentant sinners to discover a method or procedure that would protect the holiness of the nation and deal fairly with those involved in mixed marriages, in which a Hebrew was married to an unbeliever. Ezra set a good example for all who are dealing with sin in the community of believers:

1. He took the matter to God, identified with the troubles of his audience, and squarely faced the failures of the community (9:1-15).
2. He waited until some repented and confessed their unfaithfulness to God (10:2), saw their need for renewing their covenant with God, decided to obey God's word, and were willing to submit themselves to the spiritual leaders in the community (10:3-4). Ezra could not force revival, but he could show the way and invite others to follow.
3. He made sure that the leaders were repentant before he began to address the problem throughout the community (10:5).
4. He invited the whole community to consider the problem and develop a workable, practical solution that was fair and took the evidence into consideration (10:7-8).
5. He unambiguously communicated the fundamental problem without muddying the waters with other complicating factors ("you have committed a terrible sin"), identified the first step toward resolution with God ("confess your sin"), and outlined the basic changes needed if a resolution to the problem was desired ("separate yourselves from the people of the land") in 10:10-11. All the other factors could be worked out later, if everyone could agree on these few basics.
6. He listened to suggestions about creating proper procedures that were fair and orderly so that the people could avoid God's wrath (10:13-14).
7. He was aware of opposition (10:15) but did not let a minority prevent the community from moving forward with the plan that most people accepted.
8. He shared authority with other leaders in deciding what to do with mixed marriages (10:16).
9. He completed the task in relatively short order and helped the unfaithful ones to right their relationship with God (10:17-19).

The care with which Ezra dealt with this conflict is often overshadowed by the larger question of whether people today should argue for similar procedures when a believer and unbeliever marry. Should spiritual people try to break up marriages? Jesus allowed for divorce in a few cases (Matt 5:32; 19:8-9), but both Jesus and Paul discouraged divorce (1 Cor 7:10). Paul wanted believers to have a positive influence on an unbelieving spouse (1 Cor 7:12-15), but he recognized that sometimes the unbelieving spouse may divorce the believer. In the end, following God is more important than remaining married, and living a holy life is more important than having the social or financial stability of marriage.

◆ **III. Nehemiah Returns to Build the Walls of Jerusalem (Neh 1:1–7:73a)**
  A. Nehemiah's Vision to Remove Judah's Disgrace (Neh 1:1–2:20)
   1. Nehemiah asks God to remove Judah's disgrace (Neh 1:1–11)

These are the memoirs of Nehemiah son of Hacaliah.

In late autumn, in the month of Kislev, in the twentieth year of King Artaxerxes' reign,* I was at the fortress of Susa. ²Hanani, one of my brothers, came to visit me with some other men who had just arrived from Judah. I asked them about the Jews who had returned there from captivity and about how things were going in Jerusalem.

³They said to me, "Things are not going well for those who returned to the province of Judah. They are in great trouble and disgrace. The wall of Jerusalem has been torn down, and the gates have been destroyed by fire."

⁴When I heard this, I sat down and wept. In fact, for days I mourned, fasted, and prayed to the God of heaven. ⁵Then I said,

"O LORD, God of heaven, the great and awesome God who keeps his covenant of unfailing love with those who love him and obey his commands, ⁶listen to my prayer! Look down and see me praying night and day for your people Israel. I confess that we have sinned against you. Yes, even my own family and I have sinned! ⁷We have sinned terribly by not obeying the commands, decrees, and regulations that you gave us through your servant Moses.

⁸"Please remember what you told your servant Moses: 'If you are unfaithful to me, I will scatter you among the nations. ⁹But if you return to me and obey my commands and live by them, then even if you are exiled to the ends of the earth, I will bring you back to the place I have chosen for my name to be honored.'

¹⁰"The people you rescued by your great power and strong hand are your servants. ¹¹O Lord, please hear my prayer! Listen to the prayers of those of us who delight in honoring you. Please grant me success today by making the king favorable to me.* Put it into his heart to be kind to me."

In those days I was the king's cup-bearer.

1:1 Hebrew *In the month of Kislev of the twentieth year.* A number of dates in the book of Nehemiah can be cross-checked with dates in surviving Persian records and related accurately to our modern calendar. This month of the ancient Hebrew lunar calendar occurred within the months of November and December 446 B.C. The *twentieth year* probably refers to the reign of King Artaxerxes I; compare 2:1; 5:14.   1:11 Hebrew *today in the sight of this man.*

NOTES

1:1 *These are the memoirs of.* Lit., "the words of" (*dibre* [TH1697, ZH1821]). "The words" were not a series of sermons like those found in most prophetic books but a narrative story that recounts what happened in Nehemiah's lifetime. It is not improper to think that some of this information came from the diary or the memoirs of Nehemiah. First Chronicles 29:29 mentions "the events [*dibre*] of King David's reign," while 2 Chr 9:29 mentions "the rest of the events [*dibre*] of Solomon's reign."

In late autumn, in the month of Kislev, in the twentieth year of King Artaxerxes' reign. Lit., "In the month of Kislev, in the twentieth year." Kislev usually coincides with November/ December, and Neh 2:1 names Artaxerxes as the ruling monarch in Persia. Since Nehemiah's memoirs continue straight on from Ezra's memoirs, it would be natural to assume that the reader would understand these events as taking place in the 20th year (445 BC) of the same king who was ruling in Ezra 7–10, that is, in the reign of the Persian King Artaxerxes I (465–424 BC). Saley (1968:151-165) used evidence from the Wadi Daliyeh Papyri to show

the possibility that Nehemiah may have served under Artaxerxes II when another man named
Sanballat was governor of Samaria. I do not think this solution is the best interpretation, so
I do not take its late date as a basis for understanding Nehemiah's work. Similarly, Green
(1990:195-210) concludes that the evidence for placing Nehemiah in the time of Artaxerxes I
is stronger (Allen 2003:91).

the fortress of Susa. The city of Susa had a large citadel or "fortress" (*birah* [TH1002, ZH1072]).
(See Yamauchi 1990:279-303 for pictures, maps, and the history of Susa.) It is next to the
river Kerkheh in a hot region of the country (130°F in summer), about 150 miles north
of the Persian Gulf in modern Iran. The mound where ancient Susa lies stands about
70 feet higher than the plain around it and was occupied for about 3,500 years. It had a
royal palace, areas where artisans and palace workers lived, and a magnificent great hall
(the Apadana). The Persian kings had several palaces and would spend time in each one
based on which had the best weather conditions. Susa, with its warmer climate, served as
the winter palace (see Esth 2:8; Dan 8:2). The events of ch 1 occurred in the month Kislev
(November/December).

1:2 *Hanani, one of my brothers.* Although many think Hanani was a blood brother of
Nehemiah because of this passage and 7:2 (Williamson 1985:170; Fensham 1982:151), the
term "my brothers" (*'akhay* [TH251, ZH278]) could simply refer to fellow Jews. In 7:2, this man
is given responsibility for governing the city of Jerusalem, an important job that needed
a trustworthy leader. One would expect that Nehemiah would be more likely to entrust a
job like this to his blood brother (this is not proof, but strengthens the probability). The
reason for Hanani's trip from Jerusalem to Susa was not recorded. Was he part of an unof-
ficial delegation that bypassed official channels to report what was really happening in
Jerusalem, as some suppose (Myers 1965:94)? Since Hanani did not say he came to Susa to
report on Jerusalem (officially or unofficially), and since Nehemiah is portrayed as the one
asking questions about conditions in Jerusalem, Myers's reconstruction of Hanani's visit
seems unlikely. Nehemiah was probably inquiring about family and friends and in that
process received the news that Jerusalem was in bad straits. If he was Nehemiah's blood
brother, Hanani's conversation with Nehemiah could be explained as a family visit. Nehemiah's questions about the status of life in Jerusalem were a sign of his concern for others,
a quality that should characterize every believer.

1:3 *They are in great trouble and disgrace.* The "disgrace" (*kherpah* [TH2781, ZH3075]) refers
to the sense of shame and reproach people felt because foreigners had destroyed the walls
of the city of Jerusalem. Foreigners would laugh and scoff at the powerlessness of the
Hebrews' God. Was he not strong enough to help his people rebuild his city? Maybe he
abandoned them or was asleep. No doubt the people in Jerusalem would cringe in shame
when they heard this ridicule. Their disgrace was derived not just from their shameful
physical conditions and the disgraceful way the city looked (cf. 2:17), but also because they
knew that God had allowed them to be humiliated because of their past sins. They had
brought this upon themselves and could not expect God to immediately come to the rescue
of his disobedient people.

The wall of Jerusalem has been torn down. The news that Hanani communicated
described a recent setback in Jerusalem, not the Babylonian conquest in 586 BC, which
occurred 140 years earlier (Yamauchi 1988:681). It is likely that Hanani was referring to
recent events, when the Samarians stopped Jewish efforts to rebuild the walls in the reign
of Artaxerxes (Ezra 4:6-23; see Williamson 1985:172). Although Ezra 4:23 says that the
Jewish rebuilding efforts were stopped, it does not say what the Samarians did to that portion of the wall that was partially rebuilt. If the partially rebuilt walls were demolished and

the new gates were burned, as Hanani says, and if these events occurred a short time before 445 BC (Ezra 4:21-22), they could be connected with an Egyptian revolt around 460–445 BC or the revolt of Megabyzus, the satrap of Transjordan in 448 BC. If the Persians thought the Jewish rebuilding of the walls of Jerusalem was part of the broader rebellion taking place at that time (even if it was not), one can understand why the Persians would act to stop this Jewish rebuilding project. Josephus (*Antiquities* 11.159-163) gives a different version of this story that does not totally agree with the biblical story. Josephus seems to embellish the persecution, including statements like, "every day the roads are full of corpses" (referring to the persecution of the people in Jerusalem). At this point the political unrest to the south of Jerusalem had a negative impact on the people of Jerusalem. Later, when Nehemiah asked the king to send him to Jerusalem to rebuild the ruined city (ch 2), this unrest probably played an important role in motivating the king to send Nehemiah to establish Jerusalem as a stronghold of Persian authority (Hoglund 1992:86-96). The king believed he could trust Nehemiah to bring some law and order to this part of his kingdom.

1:4 *for days I mourned, fasted, and prayed.* Nehemiah responded to this bad news the same way Ezra did when he heard discouraging news (Ezra 9:3-5). His extended fasting, mourning, and praying displayed his deep feeling of distress and agony.

1:6a *listen to my prayer! Look down and see me praying . . . for your people Israel.* Lit., "Let your ears be attentive and your eyes be open to hear the prayer of your servant . . . concerning the sons of Israel, your servants." Nehemiah saw himself as God's "servant" (*'ebed* [TH5650, ZH6269]), and he believed that the people of Israel were supposed to live and act as God's servants. But he knew that God's "servants" had not always served him in the past. Thus, he appealed for God to carefully consider his request, because it was from someone who wanted to serve God. Nehemiah was not calling for God to wake up from his sleep when he asked him to listen to his prayer. Nehemiah knew that God would hear what he said; he wanted God to show that he heard his prayer by responding with acts of love that would alleviate the problems in Jerusalem (Breneman 1993:172). At this point, Nehemiah was taking on the role of an intercessor, requesting God's grace on the nation.

night and day. This phrase indicates the heaviness of the burden Nehemiah felt and his daily persistence in laboring over the way God was dealing with his people. This was a constant concern that he struggled with every day because the situation was so serious. He probably lost some sleep because he was earnestly praying for God to intervene to change the disgraceful situation in Jerusalem. Nehemiah was not a person who lightly said, "I'll pray for you" and then quickly forgot all about it.

1:6b-7 *we have sinned. . . . my own family and I have sinned! . . . We have sinned terribly by not obeying.* Twice Nehemiah confessed that the people had "sinned" (*khata'* [TH2398, ZH2627], "missed the mark") against God. To this he added that they had "acted very corruptly" (*khabol khabalnu* [TH2254B, ZH2472]—an infinitive absolute plus a finite verb; NLT, "sinned terribly"), and had "not kept" (*lo'-shamarnu* [TH8104, ZH9068]) the covenant stipulations that God gave through Moses.

1:8-9 *If you are unfaithful to me, I will scatter you. . . . But if you return to me . . . I will bring you back to the place I have chosen for my name to be honored.* Drawing heavily from the theology of Deut 4:25-31 and 30:1-5, Nehemiah reminded himself and those listening to his prayer (note that 1:11 references others who were praying, probably with Nehemiah) that God had promised curses for sin, as well as the blessing of restoration for his repentant chosen people. "Scattering" (*'apits* [TH6327, ZH7046]) would be reversed by "bringing back" (*'aqabbetsem* [TH6908, ZH7695], "I will gather them"), and going to the "ends of the earth" (lit., "the end of the heavens") is the opposite of "the place I have chosen for my name to be honored" (lit., "the place I have chosen for my name to dwell there"). These two opposite destinies will be determined by whether the Israelites remain "unfaithful" to God or "return" to have a love relationship with him.

1:10 The people you rescued . . . are your servants. Drawing on Deut 9:29 (cf. Deut 3:24; 11:2), Nehemiah spoke of the Lord's deliverance of his people by his great power and strong hand. Nehemiah knew that he and the Israelites were God's "servants" (mentioned three times in the Hebrew of 1:11; cf. KJV), those rescued (*paditha* [TH6299, ZH7009], "you pardoned, rescued") by God to serve and worship him.

1:11 Please grant me success today by making the king favorable to me. More lit., "Today, give your servant favor in the presence of this man" (*ha'ish hazzeh* [TH376, ZH408]). The NLT puts these words in the first person, "me" (rather than "your servant," used three times in this verse), and identifies "this man" as the king. This prayer ended with a specific request for divine grace. We do not know on how many days Nehemiah made this specific request before the opportunity in ch 2 actually presented itself. One would assume that he focused on confessing sins for some days and that at some later date he began to pray for God to use his own contact with the king to bring about a solution to the disgraceful situation in Jerusalem. Thus, Nehemiah believed God could influence the mind of a pagan king.

In those days I was the king's cup-bearer. The role of cup-bearer (*mashqeh* [TH4945, ZH5482]; lit., "one who gives to drink") provided Nehemiah daily access to the Persian king Artaxerxes at mealtimes. But as cup-bearer, Nehemiah could not dare to raise his own personal issues before the king. Over time, kings got to know their cup-bearers very well; consequently, a king's relationship to a cup-bearer could develop into an influential advisory role. (Fensham 1982:157 and Myers 1965:96 describe the importance of the cup-bearer to the king.) Esarhaddon made his cup-bearer the second ruler of the kingdom.

Some suggest that the cup-bearer would have to be a eunuch because he would be around the king's harem (Myers 1965:96; Fensham 1982:157), but this was not universally required (Williamson 1985:174-175). Some Greek translations have "eunuch" instead of "cup-bearer," but this is probably a spelling error in Greek, for the words are almost identical: *eunouchos* (eunuch) and *oinochoos* (cup-bearer). Yamauchi (1980:132-142) examined the arguments for concluding that Nehemiah was a eunuch and found that numerous Persian texts distinguish between the cup-bearer and the eunuchs.

COMMENTARY

If Ezra was the author/editor of Ezra-Nehemiah, the memoirs of Nehemiah became his authoritative resource for telling much of the story of Nehemiah's ministry in Jerusalem (see note on 1:1). The introductory information in 1:1 is very brief, omitting the name of Nehemiah's father, his occupation, the name of the king who was reigning at that time, and other information that is typically found in the superscription of ancient books. Since this new narrative about Nehemiah was not seen as a separate book but merely a continuation of Ezra, a full-blown superscription was not necessary or appropriate. Still, one is struck by how little information is given about Nehemiah when it is compared to the long introduction of Ezra the scribe at the beginning of his memoirs (Ezra 7:1-10), which also is found in the middle of the book.

The first chapter introduces the reader to the theological problem (Jerusalem was in disgrace, and the past and present Israelite people were sinful), the players in this drama (Hanani, the people of Judah, Nehemiah, and the king), and the potential theological solution (Nehemiah will intercede, God will have mercy, and God will give Nehemiah favor before the king). Hanani and "this man" (referring to the king; see note on 1:11) are of minor importance in the story at this point. Most of this chapter concerns Nehemiah's mourning for the conditions in Jerusalem and his prayer, wherein he confesses the nation's sins. The suffering of his relatives in Jerusalem and the great opposition to rebuilding the wall of Jerusalem were what bothered Nehemiah.

Nehemiah's mourning demonstrates how strongly this news affected his soul, and his continued fasting and prayer show his profound concern for the honor of God in Jerusalem. He did not arrange a protest march or complain bitterly to the king about how his people were being mistreated. Nehemiah prayed to God because he was helpless to change the situation. Nevertheless, he knew God cared about his people in Jerusalem and could remove their disgrace. These "days" eventually extended to months, because four months later, in the spring (2:1), Nehemiah was still visibly upset about this matter. His continual intercession illustrates the depth of his concern and how persistent he was in calling on God to intervene.

The structure of Nehemiah's prayer does not exactly fit the pattern of the laments in the book of Psalms, but it has many similarities to community laments (Pss 74, 79, 85). It is distinctively focused on the confession of sins rather than on complaints about oppression from enemies or any complaint against God (Williamson 1985:167). The prayer is heavily dependent on phrases from the book of Deuteronomy (Deut 4:27; 6:1; 7:9-10, 21; 10:17; 28:64; 30:1-4), demonstrating Nehemiah's extensive knowledge of the writings of Moses. Like Ezra (Ezra 9:5-15) and Daniel (Dan 9:4-19), Nehemiah identified with the plight of his people and confessed that "we" have displeased God. His intercession was not pointing out how bad "they" were behaving, for he took some responsibility for the spiritual status of his own people. The structure of the prayer falls into five parts: (1) an invocation to God in 1:5, (2) a petition for God to hear in 1:6a, (3) a confession of sins in 1:6b-7, (4) a petition for God to remember his promises in 1:8-9, and (5) an intercessory request for God's help in 1:10-11. This prayer, as well as the prayers of Daniel and Ezra, can serve as a model that illustrates how a believer should approach God concerning the sin in our community or nation.

The prayer opens with an invocation to God, recognizing God's mighty power and his wonderful acts on behalf of his people. Nehemiah's conception of the awesome glory of God gave him faith to bring his request to one who could change the status quo in Jerusalem. Great power (*haggadol wehannora'* [TH1419/3372, ZH1524/3707], "the great and awesome") and unfailing covenant love (*khesed* [TH2617, ZH2876]) characterized the God that Nehemiah knew. This "great power" produced awesome deeds of judgment and grace, but God's loving acts of mercy were extended only to those who faithfully responded to God by loving him with all their hearts and following his will (Deut 6:5; 10:12). God's election of Israel to be his covenant people was an act of unconditional love that was totally undeserved, but his continual granting of "unfailing [covenant] love" to his covenant people was conditioned by their faithfulness to their covenant relationship with God. There could be no covenantal solidarity between the covenant partners if both parties did not commit themselves completely to each other.

In his prayer, Nehemiah did not try to hide the root problem, made no excuses, and admitted failures on the part of himself and his family. He did not consider himself blameless or superior to anyone else. He accepted his own individual responsibility as a sinner before God and saw that he shared part of the corporate guilt because he was part of the larger covenant group that was not pleasing God. No doubt Nehemiah's leadership abilities were partially grounded in his clear thinking about the reality of his own sinfulness and status as God's servant, his close identification with the people who were supposed to serve God, and his understanding of what God required from his people. All too often people blame things on others, point to their difficult circumstances, or try to hide or excuse their sins, but Nehemiah openly admitted his failure and tried to address the nation's central problem. Sin, not the destroyed walls, was the factor that determined their destiny. Wise spiritual believers take responsibility for their own failures and, through God's grace, move beyond the present dilemma toward a solution to their problems. Getting right with God is always the first step in that process.

The standard for human behavior for Nehemiah was the revelation of God in the "commands, decrees, and regulations" given to God's servant Moses (1:7). No man-made authority or human set of laws quantify what it means to sin against God. People may try to reinterpret through situational ethics what is right and wrong, but everyone will eventually have to give an account for their actions before God. The Mosaic writings were the authoritative source of human knowledge about God's character, his desires, and his covenant stipulations. God's requirements to love him, fear him, serve him, and worship only him (Deut 6:4-5; 10:12) meant that certain other acts should not be done. Obedience to these "commands, decrees, and regulations" was not a guaranteed means of gaining God's blessing (that was based on faith and love); these regulations explained how the Israelites needed to think and what they needed to do to maintain their existing covenant relationship with God.

Overall, chapter 1 draws out the character of the people in Jerusalem in negative as well as positive terms. Though the people in Jerusalem were in "great trouble and disgrace" (1:3) and had "sinned terribly by not obeying the commands" (1:7), they were still the remnant of God's "people," his "servants," and the "rescued" (1:10). These characteristics appear contradictory at first, but the divine transformation of a wicked person into a servant of God was made possible through the confession of sins and God's forgiving grace. Before this reconciliation can happen, someone (like Nehemiah) has to recognize that a problem exists and that a solution is available. If people ignore the problem of sin or disgrace, no one will think change is needed. If the difficulty is recognized, but no one knows that God can solve this problem, there will be no resolution of the issue.

In this case, an intercessor (Nehemiah) activated the sovereign power of God's grace, not the sinful people themselves. This is no different than a faithful parent who intercedes for a wicked son who has strayed away from God. Nehemiah was the one who mourned and prayed; Nehemiah was the one who saw that God might use him to influence the king in some way to remove the disgrace of Jerusalem. As an intercessor, Nehemiah knew that a higher power controlled things and that he was only a go-between who served others. Nevertheless, this go-between, who was well connected to the divine source of power and to an earthly source of power, was able to enlist both for the benefit of the people who were suffering. Nehemiah did not try to correct the problem himself; he went to the right power sources that could bring about lasting change (spiritual and political). Nehemiah also knew the relative strength of these powers. He knew that God controlled kings; it was not the other way around. If Nehemiah hoped to be successful, God would have to graciously act in covenant faithfulness toward his people, just as he did at the time of the Exodus. God would have to cause the earthly king to act favorably toward Nehemiah and the people living in Jerusalem. Although people today and in the past tend to idolize great leaders like Nehemiah, Nehemiah simply saw himself as God's faithful servant (1:6, 11—"your servant" is translated several times as "me" in NLT) who was involved in praying and caring for God's people. Nehemiah was not a controlling, power-hungry, or proud leader; he became a leader because he was willing to serve God and serve the people he loved.

The theology of Nehemiah's prayer is powerful. He appealed to the "great and awesome God" (1:5). He recognized that God had the ability to use his power to change the terrible situation in Jerusalem. As God's servant, Nehemiah knew that prayer served God's ends and that he and the people of Jerusalem needed to act in ways that would glorify God's name. The problem that prevented God from being glorified was the sin of his people. Consequently, Nehemiah attacked the central problem of sin and did not get sidetracked with secondary symptoms or causes. He took action against sin by confessing it, even when others did not bother to fast and pray for mercy. He recognized that sin was not just a problem with other people; instead, he saw himself as partially responsible for the situation that now existed among his people. The present terrible situation did not demoralize Nehemiah or cause him to think that there was no hope for Jerusalem. He understood God's dealings with his sinful people on the basis of past experiences and past promises (1:8-9). He was not one who would give up on sinful people, and he knew God would restore repentant sinners. He prayed for God's powerful transformation of the hearts, the wills, and the circumstances of the people in Jerusalem.

God's action is directly related to the behavior of his covenant people, except when he acts in undeserved grace. There was nothing hidden or mysterious about how one should relate to God or what would be the results of rejecting God's covenantal relationship of mutual commitment. If God was not blessing his people in the downtrodden city of Jerusalem, it was logical to assume that there was a need to confess the nation's sins so that God could pour out his blessing on them in the future. The place where God's name dwelt was in the Holy of Holies (1:9), in the Temple at Jerusalem (Deut 12). This was where people came to worship and honor him with praise, confession, and thanksgiving.

Because God had rescued the Jews from the bondage of Egypt to be his people, they were his holy nation, his prized possession, his servants (see Exod 19:4-6). From beginning to end, their future and the future of every believer will always be determined by their identification with God as his pardoned servants (1:10). If believers fail to understand who has rescued them, what they were rescued from, and what their new status is, they will fail to enjoy the full pleasure of his grace.

Nehemiah ended his prayer with the recognition that God's "strong hand" would determine their future, just as it had their past (1:10). Every prayer of faith must rest on the fundamental conviction that God can sovereignly act on our behalf, but intercessory prayers dare to boldly approach God with requests for him to powerfully respond to the present needs of others. The people in Jerusalem had no claim to deserve anything from God because of their sins. But in faith, Nehemiah believed that God would delight in the prayers of a humble sinner who loved God and interceded for others. Nehemiah believed that God wanted to have his name honored in Jerusalem (5:9; 9:5-6; cf. Pss 47; 48; 99), so he confessed the people's sins and prayed for mercy and God's powerful intervention.

The theology of Nehemiah's intercessory prayer teaches us how to pray. It teaches us about how we should conceive of God and his relationship with sinful people. His prayer challenges every believer to act as an intercessor for someone else whom God can rescue from disgrace and shame. His persistence for four months serves as a powerful example to not give up until God has answered our prayers. His willingness to be part of the solution illustrates the need to be willing to put feet to our prayers, even if it means moving out of our present comfortable situation and into a conflict environment where success is not assured.

◆   ## 2. God causes the king to approve Nehemiah's vision (Neh 2:1-10)

Early the following spring, in the month of Nisan,* during the twentieth year of King Artaxerxes' reign, I was serving the king his wine. I had never before appeared sad in his presence. ²So the king asked me, "Why are you looking so sad? You don't look sick to me. You must be deeply troubled."

Then I was terrified, ³but I replied, "Long live the king! How can I not be sad? For the city where my ancestors are buried is in ruins, and the gates have been destroyed by fire."

⁴The king asked, "Well, how can I help you?"

With a prayer to the God of heaven, ⁵I replied, "If it please the king, and if you are pleased with me, your servant, send me to Judah to rebuild the city where my ancestors are buried."

⁶The king, with the queen sitting beside him, asked, "How long will you be gone? When will you return?" After I told him how long I would be gone, the king agreed to my request.

⁷I also said to the king, "If it please the king, let me have letters addressed to the governors of the province west of the Euphrates River,* instructing them to let me travel safely through their territories on my way to Judah. ⁸And please give me a letter addressed to Asaph, the manager of the king's forest, instructing him to give me timber. I will need it to make beams for the gates of the Temple fortress, for the city walls, and for a house for myself." And the king granted these requests, because the gracious hand of God was on me.

⁹When I came to the governors of the province west of the Euphrates River, I delivered the king's letters to them. The king, I should add, had sent along army officers and horsemen* to protect me. ¹⁰But when Sanballat the Horonite and Tobiah the Ammonite official heard of my arrival, they were very displeased that someone had come to help the people of Israel.

2:1 Hebrew *In the month of Nisan.* This month of the ancient Hebrew lunar calendar occurred within the months of April and May 445 B.C.   2:7 Hebrew *the province beyond the river;* also in 2:9.   2:9 Or *charioteers.*

NOTES

2:1 Nisan. The month Nisan (also called Aviv or Abib) is the first month of the Babylonian civil calendar (Exod 12:2) and falls in the spring; it fell in April and May in 445 BC (cf. NLT mg).

I was serving the king his wine. The Hebrew text appears somewhat redundant, reading "the wine [was] before him, and I took the wine and I gave it to the king." To avoid this duplication, some prefer to follow the Greek translation of the first clause: "when the wine was before *me*" = "when I had charge of the wine" (Blenkinsopp 1988:211-212). But the first phrase may simply mean that this all happened at an important event (maybe this was a New Year's banquet—Williamson 1985:178), so Nehemiah had to be there. The second phrase describes Nehemiah's act of coming into close contact with the king while he was serving the king wine. Herodotus (*Histories* 9.110-111) refers to a special banquet celebrating the Persian king's birthday, when the king would grant any request addressed to him. Blenkinsopp (1988:213) implies that Nehemiah shrewdly waited for such an occasion to make his request, but the text of Nehemiah does not say this.

I had never before appeared sad in his presence. At this close range, the king could see the "sad" or "gloomy" (*ra'* [TH7451, ZH8273]) expression on Nehemiah's face. Apparently, Nehemiah had always been careful not to let his sadness show on previous occasions, but this time he could not cover up his distress about the situation in Jerusalem.

2:2 You must be deeply troubled. Lit., "This is nothing but a troubled heart." Since the king's servants were always supposed to be courteous and cheerful, the king was suspicious of danger when he saw Nehemiah's troubled face.

2:3 I replied, "Long live the king!" First, Nehemiah reaffirmed his respect and loyalty to the king with the customary greeting, "Long live the king" (cf. Dan 2:4). He wanted to ease the king's fear by communicating that he was still completely loyal to the king.

2:4 Well, how can I help you? Lit., "What is it that you are seeking?" This is more of a request for information than an offer of help.

2:6 The king, with the queen sitting beside him. The setting in this verse has surprising characteristics—the queen was not usually invited to Persian banquets to eat with the king and his officials (Esth 1:3, 9). At some public events (Dan 5:2) women were invited. However, if she was not invited this may imply that the conversation in 2:6-8 took place some time later in a more private area (Myers 1965:98). Thus, later that evening, or a few days later, the king raised the issue again with Nehemiah to try to resolve the problem that was concerning him. The word rendered "queen" (*shegal* [TH7694, ZH8712], related to the verb "to lie with," *shagal* [TH7693, ZH8711]) is not the usual word for queen. Nevertheless, Clines (1984:142) thinks this was the queen, Damaspia, while Blenkinsopp (1988:215) does not. The word probably refers to a favorite concubine from the king's harem. Some hypothesize that this woman supported Nehemiah and encouraged Artaxerxes to be generous to him (Tarn 1985:2-3), but this is pure speculation. It was God, not Artaxerxes' female companion, who influenced the king.

How long will you be gone? The king wanted a definite commitment of time from Nehemiah; he was not going to write a blank check or free Nehemiah completely from his royal responsibilities. Unfortunately, Nehemiah did not record his answer to the king's question, so we do not know how long he suggested. No doubt he gave the king a reasonable estimate of how long it might take to build the walls and repair the gates of Jerusalem. It is unlikely that the king would have approved of a 12-year mission to Jerusalem (5:14 indicates that Nehemiah ended up staying that long), so Kidner (1979:81) suggests that Nehemiah likely gave a short period of time and then reported back to the king after the walls were completed (in less than a year). The king perhaps then renewed his stay as governor for additional years because he was doing so well.

2:8 *Asaph, the manager of the king's forest.* This forest could refer to the cedars of Lebanon (Clines 1984:143), but the Jewish name of the keeper of the forest argues for an Israelite forest close to Jerusalem. Yamauchi (1988:686) refers to a royal forest or garden six miles south of Jerusalem.

2:9 *sent along army officers and horsemen to protect me.* Nehemiah's acceptance of an armed government escort is not a sign of weak faith and should not be negatively compared to Ezra's refusal to request military protection (Ezra 8:21-22). We have no record of Nehemiah requesting troops (it was probably standard procedure for a governor to have troops to enforce the king's will—see Blenkinsopp 1988:216), but he accepted what the king sent while recognizing that all his success was based on God's gracious and powerful direction of his life.

2:10 *But when Sanballat the Horonite and Tobiah the Ammonite official heard of my arrival, they were very displeased.* Some see 2:9-10 as the center (and thus a key emphasis) of a long chiastic structure, stretching from 1:1 to 2:20 (Throntveit 1992:62). In these verses Nehemiah's long trip from Susa to Jerusalem was passed over without comment (but it did include an armed escort); instead, the focus is placed on the strong opposition to Nehemiah's mission (2:9-10). Once the surrounding officials heard the king's orders, they were angry because this new leader coming to rebuild the walls of Jerusalem would give the city greater independence and security, which might reduce their power. This new status for Jerusalem would change the balance of political power in favor of the Jewish people.

Sanballat was probably from the area of Upper or Lower Beth-horon, about 12 miles northwest of Jerusalem. One of the Elephantine Papyri indicates that he was the governor around Samaria in 408 BC, so some assume he was already the governor when Nehemiah arrived (Yamauchi 1988:687; Allen 2003:95); but Nehemiah never credits him with that official title, so one should not assume he was the governor at this time. The other opponent was Tobiah the Ammonite "official" (*'ebed* [TH5650, ZH6269], "servant"). Some think that (1) Tobiah was a Hebrew who was the Persian governor (an "official") of Ammon (Myers 1965:101); or (2) the term "servant" was a contemptuous comment about Tobiah's subservient role (Kidner 1979:82); or (3) as seems most likely, he was an Ammonite who was a powerful servant of Sanballat (Clines 1984:145; Williamson 1985:183). Their opposition to Nehemiah's goal of rebuilding the walls would test his ability to persevere in the midst of great opposition, a testing that most people in leadership positions must face when they introduce change that disrupts the status quo of any group.

COMMENTARY

Nehemiah had spent many hours with the king over the previous years, so it was not hard for the king to see that something was bothering his cup-bearer. The king was discerning enough to see that this was not just from having a cold or being tired; this was something much deeper. The king may have thought that the gloomy appearance was a sign that Nehemiah was aware of a palace plot to overthrow the king. The king knew that something was bothering Nehemiah's conscience, so he confronted him to find out what the problem was.

Nehemiah's response of fear was well founded because kings did not take chances with people they could not trust completely. Nehemiah could be banished from his prestigious job and imprisoned merely because he appeared to put the king in danger. Nehemiah was also fearful because he did not know how the king would respond if he actually told the king about his deep sorrow over the ruin of Jerusalem. He knew that the moment he had prayed about for several months was now here, but a brief moment of panic hit him because he wanted to present his concern with just the right words. He needed to be honest but not pushy or critical of Persian policies, sincere but not a whiner.

Nehemiah did not deny his sadness (thus creating greater suspicion) but tried to explain it in terms that would elicit the king's sympathy and help. He told the king, "The city where my ancestors are buried is in ruins" (2:3). Nehemiah wanted his concern for the ruined city of his ancestors to encourage a positive reaction from the king. Some commentators find Nehemiah very wise and a little crafty in not mentioning the name of this rebellious city (Jerusalem), because its walls were probably destroyed because of Artaxerxes' own decree (Ezra 4:17-22; see Brockington 1969:106; Breneman 1993:175). But certainly the king knew his private cup-bearer's background, and certainly the king would not send this man on an expensive government mission without finding out the name of the city (Fensham 1982:160). Jerusalem was not mentioned because the king already knew where Nehemiah was from.

The king believed Nehemiah's story and was impressed enough with Nehemiah's genuine concern for others that he asked Nehemiah for further information, rather than making an offer to help (see note on 2:4). The king assumed that Nehemiah knew the situation well through his contact with relatives in that city. He also assumed that Nehemiah had some good ideas about how to deal with these problems. Possibly Artaxerxes had relied on Nehemiah's informal advice on other occasions. The king's question gave Nehemiah an open invitation to carefully lay out what he wanted the king to do to help restore the ruined city of his ancestors.

A momentary prayer by Nehemiah briefly interrupted the conversation (2:4-5). This showed his piety and dependence on God to intervene on his behalf; he did not depend on the logic of his reasoning, his emotional appeal, or his ability to give a slick presentation. Nehemiah knew that the Persian king was subject to God's sovereign plan and that God could influence his acceptance of Nehemiah's ideas. Nehemiah himself also needed God's guidance so that he would carefully lay out his request to the king in a manner that was concise and complete.

After his prayer, Nehemiah boldly outlined his plan by offering to go and personally be in charge of rebuilding this city in Judah, if this was the king's desire. This shows the seriousness of his concern, his willingness to be personally involved in working out a solution, and his willingness to submissively do whatever pleased the king. Nehemiah presented a wonderful model for all who have complaints today. He did not just dwell on the problem; he had some constructive ideas to address the dilemma. He was shrewd and willing to push his ideas if he was given a chance, but he would never think of telling the king what to do. He merely suggested that if the king desired to help correct the disastrous situation in Judah, he would need to give Nehemiah the authority to carry out the king's wishes. Artaxerxes' openness to his idea may seem surprising in light of his decrees to stop the Jews in Jerusalem in Ezra 4:17-23, but the king may have seen Nehemiah's plan as a strategic way of solidifying his influence in a troubled area of his empire after a revolt a few years earlier (Blenkinsopp 1988:214). Of course, God was intervening on Nehemiah's behalf, both in guiding Nehemiah's presentation and in making the king open to what Nehemiah suggested.

It is evident that Nehemiah had thought about what he would need from the king, so he was immediately ready to make his requests. The king was no doubt impressed with his wise planning and his broad understanding of what it would take to accomplish this large task. Since Nehemiah would have to travel through several provinces, he would need permission from the king. Nehemiah was not just some wild dreamer who had no practical sense of what it would take to pull off this major rebuilding project. He was a realist who knew he would need the king's approval to get lumber from the king's forest and all the other supplies he would need. At least three rebuilding projects would need wood: (1) the gates of the fortress by the Temple (at the north end was the Tower of the Hundred; cf. 3:1), plus any other destroyed gates; (2) the scaffolding that the builders would use to raise the stone up to the higher levels of the wall; and (3) major log beams for the roofs of new homes for Nehemiah and those residents who came with him.

To our surprise (and possibly to Nehemiah's surprise), all his requests, and any others that are not recorded in detail, were freely given to him, seemingly without hesitation or qualification. This was an amazing reversal of the king's previous opposition to rebuilding the walls of Jerusalem (Ezra 4:17-23). Why did this change take place? Nehemiah did not say that this favorable response happened because of help from the queen or his own brilliant or persuasive speech; it was all an act of God's gracious, sovereign control over the situation. Nehemiah's attention was focused on God, the real power that moved the course of history. God deserved all the credit because it all happened because of his grace (lit., "because the hand of God was good to me"). This is the kind of humility every leader should mirror when they accomplish something.

In summary, the main theological point of this passage is related to Nehemiah's belief that God was in control of his situation. This is evident in Nehemiah's brief prayer for God's guidance at the crucial point when the king asked him what he wanted (2:4) and Nehemiah's summary statement that the king granted everything Nehemiah asked "because the gracious hand of God was on me" (2:8). These statements show that Nehemiah began this encounter with the king depending on God and that he ended his discussion with the king by concluding that God had acted on his behalf. This attitude of faith in God's control of his life highlights Nehemiah's understanding of his own inabilities and God's gracious abilities. His summary statement (2:8) was really just another act of praising God. Nehemiah did not take credit for persuading the king. He attributed success to divine intervention, not political pressure, favoritism, or any human causality. God accomplished far beyond what any human person could even imagine. Ephesians 3:20 says that God "is able . . . to accomplish infinitely more than we might ask or think."

This narrative seamlessly molds the theme of strong dependence on God with Nehemiah's natural fulfillment of his human responsibility. He (1) took time to fast and pray over several months, (2) patiently waited until an appropriate opening presented itself rather than prematurely forcing his agenda on the king, (3) planned well ahead of time what he would need so he would have an answer if he was asked, (4) confidently and boldly presented his proposal to the king, (5) wisely focused on the solution to the problem rather than casting blame for it, and (6) was willing to give up his own comfortable job in the king's court to solve this problem. He did not just complain about those who had not paid attention to this issue earlier. He did not blame others but confidently presented his vision as a remedy that would address that specific problem. His positive solution to Jerusalem's situation did not get involved with any of the political debates that surrounded the problem; he just wanted to help the king and his people secure Jerusalem. Nehemiah's exercise of his human responsibility did not interfere with or take the place of God's sovereign control; these two factors worked hand in hand without conflict. Human responsibility and divine sovereignty are not contradictory; both are essential in accomplishing the divine plan for the world.

Finally, the appearance of opposition to what God was doing (2:9-10) should not be unexpected or always used as a tool to identify "closed doors." Although opposition can be garbed in political undertones and involve a great deal of anger, God's servants should not allow opposition to sidetrack them from doing what they know is the will of God. Opposition from those outside the will of God should be expected (1 Pet 4:12-19). In these kinds of situations, a firm conviction about the will of God, born out of weeks of prayer, will not be sidetracked by the emotional accusations of those who would attempt to intimidate and discourage those who are trying to do the will of God. Dealing with angry opponents is never fun, but one should expect that some of God's plans will be opposed by evil people.

◆   ## 3. God's grace causes the people to accept Nehemiah's vision (Neh 2:11-20)

¹¹So I arrived in Jerusalem. Three days later, ¹²I slipped out during the night, taking only a few others with me. I had not told anyone about the plans God had put in my heart for Jerusalem. We took no pack animals with us except the donkey I was riding. ¹³After dark I went out through the Valley Gate, past the Jackal's Well,* and over to the Dung Gate to inspect the broken walls and burned gates. ¹⁴Then I went to the Fountain Gate and to the King's Pool, but my donkey couldn't get through the rubble. ¹⁵So, though it was still dark, I went up the Kidron Valley* instead, inspecting the wall before I turned back and entered again at the Valley Gate.

¹⁶The city officials did not know I had been out there or what I was doing, for I had not yet said anything to anyone about my plans. I had not yet spoken to the Jewish leaders—the priests, the nobles, the officials, or anyone else in the administration. ¹⁷But now I said to them, "You know very well what trouble we are in. Jerusalem lies in ruins, and its gates have been destroyed by fire. Let us rebuild the wall of Jerusalem and end this disgrace!" ¹⁸Then I told them about how the gracious hand of God had been on me, and about my conversation with the king.

They replied at once, "Yes, let's rebuild the wall!" So they began the good work.

¹⁹But when Sanballat, Tobiah, and Geshem the Arab heard of our plan, they scoffed contemptuously. "What are you doing? Are you rebelling against the king?" they asked.

²⁰I replied, "The God of heaven will help us succeed. We, his servants, will start rebuilding this wall. But you have no share, legal right, or historic claim in Jerusalem."

2:13 Or *Serpent's Well.*   2:15 Hebrew *the valley.*

NOTES
2:11 *Three days later.* In these three days Nehemiah may have rested (see Ezra 8:32), visited with friends or relatives, observed the Sabbath, got to know the city leaders, or simply settled into his new living quarters. The temporal notice indicates when he toured the ruined walls of Jerusalem and began to plan for their reconstruction. He did not wait long to get down to business.

2:12 *I had not told anyone about the plans God had put in my heart.* The NLT refers to the plan God "had put" in Nehemiah's heart, but the Hebrew word is *nothen* [TH5414, ZH5989], a participle ("putting"). This linguistic form suggests that Nehemiah was referring either to (1) the guidance that God was presently giving him for a reconstruction plan, or (2) the vision to rebuild Jerusalem that God had put in his heart while he was in Susa (cf. NASB). This suggests that God leads people step-by-step as they respond in obedience to earlier directions. He guides them as they understand the circumstances and face the dilemmas of each new challenge.

2:13-15 *the Valley Gate . . . the Jackal's Well . . . the Dung Gate . . . the Fountain Gate and to the King's Pool . . . I went up the Kidron Valley . . . before I turned back and entered again at the Valley Gate.* Nehemiah's survey of Jerusalem's walls covered only the City of David, south of the Temple area. Williamson (1984:81-88) thinks Nehemiah rebuilt the walls around the preexilic City of David on the eastern hill, not the larger city of Hezekiah, which extended to the western hill.

The Valley Gate was toward the northern end of the west wall of the City of David. After going through it, a person would enter into the Tyropoeon Valley (Mazar 1975:167, 182, 193). The remains of a gate with its towers dating back to the Persian period were discovered in this area by the archaeologist M. Crowfoot. Uzziah fortified this gate (2 Chr 26:9), and apparently a good part of the stone structure of the gate remained at the time of Nehemiah.

Nehemiah turned left and proceeded downhill to the south to the "Jackal's Well" (sometimes translated "the Dragon's Well" or "the Serpent's Well"). This place is not identified elsewhere in the Bible. Some hypothesize that this well refers to the spring of En-rogel, which is past the southern tip of the wall where the Hinnom and Kidron valleys meet, but this is unlikely, for it lies beyond the third landmark—the Dung Gate (Williamson 1985:188-189). This Jackal's Well may refer to the meandering, serpentine tunnel (built by Hezekiah) that brought excess water from the Gihon Spring to the Pool of Siloam area (Yamauchi 1988:689), or to an unknown spring that is now dried up (Blenkinsopp 1988:222). Nehemiah continued south to the Dung Gate (called the Gate of Broken Pots in Jer 19:2) at the southern end of the western wall (about 1,500 feet south of the Valley Gate according to 3:13). People would take rubbish and refuse out through the Dung Gate and throw it into the Hinnom Valley. Next Nehemiah came to the Fountain Gate (near En-rogel) on the southeastern corner of the wall near the King's Pool and Gardens (a pool created from the overflow of the Gihon Spring—see 2 Kgs 20:20; 25:4), which is probably the same as "the pool of Siloam" in 3:15. Then Nehemiah turned north to go up the Kidron Valley (lit., "the valley") along the eastern wall of the City of David. Because of the massive stones littering the steep hillside of the Kidron Valley, Nehemiah abandoned his mule and walked. Kenyon (1967:108-109) describes the large boulders and the extensive damage to the eastern wall.

This record does not say how far up the Kidron he traveled, but at some point he turned back, retraced his path, and reentered the city through the same gate he used when he left the city. Now he had firsthand details about the enormous job of rebuilding the walls of Jerusalem.

2:18 *They replied at once, "Yes, let's rebuild the wall!"* The people enthusiastically agreed to get started on this project. Their words of agreement in this cohortative clause could be understood as mutual encouragement, as NLT translates them, "Yes, let's rebuild the wall," or as a firm resolve, "We will arise and will build." The latter interpretation would demonstrate a firm and confident approval of Nehemiah's proposal by the community of believers. This was now their project, which they were determined to complete.

they began the good work. Lit., "so they strengthened their hands for the good." Rather than understanding "hands" as implying an immediate physical action, it seems better to see this as mental strengthening of their resolve for this good cause or as a strengthening of their commitment by mutual encouragement (Clines 1984:147; Allen 2003:99). It is premature to think that they could immediately leave this public event and begin working on the wall.

2:19 *Sanballat, Tobiah.* These were already identified as Nehemiah's enemies in 2:10.

Geshem. In 1947, a fifth-century BC silver vessel was found at Tell el-Maskhuta near the Suez Canal, which had the Aramaic name of "Qaynu the son of Geshem, the king of Qedar." This suggests that the Geshem who opposed Nehemiah was a powerful ruler over the scattered nomadic tribes in desert areas of Arabia, Edom, the Sinai, and over to Egypt. See Cross 1955:46-47 or Dumbrell 1971:33-44 for details.

What are you doing? Are you rebelling against the king? These two questions were meant to intimidate and accuse, not to find out accurate information. When these people asked, "What are you doing?" they were implying that Nehemiah was doing something incredibly stupid. The second question implied their answer to their own question: "Are you rebelling against the king?" They were not asking; they were accusing.

2:20 *you have no share, legal right, or historic claim in Jerusalem.* Nehemiah assured his audience that Sanballat, Tobiah, and Geshem did not control the people of Jerusalem, for they (1) did not even have possession of a part or "share" (*kheleq* [TH2506, ZH2750], "property, inheritance") of the land through family inheritance laws, (2) did not have any "legal right" in court (*tsedaqah* [TH6666, ZH7407]) to influence what was done in Jerusalem, and (3) did not have any "religious rights" (*zikkaron* [TH2146, ZH2355]) to participate in cultic activities at the Temple. See Williamson 1985:192 or Blenkinsopp 1988:226 for more on these terms.

COMMENTARY

Nehemiah needed to get a firsthand understanding of the problem he was facing before he could approach the people about rebuilding the walls. This information was important if he was going to present a credible plan for reconstruction (see his plan in ch 3). In order to create a plan that was not unduly influenced by people in one part of the city or another, Nehemiah had to get the facts for himself. This secrecy also kept Nehemiah's enemies, who had some information about his need for timbers from the documents he brought from the king (2:9), from knowing when and how he would carry out his plan. This example does not justify planning in secret per se; instead, it supports the idea that people need to have firsthand knowledge of the situation they are in if they are going to present a credible plan for change.

Nehemiah did not tell anyone about his plan because he did not have the whole plan God was giving him (see note on 2:12). As he traveled around the city, God clarified and filled in the pieces in this plan. He patiently waited for divine guidance rather than filling in the blanks based on his own intuition, certain natural preferences, or his own logical deductions. Once he had received God's plan, he could use his natural abilities and logical thinking to decide how best to implement it. Nehemiah carefully kept his survey of the walls and his rebuilding plans to himself. He did not inform any of the city "officials," and one can be sure he did not publicize his ideas with the Jewish priests, elders, or Persian officials. In fact, no one knew what he was really up to. Nehemiah realized that now was the time to think and plan. When these plans were complete, there would an appropriate time to publicize them. If the plan was leaked too early, before it was well thought out, it could be incomplete and open to criticism; thus, opposition could be organized for an alternative approach and seriously blunt enthusiasm for the work of rebuilding. With the information he had from his survey of the walls, he could develop a plan that would divide the work on the wall and gates into small segments of comparable work that could be rebuilt by small teams in a relatively short period of time.

We are not told when Nehemiah finally publicized his plan, where the meeting took place, or who was at the meeting. We do not even get the full text of his speech, just a brief summary of two key points. First, he emphasized the intolerable disaster that was inflicted on Jerusalem when its walls and gates were destroyed (cf. 1:3). In the first part of his speech he demonstrated the need to rebuild the walls. Nehemiah did not focus on the economic or security problems this destruction caused. He did not even need to argue his case with 10 reasons why Jerusalem was in trouble; everyone could see the broken walls and knew the city was in trouble.

Nehemiah told the people, "Let us rebuild the wall of Jerusalem and end this disgrace" (2:17). The difficult part of his job was to convince the people to do something to repair the walls. His rationale for rebuilding was not tied to gaining political independence or financial prosperity; it was connected to the theological "disgrace, scorn" (*kherpah* [TH2781, ZH3075]) the broken walls were bringing to the reputation of God. Nehemiah admitted that this problem had spiritual implications and did not minimize the importance of this degrading situation (Kidner 1979:83). The dilapidated walls said something very negative about the people who lived there and the God they followed. This did not look like the "city of the great King" that "the whole earth rejoices to see" (Ps 48:2). The surrounding nations would think this God was weak and laugh at those who trusted him, because he did not seem to care about his people or help them rebuild his city. These ruined walls were a bad testimony and a shame to God's glorious name. Even today, people have negative thoughts about those who don't take care of their homes or let their church facilities get run down.

The solution was to rebuild the walls to get rid of this public disgrace. By standing up and suggesting a plan, Nehemiah put himself in a position of potential leadership. He admitted the problem and did not try to downplay its significance, gave motivational encouragement about changing the status quo, told why this goal was worthy of their participation, and offered to get involved in the process of rebuilding (Breneman 1993:182). Real leaders do not just motivate other people to accept a plan, give of their time, and sacrifice their money. They get involved, willingly give of themselves to do the hard work of accomplishing the goal, and invite others to join them.

One of the strongest motivators for participation in any project is clear evidence of God's sovereign and providential involvement in the project (2:20). Nehemiah was able to legitimate his vision for rebuilding Jerusalem by recounting how God marvelously caused the Persian king Artaxerxes I to send him to remove Jerusalem's disgrace. If God was not in this project, how could these unusual things have happened? Since Nehemiah had prayed persistently about these issues, had the king's official permission, carried the necessary letters to get lumber, and was willing to lead the project, the audience concluded that Nehemiah was following God's guidance.

When Nehemiah's enemies heard about his plans and the people's enthusiasm for rebuilding the walls, they immediately went on the offensive to stop any progress (2:19). The leaders of the opposition are identified by name, but the number of their supporters is unknown. Not all the Jewish people helped with the project of building these walls (3:5), so the opposition was not insignificant. Some of the wealthy did not follow Nehemiah (5:6-13), and one of the prophets opposed Nehemiah (6:10-14). Initially, the number of opponents was small, but they could have a powerful influence on the population if they could discourage the people by undermining the credibility of Nehemiah or his plan. The opponents began to scoff and make contemptuous statements.

They saw Nehemiah's plan as a political move of independence that would run contrary to Persian interests, and by implication, their own interests. They intended to scare the Jewish people who might join Nehemiah by implying that the Persians would interpret their action as rebellion and stop any rebuilding, just as they had earlier (as in Ezra 4:6-23). In reality their underlying concern was probably much more selfish, for they were fearful that this new Jewish leader would gain some political advantage over them, weaken their power, and reduce their financial base for taxation. Either they did not know about Nehemiah's official letters from the king that granted permission to rebuild the walls or they believed that these documents were forgeries Nehemiah had created for his own selfish purposes. They redefined Nehemiah's positive attempt to help the people as a negative act of treason against the king.

Nehemiah did not retaliate by accusing his enemies of any evil, and there is no record that he tried to disprove their statements. He did not need to worry about what they thought of his plan because he and the Jewish population of Judah were convinced that God had sent him to accomplish this task. He had already received official permission to rebuild the walls from Artaxerxes, so their threats were not going to discourage him. This was not an act of rebellion against the king. Nehemiah's plan was based on doing the will of the king and the will of God. God's miraculous direction of the Persian king demonstrated that God was behind this project. God is the one who determines the success or failure of a project, not man. Nehemiah would have been foolish to suggest that this was his plan or that he could guarantee the successful completion of the project.

In summary, most of this passage deals with the practical steps Nehemiah took to rebuild the walls of Jerusalem (God is mentioned only three times). Although there is nothing in this passage that one could call a "theology of leadership," Nehemiah, and all who are in positions of responsibility today, are directed by their basic theological beliefs and underlying approaches to interacting with people. The first quality that stands out is that Nehemiah remained humble and did not take credit for what God was doing. God gave him the burden to request help for Jerusalem while he was in Susa (1:4-11), and God was giving him the plans for rebuilding during and after he surveyed the walls of Jerusalem (2:12). Nehemiah knew this project was not an ego trip to fulfill his own ambitions. He was not the source of these ideas, he would not get the credit, and success would not be dependent on him. After praying four months, Nehemiah recognized the hand of God marvelously working to cause the Persian king Artaxerxes I to grant all his requests about Jerusalem (2:1-8). God's action fully convinced Nehemiah that he was doing what God wanted. Any confusion about who was in charge of rebuilding Jerusalem at this stage would have pushed the project in a whole different direction. If Nehemiah did not believe this was God's plan, questions about Nehemiah's intentions or abilities could have threatened the success of the project and made him defensive when opposition arose. All people in positions of spiritual responsibility need to avoid the mistake of promoting their own agendas by spending the necessary months in prayer, waiting for God to clarify his will.

Nehemiah's theological perspective on the plan gave him confidence that God would help the people successfully complete the project in spite of opposition and the difficulty of the work (2:20). This quiet confidence gave him the ability to hear opposing views without losing hope or becoming defensive. Nehemiah did not let reason, emotions, personalities, or legal threats lessen his optimism that God would accomplish what he was setting out to do. Throughout these events, Nehemiah was a man led by God.

Once Nehemiah's theology of divine leadership was put in order, it was possible for many of his other tasks to fall into place. These tasks required the use of the practical wisdom of planning, engendering confidence, and building trust. Since it was God's work, Nehemiah gladly invested his time and effort to assist in the task that God was accomplishing. Since God had not revealed how to rebuild the wall in detail, Nehemiah knew it was his responsibility to figure out the most reasonable way to accomplish the goal. Since opposition had already appeared (2:10), Nehemiah needed to get at the work right away (after only three days; see 2:11-12) and not waste time. Although secrecy is not a virtue by itself and can often have serious repercussions, it was wise for Nehemiah to get a firsthand view of the problems rather than basing his solutions on slanted, secondhand knowledge that might not fully represent the facts. Keeping a plan quiet until it is thought through is just common sense, for one avoids making foolish statements and losing the confidence of those who follow. When the plan is put together, it is essential to gain the support of those who will do the work. Motivating people to the challenge of a bold new venture should include (1) the honest admission of the need—it should recognize both spiritual and practical aspects (2:17a), (2) a call for the mobilization of everyone in order to resolve the need (2:17b), (3) an undeniable sense that God is leading in the direction the plan proposes (2:18), and (4) confidence to respond appropriately to opposition or doubt (2:19-20). No leader can assume that everyone in his audience will immediately recognize the value of any plan (even when it is God's); therefore, the presentation should engender hope that a reliable solution to a real need is being addressed in a reasonable way. The aim is to inspire hope and willing involvement by all and not a passive assent to a plan. Of course, those who propose new ideas get their confidence from knowing the will of God, not from the response of the audience. Audience approval merely indicates that they agree with God's plan and are willing to commit themselves to implementing it.

♦ **B. God Overcomes Opposition to Building the Walls (Neh 3:1–7:73a)**
1. The whole community works to rebuild the walls (Neh 3:1-32)

Then Eliashib the high priest and the other priests started to rebuild at the Sheep Gate. They dedicated it and set up its doors, building the wall as far as the Tower of the Hundred, which they dedicated, and the Tower of Hananel. ²People from the town of Jericho worked next to them, and beyond them was Zaccur son of Imri.

³The Fish Gate was built by the sons of Hassenaah. They laid the beams, set up its doors, and installed its bolts and bars. ⁴Meremoth son of Uriah and grandson of Hakkoz repaired the next section of wall. Beside him were Meshullam son of Berekiah and grandson of Meshezabel, and then Zadok son of Baana. ⁵Next were the people from Tekoa, though their leaders refused to work with the construction supervisors.

⁶The Old City Gate* was repaired by Joiada son of Paseah and Meshullam son of Besodeiah. They laid the beams, set up its doors, and installed its bolts and bars. ⁷Next to them were Melatiah from Gibeon, Jadon from Meronoth, people from Gibeon, and people from Mizpah, the headquarters of the governor of the province west of the Euphrates River.* ⁸Next was Uzziel son of Harhaiah, a goldsmith by trade, who also worked on the wall. Beyond him was Hananiah, a manufacturer of perfumes. They left out a section of Jerusalem as they built the Broad Wall.*

⁹Rephaiah son of Hur, the leader of half the district of Jerusalem, was next to them on the wall. ¹⁰Next Jedaiah son of Harumaph repaired the wall across from his own house, and next to him was Hattush son of Hashabneiah. ¹¹Then came Malkijah son of Harim and Hasshub son of Pahath-moab, who repaired another section of the wall and the Tower of the Ovens. ¹²Shallum son of Hallohesh and his daughters repaired the next section. He was the leader of the other half of the district of Jerusalem.

¹³The Valley Gate was repaired by the people from Zanoah, led by Hanun. They set up its doors and installed its bolts and bars. They also repaired the 1,500 feet* of wall to the Dung Gate.

¹⁴The Dung Gate was repaired by Malkijah son of Recab, the leader of the Beth-hakkerem district. He rebuilt it, set up its doors, and installed its bolts and bars.

¹⁵The Fountain Gate was repaired by Shallum* son of Col-hozeh, the leader of the Mizpah district. He rebuilt it, roofed it, set up its doors, and installed its bolts and bars. Then he repaired the wall of the pool of Siloam* near the king's garden, and he rebuilt the wall as far as the stairs that descend from the City of David. ¹⁶Next to him was Nehemiah son of Azbuk, the leader of half the district of Beth-zur. He rebuilt the wall from a place across from the tombs of David's family as far as the water reservoir and the House of the Warriors.

¹⁷Next to him, repairs were made by a group of Levites working under the supervision of Rehum son of Bani. Then came Hashabiah, the leader of half the district of Keilah, who supervised the building of the wall on behalf of his own district. ¹⁸Next down the line were his countrymen led by Binnui* son of Henadad, the leader of the other half of the district of Keilah.

¹⁹Next to them, Ezer son of Jeshua, the leader of Mizpah, repaired another section of wall across from the ascent to the armory near the angle in the wall. ²⁰Next to him was Baruch son of Zabbai, who zealously repaired an additional section from the angle to the door of the house of Eliashib the high priest. ²¹Meremoth son of Uriah and grandson of Hakkoz rebuilt another section of the wall extending from the door of Eliashib's house to the end of the house.

²²The next repairs were made by the priests from the surrounding region. ²³After them, Benjamin and Hasshub repaired the section across from their house, and Azariah son of Maaseiah and grandson of Ananiah repaired the section across from his house. ²⁴Next was Binnui son of Henadad, who rebuilt another section of the wall from Azariah's house to the angle and the corner. ²⁵Palal son of Uzai carried on the work from a point opposite the angle and the tower that projects up from the king's upper house beside the court of the guard. Next to him were Pedaiah son of Parosh, ²⁶with the Temple servants living on the hill of Ophel, who repaired the wall as far as a point across from the Water Gate to the east and the projecting tower. ²⁷Then came the people of Tekoa, who repaired another section across from the great projecting tower and over to the wall of Ophel.

²⁸Above the Horse Gate, the priests repaired the wall. Each one repaired the section immediately across from his own house. ²⁹Next Zadok son of Immer also rebuilt the wall across from his own house, and beyond him was Shemaiah son of Shecaniah, the gatekeeper of the East Gate. ³⁰Next Hananiah son of Shelemiah and Hanun, the sixth son of Zalaph, repaired another section, while Meshullam son of Berekiah rebuilt the wall across from where he lived. ³¹Malkijah, one of the goldsmiths, repaired the wall as far as the housing for the Temple servants and merchants, across from the Inspection Gate. Then he continued as far as the upper room at the corner. ³²The other goldsmiths and merchants repaired the wall from that corner to the Sheep Gate.

3:6 Or *The Mishneh Gate*, or *The Jeshanah Gate*.   3:7 Hebrew *the province beyond the river*.   3:8 Or *They fortified Jerusalem up to the Broad Wall*.   3:13 Hebrew *1,000 cubits* [450 meters].   3:15a As in Syriac version; Hebrew reads *Shallun*.   3:15b Hebrew *pool of Shelah*, another name for the pool of Siloam.   3:18 As in a few Hebrew manuscripts, some Greek manuscripts, and Syriac version (see also 3:24; 10:9); most Hebrew manuscripts read *Bavvai*.

NOTES

3:1 *Eliashib the high priest . . . started to rebuild at the Sheep Gate.* The priests, led by the high priest Eliashib, the grandson of Jeshua (12:10; Ezra 5:2), worked on the northern wall around the sacred Temple. They "built" (*wayyibnu* [TH1129, ZH1215]) the Sheep Gate (indicating a major amount of work) at the northeastern corner of the wall (near the pool of Bethesda; see John 5:2). This gate was the place where people would bring their sheep into the city in order to take them to the Temple to sacrifice them.

other priests. Williamson (1985:201) thinks ch 3 was originally drawn up as a separate document by the priests, not Nehemiah, since it (1) highlights the work of the priests, (2) refers to Nehemiah as "their lord" (3:5; cf. NIV mg), and (3) interrupts the connection between 2:20 and 4:1. Throntveit (1992:74-75; cf. Myers 1965:112) agrees with this perspective because (1) 3:3, 6, 13, 14, 15 state that these workers set up the doors in the gates, while elsewhere in the Nehemiah Memoirs (6:1) it states that they did not set up the doors of the gates (thus this document does not agree with the Nehemiah Memoirs); (2) the Hebrew word for "nobles" (NLT, "leaders") in 3:5 is different from the terminology that is used in the Nehemiah Memoirs in 2:16; 5:7; 6:17; 7:5; 13:17; and (3) the prominence of Eliashab the high priest in this account. On the other hand, "their lord" could refer to a different high official at Tekoa (Clines 1984:152), or possibly God (NRSV), though most correctly believe it refers to Nehemiah. Weakening Throntveit's position is the possibility that 3:5 refers to a different kind of official than other passages do (2:16; 5:7; 6:17)—thus it is not contradictory—and that the setting of the doors in ch 3 could be a summary of what was to eventually happen and not a chronological statement reporting what happened immediately. Thus the main argument for ch 3 as a priestly document focuses on the role of the priests. There is no reason why the editor of this material could not have used a priestly document from the Temple archives, but one should not always assume that only a priest could or would write about issues related to the Temple.

They dedicated it. It would be unusual for the priests to dedicate this wall by itself, since no other section received its own dedication before the final ceremony in 12:27-43. It would also be odd to have two references to this dedication and to have the first dedication precede the completion of all the work. Some scholars (Brockington 1969:134; Williamson 1985:195) think a scribal error has entered the text, thus they change *qiddeshuhu* [TH6942, ZH7727] (they dedicated it) to *qeruhu* [TH7136A, ZH7939] (they laid the beams), which occurs in 3:3, 6, or to *qershuhu* ("they boarded it"; cf. noun *qeresh* [TH7175, ZH7983]). Nevertheless, no one should be surprised that the priests sanctified this portion of the wall that was part of the Temple complex (Fensham 1982:173). Since it is odd to have the dedication announced twice, one could accept the notion that the first usage is a corruption of "they laid the beams," thus having a more normal order with the dedication following the construction of everything (Eskenazi 1988:84-85). Or since the text does not identify when this dedication took place, it could be referring to the later dedication in 12:27-43, not a separate, earlier dedication. The reason for inserting information about the dedication here would be to assure the reader that the sanctity of the Holy Place was preserved in spite of all the construction going on around it.

the Tower of the Hundred . . . and the Tower of Hananel. This group of priests also worked on two major military towers on the north side of the Temple (12:38). It is not clear what the "Hundred" refers to. Was it a hundred cubits high, did it hold a hundred soldiers, or was this the name of a military unit? The Tower of Hananel (Jer 31:38; Zech 14:10) was probably named after some war hero or the general who built it. It served as a key military fortification to protect the northern walls from enemy attacks.

3:2 *Zaccur.* Zaccur may be the same person listed in Ezra 8:14 and/or the Zechariah listed in 10:12.

3:3 *The Fish Gate was built by the sons of Hassenaah.* The Fish Gate was on the western wall (Zeph 1:10 connects it to the Mishneh section of western Jerusalem), though some put it on the northern wall and connect it to the present-day Damascus Gate (Yamauchi 1988:694). Its name is associated with the place where people sold fish from the Sea of Galilee and the Mediterranean (2 Chr 33:14). Hassenaah could be the Senaah listed in Ezra 2:35.

3:4 *Meremoth . . . Meshullam.* A Meremoth is mentioned in Ezra 8:33, and Meshullam is the man who gives his daughter to a son of Tobiah in 6:18 and later signs the covenant in 10:20.

3:6 *The Old City Gate was repaired.* Some (e.g., NIV, NET) translate this as the "Jeshanah Gate" (cf. NLT mg). This is because the word *yeshanah* [TH3465, ZH3824] can be understood either as the name of a town (2 Chr 13:19) or (more commonly) to mean "old." If "Jeshanah Gate" is accepted (so Fensham 1982:174), the gate is usually understood as leading to Jeshanah. But "Old Gate" seems more likely because (1) Jeshanah was a minor, obscure city, (2) this city was situated far from Jerusalem (15 miles north, near Bethel), and (3) if this gate led to Jeshanah, as is often suggested, it would more likely be on the north side of the city, and this one seems to be on the west side of the city. If "Old Gate" is accepted, then it is usually understood as a gate leading into the old city (hence NLT's "Old City Gate") from the new city that grew up on the western hill. This new area of the city was surrounded by the Broad Wall, built during the time of Hezekiah (2 Chr 32:5; cf. Neh 3:8; 12:38), and was called the Mishneh (Zeph 1:10, NLT mg). On this basis, Williamson (1985:196) suggests that *hayeshanah* [TH3465, ZH3824] (the old) could be a scribal error for *hammishneh* [TH4932A, ZH5467] (the Mishneh; i.e., new city), a name known from other biblical and nonbiblical texts that refers to the same gate as the proposed Old Gate. This gate, which the workers "repaired" or "strengthened" (*hekheziqu* [TH2388, ZH2616]) but did not need to rebuild, is also mentioned in 12:39.

3:8 *They left out a section of Jerusalem as they built the Broad Wall.* It seems best to conclude that the workers "left off, abandoned" (*wayya'azbu* [TH5800, ZH6440]) parts of Jerusalem on the western hill (Clines 1984:153). In contrast, the NLT interprets this clause to say that these workers "built the Broad Wall," but a literal reading ("they abandoned Jerusalem up to the Broad Wall"; cf. NLT mg) suggests that they did not work on the Broad Wall. Fensham (1982:175) and Blenkinsopp (1988:230) (so RSV and NIV) read here the secondary meaning (known from Ugaritic) of *'azab*, which is "to prepare, to make, to restore," and conclude that they did repair the Broad Wall (see also Tuland 1967:158-180). Since there were so few people living in Jerusalem at this time, there was no need to add extra area within the city walls. This Broad Wall was located on the northern border of the western hill and was partially destroyed when the Babylonians defeated Jerusalem. If they had decided to include the western hill of Jerusalem, that would have doubled the length of the walls to be reconstructed. Avigad (1972:193-200) found portions of this wall, which was about 24 feet thick.

3:9-12 *Rephaiah . . . Shallum.* Similar to the list of faithful people in Hebrews 11, this chapter carefully chronicles the names of the faithful people who rebuilt the walls of Jerusalem. Although one might expect political officials to be directing others, two leaders of districts within Jerusalem (Rephaiah and Shallum) took on the manual labor of repairing a portion of the wall. The dedication of these people was remarkable. Shallum even got his daughters to help him; he may not have had any sons.

3:11 *another section of the wall.* Malkijah and Hasshub did their assigned portion plus an extra section beyond what they were assigned. The text never tells us what their original task was, indicating that this list of workers does not provide a complete list of all the repairs that were done.

Tower of the Ovens. The location of the Tower of the Ovens is unknown. It could refer to a portion of the wall where people baked bread or a place for baking pottery.

3:13 *Valley Gate.* The Valley Gate is a known landmark at the northern end of the City of David.

people from Zanoah . . . repaired the 1,500 feet of wall. Even people from as far away as Zanoah, about 13 miles southwest of Jerusalem, took on the big task of repairing 1,500 feet of wall between the Valley Gate and the Dung Gate (see 2:13). One must assume that this long portion of the wall was not in need of many repairs, otherwise Nehemiah would have assigned more workers to this job.

Dung Gate. The Dung Gate (called the Gate of Broken Pots in Jer 19:2) stood close to the southernmost tip of the wall, where the wall met the Hinnom Valley. Here was where people dumped and burned their trash and where people sacrificed to pagan gods during the days of Manasseh (2 Kgs 23:10).

3:14-15 *Dung Gate . . . Fountain Gate . . . wall of the pool of Siloam.* This reconstruction report is focused on the southern tip of the City of David where the Hinnom and Kidron valleys meet. The Dung Gate was near the southwestern corner, and the Fountain Gate near the southeastern corner of the wall (see the discussion of these in 2:13-14). The Fountain Gate (near En-rogel) was near the "pool of Siloam" (a pool created from the overflow of the Gihon Spring—see 2 Kgs 20:20; 25:4), which probably is the same as the "King's Pool" in 2:14 or the "lower pool" of Isa 22:9. Some (cf. NLT, NIV) think this verse is referring to the pool of Siloam partway up the western side of the City of David (Brockington 1969:116), but it is more likely that this refers to a pool further south on the eastern side of the city that was by the king's garden.

the leader of the Beth-hakkerem district . . . the leader of the Mizpah district. The people repairing this portion were not from Jerusalem but from Beth-hakkerem and Mizpah. They caught the vision and pitched in to do their share of the work. Some connect the administrative district of Beth-hakkerem with Ramat Rachel, about two miles south of Jerusalem (Clines 1984:154), or Ein Kerem, about five miles west of Jerusalem (Blenkinsopp 1988:236). People from Mizpah were mentioned in 3:7, but the person in charge here was a government official who took time off from his own political responsibilities to contribute to the community effort to rebuild Jerusalem.

3:16-32 Commentators have noted that the Hebrew style of presentation changes beginning with 3:16, with houses or angles in the wall being dividing markers in addition to the gates. This is because the eastern wall was in such bad shape that a totally new wall was built higher up the slope of the Kidron Valley (Williamson 1985:199; Blenkinsopp 1988:232). Since these features cannot be identified today with absolute certainty, it is more difficult to follow the reconstruction of the eastern wall of the City of David.

3:16 *Nehemiah son of Azbuk.* This Nehemiah (not the king's cup-bearer) was the leader of an administrative district called Beth-zur, which was just north of Hebron.

tombs of David's family . . . House of the Warriors. The royal cemetery could be the place where King David was buried (1 Kgs 2:10; 11:43; 2 Chr 21:20; Acts 2:29), and the House of the Warriors could be a tomb for David's mighty men (2 Sam 23:8-39) or a military barracks for troops guarding the eastern wall in Nehemiah's time.

3:17 *district of Keilah.* This was near Adullam and Azekah, to the southwest of Jerusalem.

3:19-21 These verses record that three groups repaired an "additional section," above and beyond what was initially requested of them. They did not just pick up their tools and go home when their work was done, but probably volunteered to help out where they were needed. Meremoth's (3:21) first assignment was described in 3:4. The people of Mizpah had an earlier assignment at the Fountain Gate (3:15, but a different leader was named there). There is no reference to Baruch's (3:20) earlier building location (a sign that this long list is incomplete). Some omit the reference to Baruch working "zealously" (*kharah* [TH2734, ZH3013]) in 3:20 because they believe this word was the result of dittography (Blenkinsopp 1988:231) or that it was confused with the typical phrase "after him" (Fensham 1982:177).

3:19 *section of wall across from the ascent to the armory near the angle.* Archaeologists do not know where the "ascent to the armory near the angle" is, but it must have marked a distinct architectural feature where there was a steep slope or a turn in the wall.

3:22-27 The repairs described in these verses were on the northern half of the eastern wall around the City of David. The specific geography of the sections, however, is unclear and beyond accurate reconstruction.

3:24 Binnui son of Henadad. He did double duty if this was the same person mentioned in 3:18, although his name was spelled Bavvai in the earlier text (see NLT mg on 3:18).

the angle and the corner. This must refer to another turn in the wall (somewhere north of the turn mentioned in 3:19).

3:25 the tower . . . the king's upper house beside the court of the guard. These refer to a royal complex on the hill of Ophel just south of the Temple area.

3:26-27 The area where the Temple servants (see Ezra 2:43-58) and the people of Tekoa worked is also difficult. Verse 27 locates their work near the hill of Ophel just south of the Temple, but 3:26 seems to associate them with the Water Gate, which one would naturally connect with the Gihon Spring (Williamson 1985:209). This is problematic because the spring was much further south. Others take the Water Gate as an internal gate of the Temple-palace complex that allowed one to go to the spring for water (Yamauchi 1988:699; Clines 1984:156); if so, it was not a part of the external wall of the city. Some think the Water Gate was an older gate that was part of the preexilic wall and functions as a well-known geographic landmark in this context, rather than a part of the wall they were reconstructing (Rudolph 1949:119).

3:28-32 the Horse Gate . . . the East Gate . . . the Inspection Gate . . . the Sheep Gate. So little information is provided that it is impossible to determine if these gates were part of the Temple-palace complex, as suggested by 2 Kgs 11:16 and 2 Chr 23:15 (Yamauchi 1988:699), or external gates, based on Jer 31:40 (Williamson 1985:210). The East Gate could even be the eastern gateway of the Temple (Ezek 40:6). The Inspection Gate would be a place where Temple animals were inspected by priests before they could be approved for sacrifice. The final group of workers brings this report on the rebuilding of the walls back to the Sheep Gate where the work started (3:1).

COMMENTARY

This chapter is a summary of the people responsible for rebuilding various sections of the wall, but the actual process of rebuilding the walls is not reported as complete until 6:15-19. The hanging of the gates is completed in 7:1-3, and the final dedication of the whole project is recorded in 12:27-43. The rebuilding of the walls and gates covering the northern section of the city was divided among eight work groups (3:1-5). These people encouraged their families to join in the hard work of changing the future direction of Jerusalem.

But not everyone was cooperative. Nehemiah 3:5 tells us that the leaders of Tekoa refused to work. No reason is given for their uncooperative spirit, but some think that Geshem (2:19), who controlled the area south of Tekoa, had a negative influence on the political leaders in Tekoa (Blenkinsopp 1988:234). This negative comment shows that this document was an honest presentation of the good and the bad side of this project. Nehemiah was not writing a piece of political propaganda to show how smoothly everything went.

Nehemiah 3:6-13 describes the repair of the wall and gates on the western side of the city. The leaders of these families are not mentioned elsewhere, but they were important people whom Nehemiah knew, appreciated, and honored by including their names. They and their families worked hard to move heavy stones into place because they wanted to help remove the disgrace of Jerusalem. It is significant that people from outside Jerusalem cooperated with this project (Gibeon and Mizpah

[3:7] were about 6-7 miles north of Jerusalem) and that people having wealth and more delicate occupations pitched in (goldsmiths and perfumers, 3:8).

The rest of the chapter names several individuals and the sections of the wall they repaired. Significantly, many of the people were priests. The Levites worked hard, not believing that they were too holy to sweat and get their hands dirty (3:17). Nehemiah 3:22-27 tells us of workers who repaired the northern half of the eastern wall around the City of David. The workers included (1) priests who lived outside of Jerusalem, (2) priests who lived just outside the Temple complex on the hill of Ophel, (3) Temple servants who lived close by, as well as (4) people living right next to the wall. The repeated reference to priests and Temple personnel suggests that they had a great deal of enthusiasm for the restoration of Jerusalem.

The last portion of the list of workers (3:28-32) includes priests (including Zadok from the family of Immer; see Ezra 2:37), gatekeepers, Meshullam (who did an earlier section, 3:4), goldsmiths, and merchants. As in 3:1-2, there were priests and Temple servants involved in repairing the area around the Temple (though no dedication is mentioned). Since they lived in the area, Nehemiah wisely assigned them to "[rebuild] the wall across from where [they] lived" (3:30). The merchants who lived here may have worked in this area selling sacrificial animals to individuals who came from too far away to bring an animal from their own flock (13:15-22; Mark 11:15-17).

When one quickly reads through chapter 3, it seems to be filled with odd-sounding names, obscure places that are hard to identify, and a mass of details that were important for the reconstruction, but unimportant for the modern reader. The rebuilding of the wall is not explicitly presented in this chapter as God's work. God is not said to be the one who intervened to help them finish the wall, and there is no mention that the work was done to glorify God. This chapter focuses on the acceptance of human responsibility by the people of Judah rather than God's divine empowerment of them.

Therefore, one should simply approach this list of names and places as a summary description of how the work was organized. This chapter outlines Nehemiah's practical plan for getting the work done by a very diverse group of people. Spiritual lessons are not trumpeted, but the practical principles of getting the work of God done are illustrated by the way people went about their work. Nevertheless, sometimes people's lives and actions can speak a more powerful theological message than their words.

Almost everyone pitched in and gave a hand (except the leaders of Tekoa; see 3:5). The high priest did not excuse himself in order to do "God's work at the Temple" (3:1-2); the goldsmiths, perfumers, and merchants did not put their profits above the work that needed to be done on the wall (3:8, 32); and people from throughout the land traveled to Jerusalem to help others remove the disgrace of Jerusalem (see McConville 1985:88-89). Master carpenters and professional block layers did not do the work, and no architects are mentioned, just common people working hard. They worked alongside one another and in cooperation with each other. This back-breaking, menial work of lugging heavy stones and timbers was a shining testimony to their internal spiritual condition and was a testimony to what God was moving them to do. They were "sharing each other's burdens" and caring for the good of their neighbors (1 Cor 10:24; Gal 6:2) instead of focusing on their own desires (Holmgren 1987:104). This cooperative effort demonstrates that a unity of purpose pervaded the workers. This was quite the opposite of what happened in the church at Corinth, where small groups were in opposition to one another (1 Cor 3–6). This cooperative spirit illustrates the unity Jesus wants for his followers (John 17).

Surprisingly, Nehemiah's role is not mentioned in this chapter at all, but one assumes his organizational planning was behind the structured approach to accomplishing this monumental task. This degree of coordination and teamwork and this level of enthusiasm and commitment (with volunteers sometimes doing two sections) do not come about unless there is a good organizer putting all the pieces together. The publication of this chapter in Scripture was Nehemiah's thank you to individuals who would otherwise be lost to history. The credit goes to each family that consistently completed the task it was given. Nehemiah delegated responsibility to the natural heads of families and districts and did not try to take any credit for their accomplishments.

At times, Nehemiah seems to be the catalyst God used to motivate these people to action (2:17-18), but in this chapter there is no focus on his role. Instead, the author highlights concepts like working to repair the wall by one's own house as a practical, motivating factor. If more leaders today would follow Nehemiah's example of humility, there would be fewer ministries built around the personality of the man in control and greater attempts to build up the roles of the faithful workers who quietly do the little things day after day.

◆ ## 2. Prayer and hard work overcome outside opposition (Neh 4:1-23)

[1]*Sanballat was very angry when he learned that we were rebuilding the wall. He flew into a rage and mocked the Jews, [2] saying in front of his friends and the Samarian army officers, "What does this bunch of poor, feeble Jews think they're doing? Do they think they can build the wall in a single day by just offering a few sacrifices?* Do they actually think they can make something of stones from a rubbish heap—and charred ones at that?"

[3] Tobiah the Ammonite, who was standing beside him, remarked, "That stone wall would collapse if even a fox walked along the top of it!"

[4] Then I prayed, "Hear us, our God, for we are being mocked. May their scoffing fall back on their own heads, and may they themselves become captives in a foreign land! [5] Do not ignore their guilt. Do

not blot out their sins, for they have provoked you to anger here in front of* the builders."

[6] At last the wall was completed to half its height around the entire city, for the people had worked with enthusiasm.

[7]*But when Sanballat and Tobiah and the Arabs, Ammonites, and Ashdodites heard that the work was going ahead and that the gaps in the wall of Jerusalem were being repaired, they were furious. [8] They all made plans to come and fight against Jerusalem and throw us into confusion. [9] But we prayed to our God and guarded the city day and night to protect ourselves.

[10] Then the people of Judah began to complain, "The workers are getting tired, and there is so much rubble to be moved. We will never be able to build the wall by ourselves."

¹¹Meanwhile, our enemies were saying, "Before they know what's happening, we will swoop down on them and kill them and end their work."

¹²The Jews who lived near the enemy came and told us again and again, "They will come from all directions and attack us!"* ¹³So I placed armed guards behind the lowest parts of the wall in the exposed areas. I stationed the people to stand guard by families, armed with swords, spears, and bows.

¹⁴Then as I looked over the situation, I called together the nobles and the rest of the people and said to them, "Don't be afraid of the enemy! Remember the Lord, who is great and glorious, and fight for your brothers, your sons, your daughters, your wives, and your homes!"

¹⁵When our enemies heard that we knew of their plans and that God had frustrated them, we all returned to our work on the wall. ¹⁶But from then on, only half my men worked while the other half stood guard with spears, shields, bows, and coats of mail. The leaders stationed themselves behind the people of Judah ¹⁷who were building the wall. The laborers carried on their work with one hand supporting their load and one hand holding a weapon. ¹⁸All the builders had a sword belted to their side. The trumpeter stayed with me to sound the alarm.

¹⁹Then I explained to the nobles and officials and all the people, "The work is very spread out, and we are widely separated from each other along the wall. ²⁰When you hear the blast of the trumpet, rush to wherever it is sounding. Then our God will fight for us!"

²¹We worked early and late, from sunrise to sunset. And half the men were always on guard. ²²I also told everyone living outside the walls to stay in Jerusalem. That way they and their servants could help with guard duty at night and work during the day. ²³During this time, none of us—not I, nor my relatives, nor my servants, nor the guards who were with me—ever took off our clothes. We carried our weapons with us at all times, even when we went for water.*

4:1 Verses 4:1-6 are numbered 3:33-38 in Hebrew text.   4:2 The meaning of the Hebrew is uncertain.   4:5 Or *for they have thrown insults in the face of.*   4:7 Verses 4:7-23 are numbered 4:1-17 in Hebrew text.   4:12 The meaning of the Hebrew is uncertain.   4:23 Or *Each carried his weapon in his right hand.* Hebrew reads *Each his weapon the water.* The meaning of the Hebrew is uncertain.

NOTES

4:1 [3:33] While ch 3 outlines the organization of the people working on the wall around Jerusalem, ch 4 describes the opposition of outsiders to the rebuilding of the wall. The chapter divisions between 3 and 4 are not the same in the English and Hebrew texts. In the Hebrew text, ch 3 has 38 verses, continuing until what is 4:6 in the English. In the Hebrew, the initial negative response to the building of the wall (4:1-6) is part of ch 3, and ch 4 does not begin until 4:7.

Sanballat was very angry. . . . He flew into a rage and mocked the Jews. The reaction of Sanballat was emotional, aggressive, and sarcastic. Three words describe his strong negative reaction: *kharah* [TH2734, ZH3013] (be hot, angry); *ka'as* [TH3707, ZH4087] (be irritated, enraged); and *la'ag* [TH3932, ZH4352] (scorn). These responses do not describe a slight irritation that he kept to himself; these were open expressions of hostility to gain the support of friends and the sympathetic military leaders in Samaria (these same military leaders probably stopped the wall construction in Ezra 4:12-23).

4:2 [3:34] *Do they think they can build the wall in a single day by just offering a few sacrifices?* More literally, "Will they restore/abandon for themselves? Will they sacrifice? Will they finish in a day?" The NLT attempts to convey the force of Sanballat's disjointed ridicule by adding logical connectors. But commentators have understood this question in various ways because they interpret the verb *'azab* [TH5800A, ZH6441] variously as "leave, abandon" (Blenkinsopp 1988:242), "restore" (NIV; NASB; RSV; Fensham 1982:180), or "commit" (Williamson 1985:213-214), and some think *lahem* [TH3807.1/1992.1, ZH4200/2157] (for themselves) should be emended to read *le'lohim* [TH430, ZH466] ("for God"; see Williamson 1985:214; Blenkinsopp 1988:243). All of these solutions are somewhat problematic, but if one avoids emending the text, it appears that Sanballat was asking if the people were going to "leave to themselves" this whole project. In other words, in parallelism with the first question, he asked, "Do they think they can leave the building of the wall to themselves, and actually finish it?" The ridicule about offering sacrifices probably mocks the people's ability to complete the wall and offer a "foundation sacrifice" as they dedicate it (12:43; Clines 1984:159).

4:4 [3:36] *May their scoffing fall back on their own heads.* The scoffing of Sanballat and Tobiah is contrasted with the prayer of Nehemiah, but the text does not indicate exactly when this prayer was spoken (immediately or some days later), nor does it describe the specific setting (at the Temple or right there by the wall). Did Nehemiah publicly interrupt Tobiah and loudly pray God's judgment on him at that moment, or was this Nehemiah's private prayer in his closet at home? The text does not answer these questions directly, but the practice of Nehemiah elsewhere in the book was to cry out immediately to God in brief, private prayers when he needed God's help (2:4; 5:19; 6:14; 13:14, 22, 29, 31).

4:5 [3:37] *Do not blot out their sins, for they have provoked you to anger.* They should be held accountable for opposing God's work in Jerusalem; their sins should not be overlooked or ignored. Nehemiah did not get involved with personal revenge because vengeance belonged to God (Deut 32:35). This was not some vendetta; this was a request for God's justice to respond appropriately to those who "have provoked you to anger." "You," however, is implied and not stated in the Hebrew; therefore, Fensham (1982:181) and Myers (1965:121) translate the passage as "they have insulted the builders." But the use of the prepositional phrase "in front of the builders" in this same verse rules out the possibility that they are the objects of the verb, thus one must infer that God is the one insulted. Many years earlier, when Goliath insulted the name of God, David also believed that God should destroy Goliath for reproaching God's name (1 Sam 17:26, 45-46). The enemies of man can mock the work of believers and get away with it, but when they provoke and defy God, he will hold them accountable for their open insults.

4:6 [3:38] *the wall was completed to half its height.* Nehemiah did not state how long it took the people to get the wall halfway done (this was the easier part, so it probably did not take too long), but he recognized this as a significant accomplishment. The text does not say whether this is half the length or half the height, but most assume it refers to the height of the wall. If so, then at this point the wall gave the people basic security from most outsiders.

for the people had worked with enthusiasm. Interestingly, Nehemiah did not credit himself, his excellent organizational skills, his comprehensive planning, or his leadership ability for this success. He knew that everything was dependent on the people's willingness and determination to work hard (lit., "the people had a heart to work"). This level of success—completing half the wall—was proof that God intervened and answered his prayer. The comments of their enemies failed to discourage the workers.

4:7 [1] *heard that the work was going ahead.* One gets the impression that the enemies of the Jews (from the north [Sanballat], the south [the Arabs], the west [Ashdodites], and the east [Ammonites]) were surprised by the speed at which the people worked. The workers in Jerusalem did not stop their efforts or slow down; instead, the breaches where the wall was destroyed were "repaired and sealed" ('arukah [TH724, ZH776], "to heal, mend," as in Isa 58:8; Jer 8:22; and lehissathem [TH5640, ZH6258], "to seal, fill up"). This substantial progress toward the goal of completing the wall infuriated these opponents and signaled the need for them to take a more aggressive posture to prevent the completion of the project.

4:8 [2] *They all made plans to come and fight . . . throw us into confusion.* Making plans was a coordinated act of "conspiring, dealing falsely" (*qashar* [TH7194, ZH8003]) in order to launch a joint attack that would cause confusion "to him" (*lo* [TH3807.1/2050.2, ZH4200/2257]). In this case the sg. pronoun "him" treats the workers as a single, unified group. Some think "to him" means "to it," that is, "to Jerusalem" (but the city would be treated as a fem., not a masc. word), while others change the text to "to me" or "to us" (Williamson 1985:221).

4:10 [4] *the people of Judah began to complain. . . ."We will never be able to build the wall by ourselves."* The project had external problems from foreign opposition, but the internal ones were much more serious. The complaints of the workers were expressed in a song of four lines, following the poetic rhythm of a lament (Fensham 1982:185). This song (cf. NASB) revealed the people's anxiety about the size of the task and their own limited abilities to accomplish the goal. This complaint may have arisen because (1) the initial excitement had worn off, (2) the workers were tired and worn out, (3) the big rocks from the rubble of the wall now had to be hoisted higher on the wall (which meant that the work would go much slower and require greater effort), or (4) they felt that they would not be able to complete the work. The Hebrew text does not include the phrase "by ourselves." This interpretive addition in the NLT suggests that the people thought they needed others to help them complete the wall. Interestingly, there was no call to God for help, or statement of trust, or claim of confidence in God—these were traditional parts of laments (see Westermann 1965:64-69; Allen 2003:108). Although we cannot conclude that the people did not petition God, trust God, or have confidence in him (this would be arguing from silence), it is significant that none of the more positive aspects of the lament are included in this narrative account.

4:12 [6] *again and again.* Lit., "ten times."

They will come from all directions and attack us! Lit., "from every place where you turn upon us"; this statement is confusing because no explicit verb (such as "attack") seems connected to "upon us." No solution is totally satisfactory, and as a result of the confusion, the major translations differ considerably. E.g., the KJV has "From all places whence ye shall return unto us *they will be upon you*"; RSV has "From all the places where they live, they will come up against us"; while NIV has "Wherever you turn, they will attack us"; and NASB has "They will come up against us from every place where you may turn." The Old Greek translation of the Hebrew has "They are coming against us from all sides." The statement does not seem to be a quotation of what the enemies of the Jews were saying, but the advice the neighboring Jewish people were giving to their friends in Jerusalem. In contrast to some of the translations, the Hebrew text says nothing about what "they" will do, but focuses on what "you" (the people in Jerusalem) should do. Two approaches are possible: (1) These words are an exhortation for the people working in Jerusalem to return to their villages to avoid being killed in the upcoming enemy attack. The friends and relatives of the workers were saying, "You must return to us" (Williamson 1985:220-221; Blenkinsopp 1988:246). This translation puts "from every place" with the preceding material: Their neighbors "from every place" came to them and told them about these plots. With this interpretation, "from every place" is connected to the warnings that come 10 times from everywhere (see previous note). Of course, if all the workers from outside of Jerusalem left, the city could not be protected, and the rebuilding of the walls would never be finished. (2) An alternative approach (as in NLT, NIV) is to imply an understood verb "attack" before the last word in the sentence, thus giving, "From every place where you turn, they will *attack* us." This warning would create fear of multiple attacks from all sides of the city that would overwhelm those defending Jerusalem. In both interpretations the purpose of the statement was to stop the rebuilding.

4:13 [7] *I placed armed guards behind the lowest parts of the wall.* At this crucial point, Nehemiah stepped forward to counteract any internal discouragement about this external threat. He did not want the wishes of concerned relatives (4:12) to discourage his workforce and cause these people to leave the city. Nehemiah's plan of action in this verse is not totally clear. Some interpretations envision this as (1) a description of the enemy, that is, "They will station themselves" (Brockington 1969:148); (2) others (cf. NLT) see this as a placement of Jewish troops along the lower and weaker portions of the wall (the vulnerable spots) to protect it; but (3) this probably refers to Nehemiah gathering the people in an open square near a low part of the wall so that he could conduct a military review by families. This was done so that their opponents outside the wall could easily see how many people were available to defend the city, thus discouraging them from acting (Williamson 1985:222). At this gathering Nehemiah reviewed the troops, encouraged them (4:14), and sent them back to work on the wall (4:15ff).

4:14 [8] *Then as I looked over the situation.* Nehemiah's action of "looking" is unqualified, though the NASB implies he "saw their fear" and the NLT adds "the situation." It may be that Nehemiah "saw, viewed, reviewed" (Clines 1984:163) the mustered troops that were gathered in the open square and then "arose" and gave them a military pep talk before he sent them to their posts.

4:16 [10] *coats of mail. The leaders stationed themselves behind the people.* The role of the "leaders" (*sarim* [TH8269, ZH8569]) is unclear in the Hebrew syntax, where it is positioned as another item in the preceding list; this, however, is illogical. Some (e.g., Clines 1984:163; Blenkinsopp 1988:250) omit the word as a dittography for "coats of mail" (*shiryonim* [TH8302, ZH9234]) since they have a similar spelling, but it seems natural for there to be "military officials" or "captains" (Allen 2003:108) who were in charge of groups of armed men. Nehemiah could not control everything by himself, so captains were put in charge of large areas so that there was an effective chain of command to organize a quick response to any potential dangers.

4:17-18 [11-12] *one hand supporting their load and one hand holding a weapon.* The "laborers" (4:17) were "carriers" of rocks and fill from the rubble outside the wall. Since they were more vulnerable to attack, they were armed and ready to respond. Those repairing the wall from the inside were more secure (4:18). They used both hands for rebuilding, but they were armed with swords and ready to fight if needed. A trumpeter stayed with Nehemiah so that he could sound the alarm and direct workers if the city was attacked.

4:20 [14] *When you hear the blast of the trumpet.* Some suppose that there were several trumpeters stationed around the wall (Josephus *Antiquities* 11.5.8 [11.177] places the trumpeters every 500 feet) or criticize this organizational system as a "dubious strategy" (Clines 1984:164). These criticisms are unnecessary because the size of the city was rather small and it would not take long for Nehemiah to be notified and redirect the resources of the city through one trumpeter. In addition, any large force of troops would be watched for hours as they prepared for their attack.

4:23 [17] *We carried our weapons with us at all times, even when we went for water.* In the Hebrew, this line is difficult. Literally it says "each one his weapon water," which does not make much sense. Fensham (1982:184, 190), Williamson (1985:223-224), and Clines

(1984:165) make the attractive suggestion that "water" may be a scribal error (involving both a Yodh-He and a Nun-Mem interchange) for "right hand," which is spelled somewhat similarly (that is, every man had his weapon at his right hand). The KJV follows the Latin Vulgate and interprets these words to mean that they kept their weapons on except when they were washing, but this is an unlikely meaning for these words.

COMMENTARY

The previous chapter gave a summary of who worked where, but this chapter describes what actually happened during the process of building the walls of Jerusalem. The walls were not completed without some opposition and a lot of sacrifice. Sanballat the Horonite was unhappy when Nehemiah arrived (see 2:10), his anger intensified when he heard about the rebuilding of Jerusalem (2:19), and it grew harsher and more cynical when the work actually began (4:1).

When Sanballat spoke to the Jewish people in Jerusalem, his words had an intimidating effect because the Samaritan military leaders were standing beside Sanballat, silently supporting him (Kidner 1979:90). The local Arabs (including Tobiah), Ammonites, and Ashdodites (see 4:7) were among the friends that Sanballat could muster as militant supporters. Similar strong objections brought a stop to work on the walls some years earlier when the Jews began to build the Temple (Ezra 4:4-5; 5:3-9) and after the first attempt to rebuild the walls (Ezra 4:12-23), so Sanballat thought it might work again. Since the Jewish people were actually rebuilding the wall (the participle form of this verb ["were building"] indicates the action was going on) and not just talking about what they might do, Sanballat knew he must act quickly to energize a broad coalition against this rebuilding activity. If he could not reverse the Persian decision to allow this rebuilding, at least he could slow down the progress. He could put pressure on some Jews so that they would not help in the rebuilding. Plus he could create an atmosphere of fear and discouragement. A good blast of psychological warfare was all it would take to stop some people who were not fully convinced of this idea and were not totally committed to doing the hard work.

Sanballat's scornful mockery (4:1-2) communicated his disrespect for the "pipe dreams" of Nehemiah and the initial accomplishments of the Jewish workers. The NLT summarizes Sanballat's comments in three questions, but the individual parts of his comments are more clearly seen if they are arranged in the five questions found in the NIV, NASB, and RSV. The first question ("What does this bunch of poor, feeble Jews think they're doing?") minimized the abilities of the Jews who were working on the walls. In one sense Sanballat was right (Breneman 1993:193); the Jewish people were a "feeble" bunch because they were not rich, powerful, or many in number. But on the other hand, his sarcastic question implied that these factors would prevent Nehemiah's workers from accomplishing anything. That assumption was patently false, for even a few dedicated workers can bring about great changes if they are fully committed to a common goal.

Sanballat's second question ("Will they restore their wall?" NIV; but see note on 4:2) questioned the people's ability to organize and accomplish this backbreaking job of lifting up large stones to erect a tall, strong wall. Sanballat was sowing seeds of doubt.

The third question asked if the people would offer sacrifices, which seems odd and inappropriate since the altar and Temple were already in use long before these events. Therefore, Sanballat must be either (1) mocking the offering of a foundation sacrifice when they began the work on the wall (Brockington 1969:146; Clines 1984:159), (2) scorning the idea that they will ever finish the work and dedicate it with a sacrifice (see 12:43; Yamauchi 1988:702), or (3) laughing at their general religious fervor and trust in God whom they have appeased with a sacrifice.

The fourth question was, "Do they think they can build the wall in a single day?" This question dealt with the amount of time it would take to finish the task of building the wall. Maybe this question was an attempt to discourage the people by reminding them that this was a big job that would take a long time. He was questioning their dedication to keep at the task and their ability to finish it. It would not be finished in just a few hours. Were they up to the task?

The fifth question ("Do they actually think they can make something of stones from a rubbish heap?") directed attention to the broken and burned stones that the people were using to restore the walls. Instead of taking the time and effort to quarry new stones and then transport them to Jerusalem, it was quicker and easier to reuse the ones available in the rubble of the destroyed wall. When the fire that destroyed Jerusalem heated these stones, some would crack, break, crumble, or become discolored. Sanballat was questioning if there was any more useful life in those stones. Could they serve any good purpose again? How could any respectable builder think of using such poor-quality stones? He was mocking the quality of their work.

Joining in the fun of mocking the Jewish efforts, Tobiah ridiculed the quality of the wall they were building. He sarcastically claimed that it was so weak and poorly built that a small animal like a fox would cause the wall to fall over if it walked on it (4:3). He was mocking the stability of the wall and implying that a breach in the wall could be established by just a little effort. These enemies of the Jews were trying to discourage Nehemiah and his workers by laughing at what they were doing. Hopefully Nehemiah would just give up on this ill-conceived project.

Nehemiah wouldn't give up. He prayed that God would stop those who opposed his will for Jerusalem (4:4-5). He requested that God would bring on his enemies what they inappropriately wished on others. Using a wordplay, Nehemiah asked God to pay attention to how the Jews and God's own name were contemptuously "scoffed at" (*buzah* [TH939, ZH999]) with taunts (cf. 1:3). In divine justice God should cause these evil wishes to bring about the "despised captivity" (*bizzah* [TH961, ZH1023]) of those who spoke these evil words. Certainly it was not wrong to ask God to destroy his enemies and make his glorious name and power known to those who sinfully and arrogantly opposed his plans (see further discussion near the end of this commentary section).

Nehemiah 4:6-23 describes how Nehemiah and the laborers responded to those who opposed their successful rebuilding efforts. The pattern is typical: (1) The enemies oppose what is being done, (2) God's people pray, (3) the people work hard in spite of danger because they believe God will help them, and (4) the enemy's plans are frustrated (Blenkinsopp 1988:247). The enemies hoped that the threat of attack on Jerusalem would create divided opinions among the workers and thus subvert their efforts to build the walls. Confusion would be created if some wanted to quit, some were overcome by fear, or if some wanted to defend the city but not continue building the wall.

The people had a twofold response: They prayed to God and guarded the city (4:9). Dependence on God and a complementary use of their own natural abilities gave a balanced approach to this threat. Trust in God and good management of human resources went hand in hand, for without God, people can do nothing. Yet it usually takes responsible and faithful people who consistently serve day after day, night after night, to accomplish God's work. It is important not to overemphasize either aspect so that God's work is not turned into a series of miracles that do not require his servants' action or a series of human accomplishments that do not require God's action. Some attribute this policy to Nehemiah's brilliant leadership (Breneman 1993:196; Kidner 1979:91), but the text is silent on this matter. The text does not enshrine Nehemiah in a cult of personality. He was just doing what made the most sense in his circumstances.

The enemies said, "We will swoop down on them and kill them and end their work" (4:11). Continual threats of physical harm by their enemies (probably the same people mentioned in 4:2 and 4:7) exacerbated the hopelessness of the workers. Their enemies were planning a secret invasion of the city (lit., "They will not know, they will not see"; 4:11), a surprise movement of soldiers when no one would expect it, a violent attack that would kill some people. They were creating fear and paranoia for the purpose of stopping the work on the wall. It is not clear if these were just empty threats to intimidate the Jewish workers or if their opponents actually intended to carry out these plans. Regardless of the intent, these words had a tremendous demoralizing effect on the people working in Jerusalem. The opponents of the Jews did not just verbally threaten the people at Jerusalem; they also would tell their plans to act against Jerusalem to Jewish people living in the towns around Jerusalem. Then the Jewish people outside Jerusalem would come and warn those working on the walls of Jerusalem (4:12).

But Nehemiah encouraged the people to stand against their enemies, saying, "Don't be afraid of the enemy! Remember the Lord, who is great and glorious, and fight for your brothers" (4:14). Nehemiah knew that the strongest motivation for hope in this difficult situation was the power and glory of God (cf. 2 Chr 32:7-8). The people did not need to be controlled by fear, for many times in the past God's power had delivered his people from mighty nations (see Exod 14:13-14; Deut 8:1-3; 20:3-4; Josh 10:25). Another key motivation for courage was that the people were doing this to protect their own homes, their families, and their friends. Thus, the hard work and bold resistance was worth the effort. It was for the right cause (for their families and God) and worthy of their effort (because God would fight for them). They should not give up and go home because of a little conflict or some hypothetical threats. Running away from the situation may be the easy way out of a problem, but it was not God's way. God's power is often marvelously displayed in those situations where his people are not able to do what needs to be done in their own strength.

The prayers of the people (4:9), the 24-hour patrol (4:9), the open display of force (4:13), and the people's confidence in God's protection had a negative effect on Judah's enemies. When these opponents heard that their plans of a surprise attack had leaked out (4:11) and that Nehemiah had prepared the city to defend itself (4:13), they abandoned this strategy. Nehemiah attributed this change of plans to human and divine causes: From a human perspective, people who lived near Judah's enemies (they became his military intelligence unit) were responsible and courageous enough to immediately communicate vital information to Nehemiah so that he was prepared for whatever might happen. Since Nehemiah knew what was going on, the enemy's plans had little chance of success. In the larger perspective, Nehemiah recognized God's involvement in frustrating these evil plans, though no explanation is provided. They had asked for God's help (4:9), and the enemy had given up. Certainly God had something to do with this sudden reversal. Nehemiah realized that God was actively involved with the daily, mundane affairs of his people, even though it was not in the form of some earth-shattering miracle. Nehemiah did not attribute this newfound hope to his own great leadership; he gave the credit to God and to the people who faithfully served him. Nehemiah preferred to talk about what "we" did, rather than what "I" did.

The last paragraph of the chapter (4:16-23) describes the working conditions that existed for the next several weeks, until the wall was finished. Half of the personal guard provided for the governor, Nehemiah, were withdrawn from the work of building, given a full array of armor, and assigned to support those on guard duty around the wall. This gave the workers on the wall a sense of security because they knew others were watching out for them. It also meant they could focus their attention on building the wall and not be constantly looking over their shoulder to see if an enemy was approaching. Having well-armed troops on guard would also discourage any enemy scouts who were looking for a good place to attack the city.

Nehemiah explained to the people that "the work is very spread out, and we are widely separated from each other along the wall. When you hear the blast of the trumpet, rush to wherever it is sounding. Then our God will fight for us!" (4:19-20). Nehemiah's purpose in saying this was to inform everyone ("nobles and officials and all the people") of the strategic plan, to encourage people to rely on one another, to assure anyone who might be attacked that a clear method of getting help was in place, and to challenge everyone to put their faith in God. Nehemiah's exhortation draws on the holy war traditions of Israel (Exod 14:14; Deut 1:30; 20:4; Josh 10:14; 23:10; 2 Chr 32:8), which demonstrate that God, the Divine Warrior, has repeatedly defeated the enemies of his people. When God fights on your side, victory is sure. This shows that the battle to rebuild Jerusalem had spiritual implications. If the leaders of God's people did not have this kind of confident faith in God's power, how would the people ever be convinced to trust God to defeat their enemies?

The job was enormous, but the people were so committed that they worked from sunup to sundown. The threat on the city was so great that a 24-hour guard was maintained. To make this work, Nehemiah needed people to be available to take a few hours of guard duty at night, plus work in the daytime. That was only possible if men who lived in the surrounding communities temporarily made their homes within Jerusalem. This change would also mean that people would not have to walk each day from their homes to Jerusalem, so more work could be accomplished. Of course, this also meant that the homes and fields of these men would be left somewhat unprotected while they were working in Jerusalem.

Nehemiah made sure that he and his close associates set a good example for the rest of the people. They were not some elite group of privileged people who could pamper themselves while the rest of the group slaved away at the wall. They wore their fighting clothes to bed so they would always be ready to fight if they were called. They were alert at all times, carrying their weapons when others might relax, even refusing to put them down when they went to get a drink at the spring.

In summary, this section deals with how believers should respond to opposition. Although today some believers experience only subtle rejection, Christians in Muslim countries are often ostracized from their families, and some are even killed. In modern Western culture, the secular push in the media for tolerance of all viewpoints sometimes casts ridicule and reproach on anyone who stands up against gay rights, abortion, or the high level of violence and sexual immorality on television. Believers who express their opinions can find themselves in just as hostile an environment as Nehemiah's. People in the past and today sometimes get angry about what believers are doing (4:1), mock them (4:2-3), and make plans to fight against them (4:7-8). Some might despise, taunt, and threaten to harm believers who do not think the same way they do. Earlier, those who had opposed the Temple rebuilding cried out for acceptance of their views (Ezra 4:2), but intolerantly opposed anyone who did not operate within their frame of reference. How did Nehemiah and his fellow laborers respond to such opposition?

Three responses are found in chapter 4. First, Nehemiah and his followers prayed (4:4-5, 9); second, they took wise and practical steps to protect themselves (4:15-20); and third, they recognized God's sovereign control of history. Their prayers were directed to God (4:4, 9), their only hope for deliverance. Nehemiah boldly asked God to bring a curse on the wicked people who opposed God. He concluded that God should not forgive their sins but should judge them in righteousness. Because this kind of talk does not sound like Jesus' teaching about loving your enemies (Matt 5:43-48), many today are uncomfortable with these aggressive requests for God to curse these enemies. Jesus even forgave those who nailed him to the cross (Luke 23:34, a verse present in some but not all manuscripts). Some have thought that Nehemiah had a rather vengeful attitude that is unacceptable for Christians today. To some his attitude seems almost sinful (Throntveit 1992:82).

Yet throughout the Old and New Testaments, God expresses his judgment on oppressors (like the enemies of Nehemiah) who mistreat the weak (like the Jewish people in Jerusalem). Many passages highlight God's grace, but does this mean that his wrath will not be poured out on the ungodly (Rom 1:18; 2:5-11)? Certainly God is not in the business of offering easy forgiveness and cheap grace. Jesus could be very blunt about the hypocrisy of the Pharisees (Matt 23), and Paul could boldly call on God to curse anyone who preaches another gospel (Gal 1:9). The key point is that vengeance belongs to God, not to those who are oppressed (Deut 32:35; Rom 12:19-20). It would be wrong for Nehemiah to avenge his anger by getting back at his oppressors, but there is nothing wrong with asking God to remove those who oppose God's work among his people. The psalmist said that he hated those who hate God (Ps 139:19-22).

Maybe the real problem that many Christians have with this strongly worded prayer is that people do not always hate sin as strongly as God hates sin. People have become so tolerant that most just accept sinners and let them do their own thing without ever confronting them. Is that love? Nehemiah was so committed to doing God's work in Jerusalem that he boldly prayed for God to remove any hindrances that might get in the way. He was asking God to give those who were opposing God's plans their just reward and not let them get away with their sinful deeds. He was asking God to fight against their present enemies just as he fought against their Egyptian enemies long ago.

The second thing Nehemiah and his followers did was to take wise, practical steps to ensure they were doing everything they could do to protect themselves and continue the work on the wall (4:6, 9, 13, 15-23). This shows that they believed they were responsible to do their part and that God would take care of the rest. They did not sit back and wait for a miracle but got to work. A delicate balance is needed. It would be wrong to depend on one's own efforts to solve all these problems, but it would be wrong to think that God was going to magically solve all these problems without his people doing anything. Hard work was combined with trusting prayers to God (4:9), with a confident assurance of God's frustration of the enemy's plans (4:15), and with faith that God would fight for them (4:20). These examples indicate that the people of Yehud believed that God would work through their efforts. God works behind the scenes, in the midst of the crisis, and he sovereignly controls what goes on among the unseen spiritual powers that influence each human character.

The third thing that Nehemiah and his workers did was to recognize God's providential control of human affairs. In the midst of this crisis when everyone was overworked and tired, Nehemiah gained inner strength for himself and encouragement for his workers by remembering the central role that God played in their lives. God would decide if the mocking enemy would face his just wrath (4:4-5). God would decide if these opponents would attack the city and create confusion (4:8, 15). If there was a military confrontation, God would decide who would win the battle. If a well-trained company of troops attacked the city, these hardworking builders were not left without hope. This was God's city, it was God's reproach that they were removing, and it was God who would be glorified when they dedicated the walls. When people work for God, he has a vested interest in getting his work accomplished.

◆   ## 3. Confrontation and the fear of God overcome internal opposition (Neh 5:1-19)

About this time some of the men and their wives raised a cry of protest against their fellow Jews. ²They were saying, "We have such large families. We need more food to survive."

³Others said, "We have mortgaged our fields, vineyards, and homes to get food during the famine."

⁴And others said, "We have had to borrow money on our fields and vineyards to pay our taxes. ⁵We belong to the same family as those who are wealthy, and our children are just like theirs. Yet we must sell our children into slavery just to get enough money to live. We have already sold some of our daughters, and we are

helpless to do anything about it, for our fields and vineyards are already mortgaged to others."

⁶When I heard their complaints, I was very angry. ⁷After thinking it over, I spoke out against these nobles and officials. I told them, "You are hurting your own relatives by charging interest when they borrow money!" Then I called a public meeting to deal with the problem.

⁸At the meeting I said to them, "We are doing all we can to redeem our Jewish relatives who have had to sell themselves to pagan foreigners, but you are selling them back into slavery again. How often must we redeem them?" And they had nothing to say in their defense.

⁹Then I pressed further, "What you are doing is not right! Should you not walk in the fear of our God in order to avoid being mocked by enemy nations? ¹⁰I myself, as well as my brothers and my workers, have been lending the people money and grain, but now let us stop this business of charging interest. ¹¹You must restore their fields, vineyards, olive groves, and homes to them this very day. And repay the interest you charged when you lent them money, grain, new wine, and olive oil."

¹²They replied, "We will give back everything and demand nothing more from the people. We will do as you say." Then I called the priests and made the nobles and officials swear to do what they had promised.

¹³I shook out the folds of my robe and said, "If you fail to keep your promise, may God shake you like this from your homes and from your property!"

The whole assembly responded, "Amen," and they praised the LORD. And the people did as they had promised.

¹⁴For the entire twelve years that I was governor of Judah—from the twentieth year to the thirty-second year of the reign of King Artaxerxes*—neither I nor my officials drew on our official food allowance. ¹⁵The former governors, in contrast, had laid heavy burdens on the people, demanding a daily ration of food and wine, besides forty pieces* of silver. Even their assistants took advantage of the people. But because I feared God, I did not act that way.

¹⁶I also devoted myself to working on the wall and refused to acquire any land. And I required all my servants to spend time working on the wall. ¹⁷I asked for nothing, even though I regularly fed 150 Jewish officials at my table, besides all the visitors from other lands! ¹⁸The provisions I paid for each day included one ox, six choice sheep or goats, and a large number of poultry. And every ten days we needed a large supply of all kinds of wine. Yet I refused to claim the governor's food allowance because the people already carried a heavy burden.

¹⁹Remember, O my God, all that I have done for these people, and bless me for it.

5:14 That is, 445–433 B.C.   5:15 Hebrew *40 shekels* [1 pound, or 456 grams].

NOTES

5:1 *a cry of protest against their fellow Jews.* The date of this strong protest is not given. Though the event can naturally fit into the period during which the people were building the wall (Yamauchi 1988:706; Kidner 1979:94), some place it much later (McConville 1985:96; Williamson 1985:235). Neufeld (1953–1954:203-204) argues for a date shortly before the completion of the wall (on the 25th day of Elul according to 6:15) because that was the time when people harvested their crops and were expected to pay their debts. The confrontation and resolution of the tension is described in 5:1-13, and then a brief additional justification of Nehemiah's unselfishness is appended in 5:14-19.

5:2 *We need more food to survive.* Lit., "Let us take grain and let us eat so that we may survive." It appears that some poor families had nothing to eat and were facing starvation. Large families needed "grain, food" (*dagan* [TH1715, ZH1841]), not money, so that they could eat and survive. Something had to give. If one places these events in the midst of the building of the wall, this problem had serious implications for Nehemiah's rebuilding efforts. Either (1) someone would have to come to the aid of these poor families by giving them food to eat, or (2) the poor men who were working on the wall would have to go home to work to support their families and stop rebuilding the walls. One can assume that those crying out in 5:1-2 did not have any land to mortgage in order to get some food for their families.

5:3 *We have mortgaged our fields, vineyards, and homes.* Joining the chorus of complaints was a group of small landowners who had mortgaged everything they owned just to survive. These mortgages (a "bartering," *'orebim* [TH6148, ZH6842], of land for food) were like a cancer that grew year after year. Now these people were so far in debt that they were in danger of losing their family inheritance. A famine had exacerbated the problem—when there was a scarcity of grain, the price of food would naturally rise and make it less affordable for the poor.

5:4 *We have had to borrow . . . to pay our taxes.* A third complaint came from landowners who were having difficulty paying their taxes. Although the people were contributing many hours of hard labor to rebuild Jerusalem, the Persians did not cancel the royal tribute that was due at harvest time. It is estimated (Yamauchi 1988:707) that the Persians collected 20 million darics a year, and a good part of that was from the annual land tax. So much was collected that the Greek conqueror Alexander the Great found over 270 tons of gold and 1,200 tons of silver stored in the treasury at Susa when he took the city (Yamauchi 1988:707). Dandamayev (1969:308) refers to similar problems throughout the Persian Empire: "Documents from Babylonia show that many inhabitants of this satrapy had to mortgage their fields and orchards to get silver for payment of taxes to the king. In many cases they were unable to redeem their property, and became landless hired laborers; sometimes they were compelled to give away their children into slavery." Loan sharks probably exacerbated the problem because they sometimes charged as much as 40 percent interest on loans, instead of the more usual 20 percent (Olmstead 1948:297-299).

5:7 *After thinking it over.* The Niphal verb is probably reflexive, yielding the rendering, "I mastered my heart," or, "I took counsel with myself." It is possible that the verb may be derived from an Aramaic or Akkadian root (cf. Cohen 1978:143).

I spoke out against. The verb *'aribah* [TH7378, ZH8189] means "to contend, bring legal charges" against someone. This was not a casual conversation where a group of people got together to chat about a minor problem. This was a confrontational meeting where Nehemiah accused the errant parties (the nobles and officials) directly with a legal charge of error. Nevertheless, he also needed the support and cooperation of the wealthy leaders in Jerusalem, so he had to be both firm and fair, corrective and redemptive, in his approach to this problem.

You are hurting your own relatives by charging interest. We do not know how long after the complaint arose that Nehemiah took this action. He could not do anything about removing Persian taxation, nor could he change the weather and end the famine. What he could do was alleviate some of the oppression caused by the wealthy Jews in Jerusalem.

According to some translations (NIV, NLT, NASB, RSV), the evil he attacked was the sin of "charging interest," but the normal Hebrew word for "interest, usury" is not used in this verse. Instead, Nehemiah used the word "loan, lending for a pledge" (*masha'* [TH4855, ZH5391]; see Deut 24:10) to describe the loans the borrowers were obligated to repay the wealthy (Clines 1984:168; Blenkinsopp 1988:259; Williamson 1985:233). The problem with these loans was that the pledges taken to insure them made it impossible for the borrowers to ever pay back the loan. Nehemiah said the lenders should return the property they had taken in pledge for these loans.

5:11 *repay the interest you charged.* The word translated "interest" is literally "the hundredth of the money," which some interpret to be one percent per month (Yamauchi 1988:709). Since this figure is far below the rate charged elsewhere in the Persian Empire at this time, the term "a hundredth" might just be a general way of referring to the interest charged, meaning "the percentage" (Williamson 1985:233) rather than a specific rate of interest. Blenkinsopp (1988:257) indicates that the interest rate at Elephantine in Egypt at this time was around 60–75 percent, so one percent per month (equaling 12 percent per year) would be extremely low. Maloney (1974:1-20) found 20 percent as the lowest rate charged in any financial documents he found.

5:12 *made the nobles and officials swear.* To ensure that the nobles would keep their word and to reassure those who were fearful of continued enslavement, Nehemiah called some priests to administer oaths concerning what would be done to resolve this problem. The wealthy probably swore self-imprecations like "May the LORD do so to me and more also, if I do not do . . ." (see 1 Sam 3:17), while the priests witnessed their promises. The oath before God put the nobles in danger of God's judgment if they failed to follow through on what they promised.

Some think that the nobles had no choice but to go along with Nehemiah (Blenkinsopp 1988:260; Fensham 1982:195) because Nehemiah, the governor, had the military resources to enforce his wishes, but that seems contrary to the way Nehemiah operated in this context and elsewhere. If that was the situation, there would be no need for the nobles to take oaths, for the governor would enforce this new policy regardless of any commitments made by the wealthy.

5:13 *I shook out the folds of my robe.* The symbolic act of Nehemiah emptying out whatever personal possessions were in the fold of his robe illustrated what God would do to empty the rich people of all their possessions if they failed to keep the oath they had spoken. As Nehemiah performed this symbolic act, he spoke a curse ("If you fail to keep your promise, may God . . .") that explained what the symbolic action meant (Williamson 1985:241).

The whole assembly responded, "Amen," and they praised the LORD. Based on the analogy of Deut 27:15-26, where the people of Israel assented to the oath of the curse by saying "amen," the assembled people accepted Nehemiah's solution to this problem.

5:15 *The former governors.* The character of Nehemiah is understood best if it is contrasted with what was done by other governors before him (probably Samarian and Jewish governors). These earlier governors included Sheshbazzar and Zerubbabel (Ezra 5:14; Hag 1:1), plus Tattenai (Ezra 5:3). Numerous seal impressions discovered on jars at excavations just south of Jerusalem at Ramat Rachel contain the names of Elnatan, Ahzai, and Yeho'ezer, a governor whom some place before Nehemiah. Avigad (1976) dates these finds to the fifth or sixth century BC based on the style of writing, but not all agree with his conclusions.

All governors had the right to expect the people to pay taxes in order to meet the daily food needs for the governor's household, but some of these governors were prone to take advantage of their power and live an extravagant lifestyle. Some commentators interpret the stipend for other expenses and a few luxuries (a pound of silver per day to pay for all these things equaled 40 shekels of silver) as being an amount in addition to the food collected, while others view these 40 shekels as the daily cost of feeding all the people at the governor's court, rather than an additional stipend (cf. Yamauchi 1988:710). No matter how one decides that issue, what is clear is that Nehemiah did not burden the people with even providing his basic needs for food (cf. 5:18). He would not dream of demanding extra luxuries because the people could not afford to pay for even the basics. He also controlled his military and government officials who worked for him. He made sure they followed his example and did not use their power to enrich themselves.

5:16 *working on the wall and refused to acquire any land.* Nehemiah was noted for what he did and did not do. He focused on accomplishing the goal God laid on his heart. He disciplined himself and his government assistants to set their priority on the primary task of building the walls of Jerusalem, not their own enrichment. Interestingly though, we never read about Nehemiah's or his assistants' role in building the wall in ch 3; instead, the attention goes to each family that worked. No doubt there were many other good projects crying out for attention in the province of Yehud, but the restoration of Jerusalem always came first in Nehemiah's thinking. He also could have gotten involved with a little speculation in the real-estate market by buying up forfeited land at a bargain price and then reselling it later for a nice profit. Instead, Nehemiah avoided putting his time and capital into schemes that would serve the sole purpose of enriching himself. If leaders today would exhibit this kind of discipline and focus their energy on the main task that God has given them, they would probably accomplish more, and fewer people would be so cynical about the real motives of religious leaders in general. Servant leaders must do everything possible to focus their efforts on serving others.

5:18 *The provisions I paid for each day.* It is impossible to estimate the cost of these animals and the wine, but it certainly was a large daily expense. Nehemiah paid for these provisions because the people were having so many financial difficulties. One might think that the difficulties refer to the hard work the people were doing on the walls of Jerusalem, but most believe this refers to the difficult burden of taxes the Persians placed on the people (Fensham 1982:198; Williamson 1985:245). Nehemiah did not want to add to this heavy burden but took pity on those who were under significant financial stress (5:1-5). He knew that when a brother was in need, it was important to help him out (cf. 1 John 3:17).

5:19 *Remember, O my God, all that I have done for these people, and bless me for it.* It is possible to interpret this as a selfish prayer for self-glorification or divine enrichment (Eskenazi 1988:151). This invocation for God's favor should rather be seen as a statement that Nehemiah had acted in good faith and with right motives; thus he was confident that God would judge him with favor and provide for all his needs (McConville 1985:102). It is not inappropriate to ask God to supply our needs or to request God's blessing on our efforts. This prayer shows that Nehemiah knew his continued success as governor in these difficult financial times would be dependent on God's continued blessing. One can hardly read the Nehemiah narratives and conclude that Nehemiah was trying to get rich or that he was interested in his own glorification. Nehemiah's request for blessing came out of his desire to continue to graciously provide for the needs of people if God would continue to bless him.

COMMENTARY

In the midst of this major building project, internal strife arose between the different socioeconomic groups of Jewish people in Yehud. Some families felt they were not being treated fairly, so they raised their voices in protest. The objections of both men and women suggest that the problem had something to do with their family interests and responsibilities. The wives were the ones who needed to put food on the table for their families, but apparently some families had no food in the house. If the husbands were away from home working on Jerusalem's walls, it may be that some husbands did not know just how bad things were at home until their wives cried out about their impossible situation.

Although many people were somewhat aware of the economic problems of the poor people in Jerusalem, it was this great cry of complaint that finally got Nehemiah and the larger community to do something about it. The tragedy of the situation was multiplied by the fact that "fellow Jews" were creating this problem for their own people, rather than trying to alleviate the problem.

Two tragedies are described. First, fellow Jews cruelly mistreated their own flesh and blood (lit., "of the same flesh as our brothers," 5:5) rather than showing them compassion. Wealthy Hebrews were the ones who were loaning money for mortgages and taxes, not Persians. Certainly this was not what one should do to his blood brother, and especially not to a brother who was selflessly giving of his time for the good of the community. Didn't these wealthy brothers care at all about their poor relatives? Did they not have any compassion? There is no accusation in the people's complaint that these acts were against the Mosaic law, but later Nehemiah would question whether their behavior was consistent with the legal instructions in Deuteronomy 15 and Leviticus 25:35-46. These laws regulate how a family might redeem a piece of property they had lost because of heavy indebtedness to a creditor and the provision for indebtedness to be canceled every seven years and in the Year of Jubilee. Provision was also made in the law of Moses for a family to pay for its debts by having a child work for a creditor until the debt was fully paid (Exod 21:1-11; 2 Kgs 4:1). But long before people ever got into this kind of serious financial trouble, the wealthy were supposed to be generous and freely give the needy some financial help (Deut 15:7-11). This was not happening in Yehud.

The second tragedy relates to the enslavement of children. When no one would loan more money to these poor people, and they had no money to pay past debts, slavery was inevitable. Logically, it would appear that daughters were sold into slavery first because the sons were needed to help the family work the fields and get out of debt. The literal wording of 5:5 speaks of these children being "subdued" (*kabash* [TH3533, ZH3899]; NLT, "must sell," "already sold"), a word that has sexual overtones in some contexts (Esth 7:8). Some commentators therefore hypothesize that creditors may have satisfied their lust by misusing these young girls (cf. Exod 21:7-11) or that they took some of these girls as second wives (Fensham 1982:192; Williamson 1985:238). But the text does not accuse anyone of mistreating the enslaved daughters; it merely reports the agonizing steps that some families had to take to survive.

When these tragedies were revealed to Nehemiah, they caused a strong negative emotional response (cf. 13:8, 25). How could the people remain united as a community and stay committed to finishing the work of God in Jerusalem if some wealthy workers were enslaving poor workers and driving others into bankruptcy? It appears that this internal crisis was about to abort any attempt to complete the rebuilding of the walls of Jerusalem. Nehemiah's anger was a direct reflection of his deep concern for the poor, as well as his strong commitment to removing this great reproach from God's city. Something had to change.

Three steps were taken to resolve this problem. First, Nehemiah wisely stopped and thought through the implications of the problem. He did not immediately blast the wealthy in a fit of rage and lose their respect. He knew that ranting and raving would not help the situation, but he could not ignore it either. His goal was not just to correct the situation but also to do it in such a way that he would gain the support of everyone. Justice and mercy would have to meet if he was going to restore the unity of the group and get the walls of Jerusalem finished.

Nehemiah decided to call for a public assembly (5:7) to address this issue, rather than deal with it privately. All the parties needed to face this problem and get it settled so that the work of rebuilding could continue. A public demonstration of opinion in favor of Nehemiah's solution would put social pressure on the wealthy to address this problem in a substantive way. At the meeting, Nehemiah said, "We are doing all we can to redeem our Jewish relatives . . . but you are selling them back into slavery" (5:8). Nehemiah made a sharp contrast in order to press his point. On the one hand, there was a group of generous Jewish brethren (including Nehemiah) who were graciously "buying back" (*qanah* [TH7069, ZH7864]) Jewish people who had been forced to sell themselves as slaves to wealthy non-Jewish people because of large debts. These generous people were paying off the debts their brothers owed so that these poor people could be released from the shame of slavery. But all this was for naught, because a few months later these same poor people were being forced back into slavery by wealthy Jewish nobles who were strictly enforcing their legal rights when the poor got behind on their payments. Although there were laws that allowed people to practice debt slavery (Exod 21:1-11; 22:25-27; Lev 25), Nehemiah demonstrated how the ungracious acts of the wealthy were nullifying the gracious acts of those who were helping people out of slavery. Nehemiah emphasized that every attempt should be made to help people avoid slavery. The wealthy should not be pushing their brothers back into such a degrading position and frustrating the efforts of people like Nehemiah. Upon hearing Nehemiah's frustration, the wealthy nobles and officials had no defense to offer.

Nehemiah made three charges against the creditors: They were (1) doing something that was "not right," (2) acting in ways that were not appropriate for those who fear God, and (3) causing foreigners to ridicule the Jews. Nehemiah did not claim they had done something sinful or illegal, which he could have if they were charging fellow Jews interest on loans (see Lev 25:36-37). Instead, the point was that they were not doing what was good for these poor people. Nehemiah seemed to suggest that they should be doing something good by helping their brothers stay out of debt (like Nehemiah and his friends), not forcing them back into slavery.

The fact that they were not doing good raised a question: Did they not fear God (5:9)? Here Nehemiah challenged his fellow Jews to live on a higher plane and act graciously out of religious convictions, rather than acting out of legal rights. Leviticus 25:36, 42-43 called on the people to fear God and help the poor, for God had already delivered his people from slavery in the Exodus. Didn't these people know that God was compassionate to the poor when they cried out for God's help in the past and that he would want his people to also be compassionate to those in slavery (Exod 22:25-27; Pss 9:9; 10:17-18; 146:9)? Finally, Nehemiah reminded the wealthy of the evil things their foreign neighbors would say when they heard that the rich men in Jerusalem were enslaving their poor brothers. The wealthy Jews would get a bad reputation for being ruthless businessmen. Neighboring peoples would ridicule and mock the Jews and their God.

Nehemiah and his relatives were people of some financial means and had legally loaned money and grain to poor people for a pledge. Although this was similar to what others (whom Nehemiah condemned) were doing, apparently Nehemiah and his associates were not collecting on these pledges and were not driving people into slavery (Fensham 1982:195). Nehemiah told the wealthy people, "Let us stop this business of charging interest" (5:10). As suggested in the note on 5:7, charging interest did not seem to be the main problem. What Nehemiah was proposing was that all lenders (including himself) give back the property they had taken in pledge against a debt (Clines 1984:169) so that the poor peasants could go back to work and earn money to pay off their debts. Some think Nehemiah absolved all loans (Fensham 1982:195) or declared an emergency Year of Jubilee (Lev 25; Jer 34:8-22; see Blenkinsopp 1988:259), but there is no evidence that he asked for a total forgiveness for all debts, just the end of seizing property. Since Nehemiah and his associates had been in Jerusalem only a short time, probably none of the poor people they helped had defaulted on a loan and lost everything. Those who had lived in Jerusalem for a long time had already seized property, and this made it impossible for the poor to have a chance to recover from their unfortunate circumstances. This was a time for grace and mercy for poor Israelites within the community, not a time for the wealthy to push their brothers in the community further into hopelessness and slavery.

Nehemiah said that they "must restore their fields . . . and repay the interest" (5:11). He did not quote any legal requirement or ancient Mosaic tradition that demanded the return of forfeited property; he simply appealed to the need to do what was best for the community in this circumstance. He did not set down a new moral or legal standard that regulated all future financial transactions; he simply proposed a means of restoring the health and unity of the community in the difficult circumstances they were facing.

Nehemiah's radical solution of returning seized property plus interest payments was a major financial concession by the wealthy. These sacrifices of financial income show how severe the problem was for the poor people in Jerusalem. Nehemiah's solution was definitely outside the legal requirements, but his bold, outside-the-box approach offered a realistic resolution to a major social and economic problem.

Surprisingly, Nehemiah's proposed solution was accepted, though no clear reason why is given. Possibly Nehemiah's example shamed the nobles who were forcing more people into slavery. Maybe they realized that their own status and the future of Jerusalem was in doubt if they did not remove the burden from the poor so that they could continue to work on the walls of Jerusalem. Perhaps the large assembly of people expressed strong support for Nehemiah and exerted social pressure on the nobles. Credit should primarily be given to God's work in the hearts of these wealthy people (cf. 5:13). By agreeing to this plan, the different social groups were united and restored together as one community. Realizing what God had done in their midst, the whole group praised God, for they knew that this solution was not

accomplished just because Nehemiah made them do this or that; it was the transforming work of a caring God who had convicted some to act positively toward their
poor brothers and stop what they were doing.

A short postscript to the story (5:14-19) describes Nehemiah's financial practices
throughout his first 12 years (445–433 BC) of service as governor of Judah. These
verses demonstrate that Nehemiah's concern for the financial needs of the people
was consistent throughout his rule and was not a temporary concern during a short
period when the problems in 5:1-13 arose. He not only used his own money to help
people out of debt (5:8) and stopped the nobles from oppressing the poor (5:8-13),
but he repeatedly denied himself the financial support (even for basics like food;
see note on 5:15) that he rightfully deserved from the taxes paid by the people of
Yehud. Nehemiah was not motivated by wealth or selfish goals; he sacrificed in
order to lighten the financial burden of others.

Nehemiah's reverence for God (5:15) caused him to be a serving governor who
cared for God's people (not one who lorded it over people; cf. 1 Cor 9). He refused
to put his needs above those of his people. The next verses (5:16-18) outline the
extent of the personal cost for food, paid out of Nehemiah's own pocket. He not
only did not charge for his services as the earlier governors had, but he went in the
hole every day as he fed his servants, officials, and guests out of his own savings.
Although one should not draw out the application from this situation that all godly
leaders should refuse to accept pay for their work, the selflessness of Nehemiah is
an exemplary model that should characterize a leader's service. This is a story that
should be required reading for all Christian workers, television evangelists, and
rich politicians.

Nehemiah was a revolutionary leader. He gave everything and asked for nothing.
What a refreshing perspective! What a precedent he set for leaders today. Probably
most leaders will want to quickly pass over these verses because few can come
close to matching Nehemiah's generosity. Out of his own savings he fed about 150
people every day for 12 years without ever turning in one expense account for reim-
bursement. This not only tells us something about the personal financial resources
Nehemiah had saved up over his years of service as cup-bearer to the king, but also
something about his attitude toward these funds. He was not spending his time
worrying about his retirement; he was concerned about providing for the needs
of others each day. It appears that Nehemiah had the spiritual gift of hospitality, a
gracious gift of service to others in need.

In summary, this chapter gives insights into practical principles of conflict management and shows how important it is to be fiscally responsible throughout life.
Financial problems are frequently a source of conflict in marriages, in the church,
and in governmental budgeting because people have different priorities concerning expenditures, different attitudes toward debt, and different philosophies about
how to address a financial crisis. People also handle conflict differently; some
want to avoid it at all costs, while others seem to love to get into a good fight and
call one another names. This means that the boss at work or the chairman of the
church board must be skilled at handling conflict so that it can be resolved to everyone's satisfaction. Of course, if someone is going to try to solve conflicts relating

to financial issues, it is absolutely necessary for them to be a blameless example of fiscal responsibility and charity.

The conflict described in chapter 5 arose because the people were heavily taxed during a time of famine. There was nothing the poor people could do about the Persian imposition of a heavy tax burden, and they had no control over the weather. Thus, there is no indication that the poor people had acted irresponsibly or wasted their money. The issue is not addressed, and one assumes that Nehemiah would have addressed that problem if the poor were at fault. If one can read between the lines and analyze the behavior of the poor, their greatest mistake was that they took on too much debt. Yet if you and your children have nothing to eat, what other choice do you have but to go further in debt? This crisis arose because the very survival of these poor people was in question. They had nowhere to turn, for some had already sold some of their children into slavery. It is interesting that the complaints of the poor never focus the problem on the rich people who were loaning them money. There is no indication that something illegal was being done. Thus, Nehemiah had to find a solution to alleviate part of the problem, even though he could not solve all their problems (the famine and heavy taxation).

Nehemiah had to address this financial crisis because there would be no chance to complete the rebuilding of the wall of Jerusalem if every poor person went home in order to help get his family out of debt. In this conflict situation, the leader listened carefully and took the complaints seriously. He even became angry about the situation (5:6) because he identified with the plight of the people suffering. He did not blame the victims, but he realized the depth of their distress and was determined to resolve this problem rather than avoid it. Before he did anything rash, he first thought it over thoroughly so that his initial reaction of anger could abate and a reasonable course of action could be devised. When one first hears of a problem, the real solution is not always obvious and one's first thoughts about a solution are not always the best. Nehemiah realized he also could do nothing about the Persian taxes or the famine, but he could do something else that could address part of the problem.

He and a few others were already helping some poor people who were in bad financial straits (5:8), so he already knew one thing that could be done to solve some of the problem. This tells us that Nehemiah was not blind to the problem before the present crisis arose and that he was quietly trying to solve the problem in his own private way. This illustrates the need for leaders to make it their business to know their people and their people's problems so they are not surprised when a crisis arises. A crisis usually does not arise without some warning signals ahead of time, and a wise leader will try to head off a crisis by honestly and practically addressing the issue so that it will not turn into a crisis. Because of the magnitude of the problem, Nehemiah's earlier attempts to solve the financial problems of the poor had failed to meet the needs of everyone.

In order to address the present crisis, Nehemiah confronted the wealthy nobles and officials, challenging them to become part of the solution with him, rather than adding to the problem. First, he confronted them privately, and then he took them to a public gathering of the people to resolve the problem (cf. Matt 18:15-17). He wisely let the group judge the actions of the wealthy, for he needed the support of the nobles to finish the walls of Jerusalem. His confrontation was direct and based on the fact that their actions were making things worse (5:7). In the public meeting, Nehemiah presented his own attempts to solve this problem (5:10) and explained how the wealthy had made the problem worse (5:8). He appealed to their sense of human justice, divine approval, and the shame their action brought on God's people. He then proposed a solution (5:11). Once the wealthy agreed to help solve the problem, priests were brought in to verify that the commitment was sure; thus, their decision was an oath to God, not to Nehemiah (5:12).

Nehemiah's reputation, based on his refusal to accept the governor's daily allowance, which rightly belonged to him (5:14-18), no doubt had a positive effect on the people's willingness to agree with his proposal to solve this problem. His care for people spoke volumes, and his practical wisdom in facing the conflict inspired confidence in his proposal. Conflict resolutions may not solve all the problems a group faces (such as the heavy Persian taxes in Nehemiah's time), but tension can be reduced and unity can be strengthened.

This text also makes an important point about a believer's role in issues of social justice, particularly as it relates to financial loans that lead people into poverty. This passage suggests that it is the responsibility of God's people to assist others in getting out of debt and poverty by giving them money or by forgiving debts. In today's high-charging profit environment, this message runs contrary to most capitalistic goals. But God's people should be motivated by their love for others and their fear of God, rather than their desire for financial profits. Some nations have followed Nehemiah's example in forgiving millions of dollars in foreign debt to poor countries in Africa and South America (cf. Williams 2002:57-74). More nations and more individuals need to follow.

◆   ### 4. God helps the people complete the wall in spite of opposition (Neh 6:1–7:3)

Sanballat, Tobiah, Geshem the Arab, and the rest of our enemies found out that I had finished rebuilding the wall and that no gaps remained—though we had not yet set up the doors in the gates. [2]So Sanballat and Geshem sent a message asking me to meet them at one of the villages* in the plain of Ono.

But I realized they were plotting to harm me, [3]so I replied by sending this message to them: "I am engaged in a great work, so I can't come. Why should I stop working to come and meet with you?"

[4]Four times they sent the same message, and each time I gave the same reply. [5]The fifth time, Sanballat's servant came with an open letter in his hand, [6]and this is what it said:

"There is a rumor among the surrounding nations, and Geshem* tells me it is true, that you and the Jews are planning to rebel and that is why you are building the wall. According to his reports, you plan to be their king. [7]He also reports that you have appointed prophets in Jerusalem to proclaim about you, 'Look! There is a king in Judah!'

"You can be very sure that this report will get back to the king, so I suggest that you come and talk it over with me."

⁸I replied, "There is no truth in any part of your story. You are making up the whole thing."

⁹They were just trying to intimidate us, imagining that they could discourage us and stop the work. So I continued the work with even greater determination.*

¹⁰Later I went to visit Shemaiah son of Delaiah and grandson of Mehetabel, who was confined to his home. He said, "Let us meet together inside the Temple of God and bolt the doors shut. Your enemies are coming to kill you tonight."

¹¹But I replied, "Should someone in my position run from danger? Should someone in my position enter the Temple to save his life? No, I won't do it!" ¹²I realized that God had not spoken to him, but that he had uttered this prophecy against me because Tobiah and Sanballat had hired him. ¹³They were hoping to intimidate me and make me sin. Then they would be able to accuse and discredit me.

¹⁴Remember, O my God, all the evil things that Tobiah and Sanballat have done. And remember Noadiah the prophet and all the prophets like her who have tried to intimidate me.

¹⁵So on October 2* the wall was finished—just fifty-two days after we had begun. ¹⁶When our enemies and the surrounding nations heard about it, they were frightened and humiliated. They realized this work had been done with the help of our God.

¹⁷During those fifty-two days, many letters went back and forth between Tobiah and the nobles of Judah. ¹⁸For many in Judah had sworn allegiance to him because his father-in-law was Shecaniah son of Arah, and his son Jehohanan was married to the daughter of Meshullam son of Berekiah. ¹⁹They kept telling me about Tobiah's good deeds, and then they told him everything I said. And Tobiah kept sending threatening letters to intimidate me.

CHAPTER 7

After the wall was finished and I had set up the doors in the gates, the gatekeepers, singers, and Levites were appointed. ²I gave the responsibility of governing Jerusalem to my brother Hanani, along with Hananiah, the commander of the fortress, for he was a faithful man who feared God more than most. ³I said to them, "Do not leave the gates open during the hottest part of the day.* And even while the gatekeepers are on duty, have them shut and bar the doors. Appoint the residents of Jerusalem to act as guards, everyone on a regular watch. Some will serve at sentry posts and some in front of their own homes."

6:2 As in Greek version; Hebrew reads *at Kephirim.*   6:6 Hebrew *Gashmu,* a variant spelling of Geshem. 6:9 As in Greek version; Hebrew reads *But now to strengthen my hands.*   6:15 Hebrew *on the twenty-fifth day of the month Elul,* of the ancient Hebrew lunar calendar. This day was October 2, 445 B.C.; also see note on 1:1.   7:3 Or *Keep the gates of Jerusalem closed until the sun is hot.*

NOTES

6:1 *Sanballat, Tobiah, Geshem the Arab, and the rest of our enemies.* See the comments on the identity of these enemies of Nehemiah in the notes to 2:10, 19. The "rest of our enemies" may refer to the Ammonites, Ashdodites, and Arabs mentioned in 4:7, plus the followers of Sanballat, Tobiah, and Geshem.

found out. Lit., "it was heard." One common way of introducing a new crisis in classical Hebrew is to indicate that something new "was heard" (*nishma'* [TH8085, ZH9048]; see 2:10, 19; 4:1, 7) by some person.

we had not yet set up the doors. This final clause was added to show that the city was not completely safe from all danger. Since the task of hanging the doors in 3:3, 6, etc., was still in progress, the enemies of Yehud decided to make a final, dramatic attempt to stop the work before it would be too late. The actual installation of the doors in the gates is reported in 7:1.

6:2 *to meet them.* The NLT reports this in narrative style, but the Hebrew records the invitation sent to Nehemiah as a direct quotation in the form of a cohortative exhortation: "Come, let us meet together." No reason for the meeting is provided, but in light of the tension between the parties, one would assume that this was presented as a gesture of peace to develop better relationships between the parties.

at one of the villages in the plain of Ono. The plain of Ono was near Lod (cf. 11:35; Ezra 2:33) and may have been located in the "Valley of Craftsmen." This was in the extreme northwest corner of the province of Yehud or possibly outside the province of Yehud in Sidonian control (Allen 2003:116) about 20 miles northwest of Jerusalem. Some think the letter mentioned a specific city, Hakkepharim or Kepharim (Williamson 1985:248; Fensham 1982:200), that was a neutral site on the border between Yehud and Samaria, though no place is known to have this name. The word means "cities, villages" (a pl. form of the word) and would be an odd name to give to one city.

I realized they were plotting to harm me. Nehemiah smelled a plot in this invitation. Why was he so suspicious? Did he receive information from undercover informants about this plot (Fensham 1982:200), was he prompted by God not to go (Brown 1998:101), or was he suspicious of the distance he would have to travel in dangerous territory to a remote city where he would have little security (Williamson 1985:255)? Since these people opposed his work in the past (2:10, 19; 4:1-3), it only makes good sense that Nehemiah should find this proposal suspect.

6:5 *an open letter.* At this time letters were usually written on leather or papyrus. A letter was made private by rolling up the document and tying it with a string that passed through a clay ball that was made secure with a seal impression. The clay seal would have to be broken to read the letter. An open letter had no seal so others could read the unsealed letter. By leaving the letter unsealed, the authors of the letter were able to spread rumors about rebellion in Jerusalem to many people. This act of intimidation was an attempt to increase the pressure on Nehemiah and force him into a corner. They thought he would have to defend himself against these charges, and of course the best way to do that would be to go to the plain of Ono and confront his accusers directly.

6:7 *appointed prophets . . . "Look! There is a king in Judah!"* Some see Sanballat saying that people were going to anoint Nehemiah as their new messianic king through the support of some prophet that Nehemiah himself planted in the community (Myers 1965:138; Throntveit 1992:86). Others correctly see this interpretation as reading too much into the text (Clines 1984:174). There is no explicit Messiah language here, and Nehemiah was not of Davidic descent, so this interpretation must be rejected. It is possible that there was an extreme nationalistic group in Yehud that wanted to make Nehemiah king (Allen 2003:119), but in the next verse Nehemiah denies this as an actual plan that he would cooperate with.

this report will get back to the king. Sanballat tried to blackmail and bully Nehemiah with these threats: "Either you come to talk to me, or I will see that the king hears about your rebellion." He ended the letter with the same invitation found in the Hebrew of 6:2: "Come, let us meet together."

6:8 *There is no truth. . . . You are making up the whole thing.* Lit., "It has not been like these words which you are speaking . . . from your mind you are inventing." The word *bada'* [TH908, ZH968] is found only here and in 1 Kgs 12:33; it means "to invent, imagine, fabricate."

6:9 *So I continued the work with even greater determination.* These few words (lit., "Now strengthen my hand") are interpreted in two quite different ways. Some imply the words "But I prayed" (NIV) before this clause or add "O God" (RSV, NASB) to make it sound like a prayer. The strongest argument that this is a prayer is the imperative verb *khazaq* [TH2388, ZH2616] (strengthen) that requests help (Yamauchi 1988:713). Others (cf. NLT) either follow the Old Greek translation "*I* strengthened my hands" (Clines 1984:174) or see the verb as an infinitive absolute taking the place of a finite verb (Williamson 1985:249; cf. NLT mg). In light of the short prayer at the end of the next paragraph (6:14) and at the end of other conflict paragraphs (13:14, 22, 29), it makes sense to view this as a prayer to God for greater strength. Although one may see Nehemiah as strong, levelheaded, wise, and principled, he knew that he could stumble at any time if he did not have God to strengthen him. He humbly asked for strengthening in order to know how to wisely handle the sly innuendos and frontal attacks on himself and the work of God. This was psychological warfare (Breneman 1993:211), and he needed strength to navigate the political minefields ahead of him.

6:10 *confined to his home.* The second section (6:10-14) describes another attempt to undermine the work of Nehemiah by creating more fear and intimidation. The word "confined" (*'atsur* [TH6113, ZH6806]) means to be "imprisoned, shut up," but it does not imply the reason why the man Shemaiah was confined to his house. Some think (1) he was confined because he was ritually unclean (cf. 1 Kgs 14:10, KJV), (2) he confined himself as a symbolic act because he also was in danger, (3) he was mentally confined or worried, or (4) he was confined by a prophetic seizure. Blenkinsopp (1988:270-271) catalogues a long list of different guesses. If Shemaiah was unclean, he would not have suggested that they go to the Temple to hide. It is also clear that he was no longer in a prophetic trance. We must admit that we do not know why he was confined, but this issue is not really significant to understanding the story. Maybe he was simply disabled and not able to walk over to Nehemiah's house.

Let us meet together inside the Temple. The reason for meeting in the Temple was for safety from the attack of enemies who might try to kill Nehemiah. According to 6:12, this idea was presented as a prophetic oracle from God to warn Nehemiah. The warning about the enemies coming to kill him was not just an idle guess. The message was in poetic form using 3 + 2 meter, which is characteristic of many laments:

> Let us meet in the house of God,
> in the midst of the Temple;
> and let us shut the doors of the Temple,
> because those coming to kill you,
> are coming to kill you tonight.

Shemaiah's willingness to go with Nehemiah might suggest that he was a priest with access to the Temple, as well as a sympathetic friend who wanted to support Nehemiah in this time of great trial. The suggestion to go for protection to the Temple was based on one of two beliefs: (1) that people could grasp the horns of the altar ("the altar of asylum"—see Exod 21:13; 1 Kgs 1:50-53; 8:64) and escape death at a time when someone wanted to kill them; or (2) that only the priests could go into certain areas of the Temple building; thus, his enemies could not enter beyond those closed doors and find him. Of course, both interpretations were based on the presumption that Nehemiah's enemies would honor Jewish religious customs, which was an unlikely assumption. Ivry (1972:35-45) suggests a bolder plot of taking over control of the Temple to make it his fortress, but this would be an extreme political and religious mistake that would not have appealed to Nehemiah. Shemaiah's suggestion was subtler and seemingly harmless.

6:11 Should someone in my position run from danger? Lit., "Should a man like me flee?" Nehemiah realized that fleeing was not a very brave response. If the governor was controlled by fear and self-preservation, what kind of example would that set for others in the province? He needed to be brave and stand up for the community, not hide. If he had accepted this plan, Nehemiah would have suffered great embarrassment in the eyes of the people. Where was his trust in God's protection?

enter the Temple to save his life. Since Nehemiah was a layman and not a priest, it was not possible for someone like him to enter the Temple to save his life. If he entered unlawfully, he would die or be under God's curse (Num 16:40; 18:7; 2 Chr 26:16-21). (Adonijah had gone to the horns of the altar that was in the courtyard, not the incense altar in the Temple, so his act was permissible [1 Kgs 1:50-53; 8:64].) Of course, if the priests found out that there was any type of inappropriate use of the Temple, Nehemiah would probably lose their support. If he was a eunuch, that would be another reason why he could not go into the Temple (Lev 21:17-20; 22:24; Deut 23:1). However, Yamauchi (1980:132-142) states that not all cup-bearers were eunuchs.

6:12 Tobiah and Sanballat had hired him. The text does not reveal how he found out that his enemies had paid Shemaiah to speak this false prophecy, but maybe Shemaiah confessed the truth. Since Tobiah's name is found first (usually Sanballat is mentioned first), this probably indicates that Tobiah was the instigator of this plot (Fensham 1982:205).

6:14 Noadiah the prophet and all the prophets like her. The narrative says nothing else about this female prophet or the other prophets who were opposing Nehemiah. One must assume that they were cooperating with Tobiah and Sanballat and that they tried to undermine Nehemiah's efforts to rebuild the wall by giving negative prophetic oracles. This indicates that Nehemiah had a considerable amount of opposition within the religious community. Since God knew what they said, he would judge them for the lies they paraded as prophecies from God.

6:15 on October 2. Lit., "on the twenty-fifth of Elul" (cf. NLT mg). The third section in this chapter (6:15–7:3) deals with the completion of the wall amidst further opposition. This was an amazing accomplishment in the relatively short time of 52 days. There is no reason to doubt this figure, though Josephus (*Antiquities* 11.5.8 [11.174-183]) says the rebuilding took two years and four months. Brewer (1924:224-226) thinks Josephus's dating may have arisen through a textual corruption in the transmission of the Greek manuscripts.

6:16 When our enemies and the surrounding nations heard about it, they were frightened and humiliated. The "enemies" probably refers to Sanballat, Geshem, and Tobiah, while "surrounding nations" probably refers to the Ammonites, Ashdodites, and Arabs (4:7). A reversal had taken place, for now the enemies were "frightened" rather than the Jews (6:9, 13-14). Now the opposition was discouraged (lit., "they fell very much in their eyes," a phrase that indicates a loss of pride and optimism replaced by a downcast look of defeat—see Prov 16:18-19) instead of the Jews (6:9).

6:17 During those fifty-two days, many letters went back and forth between Tobiah and the nobles of Judah. Nehemiah 6:17-19 gives some parenthetical remarks concerning Nehemiah's enemy Tobiah. Topically, they fit better after 6:13, but by placing them here, the author suggests that this correspondence took place after the wall was finished, and not "during those fifty-two days," as the NLT suggests. The Hebrew simply says "in those days" without defining if "those days" means throughout the 52 days of rebuilding (Breneman 1993:214) or in those days after the completion of the walls (Fensham 1982:208). Either interpretation demonstrates that Nehemiah's enemies knew what Nehemiah was saying (6:19) and doing inside Jerusalem. This put Nehemiah at a distinct disadvantage since his enemies had inside information about what was happening in Jerusalem. These letters suggest that Tobiah had some influence over the thinking of the nobles in the city. There is no way of knowing what the letters from Tobiah and his friends said, but 6:19 indicates that many of the people held Tobiah in high regard.

6:18 *many in Judah had sworn allegiance to him.* Lit., "Many are masters of the oath to him." Tobiah established an economic or political alliance with some nobles in Jerusalem. This was facilitated by Tobiah's own marriage and his son's marriage into Jewish families. It is impossible to know what these people thought of Nehemiah, though there is no indication that they opposed his plan to rebuild the walls. Maybe they liked Nehemiah's attempt to provide security for the city, but their marriages with non-Jews show that they would not agree with his exclusion of non-Jews. Nehemiah could not be flexible on things like this even though they might be unpopular with the nobles. He was firmly committed to stand on God's principles outlined in the Torah (Holmgren 1987:117), in spite of some public disagreement with his theological stance on this issue.

6:19 *Tobiah's good deeds.* The good deeds of Tobiah likely involved lucrative, money-making trading arrangements that helped people in Jerusalem make a good living. If Tobiah gave them their only access to markets outside of Yehud, they could not betray his interest or they would suffer great economic harm. Other good deeds may have involved Tobiah giving financial assistance to poor Jewish relatives who needed a loan or food during the famine. Tobiah probably used these "good deeds" as leverage to get some people to report to him what Nehemiah was saying and doing in Jerusalem.

letters to intimidate me. Though other Jews received nice letters and profited from Tobiah's good deeds, Tobiah's communication with Nehemiah was only designed to degrade, oppose, and frighten Nehemiah. The letters mentioned in 6:2-7 illustrate such attempts to frighten Nehemiah.

7:1 *set up the doors in the gates.* Soon after the walls were done, workers finished installing all the gates and put key people in charge of controlling traffic through the gates. It seems odd to appoint Levites and singers in conjunction with installing the gates. One might suggest that Nehemiah needed to use trained singers and Levites who usually guarded the Temple gates to guard the city gates on a temporary basis (Allen 2003:121) because he did not have enough regular gatekeepers (Williamson 1985:270; Yamauchi 1988:716), or that he appointed gatekeepers to watch external gates and cultic personnel to guard the inner gates around the Temple, conduct worship, and praise God (Brown 1998:113-114). These appointments indicate the end of the special focus on rebuilding the walls and a return to the normal duties that facilitated safety, commerce, and worship.

7:2 *I gave the responsibility of governing Jerusalem to my brother Hanani, along with Hananiah.* Nehemiah was still the governor of Yehud, but his trusted brother (see 1:2) and Hananiah were given responsibility for the security of Jerusalem. Since these two names are almost identical, some see Nehemiah referring to only one man. Clines (1984:178) translates this as "my brother Hanani, that is Hananiah," which is hypothetically possible. But in 7:3 Nehemiah speaks to "them," which demands more than one person. Hananiah was a key military commander of troops in the fortress at the northwest end of the Temple area (2:8; 3:1). It is not clear how their duties relate to the responsibilities of Rephaiah (3:9) and Shallum (3:12), who also ruled over half of Jerusalem. Was Nehemiah replacing old leaders with new ones, or were the two new ones put in charge of security responsibilities that did not overlap or compete with the roles of Rephaiah and Shallum?

a faithful man who feared God more than most. This was a man of truth and integrity; thus, he was trustworthy and sure to be faithful and loyal to Nehemiah. He would not follow the path of those nobles who had double-dealings with both Nehemiah and Tobiah (6:17). Hananiah was not only reliable, but he also honored God. This fear of God meant that he was guided by God's word and would conduct his military affairs ethically and in dependence on God's guidance. His piety and trust in God gave him credibility in Nehemiah's eyes.

7:3 *Do not leave the gates open during the hottest part of the day.* Often gates were open from sunup to sundown, but if one wanted to take precautions or did not have enough guards, one might limit the time when they were open in order to ensure better security for those inside the city. One can interpret this command as "not to open the gates *until* the heat of the day": They were not to open the gates early in the morning (Myers 1965:140; Yamauchi 1988:716). But the preposition *'ad* [TH5704, ZH6330] could mean "during" rather than "until" (Williamson 1985:266), which makes better sense since "the heat of the day" referred to the siesta time (cf. Gen 18:1; 1 Sam 11:9). During the heat of the day, guards (and the general populace) might be prone to fall asleep for a siesta, so the city would be vulnerable. Thus, the prudent thing to do would be to close the gates during the heat of the day.

while the gatekeepers are on duty. The text is difficult because rather than specifying gatekeepers or other individuals, it talks about unidentified persons or things as "those standing" (*'omedim* [TH5975, ZH6641]). The NLT interprets these "standing ones" as the gatekeepers who were still standing at their post on duty. They must lock the gates during the siesta time because at that time of the day many people would be lying down to rest, so the city would be vulnerable. The command to "bar the doors" refers to securing them, though no mention is made of bars. The word *'akhaz* [TH270, ZH296] ("to secure"; cf. Aramaic *'akhad*) is vocalized as an imperative, a form that does not fit with the parallel term "they will shut" just before it. The Waw on the imperative *'akhaz* suggests a continuation of the imperfect idea of the preceding word.

Appoint the residents of Jerusalem. Since there were many gates and a limited number of guards, the inhabitants of Jerusalem needed to take turns assisting the guards. Because they served near their own homes, it was in their own interest to be faithful in carrying out their guard duty so that their families and property would be safe.

COMMENTARY

After the description of Nehemiah's dealing with internal problems in chapter 5, the narrative now returns to the task of rebuilding Jerusalem's walls. Three incidents of opposition and threats from neighboring enemies are outlined (6:1-9; 6:10-14; 6:15–7:3). In each case, attempts were made to intimidate Nehemiah in order to slow or stop the rebuilding project. In each case, Nehemiah was not frightened, did not stop working on the wall, and did not act irresponsibly.

The enemies of the people of Jerusalem heard that the gaps and breaches in the wall were closed (thus connecting this story in 6:1-9 with the events recorded in 4:7). This meant the city was now much more secure from random attacks, though the wall was not yet complete. Realizing the seriousness of the situation (from their perspective), Sanballat and Geshem tried to arrange a meeting with Nehemiah. But Nehemiah said, "Why should I stop working to come and meet with you?" (6:3). Nehemiah avoided being drawn into their trap by claiming he was too busy. He maintained his focus on the work he was called to do, rebuilding the walls of Jerusalem. His question gets at the real issue, emphasizing that Nehemiah was being asked to leave the wall and go down to them. What would be gained? Nehemiah was asking them to reveal their hand and spell out their intentions. How would this meeting help the situation? Did they have an attractive offer to make to him? Obviously, Nehemiah did not think there was much to talk about since he was determined to build the walls and they were determined to stop the rebuilding. His going to them would further their cause because the rebuilding would probably slow down in his absence.

Sanballat and Geshem were persistent; they sent the same message four times (6:4). The repeated requests suggest that Nehemiah did not slam the door shut on a meeting when he replied to them the first time, and his opponents did not want to take no for an answer. Consequently, they were persistent in trying to arrange a meeting, but Nehemiah was persistent in his commitment to finish the work on the wall. He did not lower his standard or give in just to get these pests off his back. On this issue, he was 100 percent inflexible. One might be tempted to criticize Nehemiah for being stubborn, uncooperative, intolerant of other people's opinions, and not a peacemaker; but those perceptions only mirror the perspective of those who do not believe that a person should ever stand firmly and immovable on absolute biblical and ethical conviction. Uncompromising determination to do the will of God is what sets some people apart. One should never bargain with the devil; instead, one must resist him and his followers by refusing to discuss possible compromises.

Sanballat made a fifth attempt to appeal to Nehemiah using an open letter (see note on 6:5). The first line of this letter states, "There is a rumor among the surrounding nations . . . that you and the Jews are planning to rebel" (6:6). It is impossible to know if other nations were actually saying that the Jews were planning to rebel. Certainly, the enemies of Yehud (Sanballat, Geshem, Tobiah) imagined or feared it might be true, but there is no evidence to suggest that the people in Egypt or Persia thought this. This was a fear tactic. They wanted Nehemiah to panic because if other people were saying this openly, eventually the Persians would find out about Nehemiah's supposed rebellion and the people in Jerusalem would be in trouble.

Sanballat's letter ingeniously connected rebellion with wall building in such a way that the only way to prove that the Jews were not rebelling would be to stop building the wall (6:6). This repeated an earlier accusation that effectively stopped the rebuilding some years earlier (Ezra 4:7-16). The letter presented only two options: build and rebel, or do not build and do not rebel. This yes-or-no mentality excluded any other options between these two extremes. But why could they not build for defensive security purposes or in order to establish a living environment that would attract more people to settle in the city? Building a wall was not always connected to rebellion.

A second rumor was that Nehemiah was going to selfishly elevate himself to the status of king (6:6), thus subverting the authority of the Persian king. Sanballat was attributing to Nehemiah selfish, ulterior motives, claiming that he had a hidden political agenda behind his actions. Sanballat was probably hoping that even the Jewish people in Jerusalem would be aghast at this idea and put Nehemiah in his place. This was pure political propaganda to make Nehemiah look bad. But there was no evidence to prove this accusation.

Nehemiah knew that Sanballat's letter was not stating true facts. He was creating insinuations, subtle accusations, outright lies, and libelous fabrications. Wisely, Nehemiah chose not to argue every point in the accusation. These false accusations did not deserve the respect of debate, for there was no truth in them. There was no reason to dialogue with Sanballat if this was the approach he would take to try to force Nehemiah into a corner. Nehemiah realized that Sanballat was attempting to frighten and discourage those in Jerusalem (6:9). Sanballat hoped that these false accusations would "weaken their hands" and cause the work to slow down or stop, but just the opposite happened. Nehemiah did not give up, get flustered or embarrassed by the accusations, second-guess his past decisions, or become bitter and vindictive.

Sanballat and Tobiah then hired Shemaiah to speak a false prophecy to Nehemiah (6:10-13). But Nehemiah quickly realized that Shemaiah's sympathetic prophetic words, which appeared to support him, were only a thinly veiled plot that (1) did not come from God, (2) was meant to discredit and shame Nehemiah, and (3) was financed by Nehemiah's enemies Tobiah and Sanballat. Since Shemaiah's advice ran contrary to the revealed will of God in the law, it was not hard to figure out that this prophet was not speaking for God (see note on 6:11). Nehemiah saw through their fear tactics and recognized them as a plan to ruin his credibility and moral integrity. They thought desperation might cause this godly man to humiliate himself by involving himself in sin, but Nehemiah resisted the temptation to put self-preservation first. As governor he served as an example to everyone. If he could not trust God, follow God's law, and boldly face his enemies, how could he expect others to follow him? They wanted to discredit Nehemiah in order to undermine his ability to lead the people in completing the rebuilding of the wall. Rather than taking immediate revenge on Shemaiah or those who hired him (Tobiah and Sanballat), Nehemiah took his concern to God in prayer (6:14). Since vengeance belongs to God (Deut 32:35), he asked God to hold them accountable for their actions.

Since Nehemiah kept to the task at hand, so did his coworkers. Remarkably, they finished the rebuilding work in 52 days (see notes on 6:15, 17). This short time period is a testimony to the determination and speed with which the laborers worked. They were able to accomplish the task so quickly because (1) they did not quarry stones but used the stones that were at the base of the broken walls; (2) they mainly restored breaches in the wall, for some portions of the wall were still standing; (3) they focused their work on rebuilding only around the small City of David and abandoned the area on the western hill where the Broad Wall was; (4) some earlier reconstruction (see 4:7-23) fixed some portions of the wall, so part of the wall was already finished; and (5) everyone pitched in, so they were able to repair breaches all around the wall at the same time.

The text tells us that the enemies "realized this work had been done with the help of our God" (6:16). Nehemiah emphasized from the very beginning that this hard task of rebuilding the wall was the work of God (2:18) and that God would give them success (2:20). It was God who would frustrate the plans of their enemies

(4:15) and fight for his people (4:20). But when the work was accomplished so quickly, others then realized that God had been involved in this task. When unusual things happen, even unbelievers are forced to recognize that a higher power was involved in the circumstances. They could not explain this great success by saying it was just an odd coincidence; this had to be God.

In summary, the reports in chapter 6 continue the theme of conflict from chapter 5, but chapter 6 is more focused on avoiding conflict with the external opponents who were trying to undermine God's work. Nehemiah's handling of these opponents illustrates how to avoid unnecessary conflict that can sap needed emotional strength and decrease a person's ability to fulfill God's calling.

In the first event, Nehemiah managed to maintain his focus on the ministry God gave him (6:1-4) and did not put himself in a compromising situation where his enemies could capture or kill him, thus eliminating his ability to do God's work. Since his enemies could not stop the building of the wall through intimidation and ridicule (4:1-23), they attempted to stop the leader who was in charge of the rebuilding project. Using the guise of compromise, open discussion, and peace-making, Nehemiah's enemies repeatedly tried to entice him to reconsider and be open-minded in regard to the opinions of others. Like Nehemiah, those today who find themselves in a similar situation should question the underlying rationale for such an invitation. Although it sounds nice to have peace and understanding between people who have different opinions, the modern secular ideal that one has to respect another person's ideas usually requires that one has to accept the other position as a legitimate option. Nehemiah was not tempted to enter into this kind of dialogue for three reasons: (1) He was almost done rebuilding the wall and needed to finish it; therefore, he refused to get sidetracked from finishing the work. (2) The invitation was to join the enemy in a place advantageous to the enemy, but the message contained no motivation to come, no indication that his enemies had changed their hatred of him. (3) He was unwavering in his determination to faithfully accomplish what God had called him to do. He was inflexible on the issue of building the wall; there was no room for compromising on an issue that he knew was God's will. This is the kind of discernment and determination that every servant of God needs. Dialogue with the enemy is designed to weaken our resolve, soften our theological stance, destroy our reputation, and hinder God's work. Compromise on such issues should be unthinkable.

At the end of this series of letters, the potential for serious conflict was elevated by the threat that Nehemiah's enemies would undermine his credibility with the Persian king who sent him to rebuild the walls (6:5-8). Now hearsay and rumor by "everyone all around" Jerusalem was the rationale for dialogue. They tried to intimidate Nehemiah, threatening to tell the king of Persia about Nehemiah's "real" intentions of rebelling and becoming king. Although the charges sounded serious, Nehemiah did not give in because he knew the truth and was not frightened by these false rumors and threats that were the product of their imagination, confirmed by the prejudiced witness Geshem. He knew the Persian king would not believe that he had committed acts of treason to usurp royal power. Further, he knew this blackmail was an attempt to scare him into defending himself against an insincere and hostile audience. Although people sometimes do have to respond to lies and rumors, a kangaroo court that has already given its guilty verdict is not the place to do it. People do not need to let fear discourage or intimidate them (6:9), for God knows the truth, and eventually the true color of liars and blackmailers will come to light. The most important thing is for believers to walk uprightly in God's eyes so they have nothing to be ashamed of. When persecution and false accusation come, they should not be unexpected. Jesus himself predicted that acts of persecution would come to all who followed him (Matt 5:10-11; 10:16-25).

In the third incident, Tobiah and Sanballat used a prophetic man of God to tempt Nehemiah to run and hide to selfishly protect himself from danger (6:10-14). This would theoretically help Nehemiah avoid conflict and death, the very things he was trying to do in 6:1-9. But Nehemiah rejected this option because (1) it would be selfish and cowardly for the governor to hide from danger rather than help his people defeat their enemy; (2) it would be a sin for him to go into the Temple, and he would likely be struck dead or suffer some punishment; (3) this advice did not come from God but was planted by his enemies; and (4) he realized that the true motivation for this prophecy was to discredit him in the eyes of the people. This incident suggests that believers should weigh all advice, even when it comes from people in positions of spiritual leadership. One should ask several questions: (1) Does this advice seem consistent with a life of selfless service to others, or is it based on fear and self-interest? (2) Is this advice consistent with the teachings of God's word, or would it cause one to sin? (3) Does this advice further the cause of God or the cause of someone else? (4) Would following this advice discredit a person's testimony and lead to accusations of sin? Like Nehemiah, believers need to take these issues to God to receive wisdom and direction, for God will hold everyone accountable for their actions (6:14).

Finally, Nehemiah learned that even when he faithfully completed the task God called him to, some people would continue to give their allegiance to his enemies and would not perceive their sinful ulterior motives (6:15-19). It was clear that God had blessed Nehemiah's efforts and had humiliated those who were trying to stop him. Just a little common sense and a minimal amount of moral insight should have blown Tobiah's cover and revealed his true motivations. Nevertheless, Tobiah's relatives, friends, and business associates were loyal to him and helped him whenever they could. They supported him in spite of all the things he did to frighten and defeat Nehemiah. Many today have been part of similar situations during a church conflict or a family problem. Sometimes a friend is blinded by the few good deeds of a very wicked person and fails to see the serious sins that are so obvious to others. No easy solution is available in these circumstances. The Bible never promises that life will be easy, that a believer will never be misunderstood, or that everyone will like believers. Nehemiah was faithful in spite of the threatening opposition by those around him. Eventually, the true colors of those who do not love God will be revealed, and God will judge them.

The picture was not all negative and hopelessly full of conflict. The people finished rebuilding the walls in the amazingly short period of 52 days (6:15). They installed doors on the gates and stationed gatekeepers to guard the city (7:1-3). The city was secure, and the workers from around the nation could see the marvelous way God had blessed their efforts on the wall. This was a time of fulfillment, and a great sense of accomplishment must have filled the people's hearts. In spite of all the opposition within and without, they rebuilt the walls and removed the reproach of Jerusalem (1:3). Soon they would celebrate that great accomplishment and dedicate these walls and doors with singing and pageantry (12:27-43).

◆   ## 5. Nehemiah's census and the census of the first exiles (Neh 7:4-73a)

4At that time the city was large and spacious, but the population was small, and none of the houses had been rebuilt. 5So my God gave me the idea to call together all the nobles and leaders of the city, along with the ordinary citizens, for registration. I had found the genealogical record of those who had first returned to Judah. This is what was written there:

6Here is the list of the Jewish exiles of the provinces who returned from their captivity. King Nebuchadnezzar had deported them to Babylon, but now they returned to Jerusalem and the other towns in Judah where they originally lived. 7Their leaders were Zerubbabel, Jeshua, Nehemiah, Seraiah,* Reelaiah,* Nahamani, Mordecai, Bilshan, Mispar,* Bigvai, Rehum,* and Baanah.

This is the number of the men of Israel who returned from exile:
8 The family of Parosh 2,172
9 The family of Shephatiah 372
10 The family of Arah 652
11 The family of Pahath-moab (descendants of Jeshua and Joab) 2,818
12 The family of Elam 1,254
13 The family of Zattu 845
14 The family of Zaccai 760
15 The family of Bani* 648
16 The family of Bebai 628
17 The family of Azgad 2,322
18 The family of Adonikam 667
19 The family of Bigvai 2,067
20 The family of Adin 655
21 The family of Ater (descendants of Hezekiah) 98
22 The family of Hashum 328

23 The family of Bezai 324
24 The family of Jorah* 112
25 The family of Gibbar* 95
26 The people of Bethlehem and Netophah 188
27 The people of Anathoth 128
28 The people of Beth-azmaveth 42
29 The people of Kiriath-jearim, Kephirah, and Beeroth 743
30 The people of Ramah and Geba .. 621
31 The people of Micmash 122
32 The people of Bethel and Ai 123
33 The people of West Nebo* 52
34 The citizens of West Elam* 1,254
35 The citizens of Harim 320
36 The citizens of Jericho 345
37 The citizens of Lod, Hadid, and Ono 721
38 The citizens of Senaah 3,930

39These are the priests who returned from exile:
The family of Jedaiah (through the line of Jeshua) 973
40 The family of Immer 1,052
41 The family of Pashhur 1,247
42 The family of Harim 1,017

43These are the Levites who returned from exile:
The families of Jeshua and Kadmiel (descendants of Hodaviah*) 74
44 The singers of the family of Asaph 148
45 The gatekeepers of the families of Shallum, Ater, Talmon, Akkub, Hatita, and Shobai 138

46The descendants of the following Temple servants returned from exile:
Ziha, Hasupha, Tabbaoth,
47 Keros, Siaha,* Padon,

48 Lebanah, Hagabah, Shalmai,
49 Hanan, Giddel, Gahar,
50 Reaiah, Rezin, Nekoda,
51 Gazzam, Uzza, Paseah,
52 Besai, Meunim, Nephusim,*
53 Bakbuk, Hakupha, Harhur,
54 Bazluth,* Mehida, Harsha,
55 Barkos, Sisera, Temah,
56 Neziah, and Hatipha.

57The descendants of these servants of King Solomon returned from exile: Sotai, Hassophereth, Peruda,*
58 Jaalah,* Darkon, Giddel,
59 Shephatiah, Hattil, Pokereth-hazzebaim, and Ami.*

60In all, the Temple servants and the descendants of Solomon's servants numbered 392.

61Another group returned at this time from the towns of Tel-melah, Tel-harsha, Kerub, Addan,* and Immer. However, they could not prove that they or their families were descendants of Israel. 62This group included the families of Delaiah, Tobiah, and Nekoda—a total of 642 people. 63Three families of priests—Hobaiah, Hakkoz, and Barzillai—also returned. (This Barzillai had married a woman who was a descendant of Barzillai of Gilead, and he had taken her family name.) 64They searched for their names in the genealogical records, but they were not found, so they were disqualified from serving as priests. 65The governor told them not to eat the priests' share of food from the sacrifices until a priest could consult the LORD about the matter by using the Urim and Thummim—the sacred lots.

66So a total of 42,360 people returned to Judah, 67in addition to 7,337 servants and 245 singers, both men and women. 68They took with them 736 horses, 245 mules,* 69435 camels, and 6,720 donkeys.

70Some of the family leaders gave gifts for the work. The governor gave to the treasury 1,000 gold coins,* 50 gold basins, and 530 robes for the priests. 71The other leaders gave to the treasury a total of 20,000 gold coins* and some 2,750 pounds* of silver for the work. 72The rest of the people gave 20,000 gold coins, about 2,500 pounds* of silver, and 67 robes for the priests.

73So the priests, the Levites, the gatekeepers, the singers, the Temple servants, and some of the common people settled near Jerusalem. The rest of the people returned to their own towns throughout Israel.

7:7a As in parallel text at Ezra 2:2; Hebrew reads *Azariah.*   7:7b As in parallel text at Ezra 2:2; Hebrew reads *Raamiah.*   7:7c As in parallel text at Ezra 2:2; Hebrew reads *Mispereth.*   7:7d As in parallel text at Ezra 2:2; Hebrew reads *Nehum.*   7:15 As in parallel text at Ezra 2:10; Hebrew reads *Binnui.*   7:24 As in parallel text at Ezra 2:18; Hebrew reads *Hariph.*   7:25 As in parallel text at Ezra 2:20; Hebrew reads *Gibeon.*   7:33 Or *of the other Nebo.*   7:34 Or *of the other Elam.*   7:43 As in parallel text at Ezra 2:40; Hebrew reads *Hodevah.*   7:47 As in parallel text at Ezra 2:44; Hebrew reads *Sia.*   7:52 As in parallel text at Ezra 2:50; Hebrew reads *Nephushesim.*   7:54 As in parallel text at Ezra 2:52; Hebrew reads *Bazlith.*   7:57 As in parallel text at Ezra 2:55; Hebrew reads *Sotai, Sophereth, Perida.*   7:58 As in parallel text at Ezra 2:56; Hebrew reads *Jaala.*   7:59 As in parallel text at Ezra 2:57; Hebrew reads *Amon.*   7:61 As in parallel text at Ezra 2:59; Hebrew reads *Addon.*   7:68 As in some Hebrew manuscripts (see also Ezra 2:66); most Hebrew manuscripts lack this verse. Verses 7:69-73 are numbered 7:68-72 in Hebrew text.   7:70 Hebrew *1,000 darics of gold,* about 19 pounds or 8.6 kilograms in weight.   7:71a Hebrew *20,000 darics of gold,* about 375 pounds or 170 kilograms in weight; also in 7:72.   7:71b Hebrew *2,200 minas* [1,300 kilograms].   7:72 Hebrew *2,000 minas* [1,200 kilograms].

NOTES

7:4 Not everyone agrees on where to begin this paragraph. Some argue for a major paragraph division at the chapter break, thus 7:1-73a is viewed as a unit about the repopulation of Jerusalem (Fensham 1982:209; Yamauchi 1988:715). It seems better to make the new unit 7:4-73a (Throntveit 1992:93; Myers 1965:142) because 7:1-3 completes the discussion of the completion of the rebuilding of the walls and gates around Jerusalem.

the city was large and spacious. Lit., "The city was wide of two hands and large," a phrase that probably means that it was wide open in both directions—on the right-hand side and the left-hand side.

none of the houses had been rebuilt. This translation (lit., "There were no homes built") is problematic because other passages (3:10, 20, 23, 28-30; Hag 1:4) indicate there were families living in homes in Jerusalem. This must mean either (1) that the houses there had not been completely rebuilt and repaired, or (2) that "there were not enough houses" (Williamson 1985:267; Fensham 1982:211)—the Hebrew word *'eyn* [TH369, ZH401] can mean "there is not enough."

7:5 God gave me the idea . . . for registration. Nehemiah always gave God the glory rather than drawing attention to himself or his abilities. Some people might question whether this new census was the appropriate thing to do in light of God's condemnation of David for numbering the people (1 Chr 21:1). But since the registration was something that God set on his heart, this was not a sinful act, but one directed by God (as was the census of Num 1).

7:6 list of the Jewish exiles . . . who returned from their captivity. These words and the list of names included in this list are almost identical to the list in Ezra 2:1-70 (and in the apocryphal book 1 Esdr 5:4-46). Although some conclude that Nehemiah's list was the source of Ezra's list (Williamson 1985:29; Clines 1984:129), it makes more sense to imagine that both lists were copied from an independent government document. Since neither list contains the name of Sheshbazzar (7:7; Ezra 2:2) among the leaders of those who returned from exile (Ezra 1:8-11), the original list must reflect the situation some months later when the people were already settled in the towns, apparently after the death of Sheshbazzar.

7:7-67 See the discussion of this identical list of names in Ezra 2. Because of scribal errors in copying or in adding, some numbers are off by one (7:18, 23, 45) or by one hundred (7:13, 32) from the total listed in Ezra 2. A few spellings of names are different in the Hebrew (7:15, 24-25), the order is slightly changed in a couple places (7:36-37), and one name is missing between 7:33 and 34 (Ezra 2:30 lists "Magbish, 156" after Nebo).

7:39-73 [39-72] Nehemiah wanted only legitimate priests and Levites working in the Temple, so special attention is given to them in the list. This is only one of many lists of priests and Levites that can be found in Nehemiah and 1 Chronicles. Priestly genealogies were included in 10:1-8; 11:10-14; 12:1-7; and 1 Chr 9:10-13. Levitical families were also listed in 10:9-13; 11:15-18; and 12:8-11.

7:70-72 [69-71] This list of contributions is related to Ezra 2:68-70, but it is evident that this passage in Nehemiah was drawn from a much more detailed list of contributions by the leaders or that the author of Ezra 2:68-69 was only briefly summarizing what the original document said. This account includes what the governor gave, what the nobles gave, and what the rest of the people gave. These people not only gave of their time and effort, but also gave sacrificially of their limited wealth. The people who had greater financial resources (the governor and nobles) set a great example and gave the most, but everyone who was able contributed what they could. These gifts were a barometer of their love for God and their belief that God would supply their financial needs in the future. This money was supplemented by gifts from Jewish people who stayed in Babylon (Ezra 1:6).

7:70 [69] 1,000 gold coins. This refers to 1,000 darics of gold, probably the Persian gold daric rather than the small silver Greek drachma coin that weighed about 3/10 of an ounce (Yamauchi 1988:620, 721). The Persian coins were either named after Darius, a Persian king who minted them, or after the Persian word "gold" (*dari*). The figures in the two accounts are not identical: (1) Ezra 2:69 refers to 61,000 drachmas, 5,000 silver minas, 100 priestly garments; (2) 7:70-72 gives 41,000 drachmas, 4,200 silver minas, 597 priestly garments. The different figures could be due to (1) scribal errors; (2) gifts from only three groups were included in ch 7, so it is possible that a higher figure of darics and minas would have resulted if other groups (the contribution by people in Persia) were included; (3) people could have given additional priestly garments after Ezra's memoirs were written, thus Nehemiah's figures were higher.

COMMENTARY

Nehemiah's new idea of increasing the population inside the large open areas in Jerusalem is introduced in 7:4 (see note). The officials in charge of Jerusalem needed the residents of Jerusalem to function as guards at the gates and as night watchmen in order to secure the city (7:3). If the city had a small population, then it would be hard to find enough men to serve. Furthermore, if the city was now a safe place to live in because the walls were restored, Nehemiah could encourage more people to move into the city and thus develop a thriving and secure center for trade, government, and worship.

Without a growth in the population, the viability of Jerusalem was in question. There were many open areas in the city of Jerusalem, maybe as much as 30 acres (Clines 1984:179), where homes could be built, but most people had chosen to live in the countryside close to their fields. If Nehemiah was going to revive the bustling and vibrant city of Jerusalem as the center of Jewish life, he would need to increase its population. The idea of getting people to move into Jerusalem was an important step in energizing the city, but it would not be easy to convince people to make this move. They would have to leave the comfortable surroundings of friends and relatives, build new homes in Jerusalem, and either commute to their farms or find new ways of making a living in the city. Chapter 11 records the names of the people who took that bold step and moved into Jerusalem.

In the process of trying to develop a plan for repopulating Jerusalem, Nehemiah needed to know how many Jewish people were in the province of Yehud. Based on that figure, he could develop a plan that would propose that a percentage of people should move into the walled city of Jerusalem. While hunting through government records, he found a list made shortly after 536 BC (7:5). This registration list contained the names of various families and the number of people in each of those families. The text does not explain how this list would be used when Nehemiah gathered the present inhabitants of Yehud for the new registration he was conducting. Maybe it was used to identify whether all the former families were recorded in his new registry. The list would also enable Nehemiah to choose only authentic Jewish families to move into Jerusalem, thus assuring the religious purity and unity of the city. The results of the present registration would also show how much the population had grown in the past 75 years. (The commentary on Ezra 2:1-70 provides a fuller discussion of this passage.) This long list of names records, for all eternity, those who were willing to leave the familiar and comfortable confines of Persia and travel over 800 miles to the desolate land of Judah. They were the charter members of the new community of Israel that resettled the Land of Promise. Ezra and Nehemiah did not forget their courage and boldness, and neither did God.

Some took responsibility as leaders; others were priests, Levites, and Temple servants who cared for the worship of God at the Temple. It was important to have an accurate record of the true people of God in order to protect the purity of the nation and the city of Jerusalem. These were the people who had the desire to see the community of God's people restored and to establish a Hebrew presence in the land promised to Abraham. They had committed their lives, their future, and their financial resources to reestablishing the worship of God in Jerusalem many years before Nehemiah arrived.

About a hundred years after these people accepted the challenge to come to Jerusalem, Nehemiah honored their faith and commitment to God and their hard work. They had set an example for the people of Nehemiah's day. Nehemiah then challenged a new group of people to pull up stakes and leave their comfortable country farms and move only a short distance into the city of Jerusalem. Every generation of believers has a challenge to carry on the tradition of striving to do great things in the name of God. Opposition will always be present, the move will always require faith, but God will always guide and bless his people as they give themselves and their money to the work of God in this hostile world.

◆ IV. Ezra's Teaching of the Law of God Brings Covenant Renewal (Neh 7:73b-10:39)

A. The Community Understands God's Word (Neh 7:73b-8:18)

In October,* when the Israelites had settled in their towns, 8:1 all the people assembled with a unified purpose at the square just inside the Water Gate. They asked Ezra the scribe to bring out the Book of the Law of Moses, which the LORD had given for Israel to obey.

2 So on October 8* Ezra the priest brought the Book of the Law before the assembly, which included the men and women and all the children old enough to understand. 3 He faced the square just inside the Water Gate from early morning until noon and read aloud to everyone who could understand. All the people listened closely to the Book of the Law.

4 Ezra the scribe stood on a high wooden platform that had been made for the occasion. To his right stood Mattithiah, Shema, Anaiah, Uriah, Hilkiah, and Maaseiah. To his left stood Pedaiah, Mishael, Malkijah, Hashum, Hashbaddanah, Zechariah, and Meshullam. 5 Ezra stood on the platform in full view of all the people. When they saw him open the book, they all rose to their feet.

6 Then Ezra praised the LORD, the great God, and all the people chanted, "Amen! Amen!" as they lifted their hands. Then they bowed down and worshiped the LORD with their faces to the ground.

7 The Levites—Jeshua, Bani, Sherebiah, Jamin, Akkub, Shabbethai, Hodiah, Maaseiah, Kelita, Azariah, Jozabad, Hanan, and Pelaiah—then instructed the people in the Law while everyone remained in their places. 8 They read from the Book of the Law of God and clearly explained the meaning of what was being read, helping the people understand each passage.

9 Then Nehemiah the governor, Ezra the priest and scribe, and the Levites who were interpreting for the people said to them, "Don't mourn or weep on such a day as this! For today is a sacred day before the LORD your God." For the people had all been weeping as they listened to the words of the Law.

10 And Nehemiah* continued, "Go and celebrate with a feast of rich foods and sweet drinks, and share gifts of food with people who have nothing prepared. This is

a sacred day before our Lord. Don't be dejected and sad, for the joy of the LORD is your strength!"

¹¹And the Levites, too, quieted the people, telling them, "Hush! Don't weep! For this is a sacred day." ¹²So the people went away to eat and drink at a festive meal, to share gifts of food, and to celebrate with great joy because they had heard God's words and understood them.

¹³On October 9* the family leaders of all the people, together with the priests and Levites, met with Ezra the scribe to go over the Law in greater detail. ¹⁴As they studied the Law, they discovered that the LORD had commanded through Moses that the Israelites should live in shelters during the festival to be held that month.* ¹⁵He had said that a proclamation should be made throughout their towns and in Jerusalem, telling the people to go to the hills to get branches from olive, wild olive,* myrtle, palm, and other leafy trees. They were to use these branches to make shelters in which they would live during the festival, as prescribed in the Law.

¹⁶So the people went out and cut branches and used them to build shelters on the roofs of their houses, in their courtyards, in the courtyards of God's Temple, or in the squares just inside the Water Gate and the Ephraim Gate. ¹⁷So everyone who had returned from captivity lived in these shelters during the festival, and they were all filled with great joy! The Israelites had not celebrated like this since the days of Joshua* son of Nun.

¹⁸Ezra read from the Book of the Law of God on each of the seven days of the festival. Then on the eighth day they held a solemn assembly, as was required by law.

7:73 Hebrew *in the seventh month.* This month of the ancient Hebrew lunar calendar occurred within the months of October and November 445 B.C.   8:2 Hebrew *on the first day of the seventh month,* of the ancient Hebrew lunar calendar. This day was October 8, 445 B.C.; also see note on 1:1.   8:10 Hebrew *he.*   8:13 Hebrew *On the second day,* of the seventh month of the ancient Hebrew lunar calendar. This day was October 9, 445 B.C.; also see notes on 1:1 and 8:2.   8:14 Hebrew *in the seventh month.* This month of the ancient Hebrew lunar calendar usually occurs within the months of September and October. See Lev 23:39-43.   8:15 Or *pine;* Hebrew reads *oil tree.*   8:17 Hebrew *Jeshua,* a variant spelling of Joshua.

NOTES

7:73b In October. Lit., "in the seventh month" (see NLT mg). This new literary unit is connected to the beginning of the new year, which began with a day set apart for blowing trumpets (8:2; Lev 23:24; Num 29:1-6) that in later years became known as Rosh Hashanah. The year this happened during the reign of Artaxerxes I is not given. Thus, one could hypothesize that this story fits just a few days after the completion of the wall on the 25th of the preceding month (6:15) in 445 BC, or at some other hypothetical time.

8:1 all the people assembled with a unified purpose. Lit., "the people gathered as one man." There is no indication that Ezra or Nehemiah called the people together; they assembled together on their own. It was their custom each year to come together to celebrate the joy of the beginning of a new year when they heard the blowing of trumpets.

at the square just inside the Water Gate. The Water Gate (3:26; 12:37) was related to the Gihon Spring in the Kidron Valley, but it was located at the northern Ophel portion of the eastern wall, some distance north of the Gihon Spring. The Water Gate was just south of the Temple area, but not in the Temple area, because women and children were present at this gathering. It is significant that they met at this place, for it shows that they valued having everyone involved in the celebration and did not want to limit participation by holding this meeting in a restricted Temple area.

8:2 on October 8. Lit., "on the first day of the seventh month." This day was later called New Year's Day (or Rosh Hashanah) and was marked by the blowing of trumpets and a solemn assembly of the people (Lev 23:23-25; Num 29:1-6).

all the children old enough to understand. Lit., "all who had understanding to listen."

8:3 *from early morning until noon.* From the light of daybreak until midday would amount to about six hours of reading. Because of the length of time involved, the people who joined Ezra on the platform likely assisted him in reading the scroll (8:4). Some would have handled the unrolling and rolling up of the scrolls, while others would have taken their turn reading.

8:4 *high wooden platform.* This wooden tower (*migdal* [TH4026, ZH4463]) was large enough to hold 14 people and presumably functioned as a means for people in the large crowd to see Ezra and hear what he was reading. A similar but more elaborate platform was used when Solomon dedicated the Temple in Jerusalem many years earlier (2 Chr 6:13).

To his right stood . . . To his left stood. The 13 men accompanying Ezra on the platform were not identified as priests or Levites (see 8:7, which refers to a group of Levites among the crowd); they probably were important leaders in the community (Fensham 1982:217) who represented the people (maybe the elders of Israel). Their presence was a visual support to Ezra and what he was saying; plus, they may have helped with the reading of the scrolls.

8:5 *Ezra stood on the platform.* This is a rather periphrastic rendition of the parenthetical remark that "he was above all the people." This comment explains why the people could see him open the book.

When they saw him open the book, they all rose to their feet. Out of respect for God and his sacred words, the people stood when the scroll was unrolled (lit., "opened"). This was a custom when people came before a respected person (Judg 3:20; Job 29:8; Dan 1:19, KJV) or when God's word was opened (9:3). No doubt there were periodic breaks for the readers of the law, as well as for those listening to the words of God.

8:6 *Ezra praised the LORD.* This benedictory offering of praise remembered the greatness of God (see 1:5; 9:32; Deut 10:17; Dan 9:4). It was and still is a customary practice before reading the Scriptures in Jewish circles. It puts the reader in the right frame of mind, with the reader and listener in an attitude of submission to the Lord. This opens the mind's door for the Spirit to bring conviction and transformation of the heart.

Amen! Lit., "It is firm, established." This verse contains several demonstrative and emotional responses by the people listening to Ezra. There was no disunity among the worshipers, for the entire congregation expressed their agreement with Ezra's praise (see Deut 27:14-16; 1 Kgs 1:36). They exalted God for revealing to them his thoughts and instructions.

lifted their hands. This motion of the hands could be viewed as a demonstration of a need for God's help or a sign of dependence on God, as in Ps 28:2 (Williamson 1985:289), but it is also an external sign to show that one is internally directing worship to God (1 Kgs 8:22; Ps 134:2).

bowed down and worshiped. The normal posture of worship was to bow the face to the ground (Josh 5:14; Ezra 9:5; 10:1; Ps 95:6), showing submission, awe, adoration, and reverence toward God. After this initial act of worship, they stood up to listen to the word of God.

8:7 *The Levites.* Several of these 13 Levitical leaders were mentioned elsewhere (9:4-5; 10:9-13; 11:16). The Levites walked among the people explaining in more detail what the Torah said (Allen 2003:126) by speaking to the people in the Aramaic language, the language most spoke. Although Hebrew and Aramaic are similar, they are different enough that many people would have had at least some trouble understanding the Hebrew that Ezra spoke. The text does not say if these Levites answered questions, but hypothetically this too could have been part of their process of explaining what the Torah meant.

8:9 *Nehemiah the governor.* The presence of the name of Nehemiah, the Persian government official (the Persian title *tirshatha'* [TH8660, ZH9579], "governor," was also used in 10:1 [2]; Ezra 2:63), argues that Nehemiah's and Ezra's ministries overlapped. But some think their careers did not overlap and hypothesize that a later editor inappropriately added the name Nehemiah in this verse (Williamson 1985:279, Myers 1965:151). The parallel verse in the apocryphal book *3 Esdras* 5:40 does not have the name Nehemiah here, but it is present in LXX and the Hebrew of 8:9. Although Ezra is not mentioned earlier in chs 1–7 of the Nehemiah Memoirs, this does not prove that Ezra was not serving in Jerusalem during those days. The Nehemiah Memoirs are about Nehemiah's work to build the wall, not about life in Jerusalem or the work of the Levites; thus, it is not surprising that Ezra is not mentioned by name in the earlier stories in Nehemiah. The canonical positioning of this covenant-renewal ceremony suggests that it took place around 445 BC during Nehemiah's ministry and not shortly after Ezra arrived in 458 BC.

8:10 *Nehemiah continued.* Lit., "And he said." The NLT assumes that Nehemiah spoke these words, based on a similar construction at the beginning of 8:9, but 8:9 relates that Nehemiah, Ezra, and the Levites gave exhortations. Thus, it is better to conclude that 8:9 would be Nehemiah's speech, 8:10 would be Ezra's exhortation, and 8:11 records what the priests said. Additional support for this interpretation is that (1) it is more likely that Ezra would be the one instructing the people about the specifics of how to celebrate the feast; (2) a different speaker is implied in 8:10, otherwise the content of 8:9-10 would be redundant; and (3) Ezra was on the platform reading to the people and would be a natural one to authorize this change in behavior (Duggan 2001:92).

the joy of the LORD is your strength! God's "strength" is illustrated by comparing him to a strong place of "refuge, a fortress" (*ma'oz* [TH4581, ZH5057]). Such power and protection brought a sense of security and joy to the people's hearts. They could trust in this kind of God despite their other problems.

8:11 *For this is a sacred day.* The Levites helped quiet the weeping people and tried to refocus the people's attention on being joyful. The rationale that this was a "sacred day" was repeated here for the third time in three verses (8:9, 10, 11). Nehemiah, Ezra, and the Levites emphasized that God's "holy day" was to be set apart to focus on their holy God and his grace, not on the temporary problems of the people.

8:13 *On October 9.* Lit., "On the second day" (see NLT mg). The assumption is that this was the day after New Year's Day (8:2). Now that the celebration was over, most families returned to their homes (Allen 2003:127). But the leaders (lit., "the heads of the fathers") of each tribal group stayed in Jerusalem to meet with Ezra, plus the priests and Levites.

to go over the Law in greater detail. The Hiphil infinitive of the verb *sakal* [TH7919, ZH8505] relates to the idea of "being prudent, wise, having insight"; thus one would need to "ponder, look at, study, comprehend" in order to gain this insight into the meaning of the law.

8:14 *As they studied.* These words do not directly represent words from the Hebrew but were added to NLT to make a smoother transition between the previous statement about going over the law in greater detail and the following statement that "they discovered that the LORD had commanded . . ."

the LORD had commanded through Moses. Although some modern critics do not think the first five books of the Bible were written by Moses, it was the view of people in the time of Ezra that God inspired Moses to write his instructions in the Torah, usually identified as all of Genesis—Deuteronomy.

should live in shelters during the festival. One is surprised that there is no reference to the "Day of Atonement" on the tenth day of the seventh month. Some explain this by speculating that the P (Priestly) document (a theoretical documentary source of the law consisting mainly of Leviticus and Numbers) did not exist at this time, but this does not make much sense, for Ezra was reading from the law of Moses about the Feast of Trumpets and Festival of Shelters. Others conjecture that a conflict between Ezra and the other priests caused him to cancel the event, or that the Day of Atonement was a priestly event and thus did not fit this chapter's theme of community celebration (Williamson 1985:293; Breneman 1993:229). However, one might suggest that the people already knew about the Day of Atonement, so they did not require any change of behavior. What they did not know about was the Festival of Shelters. So the directive focused on reading about the celebration of the Festival of Shelters on the 15th day of the month. What is surprising about this interpretation is that the people did celebrate the Festival of Shelters shortly after they came back to Jerusalem in 537–536 BC (Ezra 3:4). It appears that the present generation around 445 BC had forgotten about observing this feast, but there is no way to know why this festival was not being observed. It is also surprising that Ezra did not make this correction and get the people celebrating the Festival of Shelters when he first came to Jerusalem in 458 BC. Why did he wait so long before he reminded people about this important festival? Allen suggests that the focus here is not on the fact that the Festival of Shelters was not being celebrated, but that Ezra was offering corrections on how it was to be celebrated (2003:127). This particular feast time was a festival that reminded them of when the children of Israel lived in tents during their wilderness journey. Although Exod 23:16 connects this feast with the ingathering of the harvest, Num 29:12-38 describes the sacrifices they were supposed to present to God, and Deut 16:13-15 mentions the joy and sharing at the feast. Only Lev 23:39-43 emphasizes the building of shelters for the families to live in during this festival. Thus, it is fairly certain that Ezra was reading from Leviticus (i.e., a portion belonging to the theoretical P document, mentioned above).

8:15 *branches from olive, wild olive, myrtle, palm, and other leafy trees.* Although these instructions are somewhat similar to the instructions in Lev 23:40, they are not exactly the same. Thus, Ezra may have adapted the instructions in Leviticus (rather than quoting them word for word) to make them practical for people to follow in his day based on the kinds of trees that were available (Clines 1984:187).

use these branches to make shelters. The Leviticus passage (Lev 23:40-42) does not say that one was to build the shelters out of these tree branches, but apparently that was what the people traditionally did with them.

8:16 *to build shelters on the roofs . . . courtyards . . . squares.* The leaders followed Ezra's instructions and proclaimed the news about the Festival of Shelters to those in their communities. People living in Jerusalem used their branches to build their temporary huts on the flat roofs of their houses, while people from out of town built their shelters in the open squares in Jerusalem.

8:17 *had not celebrated like this since the days of Joshua.* This comparative statement is similar to earlier statements comparing a present celebration to a famous one in the past (2 Kgs 23:22; 2 Chr 30:26; 35:18). The point of comparison that made this festival so great could be (1) the unusual spirit of great joy (Fensham 1982:221); (2) the unusual centralized celebration in Jerusalem was unique (Clines 1984:188); (3) this celebration was not just a harvest festival like many earlier ones, but was part of a covenant renewal (Deut 31:9-13), which drew attention to the parallelism between God's grace to those who journeyed back to the land from exile and those who first journeyed to the land after the Exodus and wilderness wanderings (Williamson 1985:296; Throntveit 1992:99).

8:18 Ezra read from the Book of the Law of God. Deuteronomy 31:9-13 indicates that the Torah was to be read every seventh year at the Festival of Shelters and that on this occasion the people would renew their covenant with God. This could indicate that this celebration also marked a Sabbatical Year of release of debts and slavery. Another possibility is that it became the practice to read the instructions from the law of God every year at this festival and not just on the seventh year.

COMMENTARY

Instead of immediately describing the resettlement of the city of Jerusalem, as one would expect (discussed in 11:1-36), an account of Ezra's reading of the Torah to a large gathering of people is now given. Since some do not think the ministry of Ezra and Nehemiah overlapped, they place this event much earlier, in 458 BC, shortly after Ezra arrived in Jerusalem (Clines 1984:182; Duggan 2001:5). Thus, the events in 7:73b–10:39, which are drawn from Ezra's Memoirs, are seen as corresponding chronologically to the events of Ezra 9 or 10 and are considered to be a ceremony of covenant renewal (Williamson 1985:279). But if Ezra continued his ministry into the era when Nehemiah built the walls of Jerusalem, there is no reason to exclude an early revival around 458 BC (Ezra 9–10) in addition to this covenant renewal ceremony about 13 years later in 445 BC. Some even hypothesize that Ezra left Yehud for a few years between these two events, but there is no evidence for this (Fensham 1982:6-7). This event and those of Ezra 9–10 are not in conflict with one another and are not the same event. Nehemiah 8–10 records another step of faith, as the people committed themselves to live according to their covenant relationship with God.

The narrative of 7:73b–10:39 can be broken down into three similarly structured sequences of events (Throntveit 1992:95) as follows:

SEQUENCE OF EVENTS	FIRST CYCLE	SECOND CYCLE	THIRD CYCLE
Time of year	7:73b; 8:2	8:13a	9:1a
Gathering the people	8:1	8:13b	9:1b-2
Hearing the law	8:3-6	8:13c	9:3
Applying the law	8:7-11	8:14-15	9:4-37
Response of people	8:12	8:16-18	9:38-10:39

This common structure unifies these three narratives to create a theological emphasis on the power of God's revelation to transform the community. The people were willing to respond positively to a clear explanation of God's instructions in his word in their own language. This rededication of the community was not the result of a change in one person's thinking, but a demonstration of the Spirit's compassionate transformation of a community of willing and obedient hearts that desired to please God.

The people eagerly wanted their gathering to have a spiritual dimension. Ezra did not force it on them or take the initiative in this case. He did not call the meeting; he did not dictate the agenda or determine what should be read. The people valued God's word and wanted to understand what it said so they would be able to follow its instructions. The people could have had many other things read (probably including treaties, royal decrees, local administrative laws, folk tales, genealogies, hymns, and prophecies, though only some texts would have been controlled by the priests), but they wisely chose to have the book of the law read to them (8:1). One could view this "book" to be (1) scrolls that contained all five books traditionally attributed to Moses, (2) just the book of Leviticus, (3) just Deuteronomy, or (4) a collection of legal material (Yamauchi 1988:723). Although Nehemiah refers frequently to theological ideas from Deuteronomy, there is no need to limit this document to just one portion of the Pentateuch (Genesis—Deuteronomy). The fact that he read from this book for only a few hours (8:3) does not prove that he did not have the whole Pentateuch (contra Fensham 1982:216).

Specific mention is made of the three groups of people at this meeting: men, women, and children (8:2). These are not exclusionary terms (eliminating younger children) but inclusive terms, showing that everyone attended and listened in order to understand what God was instructing them to do. The law of God was not just applicable to men, for it was important that a husband and wife agree on the theological beliefs and priorities that would guide their family. Parents were to instruct their children in what God said from an early age (Exod 12:26; Deut 6:7; 31:12; Josh 8:35; 2 Chr 20:13; Prov 4:1).

Since people did not have private copies of God's word in their homes and many were limited in their reading ability, they treasured those times when someone would read to them what God said in the sacred scrolls (8:3). Listening opens the mind to the thoughts and wishes of others. The person who listens is one who respects the speaker's ideas and is open to learning something new from God. These people did not passively ignore what was said, but actively soaked up and internalized the message. This is the attitude all believers should have when they hear the powerful and precious word of God read.

Part of the Levites' responsibility was to explain God's word to people so they would know the difference between what they should and should not do (Lev 10:10-11; Deut 33:10; 2 Chr 17:7-9). The text does not explain exactly the mechanics of how this was done (8:7). One could hypothesize that Ezra read a section from the scroll, and then each of the Levites explained in detail to a smaller group of people what he had read, and possibly answered some questions.

Nehemiah 8:8 is a significant text, which the NLT renders as, "They read from the Book of the Law of God and clearly explained the meaning of what was being read." This seems redundant, repeating what was just said in 8:7. But the early rabbis thought this referred to the Levitical task of translating the Hebrew into Aramaic (Myers 1965:154), the language that most of the people spoke at that time (b. Megillah 3a, 18b; Genesis Rabbah 36:8). This would then mark the beginning of providing the Scriptures in Aramaic Targums. The participle meporash [TH6567, ZH7300] (NLT, "clearly") is used adverbially in this verse and is variously taken as meaning "paragraph by paragraph" (Williamson 1985:278-279), "translate" (Fensham 1982:217), or "clearly, distinctly" (Duggan 2001:91). The use of the Aramaic form based on the same root in Ezra 4:18 is equally difficult, having possible meanings similar to those in Nehemiah 8:8 (see note on Ezra 4:18). One can conclude that the Levites made the meaning clear and suggested how the people could apply these words to their own lives. What is not known for certain is whether this clarification process involved the Levites translating the Hebrew words from the Torah into the Aramaic language. The Hebrew word *meporash* [TH6567, ZH7300] does not require this interpretation, though one would expect this to happen if there were people in the audience who did not understand Hebrew. A few years later, Nehemiah complained that many people could not read or speak Hebrew (13:24), thus an Aramaic translation would have been needed to help these people to understand what Ezra read.

After hearing the law of Moses, the people wept because they were convicted of their sin (8:9). The people truly understood the implications of the law and realized they needed to repent. Although this was a good thing, the leaders of the people reminded them that the Festival of Trumpets was a holy day and designated as a time of joy and celebration (Lev 23:23-25; Num 29:1-6; Deut 16:15). The people had repented and the leaders could now encourage them to rejoice, for God would be gracious by forgiving their sin and not punishing them. Now as the holy people of God, they could rejoice in this holy day dedicated to their holy Lord. The celebration surrounding the offering of peace offerings (cf. Lev 3) made their hearts glad because they could eat rich food (8:10). This feast boldly illustrated the unity of the nation because they all ate together, and it demonstrated their concern for others through the sharing of food with the poor (Deut 14:29; 26:12). (Similar joyful national celebrations are recorded in 2 Sam 6:18-19; 1 Chr 12:39-40; 29:22; 2 Chr 30:21-26.)

The section ends with an emphasis on the transformation of the audience (8:12). This is the response all teachers and preachers want to see when they speak. But before people can respond appropriately, they need to understand in simple and straightforward terms what God wants them to do. In other words, an explanation of God's word has to be given and application has to be made so that God's transforming power can direct people's attitudes and behavior in the right direction. God's instructions set the normative pattern for behavior for those who follow him. Part of the joy of this occasion was the assurance the people derived from knowing that they were doing what God wanted them to do.

In summary, two key themes join together in explaining the dynamics of the transformation recounted in this chapter. First, the written record of these events has a consistent emphasis on what "all the people," "the men and women and all the children," or "the Israelites," did (8:1, 2, 3, 5, 6, 9, 11, 12, 13, 17). The theological point being made is that the people were unified in their desire to celebrate the Festival of Trumpets and the Festival of Shelters. The small religious preferences of individuals or tribal groups did not divide the people on these issues. They all wanted to hear what God said in the Torah, and they all followed what Ezra told them to do. This was not a time of rebellion or divisiveness but a period of working, serving, learning, and rejoicing together. This is an example to believers today, because there are all too many people who think of themselves first, rather than putting the interests of the group first. This does not mean that one cannot disagree with others when they fall into sin or when genuine differences of opinion exist; it simply means that we should ideally be fully united together in obedience to God's word as one people.

The second main theme is the centrality of the words of God recorded in the Torah. This was the authoritative basis for determining how they should live. They asked Ezra to read the divine words in the law of Moses (8:1, 13, 15) because they knew it was important. They made sure that they had everyone there who could understand God's words (8:2-3), and then they listened closely and reverently to what was read (8:3, 5). They recognized that the authority behind these words was God himself, so they responded to the reading with humility and praise (8:6). The leadership knew that the real goal of these meetings was not just to read the law before the people; they knew that the central purpose for reading God's instructions was to get people to understand, apply, and obey what God said. Thus, they took time to explain the implications of the text and to advise people about what they needed to do (8:9-12, 14-15). The application was consistent with the original command, but it was not just a slavish repetition of the original (8:15-16). Because few copies of the Scriptures existed, it appears that many did not know what the law of Moses said. When they finally heard what God wanted them to do, they immediately wept about their sin and turned to obey God. Since there are so many copies of God's word available today, we will be held more accountable to know what God has said and to obey it.

The result of the people's spirit of unity in their desire to learn and follow God's words was a revival among the people in Jerusalem. They initially wept in an attitude of humility because they realized they had not been pleasing God (8:9). Later, they rejoiced because they had heard and understood God's word (8:12, 17) and knew God was their refuge and strength (8:10). This led to acts of obedience in which they celebrated what God had done for them in the past (8:12, 17). This presents a pattern of behavior that is worth observing. When God's people hear his words and understand how they apply to themselves, God can transform people's attitudes and behavior. The fear of not knowing what pleases God is then replaced with the joy of understanding the privilege of being the people of God. Instead of forgetting what God did for his people in the past, they can rejoice in who he is and what he has done. The word of God enlightens the eyes, and the festive commemoration of the marvelous things that God has done for his people throughout history encourages the heart to worship our powerful God and face the future with confidence and faith.

◆   ## B. The Community Hears God's Word and Prays (Neh 9:1-37)

On October 31* the people assembled again, and this time they fasted and dressed in burlap and sprinkled dust on their heads. ²Those of Israelite descent separated themselves from all foreigners as they confessed their own sins and the sins of their ancestors. ³They remained standing in place for three hours* while the Book of the Law of the LORD their God was read aloud to them. Then for three more hours they confessed their sins and worshiped the LORD their God. ⁴The Levites— Jeshua, Bani, Kadmiel, Shebaniah, Bunni, Sherebiah, Bani, and Kenani—stood on the stairway of the Levites and cried out to the LORD their God with loud voices.

⁵Then the leaders of the Levites—Jeshua, Kadmiel, Bani, Hashabneiah, Sherebiah, Hodiah, Shebaniah, and Pethahiah—called out to the people: "Stand up and praise

the LORD your God, for he lives from everlasting to everlasting!" Then they prayed:

"May your glorious name be praised!
May it be exalted above all blessing
and praise!
⁶"You alone are the LORD. You made
the skies and the heavens and all the
stars. You made the earth and the seas
and everything in them. You preserve
them all, and the angels of heaven
worship you.
⁷"You are the LORD God, who chose
Abram and brought him from Ur of the
Chaldeans and renamed him Abraham.
⁸When he had proved himself faithful,
you made a covenant with him to give
him and his descendants the land of
the Canaanites, Hittites, Amorites,
Perizzites, Jebusites, and Girgashites.
And you have done what you promised,
for you are always true to your word.
⁹"You saw the misery of our
ancestors in Egypt, and you heard
their cries from beside the Red Sea.*
¹⁰You displayed miraculous signs and
wonders against Pharaoh, his officials,
and all his people, for you knew how
arrogantly they were treating our
ancestors. You have a glorious
reputation that has never been
forgotten. ¹¹You divided the sea for
your people so they could walk
through on dry land! And then you
hurled their enemies into the depths
of the sea. They sank like stones
beneath the mighty waters. ¹²You
led our ancestors by a pillar of cloud
during the day and a pillar of fire at
night so that they could find their way.
¹³"You came down at Mount Sinai
and spoke to them from heaven. You
gave them regulations and instructions
that were just, and decrees and
commands that were good. ¹⁴You
instructed them concerning your holy
Sabbath. And you commanded them,
through Moses your servant, to obey
all your commands, decrees, and
instructions.

¹⁵"You gave them bread from
heaven when they were hungry and
water from the rock when they were
thirsty. You commanded them to go
and take possession of the land you
had sworn to give them.
¹⁶"But our ancestors were proud
and stubborn, and they paid no
attention to your commands. ¹⁷They
refused to obey and did not remember
the miracles you had done for them.
Instead, they became stubborn and
appointed a leader to take them back
to their slavery in Egypt! But you are
a God of forgiveness, gracious and
merciful, slow to become angry, and
rich in unfailing love. You did not
abandon them, ¹⁸even when they
made an idol shaped like a calf and
said, 'This is your god who brought
you out of Egypt!' They committed
terrible blasphemies.
¹⁹"But in your great mercy you did
not abandon them to die in the
wilderness. The pillar of cloud still led
them forward by day, and the pillar of
fire showed them the way through the
night. ²⁰You sent your good Spirit to
instruct them, and you did not stop
giving them manna from heaven or
water for their thirst. ²¹For forty years
you sustained them in the wilderness,
and they lacked nothing. Their clothes
did not wear out, and their feet did
not swell!
²²"Then you helped our ancestors
conquer kingdoms and nations, and
you placed your people in every corner
of the land.* They took over the land
of King Sihon of Heshbon and the
land of King Og of Bashan. ²³You
made their descendants as numerous
as the stars in the sky and brought
them into the land you had promised
to their ancestors.
²⁴"They went in and took possession
of the land. You subdued whole
nations before them. Even the
Canaanites, who inhabited the land,
were powerless! Your people could

deal with these nations and their kings as they pleased. ²⁵Our ancestors captured fortified cities and fertile land. They took over houses full of good things, with cisterns already dug and vineyards and olive groves and fruit trees in abundance. So they ate until they were full and grew fat and enjoyed themselves in all your blessings.

²⁶"But despite all this, they were disobedient and rebelled against you. They turned their backs on your Law, they killed your prophets who warned them to return to you, and they committed terrible blasphemies. ²⁷So you handed them over to their enemies, who made them suffer. But in their time of trouble they cried to you, and you heard them from heaven. In your great mercy, you sent them liberators who rescued them from their enemies.

²⁸"But as soon as they were at peace, your people again committed evil in your sight, and once more you let their enemies conquer them. Yet whenever your people turned and cried to you again for help, you listened once more from heaven. In your wonderful mercy, you rescued them many times!

²⁹"You warned them to return to your Law, but they became proud and obstinate and disobeyed your commands. They did not follow your regulations, by which people will find life if only they obey. They stubbornly turned their backs on you and refused to listen. ³⁰In your love, you were patient with them for many years. You sent your Spirit, who warned them through the prophets. But still they wouldn't listen! So once again you allowed the peoples of the land to conquer them. ³¹But in your great mercy, you did not destroy them completely or abandon them forever. What a gracious and merciful God you are!

³²"And now, our God, the great and mighty and awesome God, who keeps his covenant of unfailing love, do not let all the hardships we have suffered seem insignificant to you. Great trouble has come upon us and upon our kings and leaders and priests and prophets and ancestors—all of your people—from the days when the kings of Assyria first triumphed over us until now. ³³Every time you punished us you were being just. We have sinned greatly, and you gave us only what we deserved. ³⁴Our kings, leaders, priests, and ancestors did not obey your Law or listen to the warnings in your commands and laws. ³⁵Even while they had their own kingdom, they did not serve you, though you showered your goodness on them. You gave them a large, fertile land, but they refused to turn from their wickedness.

³⁶"So now today we are slaves in the land of plenty that you gave our ancestors for their enjoyment! We are slaves here in this good land. ³⁷The lush produce of this land piles up in the hands of the kings whom you have set over us because of our sins. They have power over us and our livestock. We serve them at their pleasure, and we are in great misery."

9:1 Hebrew *On the twenty-fourth day of that same month,* the seventh month of the ancient Hebrew lunar calendar. This day was October 31, 445 B.C.; also see notes on 1:1 and 8:2.   9:3 Hebrew *for a quarter of a day.* 9:9 Hebrew *sea of reeds.*   9:22 The meaning of the Hebrew is uncertain.

NOTES

9:1 *On October 31.* Lit., "On the twenty-fourth day of that same month" (see NLT mg).

they fasted and dressed in burlap and sprinkled dust on their heads. These outward signs represent an inner emotional feeling of grief and sorrow for sinning against God. The people saw the seriousness of their sin and expressed their grief over it. We, too, should grieve over sin.

9:2 *separated themselves from all foreigners as they confessed.* Although the NLT suggests that this separation took place while the people were confessing their sins, this reads into the text more than what is plainly there. The NASB, NIV, and RSV instead see the separation happening at a prior time. Rather than stating the precise timing, the main purpose of this clause is to indicate that only true Israelites were involved with the confession going on in ch 9. This contrasts with the situation in 8:13-18, for foreigners could participate in the Festival of Shelters (Deut 16:14; see Blenkinsopp 1988:296; Clines 1984:190). The children of Israel, not the foreigners in the land, were the ones who felt convicted of sin and worshiped God.

confessed their own sins. This brief comment is a summary statement of what happened in the rest of the chapter. The following verses indicate that this actually involved hearing God's voice through the reading of Scripture as well as a period of worship and confessional prayer. Nehemiah's prayer in 1:5-9 recognized the need for the people to confess their sins, and finally in this passage it appears that many did just that.

9:4 *The Levites . . . on the stairway of the Levites.* These Levites were not standing on stairs leading to the platform mentioned in 8:4 (Yamauchi 1988:730), but probably on steps leading up to one of the courts of the Temple (Breneman 1993:233; Allen 2003:135). The Mishnah (*Middoth* 2:5) indicates that at a later time the Levites stood on the 15 steps that led from the court of the women to the court of Israel and led the people in singing. Five of the names in 9:4 are repeated in 9:5.

9:4-5a *cried out to the* LORD *. . . called out to the people: "Stand up and praise the* LORD.*"* The Levites first led the people in crying out in distress (*za'aq* [TH2199, ZH2410]) to confess their sins to God in 9:4; then in 9:5 they led them in singing praise. In a similar situation in Ezra 9, Ezra, the spiritual leader, initially confessed the sins of the people and then later (10:1) a crowd of people gathered and joined him in confessing their sins. Blenkinsopp (1988:301) thinks that this prayer does not fit the context of the Feast of Shelters and the divorcing of heathen wives in ch 10 because the prayer pays almost no attention to those issues and because the prayer assumes the people are settled in the land. Neither of these objections are that strong, for some of the people who came back in 537 BC would have been well settled in the land by 445 BC. The prayer deals with the history of Israel in the wilderness (9:6-22) and with people not paying attention to what God said in the Torah (9:14, 16, 26, 29, 34), two important issues that relate to the events in ch 9. Thus the focus of the prayer is on the people's repeated sinfulness and God's gracious compassion that they needed once again. The need to correct the sinfulness of the people was far more important at this point than anything related to the Festival of Shelters. Once they got right with God, then they could enjoy the Festival of Shelters.

9:5 *praise the* LORD *your God, for he lives from everlasting to everlasting!* Lit., "Praise the LORD your God forever and ever." To make sense of this clause, which is difficult because the people do not continue from this point in the story to stand before the Levites and bless God forever, NLT connects it to what precedes by periphrastically adding, "for he lives" before it. The NASB adds nothing to the text and simply has the Levites calling the people to praise God forever (cf. Pss 41:13; 106:48, NASB). A second approach is to hypothesize that a line of praise ("May you be blessed, O LORD our God") has dropped out before "from everlasting to everlasting" (Williamson 1985:300, 303). A third approach is to see all of 9:5 as part of the call to praise, thus the actual prayer begins in 9:6 (Myers 1965:166). The Old Greek took this interpretation and began 9:6 with "And Ezra said," in order to make sense of this passage. But since the second-person address to God begins in 9:5b (*"your* glorious name"; my italics), it is evident that the prayer begins without any introduction in the middle of 9:5. "From everlasting to everlasting" must then refer to God, rather than the length of time people were to praise. The addition of "then they prayed" in the NLT helps the reader make sense of the unmarked transition from the call to praise in 5a to the prayer in 5b.

9:6 You made. Although not using the word "create" (*bara'* [TH1254, ZH1343]; cf. Gen 1:1), the idea of "making" (*'asah* [TH6213, ZH6913]) the world is a parallel thought.

the heavens. The literal "heavens and heavens of heavens" seems rather repetitious, but the second phrase was probably a superlative meaning the "highest heavens" (cf. Deut 10:14; 1 Kgs 8:27; 2 Chr 2:6; 6:18).

all the stars. The word *tsaba'* [TH6635, ZH7372] (NLT, "stars") literally means "hosts," which could refer to the stars but is more likely a reference to the angelic hosts or armies (1 Kgs 22:19; Yamauchi 1988:732) that inhabit heaven. It thus stands parallel to the inhabitants of the earth mentioned at the end of this verse.

You preserve. The verb could express the idea of God's power to "make alive" or "keep alive." Both ideas recognize that God is sovereignly in control of all life in heaven and earth. Without him we would not exist, and without his continuing daily gift of life nothing in heaven and earth would thrive. All life depends on God.

angels of heaven worship you. Although Israel and the nations from time to time worshiped the stars and "hosts of heaven," in heaven, the angels worship God. This reminds one of the scene of many worshipers around the throne of God that Isaiah saw (Isa 6:1-8), of Daniel's vision of the Ancient of Days (Dan 7:9-10), and of the picture of worship around the throne of God in Revelation (Rev 4:8-11; 5:8-14).

9:8 When he had proved himself faithful. Lit., "And you found his heart faithful." This statement indicates that it was important for Abraham to believe God (Gen 15:6) and demonstrates his faith through his "firm stand, fidelity, faithfulness" to God's revelation. Hebrews 11:6 proclaims that without faith it is impossible to please God.

give him and his descendants the land. The land of Israel was always supposed to be seen by the Israelites as God's gift (Gen 13:15; 15:18; 17:8), not as something the people earned or deserved. The listing of the peoples who lived in the land before it was given to Abraham's descendants is reminiscent of Gen 15:18-21, though the nations included and their order are different. Compare this list with Ezra 9:1. Ishida (1979:461-490) shows that this list follows the postexilic pattern rather than the Genesis pattern.

you have done what you promised, for you are always true to your word. Lit., "You fulfilled your words because you are righteous." God's righteousness was not an abstract idea but a character trait that was demonstrated by acts consistent with his statements. He fulfilled his promise of giving them the land. This covenant-keeping consistency provided hope for the future. God was righteous by being faithful to his promise, while God counted Abraham righteous because of his faith (Gen 15:6).

9:12 so that they could find their way. Lit., "to lighten for them the way in which they should walk."

9:18 idol shaped like a calf. In this context, the golden calf refers to the one Aaron made at Mount Sinai (Exod 32:1-8) rather than the two golden calves Jeroboam put at Bethel and Dan (1 Kgs 12:28-33). The phrase "this is your god" is sg. in Neh 9:18, but there are two ways people have interpreted a nearly identical statement in Exod 32:4, 8. In the Exodus story the people describe this idol using the pl. forms "these are your gods" (NIV, KJV, NLT, ESV, RSV, ASV, NRSV). But some translations and commentators interpret Exod 32:4, 8 as having a singular meaning (NASB, NKJV) "this is your God," since Aaron made only one idol, and he identifies this as "the LORD" (Exod 32:5). The prayer in Neh 9:18 avoids all possible confusion about this matter by using the sg. demonstrative pronoun and verb. In sum, this was not the sin of worshiping a pagan god. Aaron had claimed that the golden calf represented the God of Israel who delivered them from Egyptian slavery; thus, it was the sin of making a graven image of God himself.

They committed terrible blasphemies. Since *ne'atsoth* [TH5007A, ZH5542] is a rare word (also in 9:26), the meaning is not entirely clear. It has been translated "impieties" (Myers 1965:161), "provocations" (LXX, KJV), and "faithless murmurings" (Clines 1984:195), but its usage in Ezek 35:12 ("contemptuous word," NLT) demonstrates that it refers to scandalous or blasphemous words spoken against someone. Allen (2003:136) understands these "terrible blasphemies" as the act of "despising or rejecting God in favor of the golden calf in Exod 32:8."

9:19 But in your great mercy. Divine justice should cause great blasphemies to be met with great judgment, but instead God showed his great compassion by not killing the whole nation immediately at Mount Sinai after the golden calf incident (Exod 32:10, 14).

9:20 You sent your good Spirit to instruct them. The role of the Spirit's teaching and leading is also emphasized in Ps 143:10. Although Moses never refers to the Spirit teaching the people, this may be an interpretation of events in Num 11:24-26, where God's Spirit, which was in Moses, rested on the 70 elders of Israel and caused them to prophesy. Another, better option is to view this verse in light of Isa 63:11-14, which mentions the Spirit's presence with the people before the dividing of the Red Sea, guiding them through the sea, and giving the people rest. This reference to the "Spirit" could refer to the glory of God's presence with them in the pillar of fire. Although it is not explicitly stated in the Pentateuch that the pillar of fire is the Spirit, there is good reason to follow Kline (1972:201), who thinks it is "necessary to observe that it is the Spirit in particular who is identified with the theophanic pillar of the glory-cloud."

9:22 you placed your people in every corner of the land. "Every corner" is a possible translation in some contexts (BDB 802; cf. Lev 19:9, 27, the "corner" of a field or beard), but when the word is used of the land it often means a "side, border" (Ezek 45:7, "east side, eastern border"; 47:19, "south side, southern border"), so "border" is a preferable interpretation. Supporting the use of the word as border is the use of a similar Akkadian term (Williamson 1985:305), though others suggest it is the name of a town in Moab (Num 24:17; Jer 48:45 [KJV, "corner"]; Clines 1984:196).

King Sihon of Heshbon and . . . King Og of Bashan. The narratives reporting God's defeat of these nations in the Transjordan (Num 21:21-35; Deut 2:24–3:11) provided two examples of God's mighty conquest of their enemies.

9:23 descendants as numerous as the stars in the sky and brought them into the land. These were the two key factors in God's promises to the patriarchs: multiplication (Gen 15:5; 22:17; Deut 1:10) and giving them the land (Gen 15:18; Exod 33:1). God was faithful to keep his promise in both areas.

9:24 You subdued whole nations before them. The glory for the defeat and subduing (Deut 9:3) of these strong kings, cities, and giants belonged to God, not Joshua or Israel's army.

9:26 killed your prophets. Rejecting God's word involved rejecting both his written word and his spoken word through the prophets. First Kings 19:10, 14; 2 Chr 24:19-21; Jer 2:30; 26:20-23 are a few examples where opposition was so strong that prophets were killed. In many other examples the prophets were rejected but not killed (1 Kgs 22:13-28; Amos 7:10-17; Mic 2:6-7).

9:27 *you handed them over to their enemies. . . . they cried to you. . . . you sent them liberators.* This fits the period of the judges (Judg 2:11-18). Once again the people sinned, and God had compassion on them.

9:28 *In your wonderful mercy, you rescued them many times!* The cycle continued on and on, but God acted in compassion (better than the NLT's "mercy") to repeatedly deliver his people from oppression. The people were totally undeserving of divine compassion, for their deep-seated evil character revealed both their stubborn unwillingness to change as well as the depravity of their sinful, ingrained habits.

9:29 *they became proud and obstinate and disobeyed.* These three words describe together a pattern of selfish defiance of God's ways (see 9:16 for an earlier example). Pride makes people want to determine their own way, rather than submit to God's direction. Pride encourages a stubborn rejection of anything other than one's own way. When God's way is not given priority, disobedience will naturally follow.

people will find life if only they obey. This verse does not suggest that the future blessing of a good life and prosperity will come automatically through obeying the law. It is saying that one can continue to have a blessed life if one maintains one's covenant relationship with God by following his instructions in the law (see Lev 18:5; Deut 4:1; Ps 119:25).

9:30 *In your love, you were patient with them for many years.* If the root *mashak* [TH4900, ZH5432] is translated "you did bear" with them, the clause expresses God's patience with his people over many years (so NLT). Another option is to translate it "you extended" unto them, implying that God extended unto them "mercy" or "love"—based on other similar passages (see Pss 36:10 [11]; 109:12, NASB).

you allowed the peoples of the land to conquer them. Lit., "You gave them into the hand of the peoples of the lands." The "peoples of the lands [pl.]" were foreign conquerors; this phrase probably refers to the Assyrians who conquered and exiled the northern nation of Israel in 721 BC (2 Kgs 17). The Babylonians under Nebuchadnezzar destroyed the southern nation of Judah in 586 BC (2 Kgs 24–25). These peoples should be distinguished from the "people of the land" (sg.), which refers to the Samarian people (Ezra 4:1-4) who lived in Yehud while most of the Israelites were in Babylonian captivity. This latter group opposed the building of the Jewish Temple in Ezra 4:1-4. Since God's covenant people ignored the warning of the prophets again and again, God removed his protecting hand from them and caused their defeat. Sin exacts a terrible price when people fail to repent and turn from it.

9:31 *in your great mercy, you did not destroy them completely or abandon them forever.* Even in this great act of judgment (the destruction of these nations), God acted with compassion and grace toward his undeserving people. He did not allow all the people to be killed (see Jer 4:27; 30:11; Amos 9:8) or forsake his original plans to use this people to bless all the nations of the earth (Gen 12:3). This demonstrated God's commitment to his promises and his ability to accomplish his plan, even when his people turned against him for a time. Truly his marvelous grace is greater than all our sins.

9:32 *And now, our God, the great and mighty and awesome God, who keeps his covenant of unfailing love.* This begins a new section (9:32-37) that deals with the exilic period (9:32-35) and the present, postexilic situation (9:36-37). Both paragraphs are marked with the beginning phrase "And now/So now." The one praying confessed the nation's sins and indirectly appealed for God to recognize the difficult situation the people were in and help them.

9:34 *did not obey your Law or listen to the warnings.* Everyone failed—kings, officials, priests, and ancestors (surprisingly, false prophets are not mentioned)—because they did not do what God asked them to do in the law or listen to God's warnings via the admonitions of the prophets.

9:36 today we are slaves. Lit., "we are servants." At first this negative view of life under Persian authority is surprising because in many ways the Persians treated the Jewish people kindly (Myers 1965:170). This is the same perspective that Ezra mentioned earlier (see Ezra 9:9), for the Persians' extensive taxation system was a very heavy burden on the nation (Clines 1984:198).

COMMENTARY

It appears that this story took place two days after the end of the joyful Festival of Shelters in 8:13-18. There is no transitional statement explaining how the preceding events influenced what happened in chapter 9, but the change from joy at the Festival of Shelters to the mourning on this occasion seems rather abrupt and somewhat backward, for usually one expects confession of sin to come first and joy to follow it (Myers 1965:165). Consequently, some believe that this chapter is misplaced from its original setting after Ezra 10, which deals with the problem of divorce (see 9:2; Myers 1965:165; Williamson 1985:309-310). But the prayer in chapter 9 has a similar structure to the two paragraphs in 8:1-18, which demonstrates that chapters 8–10 belong together as a literary unit. The prayer in 9:5b-37 is not about the divorce problem; thus, the brief comment about divorce only states that this happened at some point earlier, with no indication that it happened immediately before this (Clines 1984:189). If this correctly positions the setting, it appears that the present weeping and confession arose out of the people's recognition of their sin when the law of God was read, parallel to what happened in 8:1-12.

As in 8:5, the people stood as a sign of reverence when God's word was read. This passage does not indicate who read from the Book of the Law, so one could assume that the same pattern in 8:1-3 was followed here. Thus, Ezra and some of the Levites mentioned in 9:4-5 probably did the reading (Clines 1984:191). God's instructions would give them knowledge of what they were supposed to do and what they should avoid, but head knowledge has only limited value. The goal of understanding God's word is to apply it to one's life; thus, the people needed to confess where they had failed to follow God. Then they would be in a right relationship with God and could demonstrate their humble submission by bowing in worship before him.

The Hebrew text does not indicate who prayed the long prayer in 9:5b-37. One could conclude that this was the prayer of confession made by the Levites who cried out to God in 9:4 (Throntveit 1992:102), a prayer by the people who were gathered together (Eskenazi 1988:100), or a prayer by Ezra (LXX).

This prayer has characteristics of both the historical psalms (Pss 78; 105; 106; 135; 136) and earlier prayers of confession (1:5-11; Ezra 9:6-15; Dan 9:4-19). Like the historical psalms, this prayer reviews God's gracious guidance and care throughout salvation history. It traces the history of God's great deeds from Creation (9:6) until its own time (9:32-37). It is as if the speaker were praying through Scripture and applying the lessons learned to his spiritual understanding of his present situation (Eskenazi 1988:101). In humble confession, the people acknowledged their past corporate failures and guilt, repeatedly giving recognition to God's gracious compassion when they sinned (cf. Ps 106). The first half of the prayer focuses on praising the actions of God (9:5b-31), who compassionately cared for the people in spite of their failures (9:16-18, 26, 29-30). The beginning of the second half is marked by "and now" (9:32). Its characteristics are closer to a lament.

The material can be divided into the following themes:

Praise to God (9:5b)
Creation (9:6)
Abraham (9:7-8)
Exodus (9:9-11)
Wilderness (9:12-21)
Conquest (9:22-25)
Life in the land (9:26-31)
Exile of the nation (9:32-35)
Present situation (9:36-37)

It is appropriate that the prayer should begin with words of praise to God. The worshipers wanted to exalt and glorify the Lord's name. The Lord's creative power, preservation, covenant making, faithfulness to his word, deliverance from enemies, miraculous signs, guidance, feeding, and instruction (9:6-15) demonstrate why the people praised him.

First and foremost comes a statement of the Lord's unique claim to divinity and the people's commitment to him (9:6). The Lord is incomparable, for he is the only real God (Isa 44:6, 8; 46:9). This is not just a monotheistic creedal confession (cf. Deut 6:4), but a declaration that the people's faith commitment was singularly grounded in the Lord (Yahweh) alone. In order to emphasize this idea, it is repeated at the beginning of 9:7, which then goes on to speak of how the Lord chose Abram and called him to Canaan. The Lord demonstrated his divine character by these three pivotal acts in early Hebrew history. Although the Torah does not refer to the "choosing" of Abram (Deut 4:37; 7:7; 10:15; 14:2 refer to the choosing of Israel), it does record that God brought him up (Gen 15:7) and changed his name (Gen 17:5). These acts of election, deliverance, and covenant making with Abram identify the Lord as the source of their nation's history. This recitation of the Lord's great acts recognizes the people's total dependence on him and by implication inspires hope for the future based on God's promises to Abraham.

Verses 9-12 deal with the Exodus events. It is always a comfort to know that God is aware of his people's problems and acts to alleviate their misery (see Exod 3:7; 4:31). Since he acted on behalf of his people in the past, the one praying could confidently ask that God see the people's present misery under Persian control during the time of Nehemiah (9:36-37). The plagues on the Egyptians (Exod 7-11) were repeatedly seen as irrefutable evidence of God's power over an insurmountable enemy (Deut 4:34; 6:22; 7:19). Part of the Lord's purpose in the plagues was to cause the Pharaoh, his officials, and the people of Egypt to know that he was God (Exod 7:5, 17; 8:10, 22; 9:14, 29; 10:2). This happened when his officials (Exod 8:19; 9:20; 10:7), Pharaoh (Exod 9:27; 10:16), and the Egyptian people (Exod 11:3) recognized these plagues as the hand of God.

Although the Egyptians acted in arrogance (Exod 9:17; 18:11) by refusing to acknowledge the Lord as their God, by not allowing his people to leave Egypt, and by trying to make a glorious name for their Egyptian civilization, God used the plagues to glorify his name throughout the earth (Exod 9:16). Even Rahab the harlot in Jericho knew about God's great acts of deliverance and trusted God (Josh 2:9-11). This glorious reputation inspired Israelites throughout their history and gave hope to these people in the time of Nehemiah.

Two further acts of divine grace and power led to God's glorious reputation. First, he "parted" (*baqa'* [TH1234, ZH1324]) the sea (Exod 14:16, 21-22) and enabled the Israelites to pass over on dry ground (Exod 15:16). Next he hurled "their pursuers" (*radaph* [TH7291, ZH8103]) into the sea (Exod 14:4-5, 23; 15:4-5). This was a clear miracle of God's direct intervention in history on behalf of his people. They saw and experienced a demonstration of God's power. Furthermore, the Israelites had the pillar of fire and cloud accompanying them (Exod 13:21-22; 14:24; Deut 1:33), a signal of God's continued direction of the people in the wilderness. The prayer focuses on the cloud and fire as evidence of God's guidance, rather than his powerful presence with them.

At Sinai, God not only spoke with Moses (Exod 19:3, 9, 20-21), but also directly to the people (Deut 5:22, 24, 26). This was a once-in-a-lifetime experience that the people marveled at (9:13). His thunderous words included "regulations and instructions . . . decrees and commands" that were just and good. Although some people might view the law of Moses in a very negative way, the righteous people of Israel saw it as God's just revelation of his will (Ps 119:11, 16, 18, 26-27, 35, 40, 47-48, 97, 113, 127, 140, 163), much like many today view the New Testament as a revelation of God's will.

In the instructions, God told them about the holy Sabbath (9:14). The people were not ignorant of what would please God in their relationships with others or in their relationship with him. Sabbath instructions involve the importance of keeping the day holy, resting from work, and seeing it as a sign of their covenant with God (Exod 20:8; 31:12-17; Deut 5:12). This dedication of one holy period of time to God marked the Israelites as a distinctive people, dependent on God's provision rather than on what they could earn in seven days of work.

The prayer then goes on to thank God for giving the Israelites bread from heaven and water from the rock (9:15). God's grace was abundant in many ways. The giving of the manna, like snow from heaven (Exod 16; Pss 78:24; 105:40), and springs of water from a rock (Exod 17:6; Num 20:8; Ps 105:41) demonstrated God's miraculous care for his people when they were helpless to provide for themselves. God led his people through the wilderness and on into the good land of Canaan. Joshua's conquest of the land was accomplished because of two factors working together: The people acted in faith to take the land, and God defeated their enemies (Deut 1:8; 4:1; 6:18; Josh 8:1-2; 11:6-8).

At this point (9:16), the prayer begins to contrast God's great deeds of grace and power with the Israelites' presumptuous, sinful behavior. Pride says, "I am the boss, I know best, I can do this myself; thus, I will not listen to others." A stubborn person is one who has a stiff neck (Exod 32:9; Jer 7:26) that will not change or turn. This combination is deadly, for proud and stubborn people are not even open to considering good advice that might prevent their doom. There is no way to reach them, for they refuse to listen to God's words.

God repeatedly asked the people to remember what he did for them (Deut 4:10; 5:15; 7:18) because when they remembered God's past grace and power (the miraculous plagues, the Exodus through the Red Sea, his guidance by the fire and cloud, his defeat of their enemies), it would cause them to be grateful and trust him for the future (9:17). When believers forget what God has done for them in the past, they usually do not praise God, thank him, obey him, or trust him. At Kadesh-barnea the people would not trust God to give them the land because they were afraid of the giants that the spies told them about. They forgot what God had done to their enemies in the past in Egypt; thus, ironically they wanted to appoint a new leader who would take them back to the slavery of Egypt (Num 13-14). This was not just a rejection of their earthly leader Moses; it was a rejection of God and all his promises.

The one praying then said, "You are a God of forgiveness, gracious and merciful, slow to become angry, and rich in unfailing love" (9:17b). This verse contrasts what "they" did (9:16-17a, 18) with what God did (9:17b). Israel's past experiences could be best understood through the eyes of God's love for them. In spite of their stubborn, arrogant rebellion, God acted in forgiveness and mercy by pardoning them of their sins and taking pity on them, instead of punishing them in anger; he repeatedly showed his steadfast covenant devotion to his disobedient covenant people. God faithfully and providentially cared for all the people's needs—food, water, clothes, and health. In spite of their murmuring and rebellion, they actually lacked nothing (Deut 2:7; 8:4; 29:5). Because God acted this way on many occasions, one can use the terms used in 9:17b to describe his character (Exod 34:6; Num 14:19; Ps 86:15; Joel 2:13; Jonah 4:2).

In 9:22-25, the prayer recounts all the wonderful things God did for the people during the conquest of the land under Joshua. The grace of God was evident, and his promise to bring them into a good land flowing with milk and honey was true. Moses told the people that God would give them a fertile land (Deut 6:10-11; 8:7-10; 11:10-15) and warned them not to become proud and forget God once they had all these blessings. Having received all these blessings, some became prosperous and spent their time enjoying the good life. Deuteronomy 8:11-20 warns the people about the temptation of self-sufficiency and forgetting that it is God who provides all their wealth.

Nehemiah 9:26-31 describes the people's behavior once they were settled in the land, stretching from the time of the judges, through the united monarchy, and up to the time of the Exile. This was the third round of the cycle of God's blessings and the people's rebellion. Their sin fundamentally involved an unwillingness to follow God's divine revelation and a refusal to repent, in spite of the warnings of the prophets. Instead, the wicked people of Israel killed the prophets God sent to deliver his word (1 Kgs 18:4, 13; 19:10-14; 2 Chr 24:20-22; Jer 2:30; Matt 23:29-37; Rom 11:3). It is always unwise to disregard God's instructions, but it is plainly stupid to not pay attention to God's warnings of destruction.

The next section (9:32-35) begins with words of praise to God for who he is and what he has done. The past punishments of the nation did not prove he was weak or did not love his people. Instead, past history proved that he was still Israel's God who is "great and mighty" in power, "awesome," as revealed by his miraculous deeds, and faithful to his covenant with his people (9:32). All confessions of sin and requests for divine assistance must be based on a person's submission to God, reverence for him, and personal relationship with him. In faith God's people can ask for help because they know God acts in love and faithfulness to his promises. His promises can be trusted because he has the ability to do what he has said.

The one praying was not bitter about the shame and devastation of the Assyrian or Babylonian captivity, nor did he blame God for the negative things that happened to them (9:33). In humble confession it was admitted that the people had "sinned greatly" and deserved all the judgment that God sent on the nation. The prayer encouraged the listeners to take full responsibility for their sinful actions and accept the appropriateness of God's just punishment. God is able to help his people only when they confess their sins, repent, and return to put their faith in God.

The prayer ends with a petition concerning the people's condition (9:36-37). Although God had put his people back in the fruitful land of Palestine, the riches gained from the land were not benefiting the people of Israel at this time. A good share of their wealth was being sent to the king of Persia to pay their taxes (see 5:4). Since the Persian government ruled the land, loyalty to the king and his laws was required (see Ezra 7:25-26). The Persians could require them to serve in forced labor on roads for the state, in the army, or in other state-sponsored projects. In addition, the Persians had the legal power over them to punish or kill them if they broke the Persian laws. They were still in great trouble and needed God's help to deliver them.

In summary, this long prayer involves (1) praise and acknowledgment of God's wonderful character; (2) several confessions of the nation's failures to maintain their covenant relationship with God; (3) the recognition of God's compassion, grace, and covenant faithfulness in spite of sin; (4) the admission that the nation deserved the just punishment of God for their sins; and (5) a request for God to take notice of their miserable situation. This prayer is quite different from most prayers in the Bible and in the church today: It is especially long, it traces the failures of God's people through the whole history of the nation, and it emphasizes the importance of God's compassion in the past. Nevertheless, it provides the reader with important theological perspectives that should appear in many of our prayers. People need to see God's role in the broad sphere of all history so that they properly appreciate that his work has worldwide as well as personal significance.

The Hymns of Praise in the Psalms (Pss 100; 111-113; 146-150) offer words of praise to God and call others to join in magnifying God's name. The prayer in Nehemiah begins with statements that praise God's name, exalt him (9:5), and declare his wonderful deeds (9:6-15). At the beginning of the second half of the prayer, as attention turns to confessions and requests (9:32), the prayer again repeats words of praise to God for his power, awesome presence, and unfailing covenant love. When people pray, they should always recognize the great privilege of praying to Almighty God and reverently give God honor by glorifying his name. Prayers of praise flow from a heart that desires to worship God.

The reasons for praise are related to God's miraculous acts in nature (Creation, miraculous plagues using nature, dividing the sea), his wonderful deeds on behalf of his people (election, giving the land, sending deliverers), his revelation of his will and his ways (giving the law, guiding through the pillar of fire, giving his Spirit, speaking through prophets), his personal covenant relationship with his people, his faithfulness to his promises, and his refusal to abandon his disobedient people. There is no doubt that God is wonderful, glorious, compassionate, and just. People should praise him for all the wonderful things he has done in the past and in our present time.

Prayers should include a confession of sin in order for people to restore their broken relationship with God. When people act in pride and stubbornly refuse to follow God's revealed will (9:16, 29), reject God's leaders, rebel, kill God's prophetic messengers, and blaspheme God's name (9:26), they need to confess these sins and turn from their evil ways. In the prayer, the central focus was placed on the people's disobedience to God's instructions in the law and more recent rejection of the warnings of the prophets. The people of God knew what they should do but refused to listen to or obey what God said. Such sins led to the worship of idols (9:18), which was a massive failure to maintain their covenant relationship with God. But the most depressing factor in the nation's sins was that they were repeated again and again. Although it is shameful and embarrassing to admit failures, there is no way of establishing or maintaining an intimate relationship with God unless people admit and repent of their sins.

After each description of past sin there is a counterbalancing description of God's forgiveness, grace, and compassion (9:17). God demonstrated his love by not destroying his rebellious children after they worshiped the golden calf (9:18) or when they wanted to appoint a new leader to take them back to Egypt at Kadesh-barnea (9:17). Later, after they had inherited the good land from the Canaanites and enjoyed the riches of their new land, God forgave them for rebelling against his law and rejecting the warnings of the prophets (9:26, 29). Instead of destroying his sinful and rebellious people, God was patient and compassionate with them. Even when judgment came, he did not destroy them completely (9:31). Because of the human tendency to sin, people would not survive long without God's longsuffering mercy. Truly the grace of God is wonderful and totally undeserved.

Nevertheless, since people persist in sin, continually reject God's divine revelation, and fail to maintain a close covenant relationship with God, a day of accountability will come. Such punishments are hard to endure and painful to survive, but they are God's way of justly dealing with ungodly people. Sometimes a person may receive God's justice, but at other times when kings, priests, prophets, and the people are all sinful, God will destroy a whole nation (9:32-34). When people reject God and do not serve him, there will be serious consequences. How one responds to divine judgment will determine if anything was learned through the experience. One can become bitter and blame God, or one can properly recognize that a punishment was deserved. It may be hard, but it is always best to admit a failure and learn from the punishment.

In spite of past failures and punishments, a person can always come and seek God's mercy and compassion for each new situation (9:36-37). This prayer ends with expressions of oppression and frustration because of the heavy taxation of the Persians. Although the Hebrew people were back in their own land, they were not free of foreign dictators. They knew God could address their concerns and relieve them of their pain. Thus, they cried out to God about their situation, knowing that God would hear their cries and in his sovereign wisdom answer their prayers.

Although no nation has the same relationship to God as did Israel, there are common characteristics that govern God's relationship to all nations. When foreign and Israelite nations act in ways contrary to God's will (Amos 1-2), God holds them each accountable. There are certain aspects of this prayer that could serve as a model for people in almost any nation because every nation has a history of not serving God at times. This prayer suggests that people need to confess their failures, remember God's past acts of compassion, recognize that past punishment was God's discipline, ask for God to pay attention to the miserable situation that may exist at the present time, and praise his holy name. People in every nation need to recognize that if it were not for the great compassion and patience of God, they would suffer much more for their sins.

◆   C. The Community Determines to Obey God's Word
      (Neh 9:38-10:39)

38*The people responded, "In view of all this,* we are making a solemn promise and putting it in writing. On this sealed document are the names of our leaders and Levites and priests."

CHAPTER 10

1*The document was ratified and sealed with the following names:

The governor:
  Nehemiah son of Hacaliah, and also Zedekiah.
2The following priests:
  Seraiah, Azariah, Jeremiah, 3Pashhur, Amariah, Malkijah, 4Hattush, Shebaniah, Malluch, 5Harim, Meremoth, Obadiah, 6Daniel, Ginnethon, Baruch, 7Meshullam, Abijah, Mijamin, 8Maaziah, Bilgai, and Shemaiah. These were the priests.
9The following Levites:
  Jeshua son of Azaniah, Binnui from the family of Henadad, Kadmiel, 10and their fellow Levites: Shebaniah, Hodiah, Kelita, Pelaiah, Hanan, 11Mica, Rehob, Hashabiah, 12Zaccur, Sherebiah, Shebaniah, 13Hodiah, Bani, and Beninu.
14The following leaders:
  Parosh, Pahath-moab, Elam, Zattu, Bani, 15Bunni, Azgad, Bebai, 16Adonijah, Bigvai, Adin, 17Ater,

Hezekiah, Azzur, 18Hodiah, Hashum, Bezai, 19Hariph, Anathoth, Nebai, 20Magpiash, Meshullam, Hezir, 21Meshezabel, Zadok, Jaddua, 22Pelatiah, Hanan, Anaiah, 23Hoshea, Hananiah, Hasshub, 24Hallohesh, Pilha, Shobek, 25Rehum, Hashabnah, Maaseiah, 26Ahiah, Hanan, Anan, 27Malluch, Harim, and Baanah.

28Then the rest of the people—the priests, Levites, gatekeepers, singers, Temple servants, and all who had separated themselves from the pagan people of the land in order to obey the Law of God, together with their wives, sons, daughters, and all who were old enough to understand— 29joined their leaders and bound themselves with an oath. They swore a curse on themselves if they failed to obey the Law of God as issued by his servant Moses. They solemnly promised to carefully follow all the commands, regulations, and decrees of the LORD our Lord:

30"We promise not to let our daughters marry the pagan people of the land, and not to let our sons marry their daughters.

31"We also promise that if the people of the land should bring any merchandise or grain to be sold on the

Sabbath or on any other holy day, we will refuse to buy it. Every seventh year we will let our land rest, and we will cancel all debts owed to us.

³²"In addition, we promise to obey the command to pay the annual Temple tax of one-eighth of an ounce of silver* for the care of the Temple of our God. ³³This will provide for the Bread of the Presence; for the regular grain offerings and burnt offerings; for the offerings on the Sabbaths, the new moon celebrations, and the annual festivals; for the holy offerings; and for the sin offerings to make atonement for Israel. It will provide for everything necessary for the work of the Temple of our God.

³⁴"We have cast sacred lots to determine when—at regular times each year—the families of the priests, Levites, and the common people should bring wood to God's Temple to be burned on the altar of the LORD our God, as is written in the Law.

³⁵"We promise to bring the first part of every harvest to the LORD's Temple year after year—whether it be a crop from the soil or from our fruit trees.

³⁶We agree to give God our oldest sons and the firstborn of all our herds and flocks, as prescribed in the Law. We will present them to the priests who minister in the Temple of our God. ³⁷We will store the produce in the storerooms of the Temple of our God. We will bring the best of our flour and other grain offerings, the best of our fruit, and the best of our new wine and olive oil. And we promise to bring to the Levites a tenth of everything our land produces, for it is the Levites who collect the tithes in all our rural towns.

³⁸"A priest—a descendant of Aaron—will be with the Levites as they receive these tithes. And a tenth of all that is collected as tithes will be delivered by the Levites to the Temple of our God and placed in the storerooms. ³⁹The people and the Levites must bring these offerings of grain, new wine, and olive oil to the storerooms and place them in the sacred containers near the ministering priests, the gatekeepers, and the singers.

"We promise together not to neglect the Temple of our God."

9:38a Verse 9:38 is numbered 10:1 in Hebrew text.   9:38b Or *In spite of all this.*   10:1 Verses 10:1-39 are numbered 10:2-40 in Hebrew text.   10:32 Hebrew *tax of 1/3 of a shekel* [4 grams].

NOTES

9:38 [10:1] *we are making a solemn promise and putting it in writing.* This verse begins ch 10 in the Hebrew text (cf. NLT mg), indicating the beginning of a new literary unit. There is much discussion concerning whether the contents of this section fit after the great prayer of confession in ch 9, where they are now placed; whether it would be more logical to place this section after the reforms in Ezra 8–10 (Throntveit 1992:101; Myers 1965:165); or whether it belongs with the reforms instituted in ch 13, when the governor returned from his brief stay in Susa (13:6-7; see Clines 1984:199; Williamson 1985:330-331). Although not all the material in Ezra-Nehemiah was put in chronological order and the reforms in 10:30-39 are similar to those in ch 13, it is hard to explain why Ezra would not have associated ch 10 with ch 13 if that was its original context. The connective "in view of all this" in 9:38, the "we" terminology in 9:33, 36, 37, 38, and the mention of "faithful" Abraham and "faithful covenant," (9:8, 38 [NLT, "solemn promise"]) all connect 10:1-39 with what precedes in ch 9 (Duggan 2001:241-242), so it should not be moved to fit the circumstances in ch 13.

This chapter falls into two sections. The second section, 10:30-39, describes what the people agreed to do. The first section, 9:38–10:29, records a list of the names and families that agreed with the content of this document. It is not absolutely clear if they actually signed their names to a document or if a scribe wrote their names on this document. Blenkinsopp concludes that only the civic and religious leaders signed the covenant in writing and he rejects the idea that each person who is named here affixed his seal impression on this document (1988:312), while Williamson states that "the present verse neither demands nor precludes the view that the leaders who added their names did so with seals only rather than signatures" (Williamson 1985:332). In either case these people were signifying that they were renewing their covenant relationship with God.

10:1 [2] The document was ratified and sealed. Lit., "On the seals." The NLT elaborates somewhat on the cultural importance of the seals by translating with the two words "ratified and sealed." Some take the pl. noun "seals" to refer to "those who sealed it" (cf. NIV) or to "the sealed document" (cf. NASB, NLT), but it probably refers to the multiple seals that were stamped on the document by each person or family.

Nehemiah. Nehemiah the governor set the example by signing and sealing the document first.

Zedekiah. Some hypothesize that Zedekiah was the same person as Nehemiah's scribe Zadok (13:13; cf. Blenkinsopp 1988:12; Brockington 1969:139), but this is just a guess based on a parallel context in Ezra 4:8, where Shimshai was expressly called a scribe. Another possibility is that Zedekiah was an important political leader under Nehemiah.

10:2-8 [3-9] The following priests. The NLT takes this note from the Hebrew of 10:7 [8] and places it before the list, a more familiar order for modern readers. This list of 21 priests is almost identical to the list of 22 priests who came back from exile with Zerubbabel (12:1-7). Since it is unlikely that these men were still alive at this time, these names must be family names rather than personal names (Clines 1984:201). These same 21 names are also listed in 12:12-21, where they are connected to the later period of Joiakim. This list seems to have some connection to the arrangement of the priestly families wherein 24 groups would take turns serving at the Temple (1 Chr 24:7-18).

10:9-13 [10-14] The following Levites. This list of 17 names overlaps with Levitical records in 8:7; 9:4-5; 12:8-9, 24-25. The first three seem to be the leaders. It may seem odd that the names Shebaniah and Hodiah are listed twice, but many people then and today have the same name, so these names should not be eliminated as scribal errors. These names can be compared to the Levitical genealogies in 1 Chr 6 and 23.

10:14-27 [15-28] The following leaders. Fourteen of the names in 10:14-27 are the same as those of the leaders listed in ch 7 and Ezra 2, while 13 names are mentioned in relation to those who helped Nehemiah rebuild the walls of Jerusalem (ch 3). Six names are of families who stood on the platform when Ezra read the law (8:4-14). The additional names reflect the growth of the community through additional people returning to Jerusalem from Babylon, the division of larger families into two groups, or apostate Jewish families in the land now joining with the exiles who returned to Jerusalem (Kidner 1979:115).

10:28-29 [29-30] the rest of the people. Nehemiah 10:28 delineates those who were involved in renewing this covenant of faithfulness to God, while 10:29 describes what they did. Only a few representatives of the political, religious, and influential family leaders actually sealed the document. But everyone could participate in the oral making of an oath—including men, women, and children (cf. 8:2-3). Those included in the larger congregation were gatekeepers, singers, Temple servants, and "all who had separated themselves from the pagan people of the land" (10:28). This last descriptive identification, "the rest of the people," could refer to either those who refused to intermarry with the pagan people in Samaria (Ezra 9-10; Myers 1965:177) or to a group of proselytes that converted to the worship of the God of Israel (Duggan 2001:246; Blenkinsopp 1988:314).

10:31 [32] *bring any merchandise or grain to be sold on the Sabbath . . . we will refuse to buy it.* The Torah required that the people rest on the Sabbath (Exod 20:8-11), but it did not explicitly forbid selling on the Sabbath. Other texts (Jer 17:19-27; Amos 8:5) indicate that the people understood that selling was working and thus forbidden. But the people of the land did not follow this practice, so it was necessary for the Israelites to recommit themselves to this agreed-upon interpretation of the more general Sabbatical law. Clines (1981:111-117) suggests five principles of exegesis used by priests to expand the application of earlier laws to cover new issues not directly addressed by Moses. Although the Jewish people accepted this behavior pattern, the rejection of it by non-Jews caused some real problems a few years later (13:15-18).

Every seventh year. Another related policy was to let the land rest and forgive debts in the Sabbatical year (Exod 21:2-6; 23:10-11; Lev 25:1-7; Deut 15:1-3). This would provide relief for the poor around Jerusalem (see ch 5) and demonstrate the people's trust in God to provide for their needs, since no grain would be planted in the Sabbatical year.

10:32 [33] *pay the annual Temple tax of one-eighth of an ounce of silver.* Lit., "a third of a shekel." The next couple of verses deal with caring for the Temple (10:32-33). Exodus 30:11-16 and 38:25-26 refer to a half-shekel payment to the Temple by all males over 20 years old; thus, it was not a postexilic invention (Blenkinsopp 1988:316). There is little evidence that this tax was collected yearly, though there is no evidence that it was not. When King Joash made Temple repairs, he asked people to help finance the work (2 Kgs 12:4-15). In NT times, the Temple tax was collected (Matt 17:24). Although the Persian government provided financial resources to build the Temple (Ezra 6:8) and an occasional special gift after that (Ezra 7:14-23), the leaders knew that the people needed to take responsibility for themselves. The change from a half to a third of a shekel may have been due to the use of a heavier shekel during the Persian period (Myers 1965:178).

10:33 [34] *provide for everything necessary for the work of the Temple.* These provisions included the 12 loaves of bread (Exod 25:23-30; Lev 24:5-9) to put on the golden table in the sanctuary each Sabbath. They may have functioned as a thanks offering for God's provision of bread for the people (Clines 1984:207). These people also agreed to provide regular grain and burnt offerings on the Sabbaths, new moons, and annual festivals (Exod 29:38-42; Num 28:3–29:39). The regular worship at the Temple must continue, but if it was going to continue, the people had to support it and be involved. People who love God must be responsible to arrange for the financial needs of the house of God, otherwise the activities will cease and God will not be glorified or praised by his people.

10:34 [35] *We have cast sacred lots.* Nehemiah 10:34-39 describes additional ways in which the people organized themselves to work together and supply the things necessary for the smooth functioning of the Temple. The priest would cast the lots by using the Urim or the Thummim stones in order to discover the will of God. It is interesting that everyone (priests, Levites, and common people) was responsible for a portion of this menial task; it was not something pushed off on the lower class. In today's terms, no one would be exempted from taking their turn sweeping the church floors and cleaning the bathrooms.

should bring wood. Since the altar was burning sacrifices continually (Lev 6:12), a great deal of wood was needed to keep the fire burning. Earlier the Gibeonites had the responsibility of gathering wood (Josh 9:27), but then it was spread out to all the people who returned from exile (possibly no known descendants from Gibeon returned with the exiles). Some years later, Nehemiah reinforced the need to faithfully keep up with supplying wood for the altar (13:31).

10:35 [36] *bring the first part of every harvest to the LORD's Temple.* No matter when
the grain or fruit became ready for harvest, the Israelites were to bring the firstfruits to the
Temple. God deserved the first and best of all his provisions for the people, so the people
brought them in an attitude of thanksgiving for all that he had provided for them (Exod
34:26; Num 18:12; Deut 26:1-11) This event was celebrated at the Festival of Weeks or
Festival of Harvest (Exod 23:19; Num 28:26), as well as other times when people harvested
crops. A portion from these firstfruits supplied food for the priests to eat.

10:36-37 [37-38] *give God our oldest sons and the firstborn of all our herds.* Since God
saved the firstborn from death at the Passover in Egypt, the firstborn belonged to God (Exod
13:12-13; Num 18:15-17), though a person could redeem a firstborn with a sacrifice or a payment of money (Exod 34:19-20; Lev 27:27). In addition, the people brought the first produce
from harvested crops, including the "best of our dough" from the new grain (Num 15:20-21)
and the first wine from the grapes. These were brought to the Temple storehouse (Ezra 8:29;
10:6) or to storerooms in Levitical villages to await distribution to priestly families.

10:37 [38] *bring to the Levites a tenth . . . it is the Levites who collect the tithes.* The
Levites who lived in Levitical cities scattered throughout the land collected the ten-percent
tithe (Num 18:21-24; Deut 14:22-29). The tithe showed God's ownership of their land and
was meant to help the people learn to reverence God (Deut 14:23). Deuteronomy 26:12-14
indicates that some of the tithe was used to financially assist the poor aliens, widows, and
orphans, though no mention is made of that in this chapter.

10:38 [39] *a tenth of all that is collected as tithes will be delivered by the Levites to the
Temple.* The Levites had to tithe the goods they collected by sending one-tenth to the central sanctuary in Jerusalem to support the priests there (Num 18:25-32). The exact nature
of the supervisory role of the priest who was in charge of things is unclear. Did this priest
merely receive, record, and store the tithe brought to Jerusalem, or did he go around to
the various Levitical cities and identify the kind of tithe (grain, wine, etc.) that the Temple
priests in Jerusalem needed based on what they had already received?

COMMENTARY
After the people confessed their sins to God in 9:1-37, they decided to formally
commit themselves to faithfully love and serve him by making an agreement
together (9:38). The language is similar to the earlier phrase regarding "cutting
a covenant" (Ezra 10:3, lit.), but here it refers to an "agreement of faithfulness"
(*'amanah* [TH548, ZH591]). It was voluntarily agreed to by those who signed or put their
seal to the document (10:1-27), and it was a unilateral binding agreement to remain
true to the law of God (10:29). It was put in writing to make it absolutely clear what
was agreed to and to identify those who had agreed to follow these commitments.
Maybe the leaders realized that if the people signed their names in writing or affixed
their seals to this document, they would take their oath more seriously.

Everyone knows the importance of signing your name to a document. Sealing
documents had the same force. It signified agreement with what the document said.
By signing a check, a person is agreeing to pay the amount identified on the check.
If one is selling a house, the signatures indicate that the seller and the buyer agree
on the stated price on the bill of sale. A signature is a means of holding people
accountable so they cannot come back later and change their minds, maintaining
that they did not agree to something. Accountability is required once people sign
their names.

The names of leaders, priests, and Levites were on this sealed document, but not all of them were on the clay bullae that sealed the document after it was rolled up (9:38). It is possible that each person or family wrote their name and then put an imprint of their family seal beside their name to verify that they agreed to what they had signed. (See notes on 10:2-27 for details on the names of the lists of leaders, priests, and Levites.)

After the list, 10:29 tells us that the people "bound themselves with an oath. They swore a curse on themselves if they failed to obey the Law." The ceremony involved all the people joining themselves together as one through an oral commitment to a common goal. To renew their covenant with God they had to dedicate themselves to love and obey God's covenant stipulations. To emphasize the seriousness of their commitment, everyone entered into an agreement that contained a curse on those who would break it (following the pattern established when they first received God's covenant in Deut 27-28). The people committed themselves to walking in the way God had instructed them to walk in the law of Moses. They expressed their willingness to submit themselves to God's will.

The final section (10:30-39) indicates specific commitments the people made related to (1) intermarriage with pagans (10:30), (2) keeping the Sabbath and seventh year holy (10:31), (3) caring for the Temple (10:32-33), and (4) bringing proper sacrifices (10:34-39).

The first obligation is worthy of comment in the context of Ezra and Nehemiah. (The other obligations are explained in the notes above.) The Israelites swore they would not allow their children to intermarry with the pagan people who lived in the land (based on Exod 34:11-16 and Deut 7:3-4). This was consistent with the commitment made earlier in Ezra 9-10 and with the later policy of Nehemiah 13:23-27. This prohibition was designed to protect the religious purity of the nation; it had nothing to do with any kind of racial or ethnic hatred for other people. In fact, the Israelites welcomed foreign converts who put their faith in Israel's God (e.g., Rahab and Ruth). In light of this pledge, it is odd that Nehemiah had problems with this issue some years later (13:23-27). One explanation is that some thought it was acceptable to intermarry with people in the land, so they did not join the people in this covenant renewal ceremony at this time (10:28).

In this covenant renewal ceremony, the people decided not just to say they were sorry for their past sins or that they would try to do better at following God's covenant instructions in the future. These believers wanted to challenge one another with a deeper and firmer commitment of faithfulness to God on a few key issues that were of central importance to the future spiritual vitality of the community. Thus, they made a "solemn promise" or a "firm agreement of faithfulness" (9:38) to God and one another. They realized they had not been faithful in the past (9:1-37), so they wanted to do something that would enhance their determination to serve and honor God in the future. They were recommitting themselves to God, just as Abraham did (Gen 12, 15, 17, 22). People still show their commitment this way today, such as when they sign a local church covenant or sign the Lausanne Covenant to foster evangelism and social action around the world.

A signed agreement outlines the relationship between the parties and describes certain behaviors that people willingly desire to do. Signing a document obligates the parties through oaths or sworn statements to faithfully bind themselves to one course of action, but it also eliminates other alternatives. An oath may include an expressed or implied curse for failure to remain faithful (10:29). The memory of this self-imposed curse functions as a motivator to be persistent in one's convictions. People who take oaths and swear a curse on themselves are probably more careful to follow what was agreed to and do not make excuses to absolve themselves of obligations. By signing their names to an agreement, these people did not create a legalistic setting in which they felt they must obey certain laws to gain some credit with God; instead, they freely gave themselves to God for the purpose of serving and honoring him better. There would be nothing wrong with Christians today individually or collectively making a covenant agreement that would outline those areas where they would purposely dedicate themselves to serve God.

General statements of dedication to God are good, but identifying specific attitudes and actions in a covenant document allows people to be more accountable and to measure faithfulness to a commitment more clearly. In this setting Nehemiah and the congregation knew that the people needed to get more serious about their commitments to (1) not intermarry with pagan people living around them (10:30), (2) not sell goods on the Sabbath (10:31), (3) observe the Sabbatical Year of rest (10:31), (4) pay their Temple tax (10:32), (4) bring their offerings to God (10:33), (5) provide wood to the Temple (10:34), (6) bring the firstfruits of the harvest and the firstborn children and animals (10:35-36), and (7) give the tithe to the Levites and priests (10:37).

In summary, the people "[promised] together not to neglect the Temple of [their] God" (10:39). The central purpose of these covenant renewal pledges was to encourage and support worship at the Temple so that God would continue to be glorified day after day. If no one provided wood or paid the tithe and the annual Temple tax, the Levites and priests would have to get secular jobs to make a living, and the Temple worship would stop (see 13:10). Nehemiah was not interested in getting people to agree with him or say "amen" (8:6) when they listened to God's instructions; he wanted them to act in ways that demonstrated that they were submitting their lives and money to the glorification of God.

The setting for each group of believers is different, so the areas of life where people need to make firmer commitments differ in each country and each church. But common themes will arise in many communities of believers, centering around (1) being faithful to God's instructions in the Scriptures (10:29, 34, 36), (2) proper involvement in the worship of God, (3) giving financial resources to support God's work, and (4) giving the best to God. Commitment involves faithfulness, dedication to honor God in all areas of life, and supporting God's work out of a heart of gratitude and joy. If die-hard football fans will spend untold hours watching games in terrible, cold weather, talk endlessly about their star players, spend hundreds of dollars to see their team play, and give of their time and emotional energy to further the reputation of their team, should not believers be willing to demonstrate an even greater loyalty to God? His name should be praised every week, his worship should be enthusiastically supported, and the financial needs of those who work in God's house should be met. It is time to challenge people to proclaim in some substantive way where their loyalty and dedication lie. Dedication to God is partially determined by how people spend their time and money. They support what is important to them.

◆ V. Nehemiah's Organization of the People and His Reforms
   (Neh 11:1–13:31)
   A. The Resettlement of the People (Neh 11:1–36)

The leaders of the people were living in Jerusalem, the holy city. A tenth of the people from the other towns of Judah and Benjamin were chosen by sacred lots to live there, too, while the rest stayed where they were. ²And the people commended everyone who volunteered to resettle in Jerusalem.

³Here is a list of the names of the provincial officials who came to live in Jerusalem. (Most of the people, priests, Levites, Temple servants, and descendants of Solomon's servants continued to live in their own homes in the various towns of Judah, ⁴but some of the people from Judah and Benjamin resettled in Jerusalem.)

From the tribe of Judah:
   Athaiah son of Uzziah, son of Zechariah, son of Amariah, son of Shephatiah, son of Mahalalel, of the family of Perez.
   ⁵Also Maaseiah son of Baruch, son of Col-hozeh, son of Hazaiah, son of Adaiah, son of Joiarib, son of Zechariah, of the family of Shelah.* ⁶There were 468 descendants of Perez who lived in Jerusalem—all outstanding men.
⁷From the tribe of Benjamin:
   Sallu son of Meshullam, son of Joed, son of Pedaiah, son of Kolaiah, son of Maaseiah, son of Ithiel, son of Jeshaiah. ⁸After him were Gabbai and Sallai and a total of 928 relatives. ⁹Their chief officer was Joel son of Zicri, who was assisted by Judah son of Hassenuah, second-in-command over the city.
¹⁰From the priests:
   Jedaiah son of Joiarib; Jakin; ¹¹and Seraiah son of Hilkiah, son of Meshullam, son of Zadok, son of

Meraioth, son of Ahitub, the supervisor of the Temple of God. ¹²Also 822 of their associates, who worked at the Temple. Also Adaiah son of Jeroham, son of Pelaliah, son of Amzi, son of Zechariah, son of Pashhur, son of Malkijah, ¹³along with 242 of his associates, who were heads of their families. Also Amashsai son of Azarel, son of Ahzai, son of Meshillemoth, son of Immer, ¹⁴and 128 of his* outstanding associates. Their chief officer was Zabdiel son of Haggedolim.
¹⁵From the Levites:
   Shemaiah son of Hasshub, son of Azrikam, son of Hashabiah, son of Bunni. ¹⁶Also Shabbethai and Jozabad, who were in charge of the work outside the Temple of God. ¹⁷Also Mattaniah son of Mica, son of Zabdi, a descendant of Asaph, who led in thanksgiving and prayer. Also Bakbukiah, who was Mattaniah's assistant, and Abda son of Shammua, son of Galal, son of Jeduthun. ¹⁸In all, there were 284 Levites in the holy city.
¹⁹From the gatekeepers:
   Akkub, Talmon, and 172 of their associates, who guarded the gates.

²⁰The other priests, Levites, and the rest of the Israelites lived wherever their family inheritance was located in any of the towns of Judah. ²¹The Temple servants, however, whose leaders were Ziha and Gishpa, all lived on the hill of Ophel.
²²The chief officer of the Levites in Jerusalem was Uzzi son of Bani, son of Hashabiah, son of Mattaniah, son of Mica,

a descendant of Asaph, whose family served as singers at God's Temple. ²³Their daily responsibilities were carried out according to the terms of a royal command.

²⁴Pethahiah son of Meshezabel, a descendant of Zerah son of Judah, was the royal adviser in all matters of public administration.

²⁵As for the surrounding villages with their open fields, some of the people of Judah lived in Kiriath-arba with its settlements, Dibon with its settlements, and Jekabzeel with its villages. ²⁶They also lived in Jeshua, Moladah, Beth-pelet, ²⁷Hazar-shual, Beersheba with its settlements, ²⁸Ziklag, and Meconah with its settlements. ²⁹They also lived in En-rimmon, Zorah, Jarmuth, ³⁰Zanoah, and Adullam with their surrounding villages. They also lived in Lachish with its nearby fields and Azekah with its surrounding villages. So the people of Judah were living all the way from Beersheba in the south to the valley of Hinnom.

³¹Some of the people of Benjamin lived at Geba, Micmash, Aija, and Bethel with its settlements. ³²They also lived in Anathoth, Nob, Ananiah, ³³Hazor, Ramah, Gittaim, ³⁴Hadid, Zeboim, Neballat, ³⁵Lod, Ono, and the Valley of Craftsmen.* ³⁶Some of the Levites who lived in Judah were sent to live with the tribe of Benjamin.

11:5 Hebrew *son of the Shilonite.*   11:14 As in Greek version; Hebrew reads *their.*   11:35 Or *and Ge-harashim.*

NOTES

11:1 *A tenth of the people . . . were chosen by sacred lots to live there.* There is an abrupt change of topics at 11:1, indicating the beginning of a new section. Some would see this as continuing the discussion in 7:4-5 (Blenkinsopp 1988:322; Fensham 1982:242), where the text indicates that the city of Jerusalem "was large and spacious, but the population was small." Others claim that the resumptive repetition in 11:1 points back to a continuation of 7:73, which indicates that "the rest of the people returned to their own towns throughout Israel" (Williamson 1985:268, 344; Throntveit 1992:112). Both of these threads are picked up in 11:1.

11:2 *people commended everyone who volunteered.* Lit., "The people blessed all the men who volunteered." It is difficult to know if those who "volunteered" (*nadab* [TH5068, ZH5605], "willingly offered themselves") were in addition to those chosen by lot or if those chosen by lot willingly agreed to move into the city (Brockington 1969:146).

11:3-4a *Here is a list of the names.* This is the introduction to the document the author was quoting. It informs the reader that the list includes people who lived in Jerusalem (11:4b-24) and people who lived outside Jerusalem (11:25-36).

11:4b-8 *From the tribe of Judah . . . From the tribe of Benjamin.* These are the names of the real people who gave up their comfortable life in the countryside with their friends and moved to Jerusalem. There is no assurance that this is a complete list (cf. the longer list in 1 Chr 9), but probably both lists were dependent on an official document in the government archives (Myers 1965:85).

11:9 *chief officer.* This was probably a military commander (Clines 1984:215) or an administrator (Fensham 1982:245).

Judah son of Hassenuah, second-in-command over the city. The word *mishneh* [TH4932A, ZH5467] ("second"; cf. notes on 3:3 and 3:6) can be related to Judah's role in different ways: He may have been over the "second district of Jerusalem" (Yamauchi 1988:746), or he may have been "second in command" (Breneman 1993:256; cf. NLT).

11:10-19 *From the priests . . . From the Levites . . . From the gatekeepers.* This list of priestly families parallels other lists of priests with slight differences in the spelling of various names (see 1 Chr 9:10-13), but the Harim group of priests is missing (Ezra 2:36-39).

11:11 the supervisor of the Temple of God. The "supervisor" (*nagid* [TH5057, ZH5592]) was almost certainly the high priest (Blenkinsopp 1988:324; Fensham 1982:245), based on 2 Chr 31:10, 13. This, however, leaves open the question of the role of the "chief officer" (*paqid* [TH6496, ZH7224]) Zabdiel (11:14). The term *paqid* in 11:9, 14, and 22 seems to be a military term that finds use outside of a military context (Williamson 1985:352); thus, Zabdiel may have been the one responsible for the organization of people who would keep order in and defend the Temple. Fensham (1982:246) suggests that this person had an administrative role under the high priest.

11:16 work outside the Temple of God. Some of the Levites had responsibilities for work outside the Temple, including such tasks as storing the wood people brought to the Temple, storing and distributing tithes, collecting Temple taxes, caring for the maintenance of the buildings, and a variety of other support duties. Other Levites were involved with providing praise music, prayers, and other worship activities (11:17). First Chronicles 25:1-7 indicates that David established three Levitical families to lead in the music (Asaph, Jeduthun, and Heman), but only two are mentioned here. It may be that the two choir leaders, Mattaniah and his assistant Bakbukiah, led two choirs that sang antiphonally (12:8-9, 27-42), while at other times Bakbukiah served during the hours that Mattaniah was not on duty.

11:19 gatekeepers. The gatekeepers in this context guarded the gates into the Temple area, not the external gates of the city (7:3). First Chronicles 9:17-27 refers to stationing gate-keepers at the king's gate, at the camp of the Levites, at the entrance to the Temple, and at the Temple storehouse to guard the goods collected as taxes or tithes.

11:20-24 lived wherever their family inheritance was. In some ways 11:20 seems out of order, since the paragraph about those who lived outside of Jerusalem is found in 11:25-36 (Williamson 1985:348). However, one could see 11:20 as the beginning of the list of people who were not chosen to live in Jerusalem. Thus, 11:21-24 would be a parenthetical remark within 11:20-36. Since 11:21-23 is related to the worship at the Temple, it fits into the context of 11:15-18. The family "inheritance" was the ancestral property that God gave as an eternal possession for each family. God owned the land as his possession, but he gave parts of his land to his covenant people who sojourned on it (Lev 25:23). Naturally when families returned from exile, they desired to return to their God-given parcel of land.

11:21 The Temple servants. It may well be that the author found additional information regarding people involved with Temple worship that needed to be added to his previous paragraph, and that is why these verses were added after 11:20. It is possible that the Temple servants (*nethinim* [TH5411, ZH5987]; see Ezra 2:43-54) were not listed with the earlier groups because they already lived on the hill of Ophel (3:26), just south of the Temple (Breneman 1993:259).

Gishpa. This may be an alternative spelling of Hasupha (Ezra 2:43).

11:22-23 The chief officer of the Levites . . . according to the terms of a royal command. This supplements the information in 11:17 for Mattaniah, the Levitical singer, who is mentioned in both verses. In addition to his singing, he had an official military responsibility to carry out activities in accordance with the Persian king's royal commands. Ezra 7:14-23 contains one of Artaxerxes' commands that Ezra obeyed, and one assumes that other, similar commands came year by year.

11:24 the royal adviser in all matters of public administration. It could be that Pethahiah was the Jewish ambassador to the Persian court (Fensham 1982:248) or at least one who fostered communication with the Persian royal court, but there is no evidence that he was a later governor of Judah after the death of Nehemiah, as Clines conjectures (1984:219).

11:25-36 *As for the surrounding villages.* These last few verses list the names of towns where people lived outside of Jerusalem. It is odd that some well-known towns where people lived according to other chapters are missing from this list: Tekoa (3:5), Mizpah (3:7), Beth-zur (3:16), Bethlehem (7:26), Jericho (7:36). One must conclude that this is a representative list of places and not an exhaustive list. The expression "with its settlements" (lit., "with her daughters"), which appears again and again, is another indication that not all the cities are listed. It is also significant that some towns on this list were located a long way from Jerusalem. This implies that the people were more secure and beginning to spread out into all areas of the province of Yehud, not staying in one close-knit little group of cities around Jerusalem. This list does not describe the borders of the province of Yehud following the cities listed in Josh 15 (Brockington 1969:153), but it indicates that the people were spread throughout the territory. They were free to settle the area, and they possessed the whole province of Yehud.

COMMENTARY

Although it is somewhat uninspiring to read a list of names of people and towns, one must understand what this list represents in order to appreciate the theological significance of what had happened in and around Jerusalem. The walls of Jerusalem were not rebuilt as a monument to Nehemiah or as a sign of Jewish resurgence in the land. The walls were built so that people could live in the Holy City of Jerusalem and so that the priests and Levites could maintain the regular worship of God at the Temple. If Jerusalem was not a thriving metropolis, people would not likely view it as the symbolic center of political, social, and religious life. If people did not come to visit or live in Jerusalem, there would be a natural tendency for worship at the Temple to decline in importance. If few people attended worship services, then the enthusiasm and vitality of their religious experience would be lessened.

To solve the practical problem of too few people living in Jerusalem, Nehemiah was led by God to have the priests cast lots and choose those who would move into the city of Jerusalem (11:1). In a sense, he chose the principle of the tithe and asked that the villages give a tenth of their population (Throntveit 1992:113) to populate the city where God's Temple was (11:1). The people agreed with this plan, and they encouraged those who willingly pulled up their roots in the countryside and moved to Jerusalem (11:2). This illustrated a spirit of cooperation and partnership between those who stayed and those who left. All sacrificed in the process of obeying God's will as revealed through the casting of lots. Many probably would have preferred to stay where they were with their friends, but when they were chosen, they submitted their will to the will of God and by faith moved to a new location.

The chapter is divided as follows: (1) an introduction of the problem (11:1-2), (2) a list of people who moved into Jerusalem (11:3-24), and (3) the names of the cities where people were living outside of Jerusalem (11:25-36). This list of names has much in common with a similar text in 1 Chronicles 9:2-17, though the relationship between these two passages is unknown. The purpose of these lists is to show that the theological reforms, the security provided by building the walls, and the relocation of individuals to the capital worked together to develop a strong community of dedicated believers in Jerusalem. They were committed to following God's law and maintaining vibrant worship at the holy Temple. A positive desire motivated them; they did not relocate only in order to defend Jerusalem (Williamson 1985:349).

The text of chapter 11 never mentions Nehemiah's role in this process, but one can infer from 7:1-5 that his organizational abilities were heavily responsible for the execution of this plan, for he was one of the key leaders who lived in Jerusalem (11:1). As usual, he preferred to keep himself out of the spotlight and focus on what the people did. The plan the leaders developed called for one-tenth of the people living outside of Jerusalem to move into Jerusalem. As God originally decided during the days of Joshua where each tribe should live through the casting of lots (Josh 14:2; 18:6-8), so now he chose which families should move to Jerusalem.

The narrative does not report that anyone refused to move or fought the idea of relocating, though it probably was a big adjustment and inconvenience for many of them. When they left their homes, the people in their villages supported them by praising them for sacrificing in this way. One is impressed with the community spirit, the willing cooperation, and the lack of talk about the rights of individuals to live wherever they prefer.

This kind of commitment to furthering the Kingdom of God instead of one's own individual financial or social wishes is exemplary for believers today. If God leads a congregation to plant a new church, it is often easier to stay with the mother church with all one's friends, but both the mother church and the people called by God to be involved in the new church plant need to demonstrate a spirit of partnership and cooperation to spread the worship of God in new places. Some people need to sacrifice and move out in faith, while others need to encourage them and help them adjust. The names of those who sacrifice to expand the spread of the gospel need to be remembered and held up as an example to others, just as Nehemiah remembered those who came to live in Jerusalem.

It is interesting that the lots fell on priests, Levites, gatekeepers, chief officers, Temple servants, and laypeople in Judah. This indicates that God uses all kinds of people to further his work. The city was not to be just a holy hotbed of priests and Levites; it was a normal place where everyone could use their talents to serve God by leading or joining in worship at the Temple. In fact, the priests and Levites are not even listed first. God wanted people with musical skills, singing abilities, organizational skills, diplomatic skills to work with the Persians, the ability to offer sacrifices and teach the law of Moses, and the willingness to serve in menial ways. The list does not set up some hierarchy of the important and the unimportant; it merely lists those who willingly accepted God's calling to enhance his work in Jerusalem. These people responded to God's call and submitted their will to his will. This is the essential requirement of all who desire to please God.

◆   B. A List of Authentic Priests (Neh 12:1-26)

Here is the list of the priests and Levites who returned with Zerubbabel son of Shealtiel and Jeshua the high priest:

Seraiah, Jeremiah, Ezra,
2 Amariah, Malluch, Hattush,
3 Shecaniah, Harim,* Meremoth,
4 Iddo, Ginnethon,* Abijah,
5 Miniamin, Moadiah,* Bilgah,
6 Shemaiah, Joiarib, Jedaiah,
7 Sallu, Amok, Hilkiah, and Jedaiah.
These were the leaders of the priests and their associates in the days of Jeshua.

[8]The Levites who returned with them were Jeshua, Binnui, Kadmiel, Sherebiah, Judah, and Mattaniah, who with his associates was in charge of the songs of thanksgiving. [9]Their associates, Bakbukiah and Unni, stood opposite them during the service.

[10] Jeshua the high priest was the father of Joiakim.
Joiakim was the father of Eliashib.
Eliashib was the father of Joiada.
[11] Joiada was the father of Johanan.*
Johanan was the father of Jaddua.

[12]Now when Joiakim was high priest, the family leaders of the priests were as follows:

Meraiah was leader of the family of Seraiah.
Hananiah was leader of the family of Jeremiah.
[13] Meshullam was leader of the family of Ezra.
Jehohanan was leader of the family of Amariah.
[14] Jonathan was leader of the family of Malluch.*
Joseph was leader of the family of Shecaniah.*
[15] Adna was leader of the family of Harim.
Helkai was leader of the family of Meremoth.*
[16] Zechariah was leader of the family of Iddo.
Meshullam was leader of the family of Ginnethon.
[17] Zicri was leader of the family of Abijah.
There was also a* leader of the family of Miniamin.

Piltai was leader of the family of Moadiah.
[18] Shammua was leader of the family of Bilgah.
Jehonathan was leader of the family of Shemaiah.
[19] Mattenai was leader of the family of Joiarib.
Uzzi was leader of the family of Jedaiah.
[20] Kallai was leader of the family of Sallu.*
Eber was leader of the family of Amok.
[21] Hashabiah was leader of the family of Hilkiah.
Nethanel was leader of the family of Jedaiah.

[22]A record of the Levite families was kept during the years when Eliashib, Joiada, Johanan, and Jaddua served as high priest. Another record of the priests was kept during the reign of Darius the Persian.* [23]A record of the heads of the Levite families was kept in *The Book of History* down to the days of Johanan, the grandson* of Eliashib.

[24]These were the family leaders of the Levites: Hashabiah, Sherebiah, Jeshua, Binnui,* Kadmiel, and other associates, who stood opposite them during the ceremonies of praise and thanksgiving, one section responding to the other, as commanded by David, the man of God. [25]This included Mattaniah, Bakbukiah, and Obadiah.

Meshullam, Talmon, and Akkub were the gatekeepers in charge of the storerooms at the gates. [26]These all served in the days of Joiakim son of Jeshua, son of Jehozadak,* and in the days of Nehemiah the governor and of Ezra the priest and scribe.

12:3 Hebrew *Rehum;* compare 7:42; 12:15; Ezra 2:39.   **12:4** As in some Hebrew manuscripts and Latin Vulgate (see also 12:16); most Hebrew manuscripts read *Ginnethoi.*   **12:5** Hebrew *Mijamin, Maadiah;* compare 12:17.   **12:11** Hebrew *Jonathan;* compare 12:22.   **12:14a** As in Greek version (see also 10:4; 12:2); Hebrew reads *Malluchi.*   **12:14b** As in many Hebrew manuscripts, some Greek manuscripts, and Syriac version (see also 12:3); most Hebrew manuscripts read *Shebaniah.*   **12:15** As in some Greek manuscripts (see also 12:3); Hebrew reads *Meraioth.*   **12:17** Hebrew lacks the name of this family leader.   **12:20** Hebrew *Sallai;* compare 12:7.   **12:22** *Darius the Persian* is probably Darius II, who reigned 423–404 B.C., or possibly Darius III, who reigned 336–331 B.C.   **12:23** Hebrew *descendant;* compare 12:10-11.   **12:24** Hebrew *son of* (i.e., *ben*), which should probably be read here as the proper name Binnui; compare Ezra 3:9 and the note there.   **12:26** Hebrew *Jozadak,* a variant spelling of Jehozadak.

NOTES

12:1-9 *list of the priests and Levites who returned with Zerubbabel . . . The Levites.* The author found in the nation's archives this list of 22 names of priests or priestly families from the time of Jeshua and Zerubbabel, shortly after 539 BC when Cyrus the Persian king allowed the Israelites to return to Jerusalem. This list seems to conflict with the meager list of only four priestly names in Ezra 2:36-39. But since an unusually large number of 4,289 people is included in these four families, it is safe to assume that these four major divisions represent within them the subgroupings of the 22 families listed in 12:1-7. (This list of priests is also similar to 10:2-8 and similar to the fathers of the priests listed in 12:12-21.) It is not clear why the 24 priestly groups established by David (1 Chr 24) were not all present after the return from exile, but the answer may simply be that no priests from two of the priestly groups returned with the exiles to Jerusalem.

12:10-11 *Jeshua the high priest.* This list of high priests fits into the following periods: Jeshua served as high priest when the people returned from exile until sometime in the reign of Darius I (Ezra 3:2, 8; 5:2; Zech 6:11). Joiakim the high priest is unknown and may have served after Jeshua and during the days of Ezra's ministry (Josephus *Antiquities* 11.5.1 [11.121]). Eliashib served during the time of Nehemiah (3:1, 20-21; 13:7). Eliashib's son Joiada served at the end of Nehemiah's ministry (13:28), then came Johanan (Josephus claims he took control by force, *Antiquities* 11.7.1 [11.297]), and finally Jaddua (Josephus places him in the time of Alexander the Great, *Antiquities* 11.8.3-5 [11.313-328]). An Elephantine Papyrus places Johanan as high priest around 410 BC, during the reign of Darius II. Many do not trust Josephus's accounts (Blenkinsopp 1988:336; Williamson 1985:363), so little can be said about these later high priests.

12:12-21 *Now when Joiakim was high priest.* This list comes from the time of Joiakim, but it appears to be almost identical to the list from the time of Ezra. It includes most of the names in the earlier list (12:1-7), minus Hattush (12:2), which apparently was accidentally lost in the transmission process (Williamson 1985:362), though it is also possible that Hattush had died by this time. The comparison of these lists also gives insight into the types of scribal misspellings that could happen with names: (1) Shecaniah in 12:3 is spelled Shebaniah in 12:14 (cf. NLT mg) because the letters represented by "b" and "c" looked very similar in Hebrew, (2) Rehum in 12:3 (cf. NLT mg) is spelled Harim in 12:15 because the letters represented by "r" and "h" were transposed, and (3) Maadiah in 12:5 (cf. NLT mg) is pronounced with different vowels to produce Moadiah in 12:17. Also, because all but one group has a leader listed, it appears that a name of the leader of Miniamin has dropped out of 12:17 through a scribal error, though Williamson suggests the possibility that Majamin is just an alternate spelling of his name (Williamson 1985:362). Some identify Iddo (12:16) as the (grand)father of the prophet Zechariah (Ezra 5:1; Zech 1:1), but there is no way to prove this.

12:22 *A record of the Levite families was kept.* It was very important for the Israelites to know who were members of legitimate priestly and Levitical families so that only legitimate people would serve at God's Temple. This verse is a witness to the care taken by all the priests after Jeshua and Joiakim to keep accurate written records, though these later records are not listed in detail at this point.

Darius the Persian. This was probably Darius I (522–486 BC; cf. Clines 1984:226; Fensham 1982:253; Williamson 1985:364-365) if this refers to the earlier priestly records, though some prefer Darius II (423–404 BC; cf. Clines 1984:226), or Darius III (336–331 BC) if it refers to the latest records kept as Josephus suggests (*Antiquities* 11.7.1-2). On this point, however, it appears that Josephus was confused.

12:24 Jeshua, Binnui, Kadmiel. Lit., "Jeshua son of Kadmiel" (cf. NLT mg). Earlier Jeshua was identified as the son of Jozadak (Ezra 3:2; 5:2, NLT mg), not the son of Kadmiel. The word "son of" (*ben* [TH1121, ZH1201]) is probably a scribal error for another Levite named Bani or Binnui (see 9:4 and 12:8), since the two words are spelled almost the same (Williamson 1985:357).

12:25 Mattaniah, Bakbukiah, and Obadiah. Obadiah is probably just an alternate spelling of Abda, mentioned in 11:17 (1 Chr 9:16). Mattaniah, Bakbukiah, and Obadiah were mentioned as singers in 11:17, so those names should be included with the preceding names in 12:24, for all of these people were among the Levites who provided music for the Temple worship. The three gatekeepers mentioned in 12:25b are known from other lists (11:19; 1 Chr 9:17).

COMMENTARY

This short list of names of Temple personnel shows how seriously the people took their responsibility to offer God acceptable worship at the Temple, supervised by legitimate leaders and workers. A good singing voice was not the principal requirement for being chosen for the Temple choir; rather, God had given this task to a specific group of families. This did not prevent others from singing along with the choir or singing songs of praise at home. Leading the congregation in songs of thanksgiving was a sacred responsibility that was not handed out to laypeople.

An equally heavy burden falls on those providing music in worship services in churches today. They can be instruments used by God to lead the congregation to focus on praise and thanksgiving to God, or by their dress, mannerisms, or style of presentation, they may draw attention to themselves. Care needs to be taken to ensure that only the people called by God lead in this important aspect of glorifying him.

Little is said about the responsibilities of the priests or the high priests because the purpose of this list is only to identify the true priests, not to describe their duties. Their functions at the altar when people brought sacrifices and their teaching roles were known from the book of Leviticus. Among the various responsibilities of the Levites, the only one mentioned in this section is that of singing praise and giving thanksgiving to God. These Levites were involved with singing praise to God at the Temple in two antiphonal choirs that responded to one another (see 11:22; 12:8), just as the godly King David designed their worship (1 Chr 25; 2 Chr 8:14). Although the text does not go into detail on all the aspects of worship, it is clear that a key part of worship was being thankful and praising God for his goodness and generosity to his people. Obviously, no recordings were made of their antiphonal singing, so one is left to imagine the booming sounds of the great choirs as they sang to the beat of a syncopated Hebrew melody (J. Braun 2002). No doubt these singers wrote a few of the psalms we still have in the Scriptures and sang many others at various worship services.

◆   **C. The Joyous Dedication of the Walls of Jerusalem (Neh 12:27-43)**

²⁷For the dedication of the new wall of Jerusalem, the Levites throughout the land were asked to come to Jerusalem to assist in the ceremonies. They were to take part in the joyous occasion with their songs of thanksgiving and with the

music of cymbals, harps, and lyres. ²⁸The singers were brought together from the region around Jerusalem and from the villages of the Netophathites. ²⁹They also came from Beth-gilgal and the rural areas near Geba and Azmaveth, for the singers had built their own settlements around Jerusalem. ³⁰The priests and Levites first purified themselves; then they purified the people, the gates, and the wall.

³¹I led the leaders of Judah to the top of the wall and organized two large choirs to give thanks. One of the choirs proceeded southward* along the top of the wall to the Dung Gate. ³²Hoshaiah and half the leaders of Judah followed them, ³³along with Azariah, Ezra, Meshullam, ³⁴Judah, Benjamin, Shemaiah, and Jeremiah. ³⁵Then came some priests who played trumpets, including Zechariah son of Jonathan, son of Shemaiah, son of Mattaniah, son of Micaiah, son of Zaccur, a descendant of Asaph. ³⁶And Zechariah's colleagues were Shemaiah, Azarel, Milalai, Gilalai, Maai, Nethanel, Judah, and Hanani. They used the musical instruments prescribed by David, the man of God. Ezra the scribe led this procession. ³⁷At the Fountain Gate they went straight up the steps on the ascent of the city wall toward the City of David. They passed the house of David and then proceeded to the Water Gate on the east.

³⁸The second choir giving thanks went northward* around the other way to meet them. I followed them, together with the other half of the people, along the top of the wall past the Tower of the Ovens to the Broad Wall, ³⁹then past the Ephraim Gate to the Old City Gate,* past the Fish Gate and the Tower of Hananel, and on to the Tower of the Hundred. Then we continued on to the Sheep Gate and stopped at the Guard Gate.

⁴⁰The two choirs that were giving thanks then proceeded to the Temple of God, where they took their places. So did I, together with the group of leaders who were with me. ⁴¹We went together with the trumpet-playing priests—Eliakim, Maaseiah, Miniamin, Micaiah, Elioenai, Zechariah, and Hananiah—⁴²and the singers—Maaseiah, Shemaiah, Eleazar, Uzzi, Jehohanan, Malkijah, Elam, and Ezer. They played and sang loudly under the direction of Jezrahiah the choir director.

⁴³Many sacrifices were offered on that joyous day, for God had given the people cause for great joy. The women and children also participated in the celebration, and the joy of the people of Jerusalem could be heard far away.

12:31 Hebrew *to the right.*   12:38 Hebrew *to the left.*   12:39 Or *the Mishneh Gate,* or *the Jeshanah Gate.*

NOTES

12:27 *the Levites throughout the land were asked to come to Jerusalem.* Since there were few Levites who returned from exile, it was important to bring as many Levites to this celebration as possible from throughout the land of Yehud (see 11:20). Nehemiah wanted everyone involved in this celebration.

joyous occasion . . . songs of thanksgiving. The ideas of joy and thanksgiving dominate this celebration, for truly God had done a great work through them. Similar celebrations took place at the dedication of the altar and the Temple (Ezra 3:13; 6:16-17) some years earlier.

12:28-29 *singers were brought together.* The inclusive nature of the event was emphasized. Everyone needed to feel this sense of pride and thanksgiving, so singers from the south (Netophah was near Bethlehem; see 1 Chr 2:54), east (Gilgal was near Jericho), and north (Geba was in Benjamin) came to sing God's praise.

12:30 *purified.* Before the "dedication" (*khanukkah* [ᵀᴴ2598, ᶻᴴ2853]; cf. 12:27) of the wall to God as his possession, the people, walls, and gates were purified, for this was the Holy

City of Jerusalem. This purification process could have involved fasting, abstaining from sexual relations, offering sacrifices, or washing with water (13:22; Exod 19:10, 14-15; Lev 14:49-53; Num 19:18). The people realized that they needed to be pure and holy if God was going to accept them and the walls as his possessions.

12:31 39 organized two large choirs to give thanks. Each choir included (1) a leader, (2) half the leaders of the people, (3) seven priests, (4) a music leader, and (5) eight musicians. The first choir probably started marching southward on the top of the wall from the Valley Gate on the west side of the city, around the southern end of the City of David, past the Water Gate on the east side (3:26), and ending at the Temple (12:40). Ezra (12:36) was given the honor of leading this choir. The second choir went north from the Valley Gate, past the Broad Wall (3:8), and to the Temple singing, giving thanks, playing music, and rejoicing in what God had done.

12:40 giving thanks . . . proceeded to the Temple. Having arrived at their destination, the singers, the trumpet players, and the people sang and thanked God again and again. This was an impressive time of joy and praise that was a testimony and inspiration to all who witnessed it and participated in it.

12:43 God had given the people cause for great joy. Some hypothesize that Ps 147 originated at this event (Brockington 1969:160) since it includes much praise and joy, refers to the Lord gathering his outcast people together, and refers to God strengthening the gates of the city.

COMMENTARY

This narrative is not dated, but it probably took place shortly after the completion of the walls in 6:15-19. It is impossible to date the activities recorded in 7:1–12:26. Some of what was recorded in 7:1–12:26 could fit the time period before the dedication of the walls, but that is not required. It would seem natural to assume that the dedication of the walls took place before all the people chosen to move into Jerusalem (ch 11) actually resettled in the city. The dedication of the walls was seen as a climax to Nehemiah's work, so it would be natural to put it toward the end of his writings. The integration of spiritual reforms, the resettlement of people, and the dedication of the walls in chapters 6–12 fit together as depicting one large unified effort to restore the vitality of the nation.

The dedication celebration was reported in first-person singular verbs ("I led the leaders" in 12:31), so one can assume that the author was using Nehemiah's Memoirs at this point—an eyewitness report of exactly what happened. The event involved (1) the assembling of the community (12:27-29), (2) acts of purification (12:30), (3) the two choirs walking on the walls (12:31-42), and (4) a joyous celebration at the Temple (12:43). Words of celebration and joy are repeated again and again to project a picture of this wonderful day. The joy of the Lord was freely expressed by all. People from many miles away probably heard about this joyous event, for the people who were there could not have helped talking about their unbridled joy over this great celebration.

It was appropriate to reflect on what God had done and to celebrate his goodness. A public meeting of dedication and praise signaled to everyone involved that what had been accomplished was the work of God, that he deserved the glory for it all. The builders were setting this newly constructed structure apart by giving it back to God for his use. The central focus was not on what men had done but on what God had accomplished. The act of dedication was and is a basic act of worship in which God is honored and magnified, his name is praised, and people express thanksgiving. Through worship people express their joy over God's marvelous deeds and celebrate his goodness. A dedication service can include many different aspects and involve different types of music, but the common denominator is that all of it leads to joyous thanksgiving to God. As long as the celebration brings glory to God, it is acceptable. Choirs, musical instruments, marches, eating, and a host of other activities are appropriate means of expressing thanks to God. Notice, though, there are no reports of speeches to thank Nehemiah for his excellent work in leading this project, no pats on the back for the soldiers that stood guard, no plaques hung in honor of the family that got its work done first, and not even a sermon by Ezra about what great things the Israelites were going to do in the future. The purpose of this celebration was simply for all the people to rejoice over God's grace, which had allowed them to rebuild the wall.

◆ **D. Organization of Temple Worship (Neh 12:44–13:3)**

⁴⁴On that day men were appointed to be in charge of the storerooms for the offerings, the first part of the harvest, and the tithes. They were responsible to collect from the fields outside the towns the portions required by the Law for the priests and Levites. For all the people of Judah took joy in the priests and Levites and their work. ⁴⁵They performed the service of their God and the service of purification, as commanded by David and his son Solomon, and so did the singers and the gatekeepers. ⁴⁶The custom of having choir directors to lead the choirs in hymns of praise and thanksgiving to God began long ago in the days of David and Asaph. ⁴⁷So now, in the days of Zerubbabel and of Nehemiah, all Israel brought a daily supply of food for the singers, the gatekeepers, and the Levites. The Levites, in turn, gave a portion of what they received to the priests, the descendants of Aaron.

CHAPTER **13**

On that same day, as the Book of Moses was being read to the people, the passage was found that said no Ammonite or Moabite should ever be permitted to enter the assembly of God.* ²For they had not provided the Israelites with food and water in the wilderness. Instead, they hired Balaam to curse them, though our God turned the curse into a blessing. ³When this passage of the Law was read, all those of foreign descent were immediately excluded from the assembly.

13:1 See Deut 23:3-6.

NOTES

12:45-46 *They performed the service of their God . . . as commanded by David.*
Because the needs of the Levites and priests were taken care of by the people, the spiritual leaders could concentrate on helping people worship God in the Temple. Some of the duties of the Temple workers are outlined, but this brief list is very incomplete. Twice, reference is made to David, emphasizing that the people were following the traditions established for worship when God directed David to establish the Temple. They did not ignore or reject the worship patterns set down by David as old-fashioned; they emulated them.

12:47 *in the days of Zerubbabel and of Nehemiah.* This responsible pattern of bringing food for Temple workers was not something uniquely introduced by Nehemiah; it was a consistent approach taken from the time the Temple was rebuilt in Zerubbabel's day. Such faithful consistency explains why Nehemiah was so upset a few years later when the people quit providing for the needs of the Temple workers (13:10-13).

13:1 *On that same day.* This parallels 12:44, suggesting that this happened on the day of dedication of the walls, though some view this phrase as a general reference to "the time" of Ezra and Nehemiah (Clines 1984:236).

no Ammonite or Moabite should ever be permitted to enter the assembly of God. When the portion from the book of Moses was opened, the leader read about the exclusion of certain groups from the sanctuary in Deut 23:3-6. The "assembly of God" refers to those people as a community at the Tabernacle or Temple to celebrate a festival or worship on the Sabbath (Merrill 1994:307). Two reasons explain why these people were excluded. The first was their failure to provide the Israelites the basic requirements of food and water. The second was that the Moabite king Balak had hired the diviner Balaam to curse Israel (Num 22–24). God, however, turned Balaam's curses into great blessings (Num 23:8, 20; 24:1, 10) and provided for his people (cf. Num 21; Deut 2:9-19; 2:26–3:11).

COMMENTARY

This section explains how different groups of people took responsibility for the sundry aspects of Temple worship from the time of Zerubbabel to Nehemiah. One aspect of providing for the Temple workers was the collection of offerings, the firstfruits of the land, the tithe, and the Temple tax (see 10:32-39). Certain people were responsible for collecting, storing, and distributing provisions that the Israelites gladly brought to support the Temple workers.

Although organizing, planning, collecting the offering, and a host of other jobs may not seem as glorious and spiritual as some other jobs, God has given different people different gifts so that all aspects of his work will grow together and produce spiritual fruit. Nehemiah 12:44-47 indicates that God needs behind-the-scenes workers to do the "menial" tasks so others can do more visible jobs. No task is unimportant, and all are needed if God's work on earth is to prosper. Every organization needs planning and support staff to make it possible for a few people to take visible leadership roles. Everyone has to give of themselves if the whole body of workers ever hopes to function together as a unit that glorifies God.

In 13:1-3 we read of the people's response to the words of the law. It is refreshing to see people respond in obedience when they know what God's instructions are (13:3). It is also good to see that the plain meaning of a passage can cause an "immediate" response instead of the appointment of a committee to study the problem and bring back a recommendation a year later to accommodate the rights of all parties involved. The removal of all people of foreign descent might seem at first like an overreaction, because it included all foreigners and not just the people from Moab and Ammon. This action probably was a precautionary move until the leaders in charge could identify which people were from Ammon and Moab.

Nehemiah 13:1-3 reminds us that only true believers should be included in the community of believers if a sense of theological unity and purity of worship is desired. The inclusion of pagans who might introduce foreign theological ideas and weaken the believers' total commitment to God would threaten the unity and purity of the congregation of God. This does not mean that believers should not talk to unbelievers or that foreigners that convert should be excluded from the congregation of believers in the church today. God desires that everyone should come to an understanding of the truth and that no one should perish, but those who reject God are by definition not a part of the holy family of God.

◆   ## E. Nehemiah Confronts the People's Sin (Neh 13:4-31)

⁴Before this had happened, Eliashib the priest, who had been appointed as supervisor of the storerooms of the Temple of our God and who was also a relative of Tobiah, ⁵had converted a large storage room and placed it at Tobiah's disposal. The room had previously been used for storing the grain offerings, the frankincense, various articles for the Temple, and the tithes of grain, new wine, and olive oil (which were prescribed for the Levites, the singers, and the gatekeepers), as well as the offerings for the priests.

⁶I was not in Jerusalem at that time, for I had returned to King Artaxerxes of Babylon in the thirty-second year of his reign,* though I later asked his permission to return. ⁷When I arrived back in Jerusalem, I learned about Eliashib's evil deed in providing Tobiah with a room in the courtyards of the Temple of God. ⁸I became very upset and threw all of Tobiah's belongings out of the room. ⁹Then I demanded that the rooms be purified, and I brought back the articles for God's Temple, the grain offerings, and the frankincense.

¹⁰I also discovered that the Levites had not been given their prescribed portions of food, so they and the singers who were to conduct the worship services had all returned to work their fields. ¹¹I immediately confronted the leaders and demanded, "Why has the Temple of God been neglected?" Then I called all the Levites back again and restored them to their proper duties. ¹²And once more all the people of Judah began bringing their tithes of grain, new wine, and olive oil to the Temple storerooms.

¹³I assigned supervisors for the storerooms: Shelemiah the priest, Zadok the scribe, and Pedaiah, one of the Levites. And I appointed Hanan son of Zaccur and grandson of Mattaniah as their assistant. These men had an excellent reputation, and it was their job to make honest distributions to their fellow Levites.

¹⁴Remember this good deed, O my God, and do not forget all that I have faithfully done for the Temple of my God and its services.

¹⁵In those days I saw men of Judah treading out their winepresses on the Sabbath. They were also bringing in grain, loading it on donkeys, and bringing their wine, grapes, figs, and all sorts of produce to Jerusalem to sell on the Sabbath. So I rebuked them for selling their produce on that day. ¹⁶Some men from Tyre, who lived in Jerusalem, were bringing in fish and all kinds of merchandise. They were selling it on the Sabbath to the people of Judah—and in Jerusalem at that!

¹⁷So I confronted the nobles of Judah. "Why are you profaning the Sabbath in this evil way?" I asked. ¹⁸"Wasn't it just this sort of thing that your ancestors did that caused our God to bring all this trouble upon us and our city? Now you are bringing even more wrath upon Israel by permitting the Sabbath to be desecrated in this way!"

¹⁹Then I commanded that the gates of Jerusalem should be shut as darkness fell every Friday evening,* not to be opened until the Sabbath ended. I sent some of my own servants to guard the gates so that no merchandise could be brought in

on the Sabbath day. 20The merchants and tradesmen with a variety of wares camped outside Jerusalem once or twice. 21But I spoke sharply to them and said, "What are you doing out here, camping around the wall? If you do this again, I will arrest you!" And that was the last time they came on the Sabbath. 22Then I commanded the Levites to purify themselves and to guard the gates in order to preserve the holiness of the Sabbath.

Remember this good deed also, O my God! Have compassion on me according to your great and unfailing love.

23About the same time I realized that some of the men of Judah had married women from Ashdod, Ammon, and Moab. 24Furthermore, half their children spoke the language of Ashdod or of some other people and could not speak the language of Judah at all. 25So I confronted them and called down curses on them. I beat some of them and pulled out their hair. I made them swear in the name of God that they would not let their children intermarry with the pagan people of the land.

26"Wasn't this exactly what led King Solomon of Israel into sin?" I demanded. "There was no king from any nation who could compare to him, and God loved him and made him king over all Israel. But even he was led into sin by his foreign wives. 27How could you even think of committing this sinful deed and acting unfaithfully toward God by marrying foreign women?"

28One of the sons of Joiada son of Eliashib the high priest had married a daughter of Sanballat the Horonite, so I banished him from my presence.

29Remember them, O my God, for they have defiled the priesthood and the solemn vows of the priests and Levites.

30So I purged out everything foreign and assigned tasks to the priests and Levites, making certain that each knew his work. 31I also made sure that the supply of wood for the altar and the first portions of the harvest were brought at the proper times.

Remember this in my favor, O my God.

13:6 King Artaxerxes of Persia is here identified as the king of Babylon because Persia had conquered the Babylonian Empire. The thirty-second year of Artaxerxes was 433 B.C.   13:19 Hebrew *on the day before the Sabbath.*

NOTES

13:6 *I was not in Jerusalem . . . I had returned to King Artaxerxes.* Nehemiah was governor from 445–433 BC. While Nehemiah was in Susa, Eliashib allowed Tobiah into the Temple storeroom. After staying in Susa an unknown period of time (probably only 4–6 months, but possibly as long as a year), Nehemiah returned to Jerusalem. The narrative does not say why he returned to Jerusalem or what role he had when he returned. Nehemiah probably continued on as governor until 407 BC, when Bigvai became governor.

13:9 *I demanded that the rooms be purified, and I brought back the articles for God's Temple.* Sin defiled the Temple area, so before the area could be used for the sacred utensils and the storage of tithes and offerings used in the sacrificial services, several rooms in the Temple area (not just one where Tobiah lived—13:5) had to be ritually purified (see Lev 14:4-32; 17:15-16; 2 Chr 29:15-19).

13:13 *I assigned supervisors. . . . These men had an excellent reputation.* Once Tobiah was removed from the Temple storage area for tithes and offerings (13:4-5, 7-9), a group of four honest and trustworthy (Niphal of *'aman* [TH539, ZH586]) men representing the priests (Shelemiah the priest), the governor (Zadok the scribe, to keep records), the Levites (Pedaiah), and the singers (Hanan, grandson of Mattaniah, 11:17; 12:35) was put in charge of collecting, storing, and distributing goods to their kinsmen. In Acts 6:1-6 a group of trustworthy men was similarly chosen to distribute food to the poor widows.

13:17 So I confronted the nobles of Judah. "Why are you profaning the Sabbath . . . ?" Nehemiah's confrontation is described using a term that often refers to bringing a court case (*rib* [TH7378, ZH8189]) against someone. There is no evidence that Nehemiah actually brought these accusations before a judge at a court. He apparently stated his charges in the same way one might phrase an accusation in court.

13:18 Now you are bringing even more wrath upon Israel. The demise of Judah in 586 BC was due to the fact that the people's ancestors did not obey God's instruction in the law of Moses (Jer 17:19-27). Nehemiah's rhetorical question asked whether the people had learned anything from history. Had they not promised to keep the Sabbath holy just a few years earlier (10:31)? Did these people really want to invite God's wrath to rain down destruction on the nation again? These people should have been focusing on how to make the Sabbath holy by dedicating themselves to God, not ignoring God and dedicating themselves to improving their own financial situation by working on the Sabbath.

13:21 If you do this again, I will arrest you! Lit., "I will stretch forth a hand against you." Nehemiah drove the merchants away, threatening to arrest them. One would assume that he explained to them the community's new determination to keep the Sabbath holy, but the emphasis in this verse is on discouraging these people from coming to Jerusalem on the Sabbath.

13:22 Levites to purify themselves and to guard the gates. There were two groups of gatekeepers: One stood at the city gates, and the other Levitical group served at the gates of the Temple. Since the regular gatekeepers were not guarding the gates of the city on the Sabbath, Nehemiah assigned this religious duty to the Levites who knew the importance of sanctifying the Sabbath.

13:25 So I confronted them and called down curses on them. Here again (cf. 13:11, 17) Nehemiah's confrontation was described using a term that often refers to bringing a court case (*rib* [TH7378, ZH8189]) against someone (Fensham 1982:267). Although there is no evidence that he actually brought these accusations before a judge at a court, he apparently stated his charges in the same way people would present charges in court. The curse Nehemiah spoke probably was the curse these people called down on themselves some years earlier when they renewed their covenant with God and promised not to intermarry with pagans (10:28-30).

I beat some of them and pulled out their hair. The physical beating and pulling of hair sounds like extreme abuse, but it was a common way of expressing great anger and grief in that culture.

13:27 How could you even think of committing this sinful deed and acting unfaithfully. Lit., "Should we listen to you and do all this great evil?" The NLT has "you" as the subject of the verb, but the Hebrew question inquires about what "we" should do. This is another rhetorical question that emphatically states that it would be crazy to be unfaithful to God and sinfully intermarry with pagans. Nehemiah did not mince words or soft-pedal the severity of this sin. This was not a matter of freedom of choice or a place where people could exercise their preference.

13:28 One of the sons of Joiada son of Eliashib the high priest had married a daughter of Sanballat the Horonite, so I banished him from my presence. Nehemiah "banished" or "chased away" this man. Josephus (*Antiquities* 11.7.2–8.2 [11.302-312]) tells a similar story about a priest's son Manasseh, who was exiled for marrying Nikaso, the daughter of Sanballat. This man later set up a temple at Mount Gerizim. Josephus was either referring to another person or had the details of his story confused.

13:31 *Remember this in my favor, O my God.* Once again (as in 13:14, 22) Nehemiah cried out for God to watch over him as he confronted the priests and Levites about actions that defiled their holy status and consequently made them disqualified to serve.

COMMENTARY

Nehemiah's first term of duty as governor ended after 12 years of service (13:6). He successfully accomplished many things through the power of God's grace and the determination of the people he worked with. When he came back from Susa (see note on 13:6) a few months or possibly a year later (13:6-7), the situation had changed dramatically. Nehemiah needed to institute a series of social and religious reforms that would point the people back to God's instructions in the law.

The first reform was related to the laws about the exclusion of the Moabites (13:1-3). The people's determination to exclude the Ammonites and Moabites happened a few years earlier, before Nehemiah returned to Susa for a short time to report to King Artaxerxes. Some think that the man responsible for giving Tobiah the Ammonite a place to live in the storeroom of the Temple was Eliashib the high priest (3:1, 21-22; 12:10; 13:28), but the text does not call him a high priest, and the high priest would not usually be the one put in charge of the storerooms (Breneman 1993:269). This act seems to be a family favor for Tobiah, for he was a relative, one "closely associated" (*qarob* [TH7138, ZH7940]) with Eliashib, just like Boaz was a "close relative" of Naomi (Ruth 2:20). Nehemiah 6:17-18 indicates that Tobiah's family was related to a Jewish family by marriage. Eliashib's act of giving Tobiah a room in the Temple directly contradicted what the Scriptures said (Deut 23:3-6) and what the people had decided (13:1-3).

It was bad enough to allow an Ammonite into the Temple area, but it was even more offensive to give this man a "large" room, and one that was supposed to be used for the storage of the tithes and grain offerings prescribed for priestly families, plus the utensils used in Temple worship. His presence there would interrupt the natural working of the Temple and would mean that the needs of some priests, Levites, Temple singers, and gatekeepers would go unmet. Tobiah's reasons for wanting this room are unknown, but his location at such a central place in the Temple area suggests that he was something of a commercial middleman who was buying and selling supplies needed by Temple personnel (Blenkinsopp 1988:354).

Nehemiah was the one who identified Tobiah's presence in the Temple storeroom as an "evil deed" (13:7). Others accepted Eliashib's actions, or tolerated them, but Nehemiah would not overlook evil. He acted boldly and with strong indignation. He was offended by what was happening and took action to remove this evil from the Temple. He knew that this was not a time to make peace with Tobiah and compromise his principles. It was a time to remove the heathen influence of Tobiah from the holy Temple of God. He, like Jesus, cleansed the Temple area of people who were defiling the sacred house of God (Matt 21:12-13; Luke 19:45-46).

In the process of restoring the storerooms to their proper use, Nehemiah realized that many Levites and Temple singers were not on duty in the Temple area serving the people who came to worship (13:10). Instead, these Temple workers had been forced to "flee" (*barakh* [TH1272, ZH1368]) from Jerusalem and work in their fields around the Levitical cities (Num 35:1-8; Josh 21) in order to make a living and feed their families. There is no indication that these people "fled" because of opposition from Eliashab or Tobiah; they quickly "fled" the city of Jerusalem because of the danger of having no food to eat. Nehemiah saw this situation as a disastrous reversal of his earlier work (11:1-24) of bringing priests, Levites, gatekeepers, and singers from the countryside to Jerusalem in order that they might work full-time at the Temple. A change needed to be made so that the common people would bring their tithes and offerings to the Temple. Tobiah's occupation of the Temple was preventing the Levites from collecting and distributing food to the workers in the Temple.

Nehemiah realized that the social, political, and religious leaders had allowed the situation to get out of hand and had done nothing about it (13:11). They had not confronted the people about giving God their tithes, had allowed Tobiah to live in the storeroom of the Temple, and had not prevented the Temple workers from abandoning Temple worship responsibilities. Earlier they had promised, signed their names to a covenant document, and sworn an oath to provide for the Temple services and workers (10:32-39), so Nehemiah confronted them on their failure to keep their promises. Nehemiah took the lead and called all these workers back to serve in the Temple. Once the challenge was put out, the Levites returned, and the people gave their tithes. The people responded to the leadership of Nehemiah and did what they knew was right and honoring to God (13:12).

Nehemiah knew that he was rather bold and demanding and that some people in Jerusalem probably did not appreciate his tactics or his imposing his will on others. But when he prayed, he did not confess any sins because he was not under conviction of having done anything wrong. Nevertheless, he knew he would need God's help in mending relationships and maintaining the worship at the Temple. His prayer was not a selfish request for God to make him famous or rich; he simply asked God to not forget his "faithful love" (*khesed* [TH2617, ZH2876]; 13:14) for God, which was exemplified in what he did to preserve the proper worship of God at the Temple.

While visiting in the countryside, Nehemiah noticed that many people were working on the Sabbath day: (1) Farmers were processing their grapes at the winepress, (2) merchants and farmers were transporting goods to Jerusalem to sell on the Sabbath, and (3) people from Tyre were selling fish and other goods on the Sabbath (see Ezek 26:4-14). These activities by Jews and Gentiles conflicted with earlier instructions about the Sabbath as a day of rest (Exod 16:23-29; 20:8-11; 31:14-16; 34:21), as well as later prophetic exhortations concerning conducting business on the Sabbath (Isa 56:1-6; Jer 17:19-27; Amos 8:5). Furthermore, the people had made a covenantal promise just a few years earlier regarding the Sabbath (10:31). The Sabbath was a time to remember God as the Creator and to celebrate their redemption during the exodus from Egypt. Resting on one day demonstrated that people cannot survive financially based on their own work; they must depend on God's provision. Apparently, people at this time had interpreted God's instructions more liberally or just chose to ignore what God had instructed them to do on the Sabbath. Nehemiah "rebuked" the people for defiling the Sabbath (13:15-16).

The nobles (*khorim* [TH2715, ZH2985]) had some leadership responsibilities among the people—possibly some of these people were working for one of the business enterprises of the nobles. The nobles should have stopped this activity on the Sabbath long ago instead of profiting from work done on the Sabbath. Why would the nobles encourage or allow others to "profane" or make common what was set apart as holy by God? Unfortunately, many today seem to follow this same pattern and do not set apart Sunday as a day when they do no selling or buying. Instead, they treat it as just another workday and do not set it apart as a holy day dedicated to God.

After confronting the leaders, Nehemiah himself took several practical steps to implement new procedures so that people would not profane the Sabbath. He could not go out and stop every farmer from working on the Sabbath, but he could stop commerce in Jerusalem by shutting the city gates. Secondly, he sent some of his own guards to the large gates of Jerusalem to make sure that the gates stayed shut and that no one would open the gates on the sly and bring goods into Jerusalem. Not being aware of the new plan to faithfully observe the Sabbath as a holy day dedicated to God, some merchants came as usual to sell on the Sabbath. This time they had to camp outside the gates to wait until the Sabbath was over. Nehemiah did not bend the rules for anyone (13:20-21).

After the confrontations, Nehemiah asked God to have compassion on him according to his great unfailing love (13:22; cf. 13:14). Nehemiah was standing up for what was right and bringing about real reform in the spiritual lives of the people, but the stress and opposition was great. He needed God's grace. In the midst of conflict, believers can always call on God for assurance and compassion when they stand up for the truth God teaches in his word.

Nehemiah soon confronted another problem—that of Jews marrying pagans (13:23). This problem, which Ezra had confronted (Ezra 9–10) over 25 years earlier, was reappearing. There is no indication whether there were few or many cases of inappropriate marriage. These marriages were inconsistent with the people's covenantal promise not to intermarry with pagans just a few years earlier (10:30), so this problem probably developed while Nehemiah was away in Susa. The text does not say if Nehemiah saw these mixed marriages in Jerusalem, but it is likely these were found out in country villages near Ashdod and Moab. The issue was not grounded in ethnic or racial prejudice; Nehemiah, like Ezra, saw this as a theological conflict.

The Jewish men working in the area of Ashdod must have married women from Ashdod and settled down in that area where the local language was spoken (13:24). Apparently their children had little contact with the Hebrew language, and the Jewish men did not insist that their children learn Hebrew. The severe consequences of this neglect would be that these children would not be able to read the Scriptures or easily understand what was being said if they went to worship in the Temple in Jerusalem.

Nehemiah pushed these people to reaffirm the oath they had taken earlier (10:28-30). He encouraged them to swear that they would not allow their children to intermarry with pagans. Nehemiah knew from history (1 Kgs 11:1-6) that intermarriage of this type would lead to further apostasy and ultimately the nation's destruction. The narrative does not say the people repented, but it implies that

Nehemiah convinced them to change and swear an oath. Interestingly, there was no requirement for those who had already married Ammonite or Moabite women to divorce their spouses (contrast Ezra 9–10). Does this mean that Nehemiah had a more liberal policy concerning intermarriage with pagans? Or was this a relatively small problem in a couple of small villages out in the country; thus, it was handled more informally? Or does this way of treating the problem simply mean that the Ammonite wives had all converted to follow the God of the Hebrews; therefore, it was not necessary to ask anyone to divorce? This latter interpretation might explain why Nehemiah's main focus was not on divorce, but on trying to stop this intermarriage trend from spreading into a larger problem when these people's children would marry (cf. Deut 7:2-4).

Nehemiah identified intermarriage with foreign wives as a path to sin (13:26-27). The audience knew this led to Solomon's downfall (1 Kgs 11:1-6), and Nehemiah's rhetorical question asked how the people could think of repeating the sins of the past that led to the destruction of the kingdom. If Solomon, who had a special gift of wisdom (1 Kgs 3:7-14), who was loved by God (2 Sam 12:24), and who was chosen by God to build his Temple (1 Kgs 6:1-38), was led into rebellion against God because of intermarriage with pagan wives, did the people in Nehemiah's audience really believe they could escape a similar outcome?

To make matters worse, the high priest Eliashib's grandson had married the daughter of Sanballat (13:28; see 2:10), Nehemiah's enemy. This was the last straw. This broke the clear command of Leviticus 21:14 to marry a daughter of an Israelite, as well as the high standards about intermarriage with pagans that the community set for itself (10:28-30; Ezra 9–10). This demonstrated a great deal of unfaithfulness—not only on the part of this son, but also on the part of his grandfather, the high priest Eliashib. The reason the high priest allowed this to happen is unknown. In any case, Nehemiah banished this son, exiling him from working in the Temple. Such strong action against the family of a high priest sent a clear message to the people in Jerusalem that intermarriage with pagans would not be permitted as long as Nehemiah was around.

The chapter ends with two summary statements about Nehemiah's accomplishments (13:30-31). In his view, his Temple reforms were one of the main accomplishments of his ministry in Jerusalem. If the priests did not know how to live holy lives and if the people accepted the views of the pagans they intermarried with, then the worship of the God of Israel would be perverted. If the priests, Levites, Temple servants, and singers did not know how to complete the various tasks necessary for the efficient functioning of the Temple, then God's worship at the Temple would suffer, and all the hard work of rebuilding the walls would end up being a waste of time. The second summary statement (13:31) emphasizes Nehemiah's attention to all the small details essential to worship at the Temple. Nehemiah knew that all the people had to do their part in providing wood, the Temple tax, their tithes, and their firstfruits if the priests were to be successful in leading the people in worship.

This chapter teaches us much. In order for God to be worshiped and glorified, two things are required: (1) Spiritual leaders need to live holy lives, dedicated to the service of God and those coming to worship God; and (2) the people need to reject the path of sin and provide for the needs of the spiritual leaders. Both groups will not honor God if they allow foreign influences to distract them from following what God has instructed in his word.

The first issue Nehemiah faced (13:4-14) illustrates the importance of having godly people responsible for the work at God's house. If inappropriate, unqualified, selfish, or ungodly people are allowed to take control of normal functions within the house of God, they will probably be more focused on their own interests and not on meeting the needs of others. In Nehemiah's time, Tobiah was disqualified from living in the Temple area because he was an Ammonite. Eliashab and Tobiah were irresponsible in not providing for the physical needs of the Temple and the Levites, and their actions discouraged the common people from obediently bringing their tithes and gifts to the Temple. In our time, a pastor may nominate a friend who is unqualified to be a deacon; this person may push himself forward out of self-interest and suggest innovations or changes in policy that will make it very difficult for other spiritual leaders in the congregation to accomplish their tasks. This problem points to the need for there to be shared governance of the business of the church and for the whole body of believers to sense God's leading, rather than having a powerful leader act out of self-interest and appoint a friend. This problem points to the need for godly leaders to follow God's word and prevent ungodly people from getting into key positions of responsibility.

Godly leaders also must recognize when mistakes have been made and act to correct them as Nehemiah did. When Nehemiah returned to Jerusalem, he saw that Tobiah had been inappropriately given a room in the Temple; thus, he removed him (13:6-9). Nehemiah discovered that this mistake had caused the people to quit bringing their tithe (because there was no place left to store them), with the result that the Levites quit working in the Temple because they had no food to eat from the distribution of the tithe (13:10). Nehemiah removed the problem and appointed honest and godly leaders over the Temple storerooms who represented all the groups that would use the tithe (13:13). Then Nehemiah called the Levites back to work in the Temple (13:11). In response, the common people brought food into the storerooms for the Levites to eat (13:12). These actions were probably not popular with everyone, but they were necessary in order for the people to resume worshiping God properly. Nehemiah's action was meant to undo the repercussions of Eliashib's act of favoritism, which had drastic consequences on the worship of the people. Sometimes people think their minor rule bending will not be noticed or that a little favoritism will not have lasting consequences, but this narrative is a strong warning to not put pleasing one's friends above doing what is right. We should aim to please God first above all else.

The second issue was related to keeping the Sabbath holy. Since times were tough, work needed to get done at harvest time; and since people needed to make a living, some thought that no one would mind if they did some work on the Sabbath. The non-Israelites worked and sold goods on the Sabbath; thus, there was natural economic competition with the Israelites. Once again, the nobles (13:17), who were important political leaders, allowed the people to follow the standards of unbelievers and compromise the teachings of God's word. Nehemiah boldly stood against this defilement of the Sabbath and took steps to prevent it from continuing. Similar problems have faced the church throughout the centuries and especially in our modern, materialistic economy today. Far too many nonessential services are open on Sunday, and far too many Christians willingly offer to work on Sunday to make a few extra dollars. Even more disturbing is the number of Christians who go to stores and restaurants on Sunday, thus justifying the merchant's decision to stay open. If all believers refused to buy on Sunday, probably many of the businesses now open would close because they would be losing money by staying open. Believers need to congratulate and support those few businesses that close on Sunday and refuse to work or buy anything on Sunday. It all comes down to one question: Do we want to defile the Lord's Day (cf. Acts 20:7; 1 Cor 16:2), or do we want to honor God?

The final conflict over intermarriage with pagans indicates that Ezra's reform did not totally remove this problem from Israelite society. Nehemiah recognized this as sin, and he knew that history taught them that if this sin continued, God would destroy the nation for it (13:26-27). Nehemiah boldly confronted the supposed spiritual leader, the high priest Eliashib, who allowed his grandson to marry the daughter of a foreigner (13:28). He realized that intermarriage with pagans would result in children not knowing Hebrew; thus, they would not be interested in reading or listening to God's word, plus they would be bored and not interested in going to the Temple. The New Testament also warns people not to intermarry with unbelievers (2 Cor 6:14-18), for light and darkness do not mix. Many churches can point to numerous children who grew up in the church but did not continue to attend. How many of these children have been negatively influenced by an unbelieving spouse and quit coming to church to keep peace in the family? In the interest of providing the best possible environment in which to raise children in the faith, Scripture exhorts believers to marry in the faith.

In all these reforms, Nehemiah consistently relied on God for wisdom, guidance, and compassion. He knew he was stirring up a hornet's nest that would create new enemies for him. Nevertheless, he did what was right because he loved God. He believed it was important to follow God's word, and he knew the future history of the nation depended on bringing the people to the point where they would dedicate their lives to serving a holy God.

BIBLIOGRAPHY

Ackroyd, P. R.
1972 The Temple Vessels—A Continuity Theme. *Vetus Testamentum* Supplement 23:166-181.

Allen, L. C.
2003 Ezra-Nehemiah. Pp. 3-168 in *Ezra, Nehemiah, Esther*. New International Biblical Commentary. Peabody, MA: Hendrickson.

Allrik, H. L.
1954 The Lists of Zerubbabel (Neh 7 and Ezr 2) and the Hebrew Numerical Notation. *Bulletin of the American Schools of Oriental Research* 136:21-27.

Anderson, W.
1984 The Jewish Community in Palestine in the Persian Period. Pp. 130-161 in *The Cambridge History of Judaism*, vol. 1. Editors, W. D. Davies and L. Finkelstein. Cambridge: Cambridge University Press.

Avigad, N.
1972 Excavation in the Old Jewish Quarter of the Old City of Jerusalem. *Israel Exploration Journal* 22:193-200.

1976 *Bullae and Seals from a Post-exilic Judean Archive*. Qedem 4. Jerusalem: Institute of Archaeology, the Hebrew University.

Baron, S. A.
1952 *The Social and Religious History of the Jews. I: Ancient Times*. New York: Columbia University Press.

Batten, L. W.
1913 *A Critical and Exegetical Commentary on the Books of Ezra and Nehemiah*. International Critical Commentary. Edinburgh: T&T Clark.

Bickerman, E.
1946 The Edict of Cyrus in Ezra 1. *Journal of Biblical Literature* 65:249-275.

Blank, S.
1950 The Curse, Blasphemy, the Spell, and the Oath. *Hebrew Union College Annual* 23:73-95.

Blenkinsopp, Joseph
1988 *Nehemiah*. The Old Testament Library. Philadelphia: Westminster.

Block, D. I.
1988 *The Gods of the Nations*. Winona Lake, IN: Eisenbrauns.

Bowman, R. A.
1954 Ezra and Nehemiah. Pp. 551-819 in *The Interpreter's Bible*, vol. 3. Nashville: Abingdon.

Boyce, M.
1982 *A History of Zoroastrianism*. Leiden: Brill.

Braun, J.
2002 *Music in Ancient Israel/Palestine: Archaeological, Written and Comparative Sources*. Translator, D. Stott. Grand Rapids: Eerdmans.

Braun, R. L.
1979 Chronicles, Ezra, Nehemiah: Theology and Literary History. Pp. 52-64 in *Studies in the Historical Books of the Old Testament*. Editor, J. A. Emerton. Leiden: Brill.

Breneman, M.
1993 *Ezra, Nehemiah, and Esther*. New American Commentary. Nashville: Broadman & Holman.

Brewer, J.
1924 Josephus' Account of Nehemiah. *Journal of Biblical Literature* 43:224-226.

Brockington, L. H.
1969 *Ezra, Nehemiah and Esther*. The Century Bible. London: Nelson.

Brown, R.
1998 *The Message of Nehemiah*. The Bible Speaks Today. Downers Grove, IL: InterVarsity.

Brueggemann, W.
1977 *The Land*. Philadelphia: Fortress.

Cameron, G. G.
1948 *Persepolis Treasury Tablets*. Chicago: University of Chicago Press.

Clines, D. J.
1981 Nehemiah 10 as an Example of Early Jewish Exegesis. *Journal of the Study of the Old Testament* 21:111-117.

1984 *Ezra, Nehemiah, Esther.* The New Century Bible Commentary. Grand Rapids: Eerdmans.

Coggins, R. J.
1976 *The Books of Ezra and Nehemiah.* Cambridge Bible Commentary. Cambridge: Cambridge University Press.

Cohen, H. R.
1978 *Biblical Hapax Legomena in Light of Akkadian and Ugaritic.* Missoula, MT: Scholars Press.

Cowley, A.
1923 *Aramaic Papyri of the Fifth Century BC.* Oxford: Clarendon.

Cross, F. M.
1955 Geshem the Arabian, Enemy of Nehemiah. *Biblical Archaeologist* 18:46-47.

Dandamayev, M.
1969 *Achaemenid Babylon in Ancient Mesopotamia.* Moscow: Nauka.

Drews, R.
1975 The Babylonian Chronicles and Berossus. *Iraq* 37:39-55.

Duggan, M. W.
2001 *The Covenant Renewal in Ezra-Nehemiah (Neh 7:72b–10:40): An Exegetical, Literary, and Theological Study.* Atlanta: Society of Biblical Literature.

Dumbrell, W. J.
1971 The Tell el-Maskhuta Bowls and the "Kingdom of Qedar" in the Persian Period. *Bulletin of the American Schools of Oriental Research* 111:33-44.

Ellis, R.
1968 *Foundation Deposits in Ancient Mesopotamia.* New Haven, CT: Yale University Press.

Eskenazi, T.
1988 *In an Age of Prose: A Literary Approach to Ezra-Nehemiah.* Atlanta: Scholars Press.

Fensham, F. Charles
1975 Medina in Ezra and Nehemiah. *Vetus Testamentum* 25:795-797.

1982 *The Books of Ezra and Nehemiah.* New International Commentary on the Old Testament. Grand Rapids: Eerdmans.

Gelston, A.
1966 The Foundations of the Second Temple. *Vetus Testamentum* 16:232-235.

Green, A. R.
1990 The Date of Nehemiah. *Andrews University Seminary Studies* 28:195-210.

Hallock, R. T.
1969 *Persepolis Fortification Tablets.* Chicago: University of Chicago Press.

Haran, M.
1961 The Gibeonites, the Nethinim, and the Sons of Solomon's Servants. *Vetus Testamentum* 11:159-169.

Hoglund, Kenneth G.
1992 *Achaemenid Imperial Administration in Syria-Palestine and the Mission of Ezra-Nehemiah.* Atlanta: Scholars Press.

Holmgren, Fredrick C.
1987 *Ezra and Nehemiah: Israel Alive Again.* Grand Rapids: Eerdmans.

Howard, D.
1993 *An Introduction to the Old Testament Historical Books.* Chicago: Moody.

Ishida, T.
1979 The Structure and Historical Implications of the List of Pre-exilic Nations. *Biblica* 60:461-490.

Ivry, A. L.
1972 Nehemiah 6,10: Politics and the Temple. *Journal for the Study of Judaism in the Persian, Hellenistic, and Roman Periods* 3:35-45.

Japhet, Sarah
1968 The Supposed Common Authorship of Chronicles and Ezra-Nehemiah. *Vetus Testamentum* 18:330-371.

Jastrow, M.
1900 The Tearing of the Garments as a Symbol of Mourning with Special Reference to the Customs of the Ancient Near East. *Journal of the American Oriental Society* 21:23-39.

Jones, D. R.
1963 The Cessation of Sacrifices after the Destruction of the Temple in 586 BC. *Journal of Theological Studies* 14:12-31.

Katzenstein, H. J.
1962 Some Remarks on the Lists of the Chief Priests of the Temple of Solomon. *Journal of Biblical Literature* 81:377-384.

Kent, R. G.
1953 *Old Persian*. New Haven, CT: American Oriental Society.

Kenyon, K.
1967 *Jerusalem: Excavating 3000 Years of History*. New York: McGraw-Hill.

Kidner, D.
1979 *Ezra and Nehemiah*. Tyndale Bible Commentary. Downers Grove, IL: InterVarsity.

Kline, M.
1972 *The Structure of Biblical Authority*. Grand Rapids: Eerdmans.

Larsson, G.
1967 When Did the Babylonian Captivity Begin? *Journal of Theological Studies* 18:417-423.

Levenson, J. D.
1976 *Theology of the Program of Restoration of Ezekiel 40–48*. Missoula, MT: Scholars Press.

Lipinski, E.
1970 Urim and Tummim. *Vetus Testamentum* 20:495-496.

Loewe, R.
1955 The Earliest Biblical Allusion to Coined Money? *Palestine Exploration Quarterly* 87:141-150.

Maloney, R. P.
1974 Usury and Restrictions on Interest-taking in the Ancient Near East. *Catholic Biblical Quarterly* 36:1-20.

Mazar, B.
1975 *The Mountain of the Lord*. Garden City, NY: Doubleday.

McConville, J. G.
1985 *Ezra, Nehemiah, Esther*. Daily Study Bible. Philadelphia: Westminster.

Merrill, E.
1994 *Deuteronomy*. Nashville: Broadman & Holman.

Millard, A. R.
1966 For He Is Good. *Tyndale Bulletin* 17:115-117.
1976 Assyrian Royal Names in Biblical Hebrew. *Journal of Semitic Studies* 21:1-14.

Myers, Jacob M.
1965 *Ezra, Nehemiah*. Anchor Bible 14. Garden City, NY: Doubleday.

Neufeld, E.
1953–1954 The Rate of Interest and the Text of Nehemiah 5:11. *Jewish Quarterly Review* 44:203-204.

Nickolson, E. W.
1965 The Meaning of the Expression הארץ עם in the Old Testament. *Journal of Semitic Studies* 10:59-66.

Olmstead, A. T.
1944 Tattenai, Governor of "Across the River." *Journal of Near Eastern Studies* 3:46.
1948 *A History of the Persian Empire*. Chicago: University of Chicago Press.

Oppenheim, A. L.
1965 A Note on the Scribe in Mesopotamia. Pp. 253-256 in *Studies in Honor of Benno Landsberger*. Editors, H. C. Guterbock and T. Jacobsen. Chicago: University of Chicago Press.

Rainey, A. F.
1969 The Satrapy "Beyond the River." *Australian Journal of Biblical Archaeology* 1:51-78.

Rowley, H. H.
1965 The Chronological Order of Ezra and Nehemiah. Pp. 137-168 in *The Servant of the Lord and Other Essays on the Old Testament*. Oxford: Blackwell.

Rudolph, W.
1949 *Esra und Nehemia.* Tübingen: Mohr.

Rungren, F.
1958 Über einen juristischen Terminus bei Ezra 6:6. *Zeitschrift für die alttestamentliche Wissenschaft* 70:209-215.

Sakenfeld, K. D.
1978 *The Meaning of Hesed in the Hebrew Bible.* Missoula, MT: Scholars Press.

Saley, R. J.
1968 The Date of Nehemiah Reconsidered. Pp. 151-165 in *Biblical and Near Eastern Studies. Essays in Honour of W. S. LaSor.* Editor, G. A. Tuttle. Grand Rapids: Eerdmans.

Schams, C.
1998 *Jewish Scribes in the Second-Temple Period.* Sheffield: Sheffield Academic Press.

Schmidt, E. F.
1939 *Treasures of Persepolis.* Chicago: Oriental Institute.

Smith, Gary V.
1994 *An Introduction to the Hebrew Prophets: The Prophets as Preachers.* Nashville: Broadman & Holman.

Smith, S.
1941 Timber and Brick or Masonry Construction. *Palestine Exploration Quarterly* 73:5-6.

Talmon, S.
1976 Ezra and Nehemiah (Books and Men). Pp. 317-328 in *Interpreter's Dictionary of the Bible,* Supplementary Volume. New York: Abingdon.

Tarn, W. W.
1985 Xerxes and His Successors: Artaxerxes I and Darius II. Pp. 1-4 in *Cambridge Ancient History,* vol. 6. Cambridge: Cambridge University Press.

Thomas, H. C.
1960 A Rod of Cedar Beams. *Palestine Exploration Quarterly* 92:61.

Throntveit, Mark A.
1992 *Ezra-Nehemiah.* Interpretation. Louisville: John Knox.

Tuland, C. G.
1958 'UŠŠAY' and 'UŠŠARNÂ. *Journal of Near Eastern Studies* 17:269-275.

1967 'zb in Nehemiah 3:8. *Andrews University Seminary Studies* 5:158-180.

Van Wijk-Bos, Johanna W. H.
1998 *Ezra, Nehemiah, and Esther.* Westminster Bible Companion. Louisville: Westminster John Knox.

Vaux, R. de
1972 The Decrees of Cyrus and Darius on the Building of the Temple. Pp. 63-96 in *The Bible and the Ancient Near East.* London: Darton, Longman & Todd.

Westermann, C.
1965 *The Praise of God in the Psalms.* Richmond, VA: John Knox.

Whiteley, C. F.
1954 The Term Seventy Years Captivity. *Vetus Testamentum* 4:60-72.

Williams, G. R.
2002 Contextual Influences in Readings of Nehemiah 5: A Case Study. *Tyndale Bulletin* 53:57-74.

Williamson, H. G. M.
1984 Nehemiah's Walls Revisited. *Palestine Exploration Quarterly* 116:81-88.

1985 *Ezra, Nehemiah.* Word Biblical Commentary 16. Waco: Word.

Yamauchi, Edwin M.
1976 Achaemenid Capitals. *Near East Archaeology Society Bulletin* 8:5-81.

1980 Was Nehemiah the Cupbearer a Eunuch? *Zeitschrift für die alttestamentliche Wissenschaft* 92:132-142.

1988 Ezra-Nehemiah. Pp. 563-772 in *The Expositor's Bible Commentary,* vol. 4. Editor, F. Gaebelein. Grand Rapids: Zondervan.

1990 *Persia and the Bible.* Grand Rapids: Baker.

Esther

GARY V. SMITH

INTRODUCTION TO
Esther

THE LIFE OF ESTHER demonstrates that God can use women in powerful ways to change the course of history. This young orphan girl went from having almost nothing to becoming one of the most powerful women in the Persian world. Finding herself in the midst of a major crisis, she boldly stepped forward to confront and defeat the evil man Haman. Esther's story illustrates how a woman's wisdom, patience, courage, and availability can bring hope to many. She took the opportunity to stand in the gap to save her people from certain death, and she met the challenge. With the backing of a praying community of supporters, she accepted a difficult role and put her life on the line to save the Jews from genocide.

AUTHOR

The text of Esther does not indicate who took up the pen to write its account of Esther's life (Bush 1996:294). The Babylonian Talmud (*b. Bava Batra* 15a) attributes the Esther story to the men of the Great Synagogue. Some church fathers thought Ezra wrote the book of Esther. But Josephus (*Antiquities* 11.6.13) hinted that Mordecai was the author. This seems like a possibility, for in 9:20 (see note) Mordecai is responsible for putting information about the observance of Purim in writing and for mailing this information to various Jewish communities throughout the Persian Empire. In 10:2, there is a reference to a written account of Mordecai's deeds in *The Book of the History of the Kings of Media and Persia* (cf. 6:1), but its author is unknown. These official chronicles would have focused on the official acts of Mordecai and probably included some information about Esther's role in delivering the Jews from Haman, but they would not have mirrored the exact contents of the book of Esther. Fox maintains that the author lived in Susa, was very well informed about events in the Persian royal court, and was a member of the Jewish community (1991:140).

The author of Esther may have gained some information from official court documents, but most of the book appears to contain more detailed, firsthand knowledge. Since there are many Persian words in the book and no Greek influence, it seems likely that the book was written by a Persian speaker who knew Hebrew, was acquainted with Esther's humble origin, had information about how the royal court operated, and was inspired by Esther's courage to deliver the Jewish people from the plots of Haman. In the end one must admit that there is not enough evidence to hypothesize a likely author (Jobes 1999:28). It is also less than apparent that the book went through two redactional stages as described by Bush (1996:279-294). Although some date this book much later, in the Maccabean period (e.g., Paton 1908:61, 63), believing the author was a Diaspora Jew living in Palestine, the evidence for this view is weak.

DATE AND OCCASION OF WRITING

The events in the book of Esther occurred after many Jews had already returned from Babylonian exile in 539 BC (Ezra 1–2) and before Nehemiah's ministry of rebuilding the walls of Jerusalem in 445 BC. God had used leaders like Zerubbabel the governor, Jeshua the high priest, and the prophets Haggai and Zechariah in the rebuilding of the Temple (Ezra 5–6, in 516 BC) many years before the time of Esther. But Esther and Mordecai remained in Persia and had nothing to do with these events.

The text does not reveal why Esther and Mordecai did not go back to Jerusalem with the other returnees, but for some unknown reason they and many other Jews chose to stay in the land of Persia. Through a series of unusual events, Esther was chosen to be the queen of the well-known Persian king Ahasuerus (485–465 BC), who was called Xerxes by the Greeks. The reference to the third (1:3) and seventh (2:16) years of Xerxes' reign removes any question about the date when the events in this book took place. This was an era when Persia was very strong and had expanded its empire to the far corners of the earth. Xerxes' father, Darius the Great, conquered parts of India and Europe but suffered defeat at the hands of the Greeks at Marathon (490 BC). Later, Xerxes himself accomplished great military feats, like the subjugation of Egypt, but the Greeks continued to be a significant threat on the western frontier of the empire. (The Greeks eventually defeated the Persians in 470 BC at Eurymedon near Pamphylia.) Wealth from taxes on the provinces poured into the Persian administrative capital of Susa, and Xerxes oversaw the construction of a massive, luxurious new palace at Persepolis. But Xerxes was also known as a cruel king who ruled his kingdom with tyrannical force and was known for his bizarre behavior. Artabanus, the captain of the king's bodyguard, killed Xerxes in a palace plot in 465 BC.

The beautiful Jewish girl Esther entered the king's court through a surprising series of unusual circumstances, and by God's grace she was chosen to be Xerxes' queen. There is no historical data outside this story confirming that Esther was Xerxes' queen, and it is difficult to connect either Vashti or Esther with queen Amestris, who is mentioned by Herodotus (*Histories* 7.61, 114; 9.109), though some conclude that "Esther" is a variant spelling of *Amestris* (Gordis 1981:359-388). The Murashu texts from the archaeological excavations in the city of Nippur indicate that many Jewish families stayed in Babylonia and prospered during this era (ABD 4.927-928), thus confirming the existence of Hebrew families in this area during Xerxes' reign.

The date when the book of Esther was written is unknown, though the most convincing occasion for its writing seems to be the establishment of Purim as a Jewish festival. (Outside Esther, Purim is first mentioned in 2 Macc 15:36.) In particular, Esther 8–10 supports the idea that Esther was written to explain how the feast of Purim originated. The story legitimates Purim as a miraculous deliverance worthy of celebration and explains how this festival came to be added to the original feasts designed by God in Exodus 23. It would be an annual remembrance of God's deliverance of the people from death (9:20-22), similar to his deliverance at the time of the exodus from Egypt (Exod 12–14). The name Purim ("lots") is explained in the story because Haman cast lots to choose a lucky day to tell King Xerxes about his plan to kill an unidentified evil group of people in the Persian Empire (3:7; 9:24-26). The need to write this story to legitimate the celebration of this feast would only arise some years after the introduction of Purim, probably not hundreds of years later when it was already a solid part of Jewish tradition.

Some hypothesize that the book was composed in Susa in the fourth or third century BC (Levenson 1997:26; Fox 1991:140). Others propose a date as late as the Hellenistic era, when Antiochus Epiphanes was persecuting Jews around Jerusalem in 165 BC (Paton 1908:61-62; Bush 1996:296), because (1) they find historical inaccuracies in the book, (2) Esther is not mentioned in Ben Sirach's list of biblical books, and (3) the type of Hebrew in Esther is late. Against this perspective are the following points: (1) Recent discoveries at Qumran suggest that the Hebrew of Esther is much earlier than the Hebrew language common in the Qumran period (Breneman 1993:290), (2) the lack of Greek vocabulary in spite of the inclusion of Persian words in Esther implies a location in Persia and a date before Alexander's conquest of Persia in 332 BC, (3) the book has none of the apocalyptic tendencies found in many of the scrolls written in the Maccabean period (of course, it is a historical book, not an apocalyptic book like Enoch), and (4) the accurate portrayal of the details of Persian court life requires an early date when these customs were still accurately remembered. Thus, Jobes (1999:30) prefers a date between the late fifth and third century, but a date between 450 and 400 BC, shortly after the events in Esther, is more probable (Baldwin 1984:48-49).

Alleged Historical Problems. Four major objections to the historical account recorded in Esther cause some to conclude that the story is confused, not factually accurate, was written many years after the time of Xerxes, and is probably fictional. These objections are enumerated below with comments in response.

1. There is no historical record in Persian or Greek documents of the existence of Queen Esther or the high official Mordecai. About 30 treasury tablets from Persepolis, the Persian palace of Xerxes, list a man (or more than one man) named Marduka or Mordecai (Yamauchi 1992:273), but one was an accountant, not the second-in-command over the nation (10:3). The Greek historian Herodotus claims that the Persian king had to marry from one of seven Persian families (*Histories* 3.84), and this implies he could not marry Esther, who was Jewish. Now, however, it is known that there was no official requirement that kings marry only from seven upper-class families, for Xerxes' father, Darius, married three women who were not from those families (Herodotus *Histories* 3.88). But Herodotus (*Histories* 7.61) specifically identifies one Amestris, the daughter of a Persian named Otanes, as queen in the seventh year of the reign of Xerxes. Herodotus indicates that Amestris was a brutal person who had the mother of one of Xerxes' lovers mutilated and on another occasion had 14 youths buried alive as an offering to a god (Herodotus *Histories* 7.114; 9.109-112). W. H. Shea (1976:227-246) tried to identify Esther with Amestris; however, this seems unlikely. Although secular historical evidence is limited, its failure to mention Esther does not prove she did not exist, for many facts and details are left out of every historical account. It is completely possible that Xerxes had two or more wives (Baldwin 1984:20-21).

2. According to 1:1 and 8:9, the Persian Empire was divided into 127 provinces, but Herodotus (*Histories* 3.89) knew of only 20 satraps. This seeming inconsistency (Paton 1908:72) is more apparent than real, for there could be many provinces within a satrapy. The administrative leader Daniel indicated that there were 120 provinces in the Persian Empire when Cyrus ruled the nation (Dan 6:1), so it does not seem unreasonable for there to be 127 provinces within the 20 some satrapies that existed during the reign of Xerxes.

3. Some doubt that the Persian king would authorize the extermination of the Jewish people. They also consider the slaughter of 75,000 enemies of the Jews in Persia (9:16-17) as unusually large and implausible (Clines 1984b:257). Although these are surprising events, Cicero (*Pro Lege manilia* 7) refers to all the Romans in the province of Asia being slaughtered under Mithridates VI (ruler of Pontus, of Persian descent) in the first century BC; it is estimated that 80,000 to 100,000 Romans were killed. Herodotus (*Histories* 1.106; 3.79) mentions the slaughter of large numbers of Scythians by Cyaxares and the Medes and magi by the Persians. Nothing disproves the authenticity of what the book of Esther claims, and these other historical accounts confirm that similar incidents happened.

4. Some maintain that the story of Esther contains an unusual number of coincidences and improbabilities that appear to be too good to be true or just plain implausible (Clines 1984b:259). Esther appears to be more of a romantic fiction or an exaggerated legend rather than a historical account. It is true that the book recounts many "coincidences," but that was the way the author chose to communicate to his audience how the unseen hand of God sovereignly directed the affairs of his people. No one can prove that any of these unusual things did or did not happen, but the eyes of faith see the fingerprints of God directing the affairs of his people, miraculously delivering them from the hands of those who wanted to exterminate them.

In addition, some doubt the historicity of Esther because (1) the idea that the laws of the Medes and Persians cannot be broken (1:19; 8:8; also Dan 6:8, 12) has never been confirmed by any extrabiblical Persian document; (2) no Persian law mentions that a person would be killed if the king did not raise his scepter when that person came into his presence (4:11); (3) no Persian documents ever suggest a civil war existed between the Jews and the Persians (Laniak 2003:177); (4) it seems unlikely that a feast would actually last six months (1:1-4), that Haman would give a financial gift as large as what the book of Esther suggests (3:9) or that he would tolerate Mordecai as long as the book suggests; and (5) it seems incredible that Esther would have to wait four years to see the king (2:16; cf. Paton 1908:65-77; Laniak 2003:177-182). But most of these points are based on arguments from silence (which prove very little), on an unwillingness to accept the possibility of unusual circumstances (a characteristic that is common throughout this story), or on a modern understanding of history that is different from what ancient Near Eastern people understood (Jobes 1999:31-32).

AUDIENCE

There is no direct statement about who was intended to read this story about Esther, but since it was written in Hebrew, the main audience would have been

Jewish families throughout the Persian Empire (including Yehud) who were living among non-Hebrews in the years after the death of Mordecai and Esther. The next generation needed to know that their religious freedom was made possible because (1) Mordecai and Esther had positions of high status and authority in Persian politics, (2) Mordecai and Esther were able to remove the evil opposition that was trying to kill the Jewish people, (3) the government permitted the Jewish people to defend themselves if they were attacked, and (4) there were good historical reasons why the people should celebrate the feast of Purim on the 13th and 14th day of Adar (9:17, NLT mg). Although God's name is never mentioned in the book, the plot of the story demonstrates to a Jewish believer that the unusual coincidences that allowed for Mordecai to report a plot against the king (2:19-23), for Esther to be chosen as queen (2:1-18), for Esther to enter the king's presence without being invited (5:1-8), for the vicious plot of Haman to be revealed (6:1–7:10), and for Mordecai to rise to power (8:1–10:3), all point to God's sovereign control over the details of history.

CANONICITY AND TEXTUAL HISTORY

One of the odd characteristics of the book of Esther is that the name of God is not mentioned once in its 167 verses. In addition, the New Testament authors never quote from Esther. In fact, Bishop Melito of Sardis (c. AD 170) omitted it from his list of canonical books. Even Martin Luther commented, "I am so hostile to it that I wish it did not exist, for it Judaizes too much and displays too much pagan behavior" (n.d.:13).

Although questions about the canonicity of Esther were raised by some, the Talmud (b. Megillah 7a; b. Sanhedrin 100a) defends the holy status of Esther. Esther is also listed among the sacred books in b. Bava Batra 14b-15a, and the Council of Jamnia in AD 90 affirmed its canonical place. The many fragments in the Cairo Genizah suggest that Esther was a very popular text, second only to the Pentateuch (but in contrast to this, no copies of Esther were found among the Qumran scrolls; the feast of Purim was not celebrated by the people at Qumran). Thus, there is every reason to believe that the book of Esther was considered to be Scripture at an early date (Beckwith 1985:289-293). In the Hebrew canon, Esther was placed after Song of Songs, Ruth, Lamentations, and Ecclesiastes. These five books were called the five "Megilloth" (scrolls) and were placed toward the end of the Hebrew Bible, after Proverbs and before Daniel. The five books were read at the five Jewish festivals in their liturgical calendar. In the Christian canon Esther was grouped with the historical books, where it was put after Ezra and Nehemiah.

Two difficult issues have arisen concerning the text of Esther. The first is that six additions, totaling 107 verses, appear in the Greek version of this book, as follows:

1. Seventeen verses precede chapter 1 (called A:1-17; Levenson 1997:37-42 discusses each of these apocryphal additions), giving Mordecai's dream about a fierce symbolic battle between two dragons, which ends with a promise of hope for mankind. Later, Mordecai hears the plot against the king, informs the king, and is rewarded.

2. Between 3:13 and 14 are seven verses (called B:1-7), which contain the text of the king's edict to kill the Jews on the 13th day of Adar.
3. Thirty verses follow 4:17 (called C:1-30). Verses 1-10 of this addition record Mordecai's prayer for God to sovereignly rescue the seed of Abraham, while verses 11-30 contain Esther's prayer for God to give her courage and persuasive power when she speaks to the king. These verses are followed by 16 verses (called D:1-16) that describe Esther's fearful, dramatic (she faints), uninvited approach to the king's court.
4. Between 8:16 and 17 [8:12 and 13 in LXX] are 24 verses (called E:1-24) that describe the king's condemnation of Haman, who is identified as an evil Greek, and the king's edict to make the 13th of Adar a festival.
5. Then after 10:3 are 11 additional verses (called F:1-11) that end the Greek book of Esther with Mordecai interpreting the dream he received in addition #1. He recognized God's sovereign deliverance and interpreted the two lots (one for man and one for God). Then there is a final note about the book's arrival in Egypt.

No one knows why these additions were made, if the same person added all of them, or the date of these additions. They may be pious additions clarifying the belief that all the things that happened in this story can be traced back to God, who was directing the affairs of his people. They were probably appended in Egypt to the Old Greek translation between 200 and 100 BC (Breneman 1993:299), but later, when Jerome translated the Old Testament into Latin in the Vulgate, he separated all these verses (which he found in the Greek, but not the Hebrew) into an appendix at the end of Esther. Because these verses were not in the Hebrew text he used, they were deemed to be apocryphal additions of secondary importance. (One can read these verses in the Jerusalem Bible, where the editors have put them back in their original places.) Several of these additions duplicate what is already in the Hebrew text, and a few points tend to create a contradiction, so it is not surprising that these passages were not accepted as part of the authoritative words of the book of Esther.

A second problem arises because what is known as the Greek Alpha text of Esther tells the story slightly differently than do the Septuagint and the Masoretic Text. For example, the story in 2:21-23 about the plot against the king's life is missing from the Alpha text. M. Fox (1991) hypothesizes that the Alpha text comes from a different Hebrew original. These three text types (Masoretic Hebrew, Alpha Greek, and Old Greek [LXX]) have led to much speculation about how the story of Esther was edited, expanded, and shaped before it came to the final form we have today. Fox (1991:254-266), Bush (1996:279-293), and Clines (1984a) see various versions of the Esther story growing over the years based on these different text types. They hypothesize a process in which two different stories of Esther were being written over many years before the canonical form finally stabilized. The main difficulty with this approach is that it is subjectively based on what the Masoretic and Alpha texts might have been like at some earlier stage (not their present form), but there is no evidence of this hypothetical earlier form of these texts.

LITERARY STYLE

It is natural that the book of Esther has a distinctive literary style, because it was written outside of Judah in the late Persian period. Greenstein (1987) noticed the tendency of the author of Esther to double events and pair almost synonymous words. For example, the story has two banquets at the beginning (for the men in 1:3-8 and for the women in 1:9), two banquets for the king and Haman (5:4-8; 7:1-9), and two celebrations of Purim (9:18; 9:19). The pairing of similar words like "nobles and officials" (1:3), "Persia and Media" (1:3, 14, 19), "pomp and splendor" (1:4), "greatest to the least" (1:5), "nobles and all the other men" (1:11), "made the king furious, and he burned with anger" (1:12), "contempt and anger" (1:18), "a written decree, a law" (1:19), and "to all parts of the empire, to each province" (1:22). Sasson (1987:278-284) views this as the literary style of an archivist. Niditch (1987:131) notes the use of elaborate lists (seven eunuchs in 1:10, seven wise men in 1:14, and ten sons of Haman in 9:7-9) and the tendency to say a similar thing several times ("kill, slaughter, and annihilate" in 3:13; 7:4; 8:11 or "fasted, wept, and wailed" in 4:3).

The reader will also notice the extensive use of the literary technique of irony. This results in reversals of what is expected. Thus, Haman's plan to destroy Mordecai ends up destroying himself. The sharpened pole built for Mordecai is used to kill Haman. Haman's decree allowed for people to take the wealth of the Jews, but in actuality Haman's wealth ends up in Jewish hands. Mordecai ends up with Haman's job. Haman wanted someone to glorify him on the king's horse, but he is instead commanded to glorify Mordecai, who rides on the king's horse.

Finally, the reader will see the interesting ways in which the author develops the main and secondary characters within the plot of the narrative. The evil and ill-tempered ways of the powerful are very evident, while the humble yet bold ways of those who stand for righteous principles present a stark contrast.

MAJOR THEMES

One of the central themes of the story of Esther is feasting at banquets. These banquets have special importance in the structure of the book (Levenson 1997:5), and many of the main events in the story take place at banquet feasts. One can find nine or ten banqueting events: (1) Xerxes provided for a 180-day feast for his nobles (1:2-4), (2) Xerxes gave a seven-day feast for all the people in his land (1:5-8), (3) Vashti had a banquet for the women in the palace (1:9), (4) Xerxes gave a banquet when Esther was given her royal crown (2:17-18), (5) Esther had two banquets for Xerxes and Haman (5:4-8; 7:1-9), (6) the Jewish people feasted when Mordecai came to power (8:17), and (7) there were two feast days of Purim (9:17-19). Some might consider Xerxes and Haman's drinking together (3:15) as another feast (Fox 2001:157), but this is not as clear as the other examples.

Activities at these feasts are central to the plot of the story, and each one helps develop the characterization of the people at that feast. The first two feasts show that the king is rich, powerful, arrogant, and easily angered (1:2-4, 5-8, 12). The future of queen Vashti's reign and the possibility for Esther to have a royal role was decided at this event. Another reason for the Persians to have a banquet was to honor a new person who was being given new power. The coronation of Esther (2:17-18) is a primary change in the story that determines her ability to intercede for the Jewish people and to bring Mordecai to power (8:17). These festive occasions legitimated both Esther and Mordecai in the eyes of palace officials and affirmed God's blessing on their lives. Their new places of service enabled them to intervene on behalf of Jewish people who were being oppressed.

The Purim feasts commemorated the deliverance of Jews from death (9:17-19). These feasts form the climax to the book. In the middle of the story, Esther's private banquets for Xerxes and Haman play a pivotal role in uncovering Haman's evil plan against the Jews (5:4-8 and 7:1-9). The outcome of these banquets breaks the threat against the Jewish people and leads to the resolution of the story. Since feasting together was a sign that things were going well, Haman readily came with the king to Esther's first banquet. Haman thought everything was going well (5:9), but when Esther revealed the truth at her second banquet, Haman was doomed to death (7:6-10).

This joyful idea of feasting and banqueting is contrasted with the theme of lamentation and fasting. Mordecai, the people in Susa, and all the Jews throughout the land wailed, fasted, and lamented when they heard about Haman's murderous decree (4:1-3, 16). Later, Esther, all her maidens, and the Jewish people fasted for three days before Esther attempted to enter the king's presence without an invitation (4:15-17). Fasting is a sign that everything is going badly. Surprisingly, there is no explicit indication that those who were fasting were calling on God to have mercy on them. They probably were calling on God, but the author purposely leaves the reader to infer the hidden presence and intervention of God throughout the book.

The story of Esther's life varies between these two extremes (feasting and fasting), based on the status of the Jews in the Persian Empire. These two themes demonstrate that things went well when Esther kept her Jewish origin a secret (2:7-10) and when Mordecai the Jew revealed the plot against the king's life (2:19-23; 6:1-11). Things went badly when Mordecai did not bow to Haman at the gate of the palace (3:1-6). In fact, Haman plotted to persecute and kill all the Jews because of his hatred for Mordecai (3:7-9). Later, things went well when Esther found favor in the sight of the king at the banquet (5:1-8; 7:1-3) and when she tried to have Haman's decree reversed (8:1-6). The king's new decree gave the Jews the right to defend themselves if people who followed Haman tried to persecute them (8:9-12). When the fateful day did arrive, the Jews successfully defended themselves and killed those who attacked them (9:5-16).

One might consider the "reversal of destiny" a literary device that more or less turns into a major theme in Esther (Fox 2001:158-163). For example, early in the story the king gave his signet ring to Haman to carry out the king's wishes (3:10), but by the end of the book Haman died, and the king gave his royal ring to Mordecai, Haman's enemy. The decree that Haman wrote to kill all the Jews (3:12-14) was later reversed by the king's second decree, which was written by Mordecai (8:9-13). Another example of a reversal is that Haman hoped to wear the king's royal robes as he rode on the king's horse (6:8-9), but as it actually happened, Haman put the royal robes on Mordecai and led him around the city on the king's horse (6:11). Haman also erected a sharpened pole on which to impale Mordecai (5:14), but Haman was the one who ended up dying on his own pole (7:9-10). Finally, Haman's intent was to have the Jews killed on the 13th day of Adar (3:13), but on the 13th of Adar, the Jews killed thousands who tried to kill them (9:15-18). These reversals seem to outline the plot of the story and demonstrate how good overcomes evil.

THEOLOGICAL CONCERNS

The theology of Esther is based on a foundational belief in the sovereignty of the hidden God who directs the lives of people on earth. In most of the Old Testament, God boldly speaks, acts, and directs the course of history, but in a time of foreign domination by pagan nations, he works behind the scenes through the lives of both believers and unbelievers. In many eras of history, God's face is not seen, his hand is not performing great miracles, and his voice is not heard audibly; yet, he is present. Unusual events take place, almost impossible things happen, and events fall into place in ways that are not merely accidental. Surely the hidden hand of God was at work through the events recorded in the book of Esther.

Although the book of Esther never mentions the name of God, the central purpose of this story is to demonstrate that behind people's everyday activities, as well as behind their courageous actions in times of crisis, God is providentially working to take care of his people. Xerxes' evil plans resulted in the removal of Vashti as queen. God used that event to elevate Esther (chs 1-2). Haman's evil plans to kill the Jews because of Mordecai were reversed through a series of unique circumstances that only God could have orchestrated. Although Haman tricked the king into signing an evil decree, the king assigned Haman the job of honoring Mordecai in the streets of the city (chs 3-6). Esther bravely set a trap for Haman at her banquet, and God saw to it that Haman was executed on the gallows (or "pole") he had built for Mordecai (7:1-10). In the end, Xerxes gave Haman's ring to Mordecai and canceled the order to kill all the Jewish people (8:1-17). Instead of the unjust killing of thousands of Jewish people, God ordained that hundreds in Haman's family and thousands of his supporters would be killed (9:1-18). Instead of bitter weeping by the Jewish population of Persia, the day of execution turned into a day of joy because God delivered his chosen people from extermination through a peculiar set of circumstances. This strange series of events is a reminder that God is providentially directing believers and unbelievers to accomplish his will. The world is not controlled by luck or casting lots.

Another theological concern relates to how Jewish people should live in a pagan world that opposes what the people of God believe and how they behave. The king was proud of his wealth, liked to drink, got terribly angry when he did not get his way, did not respect his wife, and used his power against those who crossed him (1:1-22). These behavior patterns would naturally raise questions for his Jewish servant Mordecai and his Jewish wife, Esther. How should these believers respond to this kind of behavior? Haman was also a powerful, rich, and arrogant man; he demanded that people bow to him, got angry when they did not bow, used deceit to get revenge on Mordecai, and plotted to kill the whole Jewish race (3:1-15; 5:1-6:9; 9:24). Since Haman was a friend of the king, both Mordecai and Esther had to interact with him. Neither Mordecai nor Esther retreated into a cloistered life to avoid people who had different political and theological beliefs. Instead, they entered the fray and lived by their own beliefs and standards of conduct. Mordecai served the king faithfully, reporting a plot in order to save the king's life rather than allowing this arrogant and angry king to be killed (2:19-23). Esther did not refuse to enter the race to become the next queen, and she impressed Hegai and the king with her beauty and her behavior (2:1-18). Mordecai refused to bow to Haman (3:1-6) because Haman was not an honorable person. Esther boldly entered the king's court without an invitation because she was willing to pay the penalty (death) in order to save her people (4:9-17). Throughout the book, the author contrasts the forthright, bold, sacrificial, and honest behavior of Esther and Mordecai with the angry, arrogant, and inappropriate behavior of the king and Haman.

The behavior of each individual is often tied up with the desire for honor and the threat of shame (Laniak 1998). Everything about the king's great banquet was designed to bring honor to Xerxes. He displayed his opulent wealth, his glory, and the "splendor of his majesty" (1:4). Of course, Vashti's refusal to come to the king's banquet was a great shame to the king, for it demonstrated that he could not control his wife. She had "wronged" the king, "despised" her husband, and brought "contempt" on men, so there was great fear that all women in Persia might not honor their husbands (1:10-20). Consequently, Vashti's honor of being the queen was taken away and given to Esther (2:17-18). Mordecai did not bow to Haman because he questioned his honorable status (3:1-6). So Haman attempted to regain his honor by getting rid of Mordecai (3:7-15). Haman did this by claiming that some people did not obey or honor the king and therefore should be destroyed. This brought a sense of shame and hopelessness to Mordecai and Esther because no one respected their lives. To end this threat, Esther was willing to give up her honorable position and even her life as queen in order to speak to the king, even if she was not invited (4:9-5:3).

Esther honored the king and Haman at her banquets, and Haman brooded on his riches and honor after that banquet (5:1-12). The night that the king could not sleep, he remembered that he had not honored Mordecai for saving the king's life and then asked Haman what should be done for someone the king wants to honor (6:1-9). Accepting Haman's suggestions, the king told Haman to honor Mordecai in exactly that way (6:10-12). The events that transpired at Esther's second banquet resulted in Haman's shame and execution (7:1-10), but later Mordecai was honored with the king's ring (8:1-2, 15-17). The shameful threat of death was later removed from the Jewish population on Purim (9:1-28), and the king's honor toward Mordecai was widely recognized (10:1-3). These events show that some try to gain honor by running over other people, and others let great honor turn into arrogance and misuse their place of status; but the greatest honor goes to those who give themselves up for the sake of others.

Finally, it is worthwhile to ask, Why isn't God's name ever mentioned in this book? Although we can only guess, a reasonable approach is that of R. Gordis (1981:359-388), who thinks that the writer was trying to compose the work in the form of an official Persian chronicle and to make it appear that it was not written by a Jew. The writer wanted his work to resemble a Persian document and not be disregarded as partisan Jewish propaganda. In addition, for aesthetic and dramatic reasons, he wanted his audience to be drawn into the suspense and irony of the story, so he told it as a historical account of real people struggling against a vicious tyrant, not as a theological treatise on the nature of God's sovereign work through providence in people's lives. The genius of the presentation is that the author reveals to sensitive readers the unseen hand of God behind the events without ever mentioning his name.

OUTLINE

The plot of the book of Esther revolves around the threat to destroy the Jewish people and the attempt to resolve that threat (Baldwin 1984:30). Haman's plan to kill every person who did not obey the king (the queen and the Jews) dominates chapters 1–5. Chapters 6–10 resolve this threat when the king kills Haman and honors Mordecai and Esther. The resolution of the problem required a reversal of everything Haman was planning to do (Fox 2001:158-163; Levenson 1997:8; Bush 1996:301-304). This plan for the book becomes clear when Mordecai receives what Haman had, Haman's decree is reversed, and the Jews gain control over their enemies (9:1). Individual verses in the later chapters repeat vocabulary and themes in earlier chapters to illustrate the reversals the author wanted to highlight (cf. 3:1 and 10:3; 3:7 and 9:24; 3:10 and 8:2; 3:12-13 and 8:9-11; 3:14 and 8:13).

I. Vashti Is Replaced by Queen Esther (1:1–2:18)
    A. Vashti Challenges Xerxes' Authority (1:1-22)
    B. Esther Becomes Queen (2:1-18)
II. Haman's Decree to Destroy the Jews (2:19–3:15)
    A. Mordecai Saves the King's Life (2:19-23)
    B. Mordecai Will Not Honor Haman (3:1-6)
    C. Haman's Decree to Get Revenge (3:7-15)
III. Esther Must Try to Reverse Haman's Plot (4:1–5:14)
    A. Esther Bravely Risks Her Life (4:1-17)
    B. Esther's Banquet for Xerxes and Haman (5:1-8)
    C. Haman's Pride and Hatred of Mordecai (5:9-14)
IV. Mordecai Is Honored and Haman Is Impaled (6:1–7:10)
    A. Haman Must Honor Mordecai (6:1-14)
    B. Haman Is Exposed and Impaled (7:1-10)
V. Haman's Decree Is Reversed (8:1–9:19)
    A. Esther Saves the Lives of the Jews (8:1-14)
    B. The Enemies of the Jews Are Killed (8:15–9:19)
VI. The Festival of Purim (9:20-32)
VII. The Greatness of Mordecai (10:1-3)

COMMENTARY ON
Esther

◆ I. Vashti Is Replaced by Queen Esther (1:1–2:18)
A. Vashti Challenges Xerxes' Authority (1:1–22)

These events happened in the days of King Xerxes,* who reigned over 127 provinces stretching from India to Ethiopia.* ²At that time Xerxes ruled his empire from his royal throne at the fortress of Susa. ³In the third year of his reign, he gave a banquet for all his nobles and officials. He invited all the military officers of Persia and Media as well as the princes and nobles of the provinces. ⁴The celebration lasted 180 days—a tremendous display of the opulent wealth of his empire and the pomp and splendor of his majesty.

⁵When it was all over, the king gave a banquet for all the people, from the greatest to the least, who were in the fortress of Susa. It lasted for seven days and was held in the courtyard of the palace garden. ⁶The courtyard was beautifully decorated with white cotton curtains and blue hangings, which were fastened with white linen cords and purple ribbons to silver rings embedded in marble pillars. Gold and silver couches stood on a mosaic pavement of porphyry, marble, mother-of-pearl, and other costly stones.

⁷Drinks were served in gold goblets of many designs, and there was an abundance of royal wine, reflecting the king's generosity. ⁸By edict of the king, no limits were placed on the drinking, for the king had instructed all his palace officials to serve each man as much as he wanted.

⁹At the same time, Queen Vashti gave a banquet for the women in the royal palace of King Xerxes.

¹⁰On the seventh day of the feast, when King Xerxes was in high spirits because of the wine, he told the seven eunuchs who attended him—Mehuman, Biztha, Harbona, Bigtha, Abagtha, Zethar, and Carcas—¹¹to bring Queen Vashti to him with the royal crown on her head. He wanted the nobles and all the other men to gaze on her beauty, for she was a very beautiful woman. ¹²But when they conveyed the king's order to Queen Vashti, she refused to come. This made the king furious, and he burned with anger.

¹³He immediately consulted with his wise advisers, who knew all the Persian laws and customs, for he always asked their advice. ¹⁴The names of these men were Carshena, Shethar, Admatha, Tarshish, Meres, Marsena, and Memucan—seven nobles of Persia and Media. They met with the king regularly and held the highest positions in the empire.

¹⁵"What must be done to Queen Vashti?" the king demanded. "What penalty does the law provide for a queen who refuses to obey the king's orders, properly sent through his eunuchs?"

¹⁶Memucan answered the king and his nobles, "Queen Vashti has wronged not only the king but also every noble and citizen throughout your empire. ¹⁷Women everywhere will begin to despise their husbands when they learn that Queen Vashti has refused to appear before the king. ¹⁸Before this day is out, the wives of all the king's nobles throughout Persia

and Media will hear what the queen did and will start treating their husbands the same way. There will be no end to their contempt and anger.

¹⁹"So if it please the king, we suggest that you issue a written decree, a law of the Persians and Medes that cannot be revoked. It should order that Queen Vashti be forever banished from the presence of King Xerxes, and that the king should choose another queen more worthy than she. ²⁰When this decree is published throughout the king's vast empire, husbands everywhere, whatever their rank, will receive proper respect from their wives!"

²¹The king and his nobles thought this made good sense, so he followed Memucan's counsel. ²²He sent letters to all parts of the empire, to each province in its own script and language, proclaiming that every man should be the ruler of his own home and should say whatever he pleases.*

1:1a Hebrew *Ahasuerus*, another name for Xerxes; also throughout the book of Esther. Xerxes reigned 486–465 B.C.   1:1b Hebrew *to Cush.*   1:22 Or *and should speak in the language of his own people.*

NOTES

1:1 *King Xerxes.* In the Persian language the king's name was *Xshayarsha* or *Khshayarshan*. The name "Xerxes" is drawn from the Greek transliteration of this name, while the name *Ahasuerus* (cf. KJV) is drawn from the Hebrew rendering of it, *'akhashwerosh* [TH325, ZH347]. King Xerxes ruled from 486–465 BC and was the son of Darius I Hystaspes (521–486 BC; mentioned in Hag 1:1, 15; 2:10; Zech 1:1; 7:1).

reigned over 127 provinces stretching from India to Ethiopia. Xerxes reigned over an expansive world empire that stretched from India (*hodu* [TH1912, ZH2064]) to somewhere in southern Egypt (*kush* [TH3568, ZH3932]; "Cush" may refer to Ethiopia or Sudan). These 127 "provinces" (*medinah* [TH4082, ZH4519]) were smaller divisions of territory within the 20 to 30 major satrapies in the empire (Laniak 2003:196; Herodotus *Histories* 3.89). The Behistun Inscription refers to 21 satrapies, but later in the same document it mentions 23, and towards the end it speaks of 29 satrapies. These political divisions of the empire were responsible to collect taxes, raise troops for the Persian army, and administer and police each local area. Jerusalem was in the province of Yehud, which was a small part of the "Satrapy beyond the Euphrates" (cf. Ezra 4:10-11).

1:2 *the fortress of Susa.* Susa (*shushan* [TH7800, ZH8809]) was formerly the capital of the nation of Elam, but at this time it functioned as the winter palace for the Persian king (Jobes 1999:59). He ruled from other palaces at Babylon, Ecbatana, and Persepolis during the other seasons, for it was too hot to stay in Susa in the summer. This palace (cf. NLT, "fortress") was set on a hill about 75 feet high (the "citadel, acropolis") with a strong wall all around it (Paton 1908:126).

1:3 *In the third year . . . he gave a banquet.* The third year was 483–482 BC. The reason for this banquet is not stated. At the beginning of his reign, Xerxes put down uprisings in Egypt and Babylon (Olmstead 1948:234-237), so it was probably not until his third year that he could sit securely on his throne and celebrate his power. The word "banquet" (*mishteh* [TH4960, ZH5492]) comes from the root meaning "to drink" (*shathah* [TH8354, ZH9272]), thus hinting at the main activity.

military officers . . . nobles. The word for "army" (*khayil* [TH2428, ZH2657]) is usually understood to refer here to "military officers" (so NLT), for the whole army could not come at once, leaving the nation unprotected. But how could these military officials abandon their responsibilities of running the army and navy for six whole months? It seems more likely that the "nobles" (*happartemim* [TH6579, ZH7312], a term borrowed from

Old Persian) and officials probably took turns attending different events during this period of celebration, thus maintaining the nation's political and military capabilities throughout the celebration. Jobes (1999:60) concludes that this event in the third year of Xerxes' reign was a "great war council" held to plan the Persians' next attack on Greece, because Herodotus (*Histories* 7.8) describes Xerxes as announcing his plans to destroy Athens. But taking advantage of a large gathering to motivate people to support the king's military causes is different from a small group of army generals planning a military strategy for the next battle.

1:4 *The celebration lasted 180 days.* Various events took place over a period of half a year, not every day for 180 days. Could this really be suggesting that "all" the military commanders spent all six months, while they left the troops in the field to defend the nation against the attacking Greek forces without any leadership? It seems the nation would have fallen into total chaos if all the nobles had spent all six months at the palace drinking. Thus an overly literal interpretation seems unlikely. One can reduce this problem by suggesting that small groups of officers came in rotations over a six-month period or by suggesting that all the officers came periodically (not every day) over six months. Bush (1996:346-347) calls this reference to a six-month banquet a "sardonic hyperbole," and he also believes the word that refers to "military leaders" (*khayil*; see note on 1:3) is a reference to "nobility, aristocracy" in postexilic texts; thus he avoids the problematic idea of having all the military officers at this banquet for six months.

1:5 *banquet for all the people . . . in the courtyard.* Everyone in Susa, rich or poor, was invited to this additional banquet, at an open house (*bithan* [TH1055, ZH1131], an open colonnaded pavilion, according to Moore 1971:7)—a reception held in the paved courtyard and lush garden area around the palace.

1:6 *beautifully decorated.* Emphasis is placed on the lavish decorations. White and violet (better than NLT's "blue") were the royal colors that hung from silver rings on marble pillars to form an awning that shaded guests from the sun. The mosaic design on the floor was an exquisite example of the opulence of the palace.

1:7 *in gold goblets . . . an abundance of royal wine.* Ancient historians (Herodotus *Histories* 1.133; Xenophon *Cyropaedia* 8.8.10, 18) testify to the king's wealth and excess, including the golden wine goblets and an unlimited supply of wine for everyone. Although this may seem excessive and hardly believable to people today, when Alexander the Great finally defeated Persia and took control of the palace at Susa, he was astonished to discover 40,000 talents (1,200 tons) of gold and silver and 9,000 talents (270 tons) of gold coins in the king's treasury (Diodorus Siculus *Library* 17.66).

the king's generosity. Lit., "according to the king's hand" (*keyad hammelek* [TH3027, ZH3338]), which could mean "to drink when the king tipped his hand to drink" or "a decree the king's hand wrote that regulated drinking" (1:8).

1:8 *By edict.* The word *dath* [TH1881, ZH2017] (law, edict) probably refers to a special rule imposed at this event: At this feast people could drink without restraint or not at all (Huey 1988:799; cf. Josephus *Antiquities* 11.188). This would still have produced a large crowd of fairly drunk men, so it is not surprising that the queen would not want to parade herself in front of this large group.

1:9 *Queen Vashti.* The word "Vashti" means "the best, desired, beloved" (Paton 1908:66). It may be an honorary title for the favored wife rather than her actual name, which may have been Amestris (Herodotus *Histories* 7.61, 114; 9.109-113). Others have suggested that Amestris was her Greek name, while Vashti was her Persian name. On the other hand, Amestris may just be another wife (Xerxes probably had many).

a banquet for the women. It was the queen's duty to entertain the wives of important guests. Laniak believes this banquet was for the 360 concubines of the king (2003:197).

1:10 *seven eunuchs who attended him.* These eunuchs have Persian names and were castrated because they would have ongoing access to the women of the royal harem. The listing of the names suggests that the author had firsthand information. These seven men probably would carry the queen into the banquet as she sat on her royal litter. All this royal pomp would make her coming a grand entrance that would impress the audience and hopefully inspire their loyalty to the king.

1:11 *He wanted the nobles and all the other men to gaze on her beauty.* The king was displaying her as another one of his possessions (Fox 2001:167). Jobes suggests that Xerxes was possibly trying to "inspire patriotism and loyalty, as appearances of the British queen do today" (1999:67). The Aramaic Targum suggests that she was asked to wear nothing but her royal crown, but this is reading into the text.

1:12 *she refused to come.* The queen's refusal is not explained, but Josephus (*Antiquities* 11.6.1) suggests that she did not want to break the protocol that women were not to attend the men's banquet. Was she fearful of being in front of a bunch of drunken men? Was the king asking something that was improper for a woman of her status? She showed courage in standing up against the king's wishes, a desire to maintain her dignity as a noble queen (Jobes 1999:73), and a willingness to stand for what was right for her to do in this situation (according to Persian custom or normal royal protocol).

This made the king furious. The king's self-centered, intemperate, cruel, and fickle character was displayed. The king's anger (*qatsap* [TH7107, ZH7911]) was probably heightened by his drunken state and by the scornful laughter of his male friends. He was furious because he had been publicly shamed by his wife's unwillingness to comply with his every wish. Vashti's action demonstrated that the supposedly all-powerful king did not have as much control as he thought (McConville 1985:157).

1:13 *his wise advisers, who knew all the Persian laws and customs.* The king did not react immediately; he followed the custom of checking with key advisers (Herodotus *Histories* 3.31). The Hebrew has the king asking about "the times" (*ha'ittim* [TH6256, ZH6961]), which could refer to court astrologers (Levenson 1997:50; Bush 1996:350 strongly rejects this interpretation) or to men who understood what to do in situations like this (Clines 1984b:280; see 1 Chr 12:32). Some unnecessarily emend the text to refer to those who knew the Persian "laws" (*haddathim* [TH1881, ZH2017]), which would parallel the inquiry about "laws and customs" later in the verse (Moore 1971:9).

1:14 *seven nobles of Persia and Media.* Ezra 7:14 also mentions the king's seven counselors. These were his closest advisers (lit., "those who see the face of the king") who held a high rank. The author of Esther probably knew them by name (they may have been famous in their time) or had access to official records that listed their names.

1:15 *What penalty does the law provide.* Lit., "according to the law (*kedath* [TH1881, ZH2017]), what to do with the queen." The king wanted to punish Vashti to the full extent of the law, but it is odd to have a despot like Xerxes worried about the Persian legal system when dealing with a family matter. One would expect this powerful king to handle these issues with his wife behind closed doors. Bush believes that this odd behavior "is intended to be farcical and humorous" (1996:350) to a Jewish reader, a satirical mockery of the Persian king. Admittedly, this behavior does put the king in a bad light, but it makes sense that he would want to know legal precedents ("the law") followed by other kings so that he would handle this embarrassing situation with what might be considered an appropriate course of action. Nevertheless, in a real sense Bush is correct in seeing this action as reducing the stature of the king. He is the king; does he not know the laws of the land? Why does he let others tell him what to do? Why doesn't the king object and prefer some reconciliation process?

1:16 *Queen Vashti has wronged.* No Persian law is quoted as a precedent to guide the king in making a decision, thus these words represent the judgment of the men in the council. They believe that the king has not been treated according to proper protocol. Memucan does not attempt to justify how Vashti's action somehow wrongs the king's seven council-lors or exactly how it harms all the people in the provinces. Apparently, he believed that the potential for disorder and disrespect (mentioned in 1:17) justified this conclusion.

1:17 *Women everywhere will begin to despise their husbands.* Fear motivated the council's advice, rather than the law. They exaggerated this event into a hypothetical national crisis that negatively impacted the authority of husbands (*ba'al* [TH1167, ZH1251], "lord, master") throughout the empire. Later Esther would disobey Persian laws but be dealt with merci-fully (5:1-4).

1:19 *issue a written decree . . . that cannot be revoked.* Memucan was quite deferential to the king ("if it please the king"), but his suggestion was unbending. This written decree would become a law that could not be changed (8:8; Dan 6:8, 12, 15), though there are no references in Persian literature that characterize Persian laws as unalterable (Huey 1988:803). Vashti, who refused to see the king at the banquet, would never see the king again.

another queen more worthy than she. This hints at the rest of the story of Esther. How would the new queen differ from Vashti? "Good, better" (*hattobah* [TH2896, ZH3202]) could point to being more beautiful, more worthy (so NLT), or possibly more obedient.

1:20 *decree.* The word *pithegam* [TH6599, ZH7330] is borrowed from Aramaic, which derived the term from the Old Persian *patigama*. Jobes finds irony and even humor in the king's acceptance of Memucan's suggestion, for the king's decree ends up publicizing his embar-rassing personal problems with his wife to people throughout the nation (Jobes 1999:80; Fox 1991:253).

1:21 *this made good sense.* Lit., "The thing was good (*yatab* [TH3190, ZH3512]) in the eyes of the king." This does not mean that it made logical sense or fit the legal requirements of Persian law.

1:22 *in its own script and language.* Royal scribes translated the decree so that it could be disseminated to every linguistic group (Paton 1908:161 lists 21 different languages). The efficient Persian postal system would distribute these decrees. Rather than accepting this at face value, Clines takes this as a conscious hyperbole, which ironically contrasts the super-efficiency of the Persian administration's fantastic ability to publish and disseminate this decree with the fact that they cannot keep their wives in order (1984b:253).

every man should be the ruler of his own home. In that culture it was unnecessary (and almost humorous) to make a decree that each man should be the ruler (*sorer* [TH8323, ZH8606]) of his house. This was already the cultural norm throughout the ancient Near East.

should say whatever he pleases. Lit., "speaking according to the language of his people." NIV removes this clause from the proclamation of the decree and puts it earlier in the sentence ("proclaiming in each people's tongue"), LXX omits this phrase, and the Targum suggests that husbands do not have to learn the language of their wives. Others unnecessar-ily emend the vowels of the text (Clines 1984b:283), changing *kilshon 'ammo* [TH3956/5971A, ZH4383/6639] (according to the language of his people) to *kol-showeh* [TH7737, ZH8750] *'immo* (whatever suits him). It is best to accept the unemended text and interpret this as the right and authority of the husband of the family to determine what language would be spoken in each household. When people intermarried with wives from other communities, the wife would want the children to learn her native language, so the second part of this decree establishes another domain where the male determines what will happen in the home. Fox (1991:23) thinks this phrase represents a Jewish concern over the lack of use of Hebrew in the postexilic period, when it was common for Hebrews to have a mixed marriage (Neh 13:23-28). This approach is unacceptable, for it removes historical value from the narrative and attributes the main theological point to a later editor's manipulation for purposes unrelated to this story.

COMMENTARY

Esther 1 provides a setting for the story of Esther in the Persian era and introduces one of the key characters in the book. This introduction reveals important facts about key people that help to create tension in the drama and hint at ways of resolving the tension (i.e., the king will seek a new wife) in the following chapters. The reader discovers the king's attitude toward his own wealth, how drinking and a quick temper lead to dire consequences, the king's feelings about women in general, and specifically how he will treat his wife if she does not do what the king thinks she is supposed to do (creating tension when Esther follows a similar pattern in chapter 5).

The extent of the king's enormous empire (127 provinces) proves that he was one of the most powerful men in the world at that time (1:1). The events at the king's drinking feast show that this monarch was prone to pride and loved to make an ostentatious display of his riches. In this situation, he showed a great ability to manipulate his followers and advisers, demonstrated rather erratic behavior when he was drunk, and exhibited a penchant to have extreme fits of irrational anger if his every whim was not responded to positively. The depravity of Xerxes' soul exposed his fleshly pleasures and his foul moods, as well as the vindictive motives behind his actions.

Although few people today can match the wealth or power of Xerxes, both poor and rich are frequently tempted to strut a new car, a new pair of shoes, a new ring or dress, or some other material object to demonstrate to others how great they are. Pride is an especially frequent temptation for the wealthy heads of companies, sports heroes, and Hollywood stars, but almost everyone is tempted to do extraordinary things to get some attention or to gain respect or honor. People will foolishly go into debt to keep up with others in their social class or with friends at church. They will display their possessions and flaunt their status to gain honor, to save face, and to show that they are important. The danger is that the desire for glory and honor can be so strong that some will even act immorally, or ask others to act immorally for them, in order to maintain their air of superiority. This contrasts with the biblical call to humble ourselves as Christ did (Phil 2) and to serve others rather than lording it over them (Luke 22:25-27).

God opposes the proud and arrogant person (Prov 3:34; Jas 4:6), for God is the one who deserves the glory and honor for everything people have or are able to do. The voice of a great singer is a gift of God, and the speed of great athletes is something they were born with. People do not make themselves powerful or rich; God does. God raises up kings to rule (Dan 2:20-23), and he gives people the ability to make wealth (Deut 8:18-20). All glory should be directed to God, who freely gives people everything they have.

King Xerxes' excessive display of wealth and opulence was a means to bring greater honor and glory to himself (Laniak 1998:36). He flaunted the "splendor of his majesty" (1:4) to the top military leaders, the highest politicians, important civic leaders, and the general population so that everyone would have an opportunity to admire him. The richly colored cloth decorations, the shining marble pillars, the exquisite mother-of-pearl mosaic (1:6), the elaborate gold cups, and an unending flow of wine all screamed a message that the king was important and a person of great glory. True greatness, of course, is not dependent on wealth, and real importance is not based on how much money one has. The royal road to success and influence in this world is firmly based on a leader's love for his people and willingness to serve them. Loyalty cannot be bought for long, and true respect comes from an admiration of a person's character, not from being dazzled by a three-karat diamond ring or a million-dollar house. Like this king, many people today pride themselves in their riches and flaunt their wealth and power, but when trouble comes, the true self is exposed with all its warts and wrinkles.

The king's goal of bringing honor to himself backfired when Vashti chose not to obey the king and refused to display her beauty before the drunken men at his feast (1:12). This simple refusal to glorify every whim of the king brought his superior status into question; it also demonstrated that it takes more than money to impress some people (especially one's wife). Vashti's behavior demonstrated that people did not have to submit to the manipulation of riches and that there were principles far higher than pleasing the whims of an arrogant, drunken king. One cannot know Vashti's motives (see note on 1:12), but it appears she determined not to be treated as just another object in the palace that displayed the king's greatness. Her presence at the king's banquet would only confirm and add to the king's high status, for what other man could attract such a beautiful woman? Consequently, she refused to enhance his glory and refused to honor the king.

Her reaction is one which may appear to be stupid—perhaps the response of a spoiled spouse who had everything—but she saw this as something that would bring shame to herself and only feed the arrogance of the king. Her decision is one that employees, politicians, and family members are faced with when an arrogant superior asks them to do an inappropriate favor that they should not do. Does one honor a drunken father and obey him, or should one refuse to cover up for his alcoholic behavior? Does one lie or fix the financial books of the company to hide the sins of a boss, or refuse to cooperate and risk being fired? Does a person heap accolades of praise on someone who has a hidden record of sexual sins, or reveal the truth and lose a friend? Vashti is an exemplary model in chapter 1, who refuses to be put in a position inappropriate for the queen and suffers great harm for her courage.

The king's reaction to Vashti was an attempt to maintain his honor by removing the problem person from the palace. Everyone would honor the king if the king simply eliminated the problem individuals (he agreed with a similar solution when Haman wanted to rid the kingdom of all Jews; 3:8-9). The king did not take decisive action against Vashti by himself, but looked to the group support of his seven counselors and then followed their advice without hearing any past precedent from law or past protocol in similar situations. He does not say no to those who make requests of him, revealing some of his inability to make decisions on his own (Laniak [2003:200] believes it is humorous that the king had to check with his advisers regarding how to deal with his wife). Jobes believes that this story mocks the inability of this great worldly power to make decisions and thus "its ultimate inability to determine the destiny of God's people" (1999:83). The king asked for a legal ruling, but his counselors' answer appears to have no basis in the laws of the kingdom. Vashti was condemned as one who "wronged" the king and every other citizen in the kingdom, a charge that was greatly exaggerated beyond anything that could be logically defended from a law. In fact, Vashti was never accused of breaking a law. The fear elicited by this one act of Vashti is evident, for it is characterized as a despising of her husband and as an act of contempt. The decree that went out to banish Vashti from the king's presence was motivated by a desire that all men throughout the kingdom should receive the "proper respect" and honor from their wives (1:20). The decree allowed a man to "be the ruler of his own home" and to "say whatever he pleases" (1:22).

The language of rule, respect, and power indicates what the true problem was. Some people in this world want to have absolute authority for themselves and at the same time remove anyone who might question their authority. They want respect, but respect is not something that one can command; it is earned. This arrogant and controlling approach to life stands in stark contrast to the leadership ideals in the Bible. The legacy of Moses that God and Joshua remembered was that he functioned as the humble "servant of the LORD" (Josh 1:1, 2, 13, 15), who never displayed any hint of glory or touted his riches. When God promised David that he would make of his dynasty an eternal house, David's prayer of thanksgiving constantly referred to himself as God's humble servant (2 Sam 7:19-21, 25-29). Christ himself did not come to earth with the glorious trappings of a world emperor but emptied himself and took on the role of a servant (Phil 2). The chief end of mankind is not to bring honor to itself, but to give all glory to God.

◆   ## B. Esther Becomes Queen (2:1-18)

But after Xerxes' anger had subsided, he began thinking about Vashti and what she had done and the decree he had made. [2]So his personal attendants suggested, "Let us search the empire to find beautiful young virgins for the king. [3]Let the king appoint agents in each province to bring these beautiful young women into the royal harem at the fortress of Susa. Hegai, the king's eunuch in charge of the harem, will see that they are all given beauty treatments. [4]After that, the young woman who most pleases the king will be made queen instead of Vashti." This advice was very appealing to the king, so he put the plan into effect.

[5]At that time there was a Jewish man in the fortress of Susa whose name was Mordecai son of Jair. He was from the tribe of Benjamin and was a descendant of Kish and Shimei. [6]His family* had been among those who, with King Jehoiachin* of Judah, had been exiled from Jerusalem to Babylon by King Nebuchadnezzar. [7]This

man had a very beautiful and lovely young cousin, Hadassah, who was also called Esther. When her father and mother died, Mordecai adopted her into his family and raised her as his own daughter.

⁸As a result of the king's decree, Esther, along with many other young women, was brought to the king's harem at the fortress of Susa and placed in Hegai's care. ⁹Hegai was very impressed with Esther and treated her kindly. He quickly ordered a special menu for her and provided her with beauty treatments. He also assigned her seven maids specially chosen from the king's palace, and he moved her and her maids into the best place in the harem.

¹⁰Esther had not told anyone of her nationality and family background, because Mordecai had directed her not to do so. ¹¹Every day Mordecai would take a walk near the courtyard of the harem to find out about Esther and what was happening to her.

¹²Before each young woman was taken to the king's bed, she was given the prescribed twelve months of beauty treatments—six months with oil of myrrh, followed by six months with special perfumes and ointments. ¹³When it was time for her to go to the king's palace, she was given her choice of whatever clothing or jewelry she wanted to take from the harem. ¹⁴That evening she was taken to the king's private rooms, and the next morning she was brought to the second harem,* where the king's wives lived. There she would be under the care of Shaashgaz, the king's eunuch in charge of the concubines. She would never go to the king again unless he had especially enjoyed her and requested her by name.

¹⁵Esther was the daughter of Abihail, who was Mordecai's uncle. (Mordecai had adopted his younger cousin Esther.) When it was Esther's turn to go to the king, she accepted the advice of Hegai, the eunuch in charge of the harem. She asked for nothing except what he suggested, and she was admired by everyone who saw her.

¹⁶Esther was taken to King Xerxes at the royal palace in early winter* of the seventh year of his reign. ¹⁷And the king loved Esther more than any of the other young women. He was so delighted with her that he set the royal crown on her head and declared her queen instead of Vashti. ¹⁸To celebrate the occasion, he gave a great banquet in Esther's honor for all his nobles and officials, declaring a public holiday for the provinces and giving generous gifts to everyone.

2:6a Hebrew *He.* 2:6b Hebrew *Jeconiah,* a variant spelling of Jehoiachin. 2:14 Or *to another part of the harem.* 2:16 Hebrew *in the tenth month, the month of Tebeth.* A number of dates in the book of Esther can be cross-checked with dates in surviving Persian records and related accurately to our modern calendar. This month of the ancient Hebrew lunar calendar occurred within the months of December 479 B.C. and January 478 B.C.

NOTES

2:1 *after Xerxes' anger had subsided.* "After" does not specify how many days or years went by. Vashti was pushed out in the third year, and the king married Esther in his seventh year (2:16). For two of these years the king was fighting the Greeks (Herodotus *Histories* 7.8). In 7:10 his anger is also said to subside (*shakak* [TH7918, ZH8896]) after Haman's proper punishment is administered.

he began thinking about Vashti. His "remembering" could reveal that the king was lonely, still in love with Vashti, or that he regretted dismissing her (Clines 1984b:285). The Old Greek says that "he no longer remembered Vashti," thus he had forgotten about her, but this interpretation misunderstands what is happening here.

2:2 *beautiful young virgins.* In this search for a new queen, the king was looking for beautiful "young virgins" (*bethulah* [TH1330, ZH1435]). Wenham (1972:326-348) argues that this word does not primarily describe virginity, though most girls of this young age (probably applicable to girls anywhere from 5 to 20 years old) would certainly be virgins.

2:3 *agents.* The use of appointed agents (*peqidim* [TH6496, ZH7224], "overseers, commission-ers") ensured a certain level of quality and prevented anxious parents from hiding their daughters (Clines 1984b:285).

beauty treatments. These are described in detail in 2:9 and 12.

2:4 *who most pleases the king.* Apparently none of the king's concubines at that time pleased him fully (lit., "were good in the eyes of the king"). This search for a new queen was not limited to the seven families that Herodotus mentions (*Histories* 3.84). Plutarch (*Lives: Artaxerxes* 23.3) mentions that some Persian kings did marry outside these seven families.

2:5-7 *Mordecai . . . Esther.* These three verses are a parenthetical comment to orient the readers to what will happen next and introduce the Jewish characters, Mordecai and Esther. In order to understand the mysterious ways that God works out all the details behind the scenes, it is necessary to understand some background information. Mordecai was the Babylonian name (related to the name of the Babylon god Marduk) of a man who worked at the gate of the palace-fortress of the king in Susa. It was not uncommon for Jews to take (or be assigned) foreign names in the Exile (as occurs in the book of Daniel; cf. Dan 1:6-7). On Esther's name, see the note on 2:7.

2:5 *descendant of Kish.* King Saul was also from the tribe of Benjamin (1 Sam 9:1; 2 Sam 16:5), so Mordecai had royal blood (Moore 1971:19). This point may prefigure the idea that a greater role may come to him at some point in the future (chs 9–10).

2:6 *His family . . . who, with King Jehoiachin of Judah, had been exiled.* "His family" is not in the Hebrew text, but is implied in the word *'asher* [TH834, ZH889] (cf. NLT, "who"), which cannot refer to Mordecai. Since the events in ch 2 happened after 483 BC and King Jehoiachin (or "Jeconiah," as in Jer 24:1, NLT mg) was exiled in 597 BC (2 Kgs 24:6-16), it is very unlikely that Mordecai was part of the group taken into Babylonian captivity— he would have been about 120 years old at this time. Therefore, the text must refer to the exile of Mordecai's father or grandfather, who was among the nobility in Judah (Laniak 2003:205, 209).

2:7 *lovely young cousin, Hadassah, who was also called Esther.* Hadassah means "myrtle," while the name Esther means "star" (a reference to the star-shaped flower of the myrtle) and is close to the name Ishtar, the Babylonian goddess of love. Some rabbis connected her name to the idea of the "hiddenness" of God (Deut 31:18; *'astir* [TH5641, ZH6259], "I will hide my face") in this story. Jobes believes Esther may not have been her real name, but the nickname given to her by her Babylonian subjects who named her after the Babylonian goddess of love, Ishtar (1999:97). Nevertheless, there is no evidence to prove this hypothesis. It was common for Jewish people in the Exile to have both a Hebrew and a Babylonian name (cf. Dan 1:6-7). R. Pierce (1992:77) interprets these Babylonian names as an example of Jewish failures to reject secularization and their will-ingness to assimilate into the culture of their day, but it is more important to evaluate a person by their actions, not just the name used in this story. The beauty of Esther related to her "form" (*to'ar* [TH8389, ZH9307]) and "appearance" (*mar'eh* [TH4758, ZH5260]), thereby fitting the king's criteria.

Mordecai adopted her. The Pentateuch has no laws explaining the Israelite legal process of adopting a child into a family, but this practice was common in Babylon. The LXX sug-gests Mordecai took Esther not as an adopted child but as a wife, but this is highly unlikely. Mordecai is pictured here as a caring (*'aman* [TH539A, ZH587], "nursing, supporting," as in Isa 60:4) and very responsible person for adopting (*laqakh* [TH3947, ZH4374], "took") this young girl when her parents died.

2:9 Hegai was very impressed with Esther and treated her kindly. Like Daniel, who was favored by a Babylonian official (Dan 1:8-9), Esther literally "gained his favor, kindness" (*khesed* [TH2617, ZH2876]), a term that may hint that this was actually God's covenant favor expressed through Hegai. In Esther, God is always active in the events, but never in the forefront.

ordered a special menu . . . beauty treatments . . . seven maids. It appears that Hegai knew the king's taste (what he would view as "good, acceptable") and separated the best prospects out for special food delicacies. This term *manoth* [TH4490, ZH4950] (portions of food) will be significant later in the story, for this is what the Jews give one another on Purim (9:19, 22). Esther never objected to the food, as Daniel did (Dan 1:8-9), possibly because Mordecai had told her not to reveal her Jewish identity (2:10). The assistance of the best maidens for Esther indicates that Hegai thought she was one of the very best candidates. God was using the king's eunuch to direct the course of history.

2:10 Esther had not told anyone of her nationality. This verse provides more parenthetical background to the story. No reason is given for hiding Esther's Hebrew origins (see also 2:20). Perhaps Mordecai had already experienced some prejudice because he was a Jew (Fox 2001:32). In the following episodes, Esther's Jewish background, combined with her position as queen, is the key to her ability to stop the terrible plot of Haman (chs 7–8). Esther is characterized as one who was careful, wise, and obedient. Interpreters sometimes attempt to read Esther's mind, and some conclude that she remained a faithful Jew throughout this period, while others condemn her for leaving her faith and the moral requirements of the law. Although it is enticing to imagine what she might have thought and consider the things she may have done, none of this is revealed in this narrative, so it is impossible to condemn or praise her. The rest of her experiences prove that she did not totally abandon her faith, but it is impossible to know how she justified all the ethical choices she faced in the pagan world of Persia.

2:11 find out about Esther. Mordecai probably never had an opportunity to talk to Esther directly, give or receive reports from Hegai, or interfere with the natural process. The text just says that he put himself in the appropriate place where he could hear the court gossip (from eunuchs—Moore 1971:23) about how the process of choosing the next queen was going.

2:12 the king's bed. Lit., "to go to King Xerxes." The NLT accurately represents what was happening in this context. The sexual encounter of the king and each girl was important (cf. 2:14), but if the new queen was going to work harmoniously with the king, he certainly would want to get to know each candidate to see if she would be a compatible spouse and capable of functioning in the official capacity as queen. The moral question of having sexual relationships outside of marriage (cf. Exod 20:14) is raised by what happened that night, and the biblical command not to marry foreigners (Deut 7:3) might have troubled the Jewish reader of this story, but neither question is directly addressed by the text. Jobes concludes that "Esther's marriage to Xerxes was the lesser of two evils, and in spite of the sin involved, led to the greater good for God's people" (1999:113). Esther's acts would not have been classified as a sin in Persian society.

six months with oil of myrrh . . . special perfumes and ointments. This report is focused solely on beautifying the skin with ointments. These oils would lighten the skin color, soften its texture, remove unwanted hair, and enhance the natural beauty of the woman. The 12 months of preparation surely involved training in court customs and royal etiquette, including what to say and how to say it. Levenson considers the 12 months of beauty treatment as an exaggeration; in fact, he views it as the editor's casting of contempt toward a "narcissistic and grossly self-indulgent body culture" (1997:61).

2:13 *she was given her choice of whatever clothing or jewelry she wanted.* Lit., "whatever she asked would be given to her." "Clothing or jewelry" is added in the NLT as indicative of the type of requests implied. Each woman would reveal something about her character by the things she asked for. This would communicate to the king what kind of person she was. Was she shy or outgoing, modest or provocative? Did she think she could impress the king with a great deal of jewelry or with the plain look of a common person? Some see these objects as a wedding gift from the king (Paton 1908:179).

2:14 *the next morning she was brought to the second harem.* Each woman would spend one night with the king in his bedroom. Unless the king remembered her name and called for her (this point is significant in 4:11), she would live the rest of her life as a concubine of the king.

under the care of Shaashgaz, the king's eunuch. The concubines in the king's harem would live an easy life, although somewhat lonely, in the luxuries of the palace, under the control of the court eunuch. As in Israel's history, polygamy was permissible in Persian culture. Laniak (2003:197) claims that the king had over 360 concubines.

2:15 *she accepted the advice of Hegai.* This is not in the Hebrew text and is somewhat redundant with the later statement in the verse that "she asked for nothing except what he suggested." Hegai knew what would be seen as good in the eyes of the king, so he gave Esther advice on what to wear and do when she met the king. Being wise and teachable, Esther relied on Hegai's counsel instead of her own wishes. She was modest in what she asked for, depending on taste and charm rather than dazzling jewelry. She exhibited a spirit of submission and humility.

2:16 *in early winter of the seventh year.* Lit., "in the tenth month." Esther's opportunity to visit the king came in the cold months of December/January in the year 479–478 BC, four years after Vashti had been removed from power (see NLT mg). The passive verbs (*wattillaqakh* [TH3947, ZH4374], "she was taken") indicate that Esther was not in control of her destiny. Hegai wisely did not bring Esther to the king early in the process because the king would have been hesitant to make his final choice quickly when he still had so many other women to evaluate. Now, after some time, the king may have tired of the process and wanted to make a decision about the next queen.

2:17 *the king loved Esther more. . . . He was so delighted with her.* The king did not just like being with Esther; he loved her. The comparative expression "more than all" (*mikkol* [TH4480/3605, ZH4946/3972]) indicates the superiority of the king's love for Esther. His delight (lit., "favor and kindness") with her emphasizes a theme already mentioned in 2:9 and 15. Although one might expect there to be some condemnation of Esther for marrying a pagan foreigner, the text offers no moral judgment on Esther's behavior. In light of her later role of saving the Jewish people from annihilation by Haman, there is no moral condemnation of her actions.

he set the royal crown on her head. There is no mention of marriage, but that must have happened. Now Esther replaced Vashti (1:11) and wore the crown that Vashti refused to wear at the king's banquet. The crown was probably a tall, stiff turban graced with precious jewels, similar to what is pictured in Persian monumental drawings.

2:18 *he gave a great banquet in Esther's honor . . . declaring a public holiday.* Now the king honored his wife instead of putting her on display (1:11). In some ways this "banquet" is a precursor to the two banquets Esther will give for the king and Haman in 5:5-8; 7:1, and to the "rest" that the Jews will later experience in 9:16-18, 22 (Clines 1984b:291). This day became a "public holiday" (*wahanakhah* [TH2010, ZH2182], "causing rest"), but did not include a remission of taxes and three years of exemption from military service as the first Targum to Esther suggests (cf. Herodotus *Histories* 3.67).

COMMENTARY

The events in chapter 2 solve the king's problem of not having a wife. He replaced the obstinate Queen Vashti with the beautiful and humble Esther. Much of the story relates to the details of how the king searched his whole empire for just the right woman, how Hegai prepared these women to meet the king, and what happened after they visited the king in his private palace quarters. These details give historical credence to the story, and they also show how difficult it was to make the final cut in this process.

God himself is not mentioned in the story, and his providential guidance of events is never referred to, yet his hand seemed to be silently guiding the process so that his plan for his people would be accomplished at some later point in time. If the hired agents of the king were out searching for the most beautiful women in all the 127 provinces of the nation (2:2-3), what chance would an orphaned Jewish girl have at becoming the next queen of Persia? If it was necessary to please a king who already had many concubines and who soon would see a new beautiful woman each night for the next several months, why would the king ever choose Esther? The drama never answers these questions, but the sheer improbability of Esther's being chosen suggests that these things did not all happen by accident. A higher hand seemed to bring Esther favor in the eyes of the king's servant Hegai, and an unseen force seemed to intervene to give Esther favor in the eyes of the king (2:17) and everyone else who saw her (2:15).

The nearly miraculous nature of what happened is heightened by the fact that several people (Mordecai, Esther, Hegai, Xerxes) just happened to be at the right place at the right time to produce these unusual results. If the king had waited a few extra years to get over his anger (2:1), Esther might have already been married. If the king had searched for a bride immediately after Vashti was deposed, Esther probably would have been too young to be chosen by the king's agents. Who would have thought that an orphan girl without many of the physical and emotional advantages of a two-parent family would even be considered? If it had not been for the compassion of Mordecai, who adopted her, she might not have survived at all.

Once she did become a possible candidate and entered the king's palace to spend a year preparing to meet the king, there probably were hundreds of other more eligible and sophisticated women who also were vying to become the new queen. Esther did not have a famous name, did not come from a prestigious family, likely had a limited education, and probably felt a little uncomfortable in these strange royal surroundings. What chance would she have of becoming the queen, if she could only spend one night with the king and then be pushed off to the second harem to be forgotten (2:14)? With her conservative moral upbringing, she would not be as forward and suggestive as some, and if the king asked about her background, she would not have any glorious stories to tell about her famous family. With all the women who would go to see the king before her, Esther may have felt the deck was stacked against her, for certainly the king would choose someone else long before it ever came to Esther's turn.

All these obstacles to success create suspense and wonder concerning the destiny of Esther. In spite of all her disadvantages, initially she was chosen because of her natural beauty (2:7). She was given every opportunity to succeed and was not disadvantaged in spite of her background. In fact, she impressed Hegai, who treated her kindly by giving her a choice spot to live and by assigning her a group of seven outstanding maidens to assist her (2:9). For at least a year Esther followed the program Hegai prescribed for her and the other candidates (2:12), and throughout that period, the staff in the palace admired her (2:15). Esther's willingness to follow Mordecai's advice and not reveal her family of origin demonstrates her willingness to listen to the counsel of others. Later she wisely paid attention to the direction of Hegai, who gave her valuable suggestions about the king's likes and dislikes (2:15). All these factors lead the reader to understand that more was happening here than just a beauty pageant. Somehow and for some reason Esther gained a distinct advantage over many of the other eligible women. She stood out from the crowd long before she was chosen as someone who might be destined to be the next queen of Persia.

When the day to meet the king finally arrived in the seventh year of the king's reign (2:16), the king responded to Esther with great love and delight (2:17). This was not just infatuation over a pretty face or the sexual thrill of being with a new woman; it appears that this was a life-transforming moment when the king was willing to make the decision that this one woman would be his new queen (2:17). The king's anger with Vashti was a thing of the past, and his desire was now focused on honoring his new wife, Esther. He openly celebrated with his palace officials and declared a public holiday to announce to the empire that Esther was his new queen (2:18). The nearly impossible had happened.

Throughout this time Mordecai was functioning in the background, but his role was important. His faithfulness and compassionate care for Esther assured that she would survive the tragic loss of her parents. Without Mordecai's commitment to Esther's welfare, it is doubtful that she would ever have become a potential candidate to be the queen (2:7). Second, Mordecai must have given permission for his unmarried orphan daughter to enter into the king's palace, implying that he did not totally withdraw from the Persian culture into a secluded Jewish ghetto to hide from the real world. Even his job at the palace gates in Susa demonstrated his openness to serve the Persian nation for the good of his own people (2:5, 19). His knowledge of the prejudice and corrupt thinking of individuals in Persia caused him to instruct Esther to not reveal her Jewish family origin (2:10). His daily concern for Esther caused him to regularly check up on her by talking to people who knew what was going on inside the palace (2:11). It is unclear whether Mordecai and Esther ever talked together privately, but he could have passed along messages of encouragement or warning to Esther through friends he knew in the palace.

The section ends with a great celebration in honor of Esther. The previous queen had refused to be dishonored by the king (1:12), but the king's heart had changed, and his desire was to bring honor to this new woman he loved (2:18). This great celebration secretly lauded a Jewish woman who surprisingly rose to power. The celebration and rest provided for the people (see note on 2:18) is parallel to another great celebration at the end of the story, when the Jewish people are victorious and have "rest" from the threats of their enemies (9:17-18, 22; see notes). In ways that are too mysterious for mankind to understand, God repeatedly places his humble and faithful people in positions of responsibility so they can function within the sinful cultures of this world to do what is right and protect the weak and innocent (4:12-16), who are often oppressed by the wicked.

◆ II. Haman's Decree to Destroy the Jews (2:19–3:15)
    A. Mordecai Saves the King's Life (2:19-23)

¹⁹Even after all the young women had been transferred to the second harem* and Mordecai had become a palace official,* ²⁰Esther continued to keep her family background and nationality a secret. She was still following Mordecai's directions, just as she did when she lived in his home.

²¹One day as Mordecai was on duty at the king's gate, two of the king's eunuchs, Bigthana* and Teresh—who were guards at the door of the king's private quarters—became angry at King Xerxes and plotted to assassinate him. ²²But Mordecai heard about the plot and gave the information to Queen Esther. She then told the king about it and gave Mordecai credit for the report. ²³When an investigation was made and Mordecai's story was found to be true, the two men were impaled on a sharpened pole. This was all recorded in *The Book of the History of King Xerxes' Reign.*

2:19a The meaning of the Hebrew is uncertain.   2:19b Hebrew *and Mordecai was sitting in the gate of the king.*   2:21 Hebrew *Bigthan;* compare 6:2.

NOTES

2:19 *transferred to the second harem.* Lit., "gathered to the second." The "second" (*shenith* [TH8145, ZH9108]) is left undefined, so one could conclude that it refers to (1) a second gathering (parallel to the first gathering in 2:8) of additional virgins for the king to choose new concubines to add to his harem (Keil 1956:341, cf. NIV; Bush [1996:372] takes it as a sarcastic depiction of the king, who continued to gather more concubines after his marriage); (2) "various virgins," by changing "second" (*shenith*) to "various" (*shonoth* [TH8138, ZH9101]; cf. Moore 1971:29-30; Paton 1908:192); (3) the gathering of a second group of virgins who arrived from a distant province sometime after the first group from the near provinces (2:8), but before Esther was chosen as queen (Paton 1908:187); or (4) the movement of all the virgins who had not yet seen the king over to the second harem with the other concubines (Breneman 1993:321; Fox 2001:38). This last view seems most likely. The movement of all the remaining virgins in the first harem to the second harem verified that the king's search for a queen was over. Though some virgins had not met with the king yet, the queen had been chosen, so all those in waiting should join the other concubines of the king.

Mordecai had become a palace official. Lit., "Mordecai was sitting at the king's gate." The gate was where court cases were decided and some of the kingdom's official business was conducted. Some, however, view the "gate" as a reference to the entire palace administrative center (Fox 2001:39). It goes far beyond the evidence to suggest that Esther had Mordecai appointed as a court official after she became queen (Gordis 1976:47; Laniak 2003:213). Mordecai's presence at the gate explains how he was able to hear about the plot against the king and how he was able to maintain at least a small amount of communication with Esther.

2:20 *keep her family background and nationality a secret.* The fact that this is mentioned twice (see 2:10) indicates its importance for the rest of the story. Although Mordecai's family origin was well known to Haman and others at the gate (3:1-4), Haman and the king had no idea that Esther had a Hebrew background.

2:21 *Bigthana and Teresh . . . guards at the door.* Bigthana may be the Bigtha of 1:10, one of the king's seven eunuchs. He and Teresh guarded the king's bedroom, so it would not be hard for them to carry out their plot.

became angry . . . and plotted to assassinate. The reason for their unhappiness is unknown—did they support Vashti, oppose Esther, dislike Mordecai, or resent the king for some other personal reason? Whatever the case, their strong anger (*qatsap* [TH7107, ZH7911]) led them to seek (*baqash* [TH1245, ZH1335]) or plan acts of political assassination (lit., "to stretch forth a hand upon the king"). Interestingly, Haman will "seek" to stretch forth his hand to take the lives of the Jews (3:6), and later his coconspirators will do the same (9:2), but Esther did not "seek" anything else for herself when she went to see the king (2:15), though later she did "seek" the protection of her people (4:8). The Aramaic Targum adds that these men were planning to poison Esther, too, but no hint of this is found in the biblical text. Since Mordecai worked in the palace area, it was possible for him to hear the rumors and bickering of the officials.

2:22 *gave the information to Queen Esther.* Mordecai did not feel safe revealing what he heard to another official in the palace because he did not know who was in on this plot. The quickest way for the information to get to the king was through the queen. This demonstrates that Mordecai could talk to or communicate with Esther through a trusted intermediary, though the frequency and occasions for these conversations are unknown. This parallels a later event in which Mordecai will give bad news to Esther so that she can tell the king about a different kind of assassination attempt (4:1-17; Levenson 1997:64).

gave Mordecai credit for the report. Esther was honest and revealed the true source of the information (lit., "in the name of Mordecai"). Mordecai's deed of saving the king's life is especially important later in the story (6:1-3). One might have expected that the king would reward or give some recognition to Mordecai for uncovering this plot, but instead Haman was elevated to a high position (3:1). There is no indication that Mordecai carried a grudge against the king or Haman. Eventually Mordecai will be rewarded at a key turning point in the story (6:1-14).

2:23 *the two men were impaled.* It is unclear whether their punishment was to be impaled on a tree/pole (NLT; Levenson 1997:65; Laniak 2003:213; Clines 1984b:292; Herodotus *Histories* 3.125) or to be "hanged on a gallows" (NIV; Moore 1971:31), or to be crucified (Josephus *Antiquities* 11.207; on LXX [see Bush 1996:373]). The Hebrew uses the terms *wayyittalu* [TH8518, ZH9434] (hang, suspend) and *'ets* [TH6086, ZH6770] (tree, wood, lumber) and could hypothetically be understood in any of these ways. Nevertheless, crucifixion was a later Roman means of execution, and hanging someone from a rope was usually only used as a way of displaying the body of a dead person. The ancient Persian custom of terrorizing and shaming criminals by impaling them on a stake is what is meant here (Bush 1996:373). This is what happened to all who opposed the king (see Haman's fate in 7:9-10).

This was all recorded. Although all of Mordecai's deeds were recorded in the king's annals (lit., "the book of the events of the days"), like Joseph (Gen 40) he was not rewarded until much later (6:1-14).

COMMENTARY

This short section illustrates the positive character traits of both Esther and Mordecai. Though she was the queen of the Persian Empire, Esther did not forget her people or the family that raised her. She did not become high and mighty as queen but still listened to the wise advice of Mordecai. She also fearlessly cooperated with Mordecai by reporting to the king that there was a plot to assassinate him (2:21-22). When doing this, she did not try to gain personally by claiming this was her discovery; instead, she gave the credit to Mordecai. In these verses, Esther is no longer the passive person controlled by others (as in 2:1-18). Now she acts responsibly and is loyal to the two key men in her life. She balanced her identity as the queen of Persia with her identity as a Jew and as the adopted daughter of Mordecai, seemingly without conflict. She proved her value to the king by transmitting information that saved his life. She did everything right to please the king and her stepfather.

Mordecai was a wise man, who did not abandon his adopted daughter when she needed him, and remained loyal to the king in the face of a palace conspiracy. He had shown wise foresight when he allowed Esther to be a candidate for the queen's position, and he maintained this mentoring relationship after she rose to power. He was a man who stood for the truth and courageously spoke the truth about the evil plot to kill the king. He demanded no reward for uncovering this plot and held no bitterness for not receiving recognition for what he did for the king. He faithfully served the king and opposed evil. His uncovering of the plot against the king is somewhat parallel to his later uncovering of a plot against the Jews in Persia. In both cases, Esther was the person who made the king aware of these evil plots. The king then killed the evil plotters, while the innocent people were saved from death. Esther and Mordecai set an excellent example for all believers, for God still opposes all forms of violence against innocent people. Believers should always reject and expose evil plots by businessmen, political leaders, and family members who try to take advantage of others.

◆   B. Mordecai Will Not Honor Haman (3:1-6)

Some time later King Xerxes promoted Haman son of Hammedatha the Agagite over all the other nobles, making him the most powerful official in the empire. ²All the king's officials would bow down before Haman to show him respect whenever he passed by, for so the king had commanded. But Mordecai refused to bow down or show him respect.

³Then the palace officials at the king's gate asked Mordecai, "Why are you disobeying the king's command?" ⁴They spoke to him day after day, but still he refused to comply with the order. So they spoke to Haman about this to see if he would tolerate Mordecai's conduct, since Mordecai had told them he was a Jew.

⁵When Haman saw that Mordecai would not bow down or show him respect, he was filled with rage. ⁶He had learned of Mordecai's nationality, so he decided it was not enough to lay hands on Mordecai alone. Instead, he looked for a way to destroy all the Jews throughout the entire empire of Xerxes.

NOTES

3:1 Xerxes promoted Haman . . . making him the most powerful official. One might have expected from 2:21-23 that Mordecai would receive the honor of being a powerful official in Xerxes' government because he saved the king's life, but instead the king promoted (*giddal* [TH1431, ZH1540]; lit., "made great") Haman. Haman is one of the main characters in the next couple of chapters. This powerful, evil man gets into a conflict with Mordecai, which leads him to plot the extermination of the Jewish people. Though some view Haman's Agagite background as a typological reminder of Saul's conflict with Agag, the Amalekite king in 1 Sam 15 (Levenson 1997:66), this connection seems very remote and immaterial to the story. The reasons why this approach is not followed in this commentary are (1) Haman was an Agagite, and there is no indication that he was an Amalakite; (2) King Agag and almost all the Amalekites were killed in the days of Saul (1 Sam 15), and there is no evidence that any son survived to create an Agagite tribe; (3) the last of the Amalekites were killed hundreds of years before Esther in the time of Hezekiah (1 Chr 4:42-43); (4) Haman and Hammedatha are Persian names, not Amalekite names (Bush 1996:378); (5) Agag is more likely the name of a Persian province (Laniak 2003:220); and (6) the story does not constantly make explicit plays on the story of Samuel and Agag in 1 Sam 15.

3:2 *bow down before Haman to show him respect . . . for so the king had commanded.* "Bowing the knee" (*yikra'* [TH3766, ZH4156]) before a superior was a common custom (Herodotus *Histories* 1.134), and there are examples of Israelites doing this elsewhere (Gen 33:3). No one knows why Mordecai refused to respect Haman at the beginning of ch 3. The speculation of the Targum is that Haman claimed the status of divinity, but that would never have been permitted by the king of Persia. To conclude that the absence of any reasonable explanation for the animosity between these two men "gives great credence to the view that the narrator assumed that the readers would recognize the tribal and racial enmity implied by the patronymics of the two men" (Bush 1996:379) is a huge assumption that is not warranted by any evidence. Since there were no Amalekites alive after the time of Hezekiah, this is a less-than-convincing conclusion.

3:3 *palace officials at the king's gate.* Mordecai's associates and some government employees at the gate noticed Mordecai's disrespectful behavior, questioned him, and tried to convince him to bow so that he would not violate the "king's command" (*mitswath hammelek* [TH4687, ZH5184]). It is not clear if these men were trying to help Mordecai or if they were trying to get him into trouble. It is also not clear exactly what the king's command was. Since this challenge did not result in Mordecai's being forced to bow before Haman, the king's command must have been worded in such a way that it did not absolutely require that Mordecai bow.

3:4 *to see if he would tolerate Mordecai's conduct.* Lit., "to see whether the words of Mordecai would stand." The word *'amad* [TH5975, ZH6641] (stand) is used here as a legal term referring to whether Mordecai's conduct would be approved in court. The tradition preserved in the noncanonical Greek addition in A:17 is that Mordecai did not respect Haman because he knew he was associated with the two eunuchs who had plotted to kill the king (Levenson 1997:41), but there is no way to confirm the value of this information. Some hypothesize that the Hebrew suggests Mordecai would not bow down to Haman because of Mordecai's arrogance (Paton 1908:197), but this is not how the rest of the book characterizes Mordecai. Fox (1991:44-45) suggests that Haman's Amalekite ethnicity meant that Haman was under God's curse, and Mordecai refused to bow because he was a Jew. But the text never fills in this point, which many read between the lines. The text simply does not explain how Mordecai's Jewishness related to not bowing. It is also interesting that Mordecai's reasoning stood under legal examination, for in this tolerant Persian society he was never forced to bow to Haman. Thus, Mordecai was within his legal rights to do what he did, so he did not have to follow the courteous practice of bowing before a high government official. Similarly, no one knows why Vashti refused to honor the king, but both choices resulted in a powerful government person doing unreasonable things out of a spirit of great anger. Many other parts of this story are left unexplained, but in spite of these unexplained events, it is evident that God used these odd situations to bring Esther to power and to protect his people from Haman's plans to destroy them.

3:6 *it was not enough to lay hands on Mordecai alone.* A law court could have decided the matter, but Haman probably did not want to take the matter to court, possibly because it became a personal matter or because he knew he could not win this battle in court. He wanted to settle it in his own way because he could manipulate the political circumstances to go around any legal rights that Mordecai might have. Haman was not interested in Mordecai's legal rights (which suggests Mordecai may have had some); he wanted revenge.

he looked for a way to destroy all the Jews. Haman wanted Mordecai to be hated by his own people. He was determined to do everything within his power to crush this "arrogant" man (following the king's pattern of overreacting to the slightest opposition). He was looking to expunge (*lehashmid* [TH8045, ZH9012], "to annihilate") an entire nationality of innocent people by massacring them in cold blood.

COMMENTARY

The narrative does not address the issue of whether Haman deserved this great promotion by Xerxes (3:1); it simply puts his rise to power and greatness immediately next to Mordecai's heroic deeds that went unrewarded. As far as anyone knows, Haman did nothing to deserve this recognition, so it appears that a great injustice was done (Moore 1971:35). This promotion may have had something to do with Haman's aspirations to become an important ruler in the land, for later he had the audacity to suggest that the one whom the king wanted to reward (and he imagined this was himself) should wear the king's robe and ride on the king's horse (6:8). His rise to power was probably based on complete and unquestioning loyalty to the king (3:8-9), a price he was willing to pay in order to get the reward he coveted.

For some legitimate reason Mordecai refused to "bow down" and "respect" Haman (3:2), even though it meant committing an act of disrespect in an era when disrespect for high officials was not well accepted. Some claim that Mordecai refused to bow because he believed that men should only bow down to God (Moore 1971:36), but there is no indication that other religious leaders like Nehemiah, Ezra, or Esther failed to bow before Persian officials. One assumes that Mordecai did bow before the king later when he was raised to a high government position (9:4), so there is more to his refusal than just an unwillingness to bow before men. Certainly the king did not raise Haman to the status of a god, nor would Mordecai think that bowing to Haman was comparable to idol worship. Somehow his Jewishness (3:4) caused him to refuse to bow. Some think that this act would be a betrayal of the honor of his nation to bow to an Amalekite (Agag was the king of Amalek in 1 Sam 15) because Amalekites were supposed to be killed (Exod 17:8-16; Deut 25:17-19; see Levenson 1997:67). But this seems unlikely since 1 Chronicles 4:42-43 indicates that the last few Amalekites died in the time of Hezekiah (see note on 3:4). The apocryphal addition to Esther indicates that Haman was a partner in the plot to kill the king (2:21), thus Haman did not deserve any honor, but the reliability of this information is suspect.

For some unknown reason, the author purposely chose to leave the reader in the dark, just as the author failed to tell the reader why Vashti refused to parade before the king and his drunken friends in chapter 1. Maybe it is more important to notice the parallelism between these two protests (by Mordecai and Vashti) and prepare for a similar consequence (rage and a desire to kill the one who does not obey). Even people today who, following their conscience, resist evil social customs and reject what seems to be an immoral legal requirement, will suffer because others hate them. Such has been the case for conscientious objectors, civil-rights marchers, and abortion foes.

This section shows a believer (Mordecai) in a compromising situation where there is legal pressure (the king's command in 3:2) and daily social pressure from fellow servants of the king (3:3) to do what his conscience says should not be done. Mordecai stubbornly maintained his beliefs and did not bow to this pressure, even when his "friends" told Haman about Mordecai (3:4). Mordecai had not previously been noticed; he apparently did not purposely try to embarrass Haman by standing tall on the front row at the gate, nor did he loudly protest to draw attention to himself. He quietly followed his conscience in spite of the danger this put him in.

Two sources of trouble opposed Mordecai. Other servants of the king, who wanted to be rewarded by Haman, squealed on Mordecai. They were not really Mordecai's friends or devoted colleagues; they were opportunists who would gladly destroy another person for personal advancement. They were motivated by selfish gain rather than hatred. By contrast, Haman, the mortal enemy of Mordecai, was motivated by pride and hatred (3:5). How dare anyone not bow down to him and honor him! (This is parallel to the king's pride being hurt when Vashti failed to honor him; cf. Laniak 1998:71.)

Haman and the king allowed their anger to turn to such a deep hatred that both sought for a way to get rid of the problem person (cf. 1:13-22). They both had exaggerated fears and thought that the implications of one small act of disobedience would have enormous implications for many other uninvolved women (1:20, 22) and many uninvolved Jews (3:6). The difference is that the king and his advisers did not propose some sort of unjust penalty to kill all the women in the land because of one woman's disobedience. But Haman's proposal did seek for a way to unjustly punish every Jewish person in the empire. Eye-for-eye retribution was not good enough for Haman. His plan was to remove every possible person who might possibly refuse to honor him in the future. The behavior of both the king and Haman illustrate the terrible danger of giving in to anger and rage. In our own times, this danger is evinced in heinous genocides—as in the Holocaust, Pol Pot's destruction of millions in Cambodia, the Serbian killing of Muslims in Bosnia, the slaughter of hundreds of thousands in Rwanda, and Saddam Hussein's slaughter of 300,000 of his own people in Iraq. On a smaller scale, many murders are committed each day in cities across America and other countries around the world because one person has offended another or will not do what they want them to do. Rage often leads to an irrational intent to destroy another person, and its expression frequently hurts bystanders and even innocent children. God declares that vengeance is his to repay (Deut 32:35; Rom 12:19), so believers are not to let anger move them to sin (Eph 4:26), nor let it turn to bitterness, rage, and revenge (Eph 4:31).

◆   ## C. Haman's Decree to Get Revenge (3:7-15)

7 So in the month of April,* during the twelfth year of King Xerxes' reign, lots were cast in Haman's presence (the lots were called *purim*) to determine the best day and month to take action. And the day selected was March 7, nearly a year later.* 8 Then Haman approached King Xerxes and said, "There is a certain race of people scattered through all the provinces of your empire who keep themselves separate from everyone else. Their laws are different from those of any other people, and they refuse to obey the laws of the king. So it is not in the king's interest to let them live. 9 If it please the king, issue a decree that they be destroyed, and I will

give 10,000 large sacks* of silver to the government administrators to be deposited in the royal treasury."

¹⁰The king agreed, confirming his decision by removing his signet ring from his finger and giving it to Haman son of Hammedatha the Agagite, the enemy of the Jews. ¹¹The king said, "The money and the people are both yours to do with as you see fit."

¹²So on April 17* the king's secretaries were summoned, and a decree was written exactly as Haman dictated. It was sent to the king's highest officers, the governors of the respective provinces, and the nobles of each province in their own scripts and languages. The decree was written in the name of King Xerxes and sealed with the king's signet ring. ¹³Dispatches were sent by swift messengers into all the provinces of the empire, giving the order that all Jews—young and old, including women and children—must be killed, slaughtered, and annihilated on a single day. This was scheduled to happen on March 7 of the next year.* The property of the Jews would be given to those who killed them.

¹⁴A copy of this decree was to be issued as law in every province and proclaimed to all peoples, so that they would be ready to do their duty on the appointed day. ¹⁵At the king's command, the decree went out by swift messengers, and it was also proclaimed in the fortress of Susa. Then the king and Haman sat down to drink, but the city of Susa fell into confusion.

3:7a Hebrew *in the first month, the month of Nisan.* This month of the ancient Hebrew lunar calendar occurred within the months of April and May 474 B.C.; also see note on 2:16.   3:7b As in 3:13, which reads *the thirteenth day of the twelfth month, the month of Adar;* Hebrew reads *in the twelfth month,* of the ancient Hebrew lunar calendar. The date selected was March 7, 473 B.C.; also see note on 2:16.   3:9 Hebrew *10,000 talents,* about 375 tons or 340 metric tons in weight.   3:12 Hebrew *On the thirteenth day of the first month,* of the ancient Hebrew lunar calendar. This day was April 17, 474 B.C.; also see note on 2:16.   3:13 Hebrew *on the thirteenth day of the twelfth month, the month of Adar,* of the ancient Hebrew lunar calendar. The date selected was March 7, 473 B.C.; also see note on 2:16.

NOTES

3:7 *in the month of April, during the twelfth year of King Xerxes' reign.* Lit., "in the first month, in the month Nisan." It is unlikely that any Jewish person would miss the significance of Nisan, the time of God's deliverance of his people from Egyptian slavery (Exod 12:1-2). Would God allow Haman to have success in finding a date to kill thousands of God's people in the month of their previous deliverance? Since this was five years after Esther became queen, the date was 474 BC (see NLT mg).

lots were cast . . . (the lots were called **purim***).* Lit., "He cast the pur, the lot." In the Hebrew the verb is active: "he cast" or "he threw the pur." The Hebrew *pur* [TH6332, ZH7052] transliterates the Akkadian term *pūru,* and the action was somewhat comparable to the throwing of dice, though it is not known if they were thrown with the hand or thrown out of a bag, nor is it clear exactly how one would interpret the lot. Although the Hebrews used the Urim and Thummim to cast lots from time to time in order to know God's will (Lev 16:8-10; Josh 14:2; Neh 10:34), they never used them to discover a lucky day to carry out an evil deed. The Persian diviners, magi, and astrologers cast lots (cf. Herodotus *Histories* 3.128) at the beginning of each new year to determine which days of the year would bring good fortune. Paton (1908:201-202) believes this throwing of lots was to discover the best day to ask the king to make a decree against the Jews, but 3:12 indicates that Haman went to the king for this decree on the 13th day of the first month, not the date chosen by lot. Bush (1996:380) rightly concludes that the day chosen in 3:7 is the date to kill all the Jewish people in the Persian Empire.

3:8 *a certain race of people scattered . . . who keep themselves separate.* Haman's vague "one people" (lit.) purposely hides the name of the people and has the significance of "only one people." Since these people were "scattered," there was less threat that they would band together and lead a revolt, but their scattered status gave them more opportunity to influence a larger number of people. Being "separate" (*umeporad* [TH6340, ZH7061]) refers to the fact that the Hebrews did not give up their culture, but purposely segregated themselves from others (Fox 2001:279). It was, however, a lie to suggest that the Jews did not keep the king's laws (Moore 1971:42). Jobes suggests that Haman is referring to Mordecai's failure to bow before Haman as one example of failure to keep the king's command (1999:121), but it would be a gross exaggeration to use this one failure to condemn a whole nation or to suggest that the Jews did not keep any of the king's laws. It seems almost unbelievable that Xerxes would agree to this plan without asking who these people were, how many there were, what evil things they had done, which laws were broken—he does not require any further investigation before he agrees to the killing of his own people. Levenson (1997:71) believes that the king's failure to ask some of these questions does not put the king in a very good light. He also notes that Haman's speech "has much in common with Memucan's in 1:16-20." In fact, *Targum Rishon to Esther* identifies Haman as Memucan (so also *b. Megillah* 12b), but there is nothing in the text of Esther to justify this identification (Paton 1908:194). Both here and in the earlier scene with Memucan, a high official is offended because someone does not honor him, the offended person becomes very angry, the situation is blown way out of proportion, and then it is decided that the offense is a crime against the whole state and the offending party must be severely punished. Haman fails to tell the king that this is all about Mordecai's refusal to bow before him.

to let them live. Lit., "to cause them to relax, remain, rest" (*lehannikham* [TH5117, ZH5663]). Haman subtly portrayed himself as a defender of the king to ingratiate himself in the king's eyes. He played on the king's fears just like Memucan in 1:16. Ironically, Haman did not want the king to "tolerate, leave them alone, let them rest," but later, at Purim, the Jews would "rest" (9:17-18, 22), just the opposite of what Haman wanted.

3:9 *10,000 large sacks of silver.* Lit., "10,000 talents" (see NLT mg). Haman tipped his hand by suggesting what he thought was an appropriate punishment and by offering to bribe the king. The 10,000 talents of silver was a huge sum (Bush 1996:381 calculates this to be over 333 tons of silver; Laniak 2003:222 thinks this is likely hyperbole), equivalent to about 68 percent of the annual tax revenue (Herodotus *Histories* 3.95 has the total at 14,560 talents) from the whole empire (Fox 2001:52). It may be that Haman was presenting this money as the cost of removing these people from the empire. He was indicating that he would cover the cost so that it would not cost the king anything. Possibly Haman thought he would raise this amount of money from the booty taken from the Jews who would be killed (Jobes 1999:121).

treasury. Heb., *genez* [TH1595, ZH1709], a Persian loan word.

3:10 *removing his signet ring . . . giving it to Haman.* By taking off the ring (used to seal a document, as in 8:8, 10), the king gave up some of his control over official government policies, and by giving Haman the ring, he signified that Haman had complete authority to seal the decree.

enemy of the Jews. This new title for Haman means he will persecute the Jews (see 8:1; 9:10, 24). This was an ominous title for such a powerful man.

3:11 *The money and the people are both yours.* Lit., "The silver is given to you and the people." It may appear here that the king did not want the bribe Haman was offering, but the comments in 4:7 (where the money is mentioned) suggest that Haman did give him the money. Thus, for public appearances or social custom the king humbly declined and said he was not interested in the money, but in reality he was. Later, Esther claims that she and her people have been sold (7:4), so it is evident that the money was given to the king. Although Bush (1996:382) finds a similarity between the king's initial response and the initial polite refusal to take money in Gen 23:3-16 when Abraham wanted to buy the cave of Machpelah from the Hittites to bury Sarah, it is dangerous to make much of these similarities because what was done in Hittite culture at 1800 BC probably has little relationship to what was done in Persian culture around 450 BC.

3:12 on April 17. Lit., "on the thirteenth day of the first month." Haman probably purposely chose to publish this decree of death the day before the beginning of the Jewish Passover (Exod 12:6) so as to destroy any joy the Jews might have in celebrating their redemption and release from Egypt. Now God would need to miraculously deliver them from another tyrant who would try to destroy them. Jobes calls this coincidence "tragically ironic" timing, but its placement at Passover time only heightens the later deliverance of the Jews (1999:123).

to the king's highest officers, the governors. "The king's highest officers" were the "satraps" ('akhashdarpan [TH323, ZH346], derived from the Persian khshastrapan) and "governors" (pekhah [TH6346, ZH7068], a Persian word). The message was quickly sent out to all the key military and political leaders serving at all different levels of government.

in their own scripts and languages. This would have included Elamite for Persians, Babylonian cuneiform, Sanskrit for India, Aramaic for the Arameans in Syria, Egyptian, Greek, Phoenician, and probably numerous minor languages that have few or no written texts that have survived until today (possibly Kassite, Vanic, and Dravidian).

3:13 swift messengers. Lit., "runners" (haratsim [TH7323, ZH8132]), even though they probably rode horses (see 8:10, 14).

all Jews—young and old, including women and children—must be killed, slaughtered, and annihilated. Haman identified which people the decree was about and left no doubt about what should be done—"kill, slaughter, and annihilate." The group of similar verbs is a stylistic feature of Persian legal documents (Baldwin 1984:75; Paton 1908:209), indicating the comprehensiveness of the slaughter.

happen on March 7 of the next year. Lit., "the thirteen day of the twelfth month, in the month Adar" (see NLT mg). It seems odd that the decree was to be carried out 11 months after it was given. This would prolong the agony of the Jews as they waited week after week, dreading the day of their demise (Bush 1996:387), but it would also give God time to reverse this decree through the efforts of a praying community and the boldness of Esther (Clines 1984b:298).

The property of the Jews would be given to those who killed them. Lit., "and to plunder their possessions." This ingenious provision of bribing the executioners assured Haman of having many helpers who would gladly kill others to gain a handsome financial reward. This contrasts with the action of the Jews in 9:10, 15-16, who refused to do this.

3:14 A copy of this decree was to be issued as law. A "copy" (pathshegen [TH6572A, ZH7358], a Persian word) of a royal decree carried the full weight of Xerxes' authority behind it.

3:15 the king and Haman sat down to drink, but the city of Susa fell into confusion. The foolish king and wicked Haman celebrated their accomplishments at a private banquet (contrast this with a later private banquet in 7:1-10), revealing just how callous and evil Haman was. But both the Jews and non-Jewish people in the city (Bush 1996:388) surrounding the palace in Susa were "perplexed, bewildered, and confused" at such a ruthless decree. What was wrong with the king? Why was he so cruel? Who would be next?

COMMENTARY

In this passage, the evil character of Haman is on full display. His plan was not just to pay back Mordecai for snubbing him at the palace gate; he wanted everyone in the empire to see what would happen to all their friends and relatives if they ever refused to honor the king's high official. He wanted all the Jews to hate Mordecai for being so foolish, to shame him before all his own people before killing them all off. In short, Haman was trying to protect his honor (a central value in most of the Middle East even today), and was going to great extremes to do so. In order to accomplish this plan, Haman needed to be clever and gain the king's assistance, for he would be requesting something that the king might not agree to. Consequently, Haman sought clairvoyant insight from the spirit world concerning the lucky day he should identify as the time these evil people should be killed (3:7).

Having that information, Haman presented a bogus complaint to transform an unnamed and obscure group into a potential threat to the king. Haman did not want the king to object to his proposal, so he had to persuade the king that the group's steadfast maintenance of cultural distinctions was subversive and then transform the failure of one man to keep the laws of the king into a nationalistic movement of rebellion. (On Mordecai's adherence to the laws of the king, see notes on 3:3, 4, 6.) There was some small thread of truth to what Haman said, but the conclusion he drew from this evidence was a fabrication. He was trying to shame the Jewish people by characterizing them with words of slander and rebellion against the king. On some issues the Jewish people did separate themselves from the pagan people in the Persian Empire. For example, many Jewish families and communities strictly prohibited intermarriage with non-Jews and resisted efforts to integrate themselves into the larger culture and religion of Persia, but others freely married with people who were not Jews (Ezra 8-10; Neh 9-10). Haman also accurately reported that the Jewish people had a unique set of laws (dietary and religious customs), but it was a vast exaggeration to say that none of them followed the laws of the king. The Israelites were to be a holy people and be separate from the sinful customs of the people around them (Lev 11:42-45; 15:31; 19:2, 26-37), but it was false to suggest that these laws caused them to disobey the laws of the king.

This extreme example of prejudice against one people was quite inconsistent with the general Persian tendency to be tolerant and respectful of other people's cultural and religious differences. Haman's accusations were a mixture of accurate observations and outright lies. But no questions were asked of Haman, not even a request for the name of this "evil" group of people. The king is presented as irresponsible and easily manipulated. At the end of the chapter, the king and Haman sat down to a banquet to drink together, celebrating that their honor would now be protected from the threats of some oddly behaving people scattered across the land. Nevertheless, the calm they sensed inside the palace walls was quite different from the anxiety they created outside them (3:15). Thus, what was designed to be an act to ensure the peace of the kingdom ended up threatening it. These men thought they had absolute authority over the people under them (3:1; 5:11), but in reality they did not understand a fraction of what God had planned or that God had already placed the Jewish queen Esther in a strategic place where she could undo the power of Haman and reverse the decrees of the king.

The rest of the book of Esther explains how Haman's revengeful deeds were reversed. In the end, God would cause Esther and Mordecai to be honored with great power and authority, while Haman would be executed in dishonor (Laniak 1998:69-84). No matter what troubles may surround a person, a believer can always be assured that God is sovereignly in charge of history. In his own time, God will rescue some from danger and diabolical plots, while at other times he will allow wickedness to rule for a time before striking it down.

Haman's plot against the Jews was facilitated by three factors. The first two applied to making a decree against the Jews and the last one to the sure implementation of that decree. First, Haman depended on the wisdom of the best religious minds in the empire to tell him when the gods would show favor to him (3:7). This indicates that his case was weak in that it might fail if the wrong day were chosen. The plan he set forth would not stand the tests of full disclosure, open inquiry into the actual facts of the case, or a response by the Jewish people to Haman's charges. Second, Haman offered the king a huge bribe (3:9). Haman was so uncertain about what the king would say that he had to entice the king with a financial reward. Bribes are not needed when legal action could accomplish the same end. Expensive bribes are only needed when a big favor is needed to approve something that is unusual or unjust. When a financial reward is offered, truth and justice are usually in short supply.

Third, to ensure the accomplishment of his goal of wiping out the Jews, Haman made sure the decree included the promise of a reward to those who would actually kill the Jewish people. Many in the empire likely worked smoothly with Jewish businessmen, while others no doubt were ready to see their competition removed, but most would not appreciate knowing that the king could decide to eradicate an ethnic or religious group on a whim. The Jews had done nothing to deserve this kind of treatment. The thought of the internal chaos—people fighting each other in the streets, Jewish revenge attacks—was not pleasant, and it would haunt these Jewish communities for almost a whole year. It would be far easier for the common person to leave the execution of Haman's decree to the government. So in order to motivate people to carry out this slaughter, Haman decided to bribe the people who killed the Jews with the reward of claiming possession of their property. These three factors demonstrate that Haman's plan could not stand on the merits of his accusations.

◆ III. Esther Must Try to Reverse Haman's Plot (4:1–5:14)
   A. Esther Bravely Risks Her Life (4:1–17)

When Mordecai learned about all that had been done, he tore his clothes, put on burlap and ashes, and went out into the city, crying with a loud and bitter wail. ²He went as far as the gate of the palace, for no one was allowed to enter the palace gate while wearing clothes of mourning. ³And as news of the king's decree reached all the provinces, there was great mourning among the Jews. They fasted, wept, and wailed, and many people lay in burlap and ashes.

⁴When Queen Esther's maids and eunuchs came and told her about Mordecai, she was deeply distressed. She sent clothing to him to replace the burlap, but he refused it. ⁵Then Esther sent for Hathach, one of the king's eunuchs who had been appointed as her attendant. She ordered him to go to Mordecai and find out what

was troubling him and why he was in mourning. [6]So Hathach went out to Mordecai in the square in front of the palace gate.

[7]Mordecai told him the whole story, including the exact amount of money Haman had promised to pay into the royal treasury for the destruction of the Jews. [8]Mordecai gave Hathach a copy of the decree issued in Susa that called for the death of all Jews. He asked Hathach to show it to Esther and explain the situation to her. He also asked Hathach to direct her to go to the king to beg for mercy and plead for her people. [9]So Hathach returned to Esther with Mordecai's message.

[10]Then Esther told Hathach to go back and relay this message to Mordecai: [11]"All the king's officials and even the people in the provinces know that anyone who appears before the king in his inner court without being invited is doomed to die

4:12 As in Greek version; Hebrew reads *they.*

unless the king holds out his gold scepter. And the king has not called for me to come to him for thirty days." [12]So Hathach* gave Esther's message to Mordecai.

[13]Mordecai sent this reply to Esther: "Don't think for a moment that because you're in the palace you will escape when all other Jews are killed. [14]If you keep quiet at a time like this, deliverance and relief for the Jews will arise from some other place, but you and your relatives will die. Who knows if perhaps you were made queen for just such a time as this?"

[15]Then Esther sent this reply to Mordecai: [16]"Go and gather together all the Jews of Susa and fast for me. Do not eat or drink for three days, night or day. My maids and I will do the same. And then, though it is against the law, I will go in to see the king. If I must die, I must die." [17]So Mordecai went away and did everything as Esther had ordered him.

NOTES

4:1 *tore his clothes, put on burlap and ashes . . . crying with a loud and bitter wail.* Mordecai's intense grief was shown by tearing his clothes (as in Gen 37:34; 2 Sam 1:11) and wearing sackcloth and ashes (Job 2:7-8; Dan 9:3), common practices in the OT and Persia (Herodotus *Histories* 8.99 describes a similar response by the Persian army when it was defeated by the Greeks at Salamis). There was no effort to hide his bitter sorrow. This would be Mordecai's way of alerting Esther that there was a problem she needed to know about.

4:2 *the gate of the palace.* The king isolated himself from the sad stories of people pleading for mercy; therefore, Mordecai could not come into the palace area. He came to the gate to get Esther's attention, for she probably knew nothing about this decree (Fox 2001:57). As Bush (1996:394) argues, there is no indication that Mordecai came to present a formal legal complaint about the king's decree to the court that met at the king's gate.

4:3 *great mourning among the Jews.* In all these reports of lamenting throughout the Persian Empire, God's name is not specifically mentioned (see "Theological Concerns" in the Introduction). Elsewhere when Jewish people were oppressed, they lamented, fasted, and always cried out for God to intervene and save his people (Exod 2:23-25; Ezra 9:5-15; Dan 9:1-19). The text does not justify the idea that Mordecai was leading the community in this time of lamenting as Laniak suggests (2003:225).

4:4 *she was deeply distressed.* Some of Esther's maidens and eunuchs lived outside the palace and probably saw Mordecai as they came to work. One need not hypothesize that they knew of the relationship between Mordecai and Esther. Esther's reaction initially was probably closer to being "perplexed" (Hitpalpal of *khil* [TH2342A, ZH2655]) and confused (Moore 1971:48), rather than "agitated" at his inappropriate dress (Levenson 1997:79). It is somewhat ironic that Mordecai, who lived outside the palace, knew more about what the king was planning to do than Esther, who lived inside the palace with the king. Possibly the king thought that Haman's request was of little significance and would involve very few people, so he put it out of his mind.

She sent clothing . . . but he refused it. The new clothes would enable Mordecai to come into the palace to talk to Esther (Clines 1984b.300). His refusal to take the clothes indicates that new clothes would not solve this problem. Mordecai communicated that the problem was much greater than Esther ever imagined.

4:5 find out what was troubling him and why he was in mourning. Lit., "to know (*lada'ath* [TH3045, ZH3359]) what is this and why is this?"

4:7 Mordecai told him the whole story. Mordecai told Hathach everything, including his refusal to bow to Haman, Haman's decree, and the exact amount of money (see 3:9) Haman was paying to bribe the king. By mentioning the huge amount of money Haman was willing to pay, Mordecai would demonstrate to Esther the seriousness of the plot and would hopefully rouse her to action. Palace gossip must have let slip the price Haman offered the king. Mordecai wanted Esther to know who the real enemy was and how serious the problem was.

4:8 a copy of the decree. A copy (*pathshegen* [TH6572A, ZH7358], as in 3:14) of the decree with the king's seal would prove to Esther its authenticity. The explanation would provide Mordecai's interpretation of the dire significance of the decree.

explain the situation to her. He also asked Hathach to direct her to go to the king to beg for mercy. Some suggest that Hathach was "to explain" the decree to Esther because she could not read Persian (Paton 1908:218; Clines 1984b:301), but "explain, inform" does not require this interpretation. Explaining probably refers to telling Esther about the past relationship between Mordecai and Haman that was the background to the origination of this decree (Bush 1996:395). Hathach was "to command" (the infinitive construct *uletsawwoth* [TH6680, ZH7422]) Esther to go directly to the king. The only hope was Esther's ability to "ask for mercy" (Hitpael stem of *khanan* [TH2603, ZH2858]) on behalf of her own people.

4:11 anyone who appears . . . without being invited is doomed to die. Esther found Mordecai's plan nearly impossible to execute. Access to the king was by invitation only, as Herodotus confirms (*Histories* 3.72, 77, 118). The Aramaic Targum wrongly attributes this law to Haman, who wanted to keep Esther from seeing the king. Apparently she ruled out the possibility of requesting an audience with the king through a messenger who was regularly in his presence, possibly because she would have to tell the messenger what she wanted to talk to the king about.

has not called for me to come to him for thirty days. The honeymoon was over after five years of marriage. Undoubtedly, the king was seeing other women in his harem. Furthermore, the king may have been upset with Esther. Esther could have manufactured many good excuses that would justify her doing nothing. Could this be a chance for the king to get rid of her? Fear overwhelmed Esther.

4:13 Don't think . . . you will escape. Mordecai's response was strong and confrontational. In the face of this problem, he challenged Esther not to "think, imagine" (*damah* [TH1819, ZH1948]) that she would be able to escape when the decree was executed. This implies that Mordecai thought the king would not nullify his decree and save her on that fateful day when the rest of the Jews would be killed.

4:14 If you keep quiet at a time like this. The verb "silent" is repeated twice to emphasize the idea "if you really remain silent" (*ki 'im-hakharesh takharishi* [TH2790A, ZH3087]; lit., "If being silent, you will be silent"). The time is merely "at this time," without any comparative.

R. Pierce (1992:87) believes Mordecai is threatening to expose Esther's Jewish background; thus, when she goes to see the king it is not because of her bravery but because she has to. This is possible, but this interpretation does not seem consistent with the characterization of Mordecai elsewhere in this story.

deliverance and relief for the Jews will arise from some other place. Wiebe (1991:409-415) makes this a question, thus implying that there is no other place where help will come from. The Targum, the Alpha Greek text, and Josephus (*Antiquities* 11.6.7) all view God as that "other place" (Moore 1971:50), though one could just as easily understand Mordecai as referring to another person (Fox 2001:63). Bush (1996:396) supports this approach because if this statement refers purely to God's intervention, this would portray people and God as not working together. This idea would run contrary to the rest of the story, which is all about how God works in mysterious ways through people. Nevertheless, it is not impossible for Mordecai to suggest that God might have to work outside of his normal pattern of using his people when his people refuse to get involved. The Greek Alpha text reveals how later Jews interpreted this verse: "If you neglect your people by failing to come to their aid, God will be their aid and deliverance." Mordecai's statement must be grounded in his faith in God, God's powerful ability to deliver, and past promises concerning God's plans for his people.

Who knows if perhaps you were made queen for just such a time as this? Possibly Xerxes' choice of Esther as queen five years earlier was not totally accidental, not just luck. Maybe there was a providential purpose. Mordecai suggested that as wife and queen, Esther might have a divinely designed role to influence the course of history for the Jewish people.

4:16 *gather together all the Jews of Susa and fast for me. Do not eat or drink for three days.* Esther accepted Mordecai's reasoning, but she needed the spiritual support from her people. The imperatives "to gather" (*kanas* [TH3664, ZH4043]) and "to fast" (*tsum* [TH6684, ZH7426]) indicate a concerted effort to intercede with God (though God is not mentioned). A total fast without any food or water for three days showed the seriousness of the need for help (fasts often lasted only one day; cf. Lev 16:29-31; Judg 20:26). Bronger (1970:1-21) describes aspects of a typical Jewish fast. Fasting without drinking contrasted with the Persian feasting with much drinking (1:3-9; 2:18) and with the Jews' celebrations after they were delivered (ch 9).

My maids and I will do the same. These were apparently Esther's seven maids (2:9). In seeing to their involvement in fasting and prayer, Esther must have spoken to her servants about her fate and her faith, explaining to them the consequences of the king's decree.

though it is against the law, I will go in to see the king. Esther determined to risk her life by doing something that was "not according to the law." Praying and fasting would request God's control over her action. Through faith she also believed that God made her queen for this purpose.

If I must die, I must die. The threat of death was real, so Esther's commitment and boldness were exemplary. She, like Vashti, would do what she felt was the right thing to do in spite of the personal cost. This was not an expression of fatalistic despair (Paton 1908:226).

4:17 *So Mordecai . . . did everything.* Mordecai was faithful in his role as intercessor and leader of his people.

COMMENTARY

The narrative addresses how certain believers responded to bad news, specifically the threat of death. The text does not outline a series of abstract principles concerning civil disobedience or idealize the goal of being a martyr for a good cause. The story merely recounts what one group of people did in a very difficult situation.

Not every disagreement is worth dying over, and not every conflict will result in a threat against someone's life. Nevertheless, the response of Mordecai and Esther can illuminate and encourage believers who may face severe opposition from people who hate them.

The immediate reaction to the threat of death in Haman's decree was lament (4:1). Mordecai did not hide his anguish or try to pretend that everything was fine. He was not intimidated by social pressure, public opinion, or other officials in the king's gate at the palace. Instead, he followed the traditional custom of tearing his clothes, putting on clothes made of sackcloth, and covering himself with ashes as he loudly wept and wailed (4:1). This funeral dress and lamenting behavior symbolized to everyone who saw Mordecai that something terrible had happened and that death was at hand. Other Jews throughout the Persian Empire joined Mordecai, for Haman's decree was essentially a death sentence for all Jews. These mourners drew attention to a terrible injustice, their own approaching death.

All hope was lost because of the king's stamp on the decree, so all that the Jewish people could do was to mourn their approaching demise. Mordecai openly revealed to everyone that great shame was about to fall on him and his people. If he kept quiet, nothing could possibly be done to reverse this royal decree. The behavior modeled in this section suggests that when people do evil things to plot and take advantage of others as Haman had done, someone like Mordecai needs to reveal the ugly truth to the world around them, so that others will know and possibly do something (following the example of Esther) to change the situation.

In this situation, Mordecai put himself in a position where someone important (Esther) could see him, so that something could be done to reverse the threat of death. His rejection of new clothes from Esther demonstrated that this was not a minor problem that could be quickly remedied (4:4). His private discussion with Esther's assistant Hathach provided a more appropriate venue for Mordecai to explain the full details of Haman's actions, how he had bribed the king, and what the decree actually said (4:7-8).

Mordecai knew that as long as the people who could possibly do something about this situation were in the dark about this decree, nothing would ever happen. But he assumed if Esther knew the truth about what her husband had allowed Haman to do, she might be able to speak to him about this matter (4:8). The principle of taking complaints to the proper civil or religious authorities who can address the issue is still valid. If the offending party is a high official, a king, pastor, or president of an organization, it makes this process more difficult. But usually the right word spoken in the right way can have some impact on board members, friends, or trusted associates who can attempt to influence the person in authority.

In the midst of this crisis, the Jewish people throughout the nation maintained their loyalty and commitment to one another by mourning together (4:3). No Jew was alone, for they had family members who could identify with their sorrows. They stuck together in the midst of this trial. Although Queen Esther did not know about the problem at first (4:4-6), she was disturbed by what she saw and did everything possible to find out what the problem was. She was in an isolated position of power and privilege in the palace, but she still cared about Mordecai's welfare. The problem was that Esther felt powerless to confront the king and oppose this decree (4:11). She could not even go to speak to the king without putting her life in danger. This is the feeling of many people who are oppressed and mistreated by powerful political, business, and religious leaders. People often feel so powerless that they see no way to adequately address their issues. They may be able to speak to a superior, but they know that they will not be heard.

This problem should be a concern to every person with some degree of control over other people. Every leader needs to have a touch of humility and assume that they may make mistakes from time to time, or that they may get bad advice from trusted friends or professional advisers. Leaders need to devise methods for receiving feedback that will allow people with different perspectives to express contrary opinions in a nonthreatening environment so that they can have the possibility of looking at issues differently. This advice may be rejected, but at least it should be heard in order to avoid making foolish mistakes. Simply listening to others and not pretending to always be right could prevent many church splits and denominational crises. Some view power and leadership as something one gains and keeps by maintaining tight control and micromanaging every detail, but true kingly, pastoral, and organizational leadership is granted to servant leaders by followers who gladly recognize the talents of the person in charge.

In order to solve this crisis, one person (Esther) had to put her reputation and life on the line for the sake of others. She counted the cost to herself and her people and determined to act courageously, even if it meant that she might be killed (4:16). She realized that God had miraculously raised her up and put her in the position of queen for this very reason (4:14). She was willing to act in faith and boldly enter the king's throne room without an invitation, but first she needed to prepare her heart (4:16) and seek the merciful intervention of God. Esther, her maids, Mordecai, and many Jewish people spent three days in prayer and fasting, crying out to God for grace to spare the queen's life and for the words to say to transform the king's thinking (4:16). This was not a time to take things for granted or foolishly appear before the king. Only God could intervene to cause the king to accept Esther.

This truth applies to many of the conflicts that people have today, for when emotions run high and power-hungry people are defensively protecting their backsides, only the power of God can bring about a softening of the wills and an openness to forgive and work together. Every organization needs that person of faith who will put their reputation on the line and step forward to mediate disagreements and call both parties together to resolve a conflict.

◆   B. Esther's Banquet for Xerxes and Haman (5:1-8)

On the third day of the fast, Esther put on her royal robes and entered the inner court of the palace, just across from the king's hall. The king was sitting on his royal throne, facing the entrance. ²When he saw Queen Esther standing there in the inner court, he welcomed her and held out the gold scepter to her. So Esther approached and touched the end of the scepter.

³Then the king asked her, "What do you want, Queen Esther? What is your request? I will give it to you, even if it is half the kingdom!"

⁴And Esther replied, "If it please the king, let the king and Haman come today to a banquet I have prepared for the king."

⁵The king turned to his attendants and said, "Tell Haman to come quickly to a banquet, as Esther has requested." So the king and Haman went to Esther's banquet.

⁶And while they were drinking wine, the king said to Esther, "Now tell me what you really want. What is your request? I will give it to you, even if it is half the kingdom!"

⁷Esther replied, "This is my request and deepest wish. ⁸If I have found favor with the king, and if it pleases the king to grant my request and do what I ask, please come with Haman tomorrow to the banquet I will prepare for you. Then I will explain what this is all about."

NOTES

5:1 *her royal robes and entered the inner court.* Royal clothes stand in contrast to the sackcloth and ashes of the preceding days. Wearing sackcloth would not have been permissible in the king's presence, and Esther had to gain access to the king. She wanted him to immediately recognize her and raise his scepter. Jobes assumes that Esther "did not try to make herself beautiful" (1999:144) as she entered the king's presence, but there is no way to determine how she looked or what her attitude was (with tears or a smile; fearful or confident). There is no basis for the Aramaic Targum's addition that she had tears running down her face. She stood in "the house of the king," that is, in his private quarters, at the entrance to the throne room awaiting permission to enter to see the king.

5:2 *he welcomed her and held out the gold scepter to her.* Lit., "And she gained/found favor in his eyes" (*nas'ah khen* [TH2580, ZH2834] *be'enayw;* see also 2:9, 15, 17, where other people have a similarly unexpected reaction to Esther). The human "favor" of others actually appears to be a result of divine intervention, although this is never reported in conjunction with any of these events. When the scepter was extended, one of Esther's greatest fears was alleviated and one of her prayers answered. She did not obey the king's laws (like Vashti in 1:12), but she was not killed for coming without an invitation from the king (4:11).

5:3 *What do you want, Queen Esther?* Lit., "What for you?" or "What's with you?" Fox maintains that this phrase suggests someone is disturbed and means, "What troubles you?" (1991:281), but this probably implies too much. Xerxes' second question, "What is your request?" simply asks "What can I do for you?" and does not indicate that Esther is upset. The king knew (or assumed) that Esther came to the court uninvited because of something important. Maybe he thought that she had heard about another plot against his life (see 2:21-23).

I will give it to you, even if it is half the kingdom! "Half the kingdom" is an idiom or conventional saying that should not be taken literally (Clines 1984b:304). The king's exaggerated hyperbole of generosity sounds like it means that he would give anything, no matter how costly, but everyone knew that it was not meant to be taken literally.

5:4 *If it please the king . . . come today to a banquet.* Esther spoke politely, asking if it would please the king to come (see 1:19; 3:9) and bring Haman to a banquet. This delays the moment when Esther has to tell the king the terrible news that his trusted prime minister Haman wants to kill her and her people, so it creates suspense and a good deal of tension in the story. The reader naturally wonders whether she will have the courage to tell the king about the terrible evil that Haman is up to, how she will make this accusation, and how the king will react.

5:5 *as Esther has requested.* Lit., "to do according to the word of Esther." There is irony here in that Haman was ordered to do what Esther said.

5:6 *What is your request?* This meal probably involved the normal courses of food and then some wine after dinner. Following the normal cultural patterns of behavior, the king did not address the queen's request until the appropriate time at the end of the meal. The king probably assumed that Esther had delayed revealing her wishes to him at his throne room in order to ask him for her request at a more appropriate, private time and place.

5:8 *if it pleases the king to grant my request.* One wonders about the wisdom of Esther's delaying tactics. Do they reflect an oriental custom to not be too eager about asking for a favor? Esther's new invitation added a condition for its acceptance: By coming the king assured Esther that he would grant her request before knowing what it was.

COMMENTARY

Esther did what she promised Mordecai (4:16). She boldly determined to do what she could do in order to reverse Haman's decree. Having prepared herself spiritually and physically for her meeting with the king, she stepped into the royal hallway to walk to the entrance of the throne room. She had no way of knowing what the king was doing at this time, how busy he was, whether another woman was with him, what guests were talking to him, or what mood he was in on that day. She simply put herself in a position where the king could see her standing in the court as he was sitting on his throne. An important principle is illustrated by this act. People who hope to be used by God must boldly put themselves in a position where God can work through them, rather than sitting back, doing nothing, passively hoping or waiting for God to do something. For example, Daniel was serving the Babylonian king Nebuchadnezzar when the king had a dream (Dan 4); thus, he had the opportunity to interpret the dream when the other wise men failed to explain what the king saw in his dream. Likewise, Nehemiah, who was concerned about the disastrous situation in Jerusalem, was serving as King Artaxerxes' cup-bearer (Neh 1:3-11). In that position, he was given an opportunity to explain why he was sad, so he told the king about Jerusalem and offered to go rectify the situation if the king wished to send him (Neh 2:1-8).

Esther dressed appropriately by wearing her royal garments, behaved properly when the golden scepter was stretched out to her, and responded to his generous offer by modestly offering to serve the king. She did not act like an emotional basket case who was about to fall apart, like an angry spouse who was jealous because she was ignored, or like someone who was trying to push her agenda on the king. Since her primary goal was to "find favor in the eyes" of the king, she did what she was supposed to do. She knew that people first have to present themselves in such a way that they will be able to get a hearing with the person they hope to influence.

At first one is surprised that Esther simply asked to meet with the king and Haman that evening at a private banquet she was preparing. Was she afraid or unprepared for the king's direct offer of help? Were some of Haman's friends present, so it seemed like an inappropriate situation? And why would Esther invite the wicked man Haman to her banquet? Would it not be better to tell the king the truth about Haman in private, without Haman's being present? And why would she delay her request of the king a second time when she had the king and Haman alone at her banquet that first night? This creates great tension in the story (Levenson 1997:90), but this was not Esther's concern (Fox 2001:71).

The delay could have subjected Esther's plans to many new dangers. Perhaps the king or Haman would not be able to come, or maybe the king would change his attitude and be much less generous the next day. In spite of these dangers, Esther probably delayed her request because she was not yet certain that the king meant what he said when he agreed to do whatever she asked (Fox 2001:71). Esther's second invitation pushed the king to admit that he truly would do what Esther asked before she ever made her request (5:8; Clines 1984b:305). If this was the king's real desire, she would ask him at the next banquet.

These negotiations reveal that there is a right time and place to accomplish a task and a wrong time and place. Some people want things done now and believe an immediate decision is necessary, but the person they are talking to may not be ready to make the desired decision. Sometimes one has to be content to sow the seeds of an idea and then let them germinate for a while before it is possible to push for a decision that will reap the harvest. Unusual accomplishments are possible for those who have the wisdom and patience to wait for just the right time and place.

◆ C. Haman's Pride and Hatred of Mordecai (5:9-14)

⁹Haman was a happy man as he left the banquet! But when he saw Mordecai sitting at the palace gate, not standing up or trembling nervously before him, Haman became furious. ¹⁰However, he restrained himself and went on home.

Then Haman gathered together his friends and Zeresh, his wife, ¹¹and boasted to them about his great wealth and his many children. He bragged about the honors the king had given him and how he had been promoted over all the other nobles and officials.

¹²Then Haman added, "And that's not all! Queen Esther invited only me and the king himself to the banquet she prepared for us. And she has invited me to dine with her and the king again tomorrow!" ¹³Then he added, "But this is all worth nothing as long as I see Mordecai the Jew just sitting there at the palace gate."

¹⁴So Haman's wife, Zeresh, and all his friends suggested, "Set up a sharpened pole that stands seventy-five feet* tall, and in the morning ask the king to impale Mordecai on it. When this is done, you can go on your merry way to the banquet with the king." This pleased Haman, and he ordered the pole set up.

5:14 Hebrew *50 cubits* [22.5 meters].

NOTES

5:9 *Haman was a happy man.* Lit., "He was glad and good of heart." This shows how confident Haman was—he did not suspect Esther's plan and did not know she was a Jew. The reason for his gladness is explained in 5:11-12. The king was favoring him, plus only Haman was invited to enjoy a banquet with the king and queen. His pride (5:11) would precede his fall by only a few hours. His joy will be proven to be unfounded and foolish, and it will last only for a few moments.

he saw Mordecai sitting at the palace gate, not standing up or trembling. Mordecai's fast had ended; he was back at work in the palace gate. Mordecai refused to honor Haman by rising when he came to the gate. Although Mordecai knew about the decree to kill him and all the Jews in the kingdom, he did not grovel at Haman's feet to plead for mercy. When severe pressure was on Mordecai, he did not quickly change his beliefs or his behavior in order to soften Haman's hatred. Mordecai continued to show no respect for Haman. Both the act of bowing (3:2, 5) and the act of standing and bowing (5:9) are ways of recognizing the importance of a person. This later act of not even standing shows even less respect for Haman, so one is not surprised that this filled Haman with emotional rage. It appears that Mordecai is acting as if Haman deserves no respect.

5:10 *he restrained himself.* Haman's mood swings (from 5:9) were radical, like King Xerxes' (1:12). Haman's "restraint" (*wayyith'appaq* [TH662, ZH706]) does not reveal a positive character trait, just a deep determination to get revenge at a later time. Haman's restraint is only momentary, for soon he will determine to get rid of Mordecai immediately (5:13-14) and not wait almost a year until the king's decree allows him to kill Mordecai.

Haman gathered together his friends. This stands in contrast to Esther's gathering of her friends to fast and pray (Levenson 1997:92). Levenson calls this gathering at Haman's house a "comic inversion of Esther's action" (1997:92). Esther gathered people together to support her selfless act of going before the king unannounced so that others could live. Haman gathered people together to hear his selfish boasting about his greatness and to support his plan to bring about the death of Mordecai.

5:11 *and boasted.* His boasting was the act of "recounting" (*wayesapper* [TH5608, ZH6218]) before others all his glory, wealth, greatness, and promotion above all others. This created a false sense of importance and security for Haman, a feeling that will soon be dashed by the unusual turn of circumstances in chs 6 and 7.

5:12 *only me.* Haman's emphasis was on the exclusive honor that was on "me" (*'othi* [TH853A/2967.1, ZH906/3276]) and the fact that a second time "I was called to her" (*'ani qaru'-lah* [TH589, ZH638]). These are two illustrations of his pride.

5:13 *But this is all worth nothing.* All the other joys, rewards, accomplishments, and honors Haman enjoyed could not fully satisfy him or change the fact that Mordecai continued to remain seated at the gate. Note that Haman never admits what the real problem is, that his pride was hurt because Mordecai would not bow down and honor him.

5:14 *Zeresh.* Jobes (1999:145) and Laniak (2003:236) compare Zeresh's advice to that of Jezebel, who, wanting to encourage and satisfy her pouting husband's desire to have some property owned by Naboth (1 Kgs 21:1-16), plotted to kill Naboth so that Ahab could take the land. Jobes (1999:146) finds irony and humor in the fact that Haman depends on his wife's advice, just the opposite of what one would expect of a strong and powerful man who was supposed to be the ruler over his house (1:22).

Set up a sharpened pole that stands seventy-five feet tall . . . impale Mordecai on it. The exact form of punishment is open to interpretation. Some interpret this "pole" (*'ets* [TH6086, ZH6770], "tree, wood") as a gallows for hanging (Moore 1971:60), while others see this as a pole to be impaled on (Clines 1984b:306). The height of 75 feet seems very tall in either case, but if the pole was placed on the high platform of the palace grounds (see note on 1:2) to reach this height, then the pole by itself was not that tall. Haman wanted everyone to see Mordecai's dead body so that Mordecai would be visibly shamed before his countrymen. He wanted to disgrace and dishonor Mordecai as much as he possibly could so that no one else would dare to follow Mordecai's example and dishonor Haman. Cf. note on 2:23.

COMMENTARY

This brief interlude (5:9-14) provides important parenthetical information about the villain in the story and further emphasizes the depth of Haman's hatred for

Mordecai. However, Haman saw himself as the most powerful and privileged person in the land, the right-hand man of the king. He was proud of his family, impressed with his own wealth, felt important because he dined with the king and queen, and had received great honors. These factors gave him great satisfaction, and he was proud of who he was. He sounds and acts very much like many of the powerful and rich people of our world today. They flaunt their wealth and will mercilessly crush anyone who gets in their way.

But not everything went Haman's way, for he had one archenemy, Mordecai, the stubborn Jew who would not honor him. Haman was angry with Mordecai and despised him intensely. In spite of the king's decree to kill all the Jews in 11 months, Mordecai refused to bend the knee to Haman, publicly embarrassing Haman in the gate. Here, Mordecai's actions are more intentional than in chapter 3. Mordecai courageously refused to honor this dishonorable man. By not standing when Haman came through the palace gate, Mordecai demonstrated that Haman did not have complete power over him. Mordecai behaved like every righteous person should. No one should bow to or do things to honor ungodly people (who in other situations often present themselves as saints), especially those who bully or intimidate others because of their arrogance and power. Godly people should stand for what they believe and be willing to go against the social pressure of the crowd, even when this means they will suffer negative consequences. Conscience should rule moral behavior, not fear.

When trouble came to Mordecai and Esther, they gathered their friends together and fasted (4:1-17). So it is not surprising to find Haman doing something similar when he was upset. People gain confidence and courage from friends, plus good advice that can help them through their trials. Haman's recital of his glory and wealth before his family and friends was readily accepted and appreciated, so they would naturally affirm him. He was an important man who deserved to be honored. This no doubt lifted his spirits, but still life was not perfect. Haman needed some advice from his trusted friends who loved him and had his best interests at heart. What should or could be done to remove that thorn in the flesh, Mordecai? Haman's wife and friends all agreed that Mordecai should be killed and publicly dishonored before everyone in the city.

People still follow these kinds of tactics today. If a powerful person cannot intimidate his or her enemies or bully them into submission, the only thing left to do is to eliminate them by some means, such as firing them, revoking their membership, or bringing false charges against them. If they no longer exist as a problem, then a deceptive worldview of peace and superiority can appear to be established as normal. When the problem people are run off, then everyone will fit into their appropriate roles, life will be wonderful again, and everyone can merrily go to their parties and have a great time (5:14). Although the mighty may rule for a brief time, when they do not promote what is right, God sees what happens and eventually intervenes. Those controlled by anger, jealousy, revenge, and the oppression of others often forget that God is still sovereignly in control of this world. He hates the proud oppressors and will hold them accountable for their action.

◆ IV. Mordecai Is Honored and Haman Is Impaled (6:1–7:10)
A. Haman Must Honor Mordecai (6:1–14)

That night the king had trouble sleeping, so he ordered an attendant to bring the book of the history of his reign so it could be read to him. ²In those records he discovered an account of how Mordecai had exposed the plot of Bigthana and Teresh, two of the eunuchs who guarded the door to the king's private quarters. They had plotted to assassinate King Xerxes.

³"What reward or recognition did we ever give Mordecai for this?" the king asked.

His attendants replied, "Nothing has been done for him."

⁴"Who is that in the outer court?" the king inquired. As it happened, Haman had just arrived in the outer court of the palace to ask the king to impale Mordecai on the pole he had prepared.

⁵So the attendants replied to the king, "Haman is out in the court."

"Bring him in," the king ordered. ⁶So Haman came in, and the king said, "What should I do to honor a man who truly pleases me?"

Haman thought to himself, "Whom would the king wish to honor more than me?" ⁷So he replied, "If the king wishes to honor someone, ⁸he should bring out one of the king's own royal robes, as well as a horse that the king himself has ridden—one with a royal emblem on its head. ⁹Let the robes and the horse be handed over to one of the king's most noble officials. And let him see that the man whom the king wishes to honor is dressed in the king's robes and led through the city square on the king's horse. Have the official shout as they go, 'This is what the king does for someone he wishes to honor!' "

¹⁰"Excellent!" the king said to Haman. "Quick! Take the robes and my horse, and do just as you have said for Mordecai the Jew, who sits at the gate of the palace. Leave out nothing you have suggested!"

¹¹So Haman took the robes and put them on Mordecai, placed him on the king's own horse, and led him through the city square, shouting, "This is what the king does for someone he wishes to honor!" ¹²Afterward Mordecai returned to the palace gate, but Haman hurried home dejected and completely humiliated.

¹³When Haman told his wife, Zeresh, and all his friends what had happened, his wise advisers and his wife said, "Since Mordecai—this man who has humiliated you—is of Jewish birth, you will never succeed in your plans against him. It will be fatal to continue opposing him."

¹⁴While they were still talking, the king's eunuchs arrived and quickly took Haman to the banquet Esther had prepared.

NOTES

6:1 *the king had trouble sleeping.* It was no mere coincidence that the king's sleep "fled, forsook, left" (*nadad* [TH5074, ZH5610]) him this night (cf. Dan 6:18). Unlike the MT, the Aramaic Targum and Old Greek explicitly attribute this to God's action. Jobes (1999:152) calls this the "most ironically comic scene in the Bible" because a very unusual series of unexplainable coincidences happen in rapid succession.

book of the history of his reign. Lit., "in the book of remembrances of the deeds of the days." Some of Persia's national history is found in their sacred book, the *Zend-Avesta*, but not these events. Archaeologists have not yet found the original Persian annals that are mentioned here and probably never will. Nonetheless, evidence of the Persians' meticulous record keeping is illustrated in Ezra 6:1, where scribes in 520 BC found an original document signed by Cyrus that was written in 538 BC.

6:2 *Mordecai had exposed the plot.* It was providential that the king should remember that Mordecai had once saved his life (2:19-23) on the very morning that Haman was planning to kill Mordecai. The irony is thick, and it permeates the scene, including the king's sleep-lessness, the attendant's choice of a text for reading, and the king's concern about whether Mordecai had been rewarded. There are just too many unusual coincidences here to believe that it all happened by chance.

6:3 What reward or recognition did we ever give Mordecai for this? According to Herod-otus (*Histories* 3.138-141), Persian kings normally honored and rewarded those who helped them immediately. For example, a man who saved the life of Xerxes' brother was immediately rewarded by being appointed the governor of Cilicia (Herodotus *Histories* 9.107). Thus, it is surprising that the king should ask such a question and more astonish-ing that the servant found nothing in the annals about any reward for Mordecai.

6:4 As it happened, Haman had just arrived. The NLT captures the astonishing turn of events by adding "as it happened" and "just." The hour was very early, and only Haman was in the palace at this time of day.

6:5 Haman is out in the court. Just like Esther (5:1), Haman was "standing" in the right place, hoping to be noticed and invited in to speak with the king. Earlier Esther was stand-ing at the entrance to the court, hoping to influence the king to save many lives, while now Haman is standing at the entrance to the court, hoping to influence the king to destroy Mordecai's life.

6:6 What should I do to honor a man who truly pleases me? The king did not reveal to Haman who he wanted to honor, just as Haman did not reveal the name of the people he wished to destroy in 3:8-9 (Clines 1984b:306).

6:7 If the king wishes to honor someone. Haman did not begin his answer like other responses to the king—"if it please the king" (1:19; 3:9; 5:4, 8; cf. Bush 1996:415)—or even grammatically connect his initial thoughts to the rest of the sentence in 6:8 (Moore 1971:64). The word "if," not in the Hebrew, is added in NLT. It seems that Haman was musing over the idea out loud—"The man whom the king wishes to honor . . ."—as he thought of some honor to suggest. Bush (1996:415) attributes this initial ungrammatical response to Haman's eagerness to describe the honor he wished for himself. It is ironic that Haman suggested something that would be a fitting honor for himself, but in reality the honor was for Mordecai, his hated enemy. His arrogance led to his downfall.

6:8 one of the king's own royal robes . . . a horse that the king himself has ridden . . . a royal emblem on its head. In Haman's thinking, honor was based on looks, association with the king, and public acclaim. He wanted to be honored as the king, a request that would probably not make the king very comfortable (Levenson 1997:97). Since he was second-in-command to the king, Haman could not ask for a higher position, and he already had a great deal of power (he held the king's ring—3:1, 10). He was likely a wealthy man, based on the bribe he intended to give the king (3:9), so his main wish was for recognition and honor. He wanted to fantasize about what it would be like to be treated like a king for a few moments, what it would be like to have hundreds of people bowing before him and honoring him. Levenson (1997:97) suggests that Haman provides an effective contrast between Joseph's rise to leadership to save Egypt from a coming famine and Haman's concern for personal glory.

6:9 be handed over to one of the king's most noble officials. Haman's words are ironic. He thought someone else would honor him through the streets of Susa, but the reality of the situation was that as a noble official of the king (3:1), he would be honoring someone else in the streets. Moreover, that individual would be Mordecai—"handed over" to him for exaltation rather than destruction (3:6).

6:10 do just as you have said for Mordecai the Jew. This was the first time the king men-tioned that Mordecai was a Jew. We have no idea how the king found out that Mordecai was of Jewish descent unless it was written in the portion of the king's annals that was read to him that very morning. The emphasis on Mordecai's Jewish background was intended by the storyteller to provide an ironic crushing reversal and an enormous embarrassment for Haman, for the king explicitly required one who hated the Jews to honor the Jew he most hated. Surely Haman was shocked and utterly dumbfounded at the king's command. How humiliating for Haman to proclaim Mordecai's greatness. Haman could not disobey the king; every last detail Haman suggested must be followed.

6:12 Haman hurried home dejected and completely humiliated. Haman was "mourning" (*'abel* [TH57, ZH63]); he "covered his head" (*wakhapuy ro'sh* [TH2645/7218, ZH2902/8031]) in shame and humiliation (cf. 2 Sam 15:30; Jer 14:3-4). This contrasts with the mourning and weeping of Mordecai, Esther, and the Jews in the city of Susa in 4:1-3, 16. This reversal provides hope that it might be possible to stop some of Haman's evil plots.

6:13 his wise advisers and his wife. Haman's wife, friends, and "wisemen" (*khakam* [TH2450A, ZH2682]), understood that Mordecai was Jewish (5:13). Therefore, they predicted that Haman would never be successful against Mordecai. They knew that these ironic events were more than just a series of coincidences.

this man who has humiliated you—is of Jewish birth, you will never succeed in your plans against him. Lit., "This man of Jewish birth, before whom you have begun to fall—you will not overcome him." Although some commentators conclude that Haman will never succeed because he is one of the cursed Amalekites, the biblical text never makes that point, and he is not called an Agagite in this verse. In fact, Clines (1984a:43) concludes that these negative statements are the convictions of the narrator, not Haman's wife and friends, for his wife and friends were strong supporters the previous evening (Bush 1996:417). Nevertheless, this story is full of unusual and unexpected reversals, so it is not impossible that Haman's own friends and family turned against him after Haman was forced to honor Mordecai.

It will be fatal to continue opposing him. Lit., "To fall you will fall before him." The verb (*napal* [TH5307, ZH5877]) is repeated to emphasize "You will surely fall." His best friends had no doubts about his failure. Haman would not only fail; he himself would be destroyed. Laniak (2003:242) believes "to fall" is an important motif in the book of Esther because (1) the lot "fell" on a certain month (3:7), (2) the king told Haman to not let anything "fall, fail to be done" (6:10) that he had commanded, (3) Haman "fell" (7:8) on the couch where Esther was reclining, (4) fear "fell" on the people (8:17; 9:3), and (5) in the present passage Haman's "fall" is predicted.

6:14 quickly took Haman to the banquet Esther had prepared. Still in shock, with no control over his life or his fate (Laniak 2003:241), Haman was taken by the king's eunuchs to face Queen Esther and King Xerxes. One can imagine the fear overwhelming Haman as he tried to balance his recent misfortune with the great honor of being present at this special banquet. He must quickly pull himself together for the queen's banquet, act like a prime minister, and do his best to preserve his dignity.

COMMENTARY

This narrative is full of unusual coincidences that appear to be much more than just accidental events. The coordination of so many exceptional circumstances in such a short period of time seems to be a sign that God's sovereign hand was guiding and controlling the lives of the king, his attendants (6:1, 3), Haman, and Mordecai. Why did the king just happen to have trouble sleeping that night—the night before

Haman was going to ask the king to give him permission to kill Mordecai? Why did the king get up instead of turning over in his bed and trying to get back to sleep? Was it just an accident that the king's attendant turned to read the exact page that recorded the events surrounding Mordecai's warning the king about the assassination plot? Why did the king happen to remember that he had not rewarded Mordecai? Was it just another coincidence that at the very time that Haman was in the palace to seek Mordecai's death, the king would call Haman in to talk to him about how to reward Mordecai? No believer can read this story and conclude that this was just a lucky break for Mordecai and an unlucky break for Haman. This must be something more than blind chance.

The theological lesson one can take from these events is that every believer can have hope in dark days because God has the ability to control the circumstances of every person's life. Things may seem totally out of control from the human perspective, but behind the scenes God is silently orchestrating the affairs of each person so that his plan will be accomplished according to his timing. This does not mean that believers will always be rescued from every evil person who tries to take advantage of them, or that Christians should conclude that they will never suffer any harm. For some, it is God's will that they suffer or die (Dan 7:21-25), but for others he marvelously delivers them from the evil people who try to destroy them (Dan 3, 6).

Throughout these events the theme of "honor" is addressed. It is that ulterior motive that compelled Haman to get his revenge against Mordecai, but as it actually worked out, Haman's excessive desire for honor was what eventually led to his ruin. Haman came to the palace with a devious plan to regain his honor by requesting that the king make a decree to kill Mordecai (5:14). But Haman did not realize that at that very moment the king was intent on honoring Mordecai for his past deed of kindness in saving the king's life (6:3). The king asked Haman to describe what should be done to honor someone who pleases the king (6:6), but he did not tell him whom he wanted to honor (just as Haman never told the king the name of the people he wanted to dishonor). The arrogant Haman wrongly assumed that the king wanted to honor him, so he mulled over in his mind what it would be like to be king for a day (Laniak 1998:101). He wanted to be honored by everyone publicly, he wanted one of the king's nobles to honor him with shouts in the public square, and he wanted to be honored by wearing the king's royal robes and by riding on the king's horse (6:7-9). Surely this overstepped the boundaries of proper behavior for a noble. How could anyone be so arrogant and foolish as to tell the king that they wanted to replace him? Although the king was likely suspicious of Haman's desires for so many honors, he didn't challenge Haman's inappropriate pipe dream of taking the role of the king, since the real honor was actually going to go to Mordecai. However, the king did gain insight into Haman's thinking, and this insight may have helped him quickly decide what to do with Haman when he again acted inappropriately by touching the queen at Esther's banquet (7:5-8).

Haman had to honor Mordecai as the king commanded (6:11), but this was an act of great humiliation and shame for Haman (6:12). Mordecai, the one who lamented loudly in sackcloth and ashes at the palace gate, would now be loudly praised as he wore the king's robe through the streets of Susa. Haman, the man who wanted to kill Mordecai by putting his dead body on a pole for everyone to see, was now publicly honoring him before the people in the capital. What a reversal of fortunes! A Jewish man was receiving the honor that Haman desired. Consequently, Haman went home dejected and ashamed. He bewailed the loss of his honor before his wife and advisers (Fox 2001:79). The king had just gloriously honored the one Haman wanted to shame. Even Haman's wife and wise friends saw the hopelessness of the situation and encouraged Haman not to shame Mordecai further, lest Haman be humiliated further or endanger himself (6:13). Although Haman's wife and friends did not claim that God was working against the aims of Haman, they certainly saw that fate was turning against Haman and believed further opposition would only lead to further shame. They realized that something or someone greater than Mordecai the Jew was bringing about the humiliation of Haman, for too many things were going against Haman for it to be mere accident. This reversal of fortunes for the Jewish heroes in the story will be picked up again in chapter 8, when the king gives these heroes Haman's property and allows them to write a second edict that permits the Jews to defend themselves.

In the midst of this mental confusion and emotional uncertainty, Haman was whisked away to go to Esther's second banquet. According to the earlier chapters, Haman was confident that everything was going his way, but now in shame he had to appear before the king again, and he did not know what to say or do about his situation. Could he rescue the situation, or would it be a fatal mistake to oppose Mordecai any further (6:13)?

This chapter of Esther brings to light the human desire to gain ever greater honors and glory. There is certainly nothing wrong, for example, with working hard for good grades in school in order to be included on the honor roll, nor is there anything wrong with being honored with a plaque for winning more business and profits for one's employer. The problem relates to why one works hard to achieve success. If the primary reason for excelling is an ego trip to gain greater recognition, then the motivation is selfish and the results will produce arrogance. When people do all things to glorify God, then selfish, egotistical motivations are left behind, and work becomes a service to others in the group. Far too many people are worried about other people respecting, honoring, and giving them recognition. Instead of trying to save face, they should be concerned with serving others, which will produce something much greater than just respect.

◆   ## B. Haman Is Exposed and Impaled (7:1-10)

So the king and Haman went to Queen Esther's banquet. [2]On this second occasion, while they were drinking wine, the king again said to Esther, "Tell me what you want, Queen Esther. What is your request? I will give it to you, even if it is half the kingdom!"

[3]Queen Esther replied, "If I have found favor with the king, and if it pleases the king to grant my request, I ask that my life and the lives of my people will be spared. [4]For my people and I have been sold to those who would kill, slaughter, and annihilate us. If we had merely been

sold as slaves, I could remain quiet, for that would be too trivial a matter to warrant disturbing the king."

⁵"Who would do such a thing?" King Xerxes demanded. "Who would be so presumptuous as to touch you?"

⁶Esther replied, "This wicked Haman is our adversary and our enemy." Haman grew pale with fright before the king and queen. ⁷Then the king jumped to his feet in a rage and went out into the palace garden.

Haman, however, stayed behind to plead for his life with Queen Esther, for he knew that the king intended to kill him. ⁸In despair he fell on the couch where Queen Esther was reclining, just as

the king was returning from the palace garden.

The king exclaimed, "Will he even assault the queen right here in the palace, before my very eyes?" And as soon as the king spoke, his attendants covered Haman's face, signaling his doom.

⁹Then Harbona, one of the king's eunuchs, said, "Haman has set up a sharpened pole that stands seventy-five feet* tall in his own courtyard. He intended to use it to impale Mordecai, the man who saved the king from assassination."

"Then impale Haman on it!" the king ordered. ¹⁰So they impaled Haman on the pole he had set up for Mordecai, and the king's anger subsided.

7:9 Hebrew *50 cubits* [22.5 meters].

NOTES

7:2 *Tell me what you want. . . . What is your request? I will give it to you.* The story skips over the meal and goes directly to the drinking of wine after dinner, focusing on the dramatic moment when Esther will make her request of the king. Twice the king asked Esther to reveal her secret, using two different words: "request" (*she'elah* [TH7596, ZH8629]) and "petition" (*baqqashah* [TH1246, ZH1336]). He thus indicated his strong desire to understand and please the queen. He repeated his offer to do what she asked (see 5:3, 6) and met her condition for attending the banquet (5:8) by promising to grant her request.

7:3 *If I have found favor with the king.* Esther followed proper, humble etiquette without presuming anything. There is a shift here in Esther's address of the king—an element of direct address not represented in the NLT. Earlier she speaks impersonally ("If it please the king," 5:4), but now she more personally says (lit.), "If I have found *your* favor, O king." This brings into the issue the personal, affectionate relationship she has with "you," the king, because if her request is not granted, it will impact their relationship.

I ask that my life and the lives of my people will be spared. Lit., "Let my life be given to me as my petition and the lives of my people as my request." The repetition of the king's phraseology in 7:2, using *she'elah* [TH7596, ZH8629] (request) and *baqqashah* [TH1246, ZH1336] (petition) connected her concerns with the king's promise. She earnestly interceded not just for herself, but for the future of her people.

7:4 *I have been sold to those who would kill, slaughter, and annihilate.* Esther chose her vocabulary carefully. Being "sold" (*makar* [TH4376, ZH4835]) by someone else implied that money was paid to accomplish the sale. Esther was obliquely referring to the huge price Haman paid (3:8-11). She used the exact terms of Haman's decree, which declared that all Jews must be killed, slaughtered, and annihilated (3:13). In saying this, Esther was careful not to accuse the king of any wrongdoing or mention who did this to her. At this point she wanted sympathy because of the grave danger she was facing.

If we had merely been sold as slaves, I could remain quiet. Esther justified her request because of the severity of the attack on herself and her people. She would humbly and quietly accept slavery if that were the king's will.

that would be too trivial a matter to warrant disturbing the king. Lit., "the *tsar* would not be equal/suitable to the *nezeq* of the king." The meanings of the terms *tsar* [TH6862/A, ZH7639/7640] and *nezeq* [TH5143, ZH5691] are uncertain. The NLT (cf. NIV, NASB, ESV) translates *nezeq* as "disturbing," thus giving the idea that Esther did not want to bother the king about personal afflictions (*tsar*). Others (Paton 1908:258; Levenson 1997:99) see the statement referring to an "enemy" (*tsar*) not being able to compensate the king enough for the king's "loss" (*nezeq*) of income from killing the Jews. This interpretation results in a rendering such as "I would have kept my silence, for the adversary cannot compensate the loss to the king" (cf. KJV, ASV, NRSV). Either interpretation is hypothetically possible for this cryptic clause. Bush (1996:427) makes a stronger case for the translation "for the trouble would not be commensurate with the annoyance to the king," which is similar to the NLT's rendering since both avoid translating *tsar* as "enemy" and both interpret *nezeq* as "annoy, disturb."

7:5 *Who would be so presumptuous as to touch you?* Lit., "Where is this one who has filled his heart to do so?" The king's questions were filled with emotion and anger. He could not imagine someone doing this atrocious thing. He did not doubt her accusation; he assumed it was true. It seems that up to this point neither the king nor Haman knew that Esther was a Jew, so both were probably astonished and perplexed at Esther's statements. The king probably did not initially connect what she was saying to Haman's earlier decree (3:8-9). By gradually introducing the facts and arousing the king's anger against the one who would dare to threaten her life, Esther sealed the fate of the one she would later name.

7:6 *This wicked Haman is our adversary and our enemy.* The king thought of Haman as a friend and his right-hand man, but actually he was an "enemy" (*'oyeb* [TH341, ZH367]), the adversary (*tsar* [TH6862/A, ZH7640]) of the king and queen. The NLT adds "our" to the phrase "our enemy," a factor not present in the Hebrew text. Levenson (1997:103) observes that at this point Esther does not call Haman an enemy of the Jews, the formula used in 3:10; 8:1; 9:10, 24, so the implication is that now he is "an enemy," both of the Jews and the Persians. The king's anger, which earlier raged against Vashti, now rages against Haman (Levenson 1997:104).

Haman grew pale with fright. Lit., "Haman was terrified." This surprisingly aggressive accusation by the queen, plus the anger of the king, made Haman fearfully aware of the seriousness of the situation. The warning of Haman's wife and advisers (6:12-13) was coming true.

7:7 *plead for his life with Queen Esther.* In most examples in this story, the king does not make decisions on his own, but always appeals for advice from others. At this point he has no one to consult, so he must decide what to do on his own. While the king was out of the room trying to decide what to do with his wicked prime minister, Haman probably sought for a reprieve, mercy, or forgiveness from Esther. Haman knew that the king's mind would probably be dead set against him, so the only hope he had was for Esther to intervene on his behalf (Jobes 1999:165). Minutes earlier Esther was pleading for her life; now Haman pleads for his (Clines 1984b:312).

7:8 *In despair he fell on the couch . . . just as the king was returning.* The words "in despair" are not found in the Hebrew text. Jobes (1999:165) reports that harem protocol required that a man not be left alone with a woman and that he should not come within seven steps of her; thus Haman's conduct was unthinkable in the Persian royal court. It is possible to understand here that Haman lost his balance and fell on the couch where the queen was reclining, possibly landing on her. But it is also possible (probably less likely) to picture Haman purposely falling on his knees at Esther's feet and kissing them as he begged for mercy. Both options make Haman look very bad, and the king sees it all. This bizarre scene has some ironic humor, for the once wise and powerful Haman, who had every break fall in his favor in the first half of the story, totally self-destructs as if he is a bumbling fool in this part of the story.

Will he even assault the queen right here in the palace, before my very eyes? Though it is hard for us to imagine that the king actually thought Haman was attempting to "rape" (*kabash* [TH3533, ZH3899], "subdue, conquer") his wife while he was in the house, the angry king saw Haman's inappropriate contact with the queen and attributed the worst possible motives to Haman: "Who does he think he is? Is he actually trying to make a move on the king's wife?" Seeing Haman's disgusting behavior, the king had an easy time deciding what should be done next. The Aramaic Targum suggests that the angel Gabriel pushed Haman at just the right moment.

his attendants covered Haman's face, signaling his doom. The clause "signaling his doom" correctly interprets the act, but the words are not in the Hebrew. This custom of covering the face of a condemned person was also known among the Greeks and Romans (Paton 1908:264) and is still used in capital cases even today.

7:9 *He intended to use it to impale Mordecai.* Harbona, one of the king's seven eunuchs (1:10), brought a second accusation, for he was aware of Haman's plan to kill Mordecai by impaling him on the tall pole. How ironic, but how fitting. One might almost suspect that a higher power was controlling what was happening. Could all these pieces of the puzzle fall into place so flawlessly just by coincidence? Perhaps Harbona was the eunuch who read to the king about his failure to reward Mordecai earlier that morning (6:1-3) and saw the pole when he picked up Haman from his house that evening.

impale Haman on it! Justice was served. God is not mentioned as the one who brought about this great reversal, but the Hebrew reader would see the hand of God directing these events.

COMMENTARY

In this chapter, we see Esther acting as an intermediary or intercessor, standing in the gap in order to save the lives of others. Like Moses, who pleaded with God for mercy on the people of Israel after they worshiped the golden calf (Exod 32, though Moses's life was not threatened), Esther pleaded for mercy with the powerful king of Persia so that she and her people would not be slaughtered (Levenson 1997:101). The difference, of course, is that the people who worshiped the golden calf deserved to be judged, while the Jews that Haman wanted to kill were innocent. The similarity in the accounts is that key people (Moses and Esther) had the courage to put their life on the line for the sake of their people. Esther waited until the proper situation to ask for compassion from the king and then confronted the injustice of Haman's plan to kill thousands of Jews. This person, who appeared on the outside to be the cordial friend of the king and queen, would now be exposed for who he really was. He acted like a friend, but in fact he was an enemy who wanted to "kill, slaughter, and annihilate" the queen and all her relatives.

This hypocrisy is similar to that of many people. When they are in the public eye, they appear to be happy, normal, and friendly (the smiling and proud Haman at home and at the banquet with the king, 5:10b-12), but that public front actually hides a sinister private life, controlled by a vengeful inner hatred for someone (Haman actually wanted to kill thousands of innocent people who had nothing to do with him). It is emotionally difficult for people (in this case the king) to accept the new reality when the truth is exposed and a well-respected friend in the community is identified as an evil person. The king had previously thought that Haman was a very responsible government official who could be completely trusted to act in the king's interest. He was so trustworthy that the king even gave him the royal ring to sign official government documents (3:1-2, 10). Instead of telling the king what he was really doing (getting personal revenge on someone), Haman had presented his plan as if he were a hero who would defend the king's laws and interests (3:8-9). The perpetrators of these kinds of evil deeds want to secretly continue their evil behavior without interruption, no matter how destructive and shameful that is to others. If someone is brave enough to confront such behavior (like Esther), change is possible.

The king responded with typical anger (as in 1:12) against Haman, even though he had foolishly approved of Haman's plan and had given him the king's ring to enact this decree (3:8-10). The king now realized that Haman had duped him and taken advantage of his trust. Rather than immediately condemning Haman to death on the spot, the king wisely left the room to think for a while so that he would not do something foolish against Haman that he might regret later (7:7). The text does not say if the king decided to have mercy on Haman or not, but when he reentered the room, he found Haman in an inappropriate position with the queen (7:8). This was a major mistake, for no one should touch the queen, much less be on the same couch with her. The text does not say if she screamed when he fell on her, but at that most inopportune time, the king came in from the palace garden and saw that Haman had transgressed the boundary of proper behavior regarding the queen. Haman was so frantic that he lost control of what he was doing. He would not have acted this way if the king was present; he would have been more careful. His actions demonstrated to the king that Haman had no respect for the queen or the king. Haman would do anything to get his way. He demonstrated that he was truly the enemy of the king. The whole situation is somewhat ironic, because the powerful and arrogant Haman was now found begging for his life from the Jewish woman he wanted to kill. His act of begging for his life was the very act that assured his demise.

The final verses of this chapter demonstrate that one cannot get away with evil behavior forever. The queen eventually revealed Haman's evil secret, she exposed the irrationality of Haman's evil decree, the king finally saw that Haman was his enemy, and Harbona testified about Haman's secret plan to kill Mordecai, the man who saved the king's life (7:9). Although people can plot to cover their tracks and can seem to get away with evil behavior for days and years, their acts are known to others and to God. Eventually, others will tire of mistreatment and refuse to cover up their wickedness. God will also have a day of accountability when the wicked will be justly punished for their sins. This belief spurs the righteous sufferer to trust God each day in spite of the present evil deeds of the wicked. God's defense of justice also encourages people to confront evil behavior head-on, rather than cover it up. Although such action may involve considerable risk, those who follow the example of Esther will realize that God has placed them where they are at the right time in order to accomplish God's purposes (4:13-14).

◆ V. Haman's Decree Is Reversed (8:1-9:19)
  A. Esther Saves the Lives of the Jews (8:1-14)

On that same day King Xerxes gave the property of Haman, the enemy of the Jews, to Queen Esther. Then Mordecai was brought before the king, for Esther had told the king how they were related. ²The king took off his signet ring—which he had taken back from Haman—and gave it to Mordecai. And Esther appointed Mordecai to be in charge of Haman's property.

³Then Esther went again before the king, falling down at his feet and begging him with tears to stop the evil plot devised by Haman the Agagite against the Jews. ⁴Again the king held out the gold scepter to Esther. So she rose and stood before him.

⁵Esther said, "If it please the king, and if I have found favor with him, and if he thinks it is right, and if I am pleasing to him, let there be a decree that reverses the orders of Haman son of Hammedatha the Agagite, who ordered that Jews throughout all the king's provinces should be destroyed. ⁶For how can I endure to see my people and my family slaughtered and destroyed?"

⁷Then King Xerxes said to Queen Esther and Mordecai the Jew, "I have given Esther the property of Haman, and he has been impaled on a pole because he tried to destroy the Jews. ⁸Now go ahead and send a message to the Jews in the king's name, telling them whatever you want, and seal it with the king's signet ring. But remember that whatever has already been written in the king's name and sealed with his signet ring can never be revoked."

⁹So on June 25* the king's secretaries were summoned, and a decree was written exactly as Mordecai dictated. It was sent to the Jews and to the highest officers, the governors, and the nobles of all the 127 provinces stretching from India to Ethiopia.* The decree was written in the scripts and languages of all the peoples of the empire, including that of the Jews. ¹⁰The decree was written in the name of King Xerxes and sealed with the king's signet ring. Mordecai sent the dispatches by swift messengers, who rode fast horses especially bred for the king's service.

¹¹The king's decree gave the Jews in every city authority to unite to defend their lives. They were allowed to kill, slaughter, and annihilate anyone of any nationality or province who might attack them or their children and wives, and to take the property of their enemies. ¹²The day chosen for this event throughout all the provinces of King Xerxes was March 7 of the next year.*

¹³A copy of this decree was to be issued as law in every province and proclaimed to all peoples, so that the Jews would be ready to take revenge on their enemies on the appointed day. ¹⁴So urged on by the king's command, the messengers rode out swiftly on fast horses bred for the king's service. The same decree was also proclaimed in the fortress of Susa.

8:9a Hebrew *on the twenty-third day of the third month, the month of Sivan,* of the ancient Hebrew lunar calendar. This day was June 25, 474 B.C.; also see note on 2:16.   8:9b Hebrew *to Cush.*   8:12 Hebrew *the thirteenth day of the twelfth month, the month of Adar,* of the ancient Hebrew lunar calendar. The date selected was March 7, 473 B.C.; also see note on 2:16.

NOTES

8:1 *Xerxes gave the property of Haman, the enemy of the Jews, to Queen Esther.* Esther did not ask for a reward, but Xerxes gave her the property of Haman, the man characterized as the "enemy of the Jews" (3:10). Normally the state would confiscate the property of a traitor (Josephus *Antiquities* 11.1.3 [11.17]; Herodotus *Histories* 3.128-129). This is one of many reversals of destiny that happen in chs 7–9.

8:2 *The king took off his signet ring . . . and gave it to Mordecai.* The ring (*tabba'ath* [TH2885, ZH3192], related to Akkadian *timbu'u*), contained the king's seal, which signified his authority. Haman used the seal to authenticate the decree to destroy the Jewish people (3:10), but now his enemy Mordecai had this power. What an ironic reversal of social standing and political power (Jobes 1999:177).

8:3 *Esther went again . . . begging him with tears to stop the evil plot.* One might consider this a new audience with the king, as in 5:1-8, because the gold scepter was extended (8:4), but the verb *wattosep* [TH3254, ZH3578] (and she added) suggests a continuation of the same conversation in 8:1 (Moore 1971:77; Bush 1996:444). Bowing, begging, and tears are symbols of her strong emotional appeal. Although the king was very gracious to Esther and Mordecai, giving them things that they did not ask for in 8:1-2, the king did not do what was most important. He did not reverse Haman's decree to kill all the Jewish people in the Persian Empire (Levenson 1997:107).

8:4 *held out the gold scepter.* Since the queen was already crying in the king's presence, the raising of the scepter did not give her permission to enter his presence as in 5:2; instead, it gave approval for her to present her specific request (Fox 2001:92).

8:5 *If it please the king, and if I have found favor with him.* Esther reverted to humble royal court etiquette. These two conditional clauses (using *'im* [TH518, ZH561], "if") are followed by two implied conditional clauses without *'im* (see next note). These show deference to the king's wishes, relying on her relationship to the king and trusting in his sense of justice.

if he thinks it is right. The verb *kasher* [TH3787, ZH4178] is a late Hebrew term that refers to something being "proper, suitable, advantageous, appropriate." Esther had been around the royal court long enough to know not to demand anything, and she knew that the king would most likely act in ways that he deemed appropriate. Unfortunately, the ethics of the court seem to have been based more on what the king considered advantageous, rather than on what was morally right or wrong.

let there be a decree that reverses the orders of Haman. Lit., "Let it be written to reverse the letters Haman devised." Esther asked the king to reverse the "letters" Haman wrote, putting the blame where it belonged (no blame falls on the king; Laniak 2003:249). We do not know if she thought the king was involved with this plot. If she was aware of his rather negligent role in allowing Haman to make this decree, she ignored it at this time, for blaming the king would not likely encourage him to grant her request.

8:6 *For how can I endure to see my people and my family slaughtered and destroyed?* Lit., "For how can I see (*ra'ah* [TH7200, ZH8011]) the evil that will fall on my people, and how can I look (*ra'ah*) at the destruction of my relatives?" Esther appealed to the king's sympathy for her happiness as queen and for her love for her people.

8:7 *I have given.* The Old Greek translation makes this a rebuke, but the statement in the MT merely claims that the king's past action demonstrated that he agreed with Esther and had already been gracious to her (8:1). On the other hand, Bush maintains that the initial word, "Look" (omitted in NLT), and the emphatic use of the pronoun "And you" in 8:8 (cf. NASB) suggest that "the words are spoken in a sharp and exasperated tone" (1996:445). Laniak (2003:250) speaks of the king's "impatience," while Bush (1996:445) refers to the king's making "an exasperated concession." This fits Bush's characterization of the king as rather callous and concerned only with his own honor.

8:8 *send a message to the Jews in the king's name, telling them whatever you want.* Lit., "And you write unto the Jews." The emphatic pl. "you" (*'attem* [TH859C, ZH917]) before the imperative "write" gave responsibility to Esther and Mordecai. Xerxes empowered them to construct a message and seemed to abdicate responsibility in this matter, just as he did in 3:10.

whatever has already been written . . . can never be revoked. Lit., "but the letter which was written . . . there is not to return." This new letter could not directly revoke the king's previous decree, so it could only act to neutralize or minimize some of the impact of the previous decree. A new letter with the king's seal could give different directions and allow the Jews to take up arms if someone should choose to attack them. For all practical purposes, the effect was that the new decree gave the Jews legal protection to fight back, stripping any attackers of a favored legal position. Nevertheless, it did not remove the threat against the Jewish people.

8:9 *So on June 25 . . . a decree was written exactly as Mordecai dictated.* Lit., "in the third month, the month Sivan, on the twenty-third" (see NLT mg). This decree was written 70 days after Haman's first decree (3:12). This decree was sent to "the Jews" (Haman's decree in 3:12 was not written to the Jews), as well as to the key political leaders in all the provinces of Persia.

8:10 *swift messengers, who rode fast horses especially bred for the king's service.* It is difficult to be certain of the precise meaning of the Hebrew (cf. KJV). The first phrase, literally "runners on horses" (*haratsim bassusim* [TH7323/5483, ZH8132/6061]), is translated here as "swift messengers" (cf. Bush 1996:436, "mounted couriers"). "Fast horses" (*rekesh* [TH7409, ZH8224]) seems to refer to some royal horse, but its meaning is vague (Bush 1996:436 tentatively renders it "post-horses"). The word *ha'akhashteranim* [TH327, ZH350] is borrowed from a Persian term meaning "royal, kingdom" (Paton 1908:273; Bush 1996:436 has "from the state service"), reflected in NLT's "for the king's service." The last phrase of the verse can be taken in apposition to the preceding and speaks of "offspring of *harammakim* [TH7424, ZH8247]"; this is also a Persian term, possibly meaning "royal stud," hence NLT's "especially bred."

8:11 *authority to unite to defend their lives.* The decree allowed Jews "to gather, assemble together" (*qahal* [TH6950, ZH7735]), which could include joint planning or military training, "to defend themselves" (*'amad* [TH5975, ZH6641], "to stand"), to kill, to slaughter, and to annihilate—the exact things Haman's decree provided for against the Jews (3:13). In effect, this decree counteracts the decree of Haman (Jobes 1999:178).

anyone of any nationality or province who might attack them. Lit., "any army of people or province that attacks."

and to take the property. Mordecai's letter did not permit the Jews to start a civil war or insurrection, but to have the freedom to defend themselves and plunder property (similar to Haman's letter in 3:13).

8:12 *The day chosen . . . was March 7.* Lit., "the thirteenth of the twelfth month, the month of Adar" (see NLT mg). The Jewish forces could defend themselves in this fashion only on the day that Haman's decree had specified for killing the Jewish people. This decree did not allow for any preemptive plot before that day or a continuation of killing beyond the decree of the king.

8:13 *ready to take revenge on their enemies.* The word translated "revenge" (*naqam* [TH5358, ZH5933]) refers to the "establishment of justice" (Baldwin 1984:100-102). If the civil government and army of Persia could not exercise authority over all the parties in a conflict, the attacked party could establish justice by personally redressing a wrong committed against them or their family.

COMMENTARY

The events in the narrative take a dramatic turn toward the resolution of the problems faced by Esther and Mordecai. When Haman was removed from the scene (7:10) and exalted to the highest point, his plan to kill Mordecai on a tall pole was removed.

Yet the deeds and decrees of Haman's administration still remained in force and would be carried out if there was no intervention. Esther had to marshal her will and resources to reverse the decree that Haman had sent with the king's seal (3:8-15).

Esther strengthened her position of influence and reinforced her ability to bring about change by telling the king about her relationship with Mordecai (8:1). The king had already rewarded Mordecai (6:10-12), but now the king realized that this loyal servant who saved his life (2:21-23) could fill Haman's position. In this stark reversal, Haman was executed, Mordecai was delivered, and Mordecai received Haman's former status and power (8:2). Justice was established by having the Jewish person who exposed Haman inherit his possessions, for this is what Haman wanted to happen when people killed the Jews (3:13). A further reversal is observed when Esther appointed Mordecai to manage Haman's property, which the king gave to her. The irony is overpowering.

But Haman's long legacy of evil was not yet totally erased from history. Esther probably wished that the king could reverse Haman's decree to slaughter the Jews right after Haman was killed, but that did not happen and apparently could not legally happen in this Persian culture. This meant that she would need to intercede with the king again in order to deliver her people from this curse. This time she was much more emotional (8:3) than on her previous visit (5:1-4) and much more insistent on raising the issue of Haman's plot against her people. Because of these changes in her approach, it appears that she felt the danger was much greater now than when she made her original request. Although she avoided casting any blame on the king, she asked the unusual favor of reversing a law signed with the king's own seal. She could not accuse the king of evil or injustice, so she asked if it might not be the "right, proper" thing to do. To this she added a more personal plea, "if I have found favor with [the king]" (8:5), which played on the sympathies of the king. This comment was meant to take advantage of her good relationship with the king at the time.

Surprisingly, she did not even mention that this decree would also require that she and Mordecai be slaughtered. Instead, she focused on the misery of seeing her own innocent people slaughtered (8:6). Finally, the king agreed, though he distanced himself from the task (8:7-8). The king's only concern was in defending his reputation and the law, ensuring that this new decree should not "revoke" the previous decree. These factors heighten the reader's perception that God was enabling Mordecai and Esther to do something impossible in Persian law, but possible through divine intervention and guidance.

The details of writing and sending the new decree (8:9-10) purposely match the account of the sending of Haman's decree in 3:12. This new decree would be just as official (written by the king's scribal secretaries), sent to the same important people as the first decree (the highest political officers), written in all the same languages throughout the kingdom, sealed by the same ring of the king, but this important message was delivered by messengers on fast horses so that the word would get out quickly.

The difference is in the content of the decree and its dissemination to all the Jewish communities in the empire (8:9). This decree allowed the Jewish people to put together a coordinated defense plan to combat anyone who might try to carry out Haman's earlier decree. This new decree did not repeal or fully negate Haman's earlier decree; it only gave the Jewish people the ability to meet deadly force with deadly force. It discouraged aggressive action against Jewish people by approving similar aggressive action against any attacker. The purpose was not to give any group permission to go out and slaughter anyone at will; it merely assured that justice and a fair playing field would be established.

This narrative raises questions about how believers should respond when their lives are threatened with violence. We know that Jesus told his disciples to "offer the other cheek" (Matt 5:39) when they are attacked, and we know that Paul willingly suffered great persecution (2 Cor 11:23-27) for the cause of Christ. But these examples speak of personal attacks on people spreading the gospel, which is different from the mass annihilation of an ethnic and religious community. In this case, it is proper to defend the cause of justice for the weak, the widow, and the orphan and to reprove the ruthless who oppress them (Deut 24:17; Ps 82:3; Isa 1:17). Thus, Esther and Mordecai as government officials were right to try to reverse the injustice done by Haman against the innocent Jewish people. Because the Persian decree of the king could not be revoked, the only option was to give those attacked the right to defend themselves when they were attacked.

◆   **B. The Enemies of the Jews Are Killed (8:15–9:19)**

[15]Then Mordecai left the king's presence, wearing the royal robe of blue and white, the great crown of gold, and an outer cloak of fine linen and purple. And the people of Susa celebrated the new decree. [16]The Jews were filled with joy and gladness and were honored everywhere. [17]In every province and city, wherever the king's decree arrived, the Jews rejoiced and had a great celebration and declared a public festival and holiday. And many of the people of the land became Jews themselves, for they feared what the Jews might do to them.

CHAPTER 9

So on March 7* the two decrees of the king were put into effect. On that day, the enemies of the Jews had hoped to overpower them, but quite the opposite happened. It was the Jews who overpowered their enemies. [2]The Jews gathered in their cities throughout all the king's provinces to attack anyone who tried to harm them. But no one could make a stand against them, for everyone was afraid of them.

[3]And all the nobles of the provinces, the highest officers, the governors, and the royal officials helped the Jews for fear of Mordecai. [4]For Mordecai had been promoted in the king's palace, and his fame spread throughout all the provinces as he became more and more powerful.

[5]So the Jews went ahead on the appointed day and struck down their enemies with the sword. They killed and annihilated their enemies and did as they pleased with those who hated them. [6]In the fortress of Susa itself, the Jews killed 500 men. [7]They also killed Parshandatha, Dalphon, Aspatha, [8]Poratha, Adalia, Aridatha, [9]Parmashta, Arisai, Aridai, and Vaizatha—[10]the ten sons of Haman son of Hammedatha, the enemy of the Jews. But they did not take any plunder.

[11]That very day, when the king was informed of the number of people killed in the fortress of Susa, [12]he called for Queen Esther. He said, "The Jews have killed 500 men in the fortress of Susa alone, as well as Haman's ten sons. If they have done that here, what has happened in the

rest of the provinces? But now, what more do you want? It will be granted to you; tell me and I will do it."

¹³ Esther responded, "If it please the king, give the Jews in Susa permission to do again tomorrow as they have done today, and let the bodies of Haman's ten sons be impaled on a pole."

¹⁴ So the king agreed, and the decree was announced in Susa. And they impaled the bodies of Haman's ten sons. ¹⁵ Then the Jews at Susa gathered together on March 8* and killed 300 more men, and again they took no plunder.

¹⁶ Meanwhile, the other Jews throughout the king's provinces had gathered together to defend their lives. They gained relief from all their enemies, killing 75,000 of those who hated them. But they did not take any plunder. ¹⁷ This was done throughout the provinces on March 7, and on March 8 they rested,* celebrating their victory with a day of feasting and gladness. ¹⁸ (The Jews at Susa killed their enemies on March 7 and again on March 8, then rested on March 9,* making that their day of feasting and gladness.) ¹⁹ So to this day, rural Jews living in remote villages celebrate an annual festival and holiday on the appointed day in late winter,* when they rejoice and send gifts of food to each other.

9:1 Hebrew *on the thirteenth day of the twelfth month, the month of Adar,* of the ancient Hebrew lunar calendar. This day was March 7, 473 B.C.; also see note on 2:16.   9:15 Hebrew *the fourteenth day of the month of Adar,* of the Hebrew lunar calendar. This day was March 8, 473 B.C.; also see note on 2:16.   9:17 Hebrew *on the thirteenth day of the month of Adar, and on the fourteenth day they rested.* These days were March 7 and 8, 473 B.C.; also see note on 2:16.   9:18 Hebrew *killed their enemies on the thirteenth day and the fourteenth day, and then rested on the fifteenth day,* of the Hebrew month of Adar.   9:19 Hebrew *on the fourteenth day of the month of Adar.* This day of the Hebrew lunar calendar occurs in February or March.

NOTES

8:15 *the royal robe of blue and white, the great crown of gold.* Mordecai did not become king, but he retired from the king's chamber clothed with all the signs of great power (*tekeleth* [TH8504, ZH9418] is probably "violet," not "blue"; see note on 1:6; Paton 1908:279) and authority (*'atarah* [TH5850, ZH6498] is a "turban," not a traditional "crown"; Bush 1996:436). Pictures and stone carvings of Persian royalty (the treasury relief) show the turban-like hat the Persians wore (Yamauchi 1990:145). The "gold" could hypothetically refer to the color of the turban, but it more likely refers to gold ornaments that were affixed on this turban. What a reversal from the mourning clothes Mordecai wore in 4:1-2 (Jobes 1999:178). Mordecai's brief wearing of the royal attire in 6:10-11 proved to be a positive omen, as Haman's wife predicted in 6:12-13, of a much greater rise to power here in ch 8.

the people of Susa celebrated the new decree. Lit., "the city of Susa shouted and rejoiced." Susa's confusion after Haman's original decree (3:15) was reversed (Laniak 2003:251); now there was great rejoicing by all the people of Susa, not just the Jews.

8:16 *The Jews were filled with joy and gladness and were honored everywhere.* Lit., "And to the Jews there was light and gladness, joy and honor." Mourning, weeping, darkness, and lamenting disappeared (a reversal of 4:3; Levenson 1997:116) because a new era in Jewish history had dawned. Before, the Jewish people had no hope, but now there was great joy as they looked to the future. "Light" (*'orah* [TH219, ZH245]) represents hope, the reverse of darkness; "joy" (*simkhah* [TH8057, ZH8525]) describes their emotional exuberance.

8:17 *many . . . became Jews themselves, for they feared what the Jews might do to them.* "Many" is left undefined. The interpretation of "becoming Jews" out of fear is problematic. Did they "become Jews" (Hitpael stem of *yahad* [TH3054, ZH3366]) by conversion (Clines 1984b:318) or just "identify themselves" (Levenson 1997:117) with the Jewish cause? Fear of God would suggest conversion, but not fear of man, as is the case in this verse. Levenson thinks that full conversion is not necessarily in view here; instead, this refers to people joining or identifying with the Jews. This might mean that they adopted Jewish customs and practices (Fox 1991:112). Bush also questions Clines's view that full conversions are in view because it was not God who convinced these people to change; it was the political power of Esther, Mordecai, and the Jewish community that influenced their decision (1996:448-449). Probably both interpretations are partially true; some people identified with the Jews because of their political power, but there is no reason to deny that some Persians were truly converted to believe in the Hebrew God after what he accomplished on behalf of his people.

9:1 *hoped to overpower them, but quite the opposite happened.* Some people hoped "to have mastery over" (*shalat* [TH7980, ZH8948]) their Jewish neighbors, but "it was turned" (*hapak* [TH2015, ZH2200]) so that the Jewish people gained mastery over them (this is another reversal; cf. Jobes 1999:119; Laniak 2003:254-255). Because chs 9–10 are said to have "an unsavory morality . . . surrealism" and are "clumsy," Clines (1984b:320) attributes them to a later, inferior author. But Bush (1996:458-460) rightly counters the arguments that support Clines's interpretation.

9:2 *no one could make a stand against them, for everyone was afraid.* Not being able to "stand" (*'amad* [TH5975, ZH6641]) does not imply there were no attacks (see 9:6-16) or that no Jews were ever killed. But no group successfully stood against the Jews; all were defeated. There is no indication this was fear (*pakhad* [TH6343, ZH7065]) of God (Baldwin 1984:103). These people were afraid of the power of Mordecai and the Persian support he had gained through the cooperative efforts of local satraps and governors (9:3).

9:3 *the royal officials helped the Jews for fear of Mordecai.* The highest government officials and administrators "supported" (*nasa'* [TH5375, ZH5951], "were lifting up") the Jewish people because Haman was dead and Mordecai was in power. Clines (1984b:322) attributes this to a fear of the God of the Jews, but Levenson (1997:120) rejects this option. Since the king favored Esther and Mordecai and entrusted Mordecai with the king's ring, Mordecai's word carried great power. When the tide turns and a new leader is installed, lower government officials know that if they hope to stay in power or get ahead, it is best to cooperate and develop a healthy fear of the one who has the power.

9:4 *his fame spread.* Mordecai was "great" in status, and his "report, reputation" (*shoma'* [TH8089, ZH9053]) was also great. Levenson (1997:121) compares this to Moses's high status in the eyes of the Egyptians (cf. Exod 11:3), but the two situations are quite different. Moses was honored not because he was a powerful politician but because the God of Israel miraculously used him to announce the plagues on Egypt and the defeat of their gods (Exod 7–12). In contrast, Mordecai did no miracles and did not destroy Persia or its gods. Mordecai was honored because he was a powerful politician.

9:5 *did as they pleased with those who hated them.* To some this does not sound like self-defense (Huey 1988:833). Doing "as they pleased" (*kirtsonam* [TH7522, ZH8356]) relates to acting with imperial backing, as in Ezra 9:7-9 (Clines 1984b:322), not to wild, indiscriminate killing. Paton (1908:283) understands this as aggressive offensive action by Jews, but Bush (1996:463-464) and Fox (1991:220-226) rightly interpret this as justified defensive action within the limits of the king's decrees. "Those who hated them" would refer to the enemies who attempted to kill the Jews.

9:6 *In the fortress of Susa itself, the Jews killed 500 men.* A revolt by 500 men was suppressed in the palace (viewed as hyperbole by Fox [2001:110]). These probably were close supporters, relatives, and the sons of Haman. In light of the rejoicing throughout Susa in 8:17 and the strong support for and fear of Mordecai in 9:3-4, it is surprising to find such a large group of people still resisting and attacking the Jews within the palace citadel.

9:7-10 *the ten sons of Haman.* The sons of Haman probably tried to avenge their father's death by killing Mordecai. Now everything that Haman had boasted about (5:11) was gone, even his ten sons. By naming each one in this long list, the narrative emphasizes the great loss—one son after another, after another, even to the very last one. These names are arranged in many traditional Hebrew texts (such as Codex Aleppo) in an unusual way, with only one name per line of text. This arrangement attracts attention to Haman's great loss and underscores just how many were killed (Josh 12:9-24 has a similar listing of enemies who were defeated).

9:10 *did not take any plunder.* Taking plunder was permitted (8:11); but with pure motives, the Jewish people rejected the defiled wealth of Haman's sons. Jobes (1999:196-198) traces this practice of not taking booty to the Israelite practices in holy war. Abram did not take any booty when he was offered a reward for saving Lot and the king of Sodom (Gen 14), the Israelites were not to take any booty when they defeated Jericho (Josh 6, but Achan sinned and did take booty), and Saul failed to utterly destroy the Amalekites and sinned by saving some of the good cattle and their king (1 Sam 15). The Jewish decision to not take booty is emphasized by its repetition in 9:10, 15, 16, so Jobes (1999:196) concludes that the Jews understood this to be holy war. In addition, this practice indicates that the Jews were disciplined and not motivated by personal greed (Laniak 2003:258).

9:12 *If they have done that here, what has happened in the rest of the provinces?* "If they have done that here" is not in the Hebrew text. The number of people killed did not disturb the king, for he allowed another day of fighting (9:14-15). Bush (1996:475) considers the king's statement (taken as an approval of what happened) as the grounds for Esther's request in the next verse.

9:13 *give . . . permission to do again tomorrow.* "Give . . . permission" is literally "give . . . according to the decree" (*dath* [TH1881, ZH2017]). Esther knew that some of their enemies in the palace escaped into Susa and might plan to get revenge for the death of Haman at some later date. Thus the Jews in Susa were again allowed to assemble together, defend themselves, kill any attackers (8:11), and avenge themselves of their enemies (8:13). Paton (1908:287) castigates Esther for this horrible, unjustified request, while Fox (1991:112) thinks Esther was punitive and somewhat vindictive, quite the opposite of the sweet, innocent girl in earlier chapters. Jobes (1999:201) even suggests that Esther got her name from this incident, for the people were naming her after Ishtar, the goddess of love and war, but there is no textual basis for this hypothesis. Some condemn Esther as power hungry and wicked, while others defend her action because there still were many vile enemies in Susa not killed on the first day.

9:14 *the decree was announced.* This new decree (*dath* [TH1881, ZH2017]) paralleled the earlier one but applied to the next day and to the city outside the palace. The public display of the dead bodies of Haman's sons probably escalated tension, but it was a common ancient Near Eastern custom that was intended to humiliate the defeated enemy (cf. 1 Sam 31, where Saul's and Jonathan's bodies were hung in shame).

9:15 *again they took no plunder.* The Jews took the high moral ground and did not take plunder as they were legally permitted to do (8:11; 9:10).

9:16 *killing 75,000 of those who hated them.* Seventy-five thousand is quite a large number. The Old Greek translation has 15,000; the First Targum has 75,000; the Greek Alpha text has 70,100; but Josephus, like MT, has 75,000 (*Antiquities* 11.6.13 [11.291]). Since the word for "thousands" (*'elep* [TH504A/505, ZH547]) also means "families," it is possible that 75 extended families (clans) were killed.

9:17 *on March 8 they rested . . . with a day of feasting.* Lit., "on the fourteenth day [of Adar] they rested" (see NLT mg). In 9:16, the people "gained relief" (*nuakh* [TH5117, ZH5663]), and now they "rested" (again, *nuakh*), so Purim became the day when they remembered that they had "relief" (9:22) from their enemies.

9:18 *rested on March 9, making that their day of feasting.* This parenthetical comment (see NLT mg) explains why the Purim celebration happened at different times at different places. Since the fighting lasted one day longer in Susa, their celebration was one day later.

9:19 *Jews living in remote villages . . . rejoice and send gifts of food to each other.* Later practice continued the tradition of celebrating Purim on different days (cf. 9:21, 27). The exchange of "gifts of food" (*manoth* [TH4490, ZH4950], "choice portions"; 2:9; Neh 8:10-12) demonstrated their unity and care for one another and spread joy to everyone at the festival.

COMMENTARY

The reversal of Haman's plot took place on the very day Haman identified as a lucky day for destroying the Jews (9:1; cf. 3:7). On that day the enemies of the Jews could follow Haman's decree to kill their Jewish neighbors and take their property (3:13), but the Jews could follow Mordecai's decree and defend themselves and take the property of their enemies (8:11-12). The Jewish people gained mastery over their enemies in several ways. First, the Jewish people in Persia helped themselves by uniting together in all the cities where they lived in order to defend one another (9:2). Second, the Persian nobles, politicians, and government officials saw that somehow, someway, something (possibly God) brought the Jews through an almost miraculous set of "coincidental circumstances" in the king's palace that ended with Esther revealing to the king Haman's plan. They knew that Haman's attempt to annihilate all the Jews had backfired. They also knew that Haman was dead and Mordecai was in power. Common sense, therefore, dictated that it would be wise to side with the Jewish cause at this time. Third, Mordecai had become very popular and famous among the people of Persia (9:4), so an official would have to ignore public opinion if he went against Mordecai's wishes.

Finally, the miraculous reversal that rescued Mordecai from death and brought Esther and Mordecai great power caused many Persian citizens to "identify with" the Jews. Although some believe these people were converts, one has to question why they wanted to become Jews (see note on 8:17). Did they change just because they feared the Jewish people would kill them, or was this a true fear of the God of Israel that resulted in repentance? Since God is not mentioned, it appears that people saw that Haman was mistreating innocent people. Therefore, many sided with the Jewish perspective against Haman's decree. They also feared the Jews because Esther and Mordecai fought to preserve and defend the Jews, plus King Xerxes had sided with them. This identification probably caused some to actually convert to worship the God of Israel, but for the majority, this identification with the Jews was a political decision of expediency to protect themselves. Another key factor in this narrative is the silent and unseen hand of God sovereignly controlling the life of every person in the story. Although his name is absent, God's providential presence is felt undergirding both Mordecai and Esther, delivering his people once again from the threat of annihilation (comparable in a few broad ways with the Exodus deliverance).

When that fateful day arrived, the day that Haman had set as the time to kill all the Jews in the empire, there were some people around who dearly wanted to carry out Haman's wishes. Although they wanted "control over" their Jewish neighbors (see note on 9:1), to dominate them and determine their future, the Jewish people gained "control over" them. This deliverance is not attributed to God's intervention in the text, but certainly every believer must assume that God was the real source of deliverance for the Israelite people on that day. The people were ready to defend themselves and go after anyone who would dare to harm their people, but God gave an overwhelming victory. The Jews fought to protect themselves so that those who tried to stand against them would fail, but this victory was not just due to their efforts. Many did not join in this fight because they feared the Jews. Could this fear actually be a fear of Israel's God, who had vindicated the righteous cause of the Jews through the events described in the last few chapters?

Mordecai's rapid rise to power enabled him to control more and more areas of the government. His fame and power brought him a respected reputation so that people in government obeyed his words (9:4). People saw that Mordecai was the man in charge, so they knew it would not be wise for them to oppose him. When the appointed day arrived, the Persian people did not see a Jewish attack on defenseless people or a ruthless, uncontrolled killing spree to take revenge on their enemies. The Jewish people were allowed to do "as they pleased" (9:5) without governmental interference from troops; thus, the forces of Haman were not successful in doing as they pleased against the Jews (3:11). This statement simply means that the Jewish people, with the aid and cooperation of government forces, were victorious in defending themselves against those who hated them (which was the Jews' intent) while Haman's sympathizers lost this battle, and 75,000 were killed.

It is hard to judge the significance of the slaughter on that day. Five hundred men in the palace (9:6) and 300 in Susa (9:15) sounds like a lot, but there is no way of knowing how many thousands of people were unaffected by these conflicts. One would expect many supporters of Haman to be present in the palace and in Susa. The 75,000 in the rest of the provinces (9:16) sounds like a very high number, and some doubt that the Persian king would have allowed the Jews to kill that many people (Clines 1984b:257). Although these are surprising events, Cicero (*Pro Lege manilia* 7) refers to all the Romans in the province of Asia being slaughtered in the first century BC by Mithridates VI of Pontus (a ruler who claimed Persian descent); it is estimated that 80,000 to 100,000 Romans were killed. Herodotus (*Histories* 1.106; 3.79) mentions the slaughter of large numbers of Scythians by Cyaxares and the Medes and magi by the Persians. (The magi were Medes who functioned as a tribe of priests in the Persian Empire, according to Herodotus in *Histories* 1.101-132. This fits with the description of the wise men in Daniel.)

No historical documents disprove the authenticity of these numbers, and other historical accounts confirm that similar incidents happened. There is no indication that the king was angry about the death of all these people, for he was probably more concerned with establishing political stability in the empire. It was not in the king's interest to have warring parties within the palace plotting to kill one another, so it was best to get the opposition identified and eliminated so that no further problems would undermine the peace of the empire.

The Jews declined to take the property of any people they killed, even though the king's decree allowed them to do so. Many years earlier Abram had refused a portion of the plunder from the king of Sodom (Gen 14:21-23; Baldwin 1984.105). Then, as in Mordecai's day, there seems to have been a desire to act ethically, in a way that was above reproach, in order to avoid any criticism that the Jews became rich by taking advantage of others, and to separate themselves and not obligate themselves in any way to ungodly people.

The celebration of Purim began that very year. The Jews did not celebrate the death of their enemies, but that they had "rest" from their enemies, an important theological concept of the covenant. They always looked forward to that day when they would receive God's blessing of peace and rest (see Deut 25:19; Josh 21:44; 2 Sam 7:11). Another aspect of Purim was the exchange of "gifts of food" (9:19). These acts of kindness strengthened the unity of the people, demonstrated that they cared for one another, and encouraged an atmosphere of joy for everyone celebrating the festival. God's name is not mentioned in regard to this festival, but surely they must have thanked God on this day for their deliverance from Haman.

◆ VI. The Festival of Purim (9:20-32)

20Mordecai recorded these events and sent letters to the Jews near and far, throughout all the provinces of King Xerxes, 21calling on them to celebrate an annual festival on these two days.* 22He told them to celebrate these days with feasting and gladness and by giving gifts of food to each other and presents to the poor. This would commemorate a time when the Jews gained relief from their enemies, when their sorrow was turned into gladness and their mourning into joy.

23So the Jews accepted Mordecai's proposal and adopted this annual custom. 24Haman son of Hammedatha the Agagite, the enemy of the Jews, had plotted to crush and destroy them on the date determined by casting lots (the lots were called purim). 25But when Esther came before the king, he issued a decree causing Haman's evil plot to backfire, and Haman and his sons were impaled on a sharpened pole. 26That is why this celebration is called Purim, because it is the ancient word for casting lots.

So because of Mordecai's letter and because of what they had experienced, 27the Jews throughout the realm agreed to inaugurate this tradition and to pass it on to their descendants and to all who became Jews. They declared they would never fail to celebrate these two prescribed days at the appointed time each year. 28These days would be remembered and kept from generation to generation and celebrated by every family throughout the provinces and cities of the empire. This Festival of Purim would never cease to be celebrated among the Jews, nor would the memory of what happened ever die out among their descendants.

29Then Queen Esther, the daughter of Abihail, along with Mordecai the Jew, wrote another letter putting the queen's full authority behind Mordecai's letter to establish the Festival of Purim. 30Letters wishing peace and security were sent to the Jews throughout the 127 provinces of the empire of Xerxes. 31These letters established the Festival of Purim—an annual celebration of these days at the appointed time, decreed by both Mordecai the Jew and Queen Esther. (The people decided to observe this festival, just as they had decided for themselves and their descendants to establish the times of fasting and mourning.) [32] So the command of Esther confirmed the practices of Purim, and it was all written down in the records.

9:21 Hebrew *on the fourteenth and fifteenth days of Adar,* of the Hebrew lunar calendar.

NOTES

9:20 *Mordecai recorded these events.* When the text says that Mordecai recorded "these things" (*hadebarim* [TH1697, ZH1821] *ha'elleh*), one could assume that it refers to the preceding events in 1:1–9:19, or at least a summary of most of what is in the book of Esther. But some (Paton 1908:292; Moore 1971:93) reject this approach and suggest Mordecai wrote about the institution of Purim in the court annals (9:21-22). Laniak (2003:262) suggests that this would have included "the battle report and at least a summary of the events recorded in chs 1–8," while Bush (1996:479) concludes that this writing was meant to "obligate the Jews to the annual celebration of the festival" and "must have included at least a précis of the events that led to Haman's edict," similar to what is found in 9:24-25. It is most unlikely that the content of Mordecai's letter was the present biblical book of Esther, but it had to be a summary of what is included here (the threat by Haman, the resolution that came through Esther, and the final deliverance of the Jews from annihilation) because this letter and the experience of the Jews at that time led to the establishment of Purim (9:26-27).

9:21 *calling on them.* Mordecai did more than call; he "established, validated, authorized" (Piel stem of *qum* [TH6965, ZH7756]) the legitimacy of this feast. Bush (1996:479) understands Mordecai to be "imposing, requiring, making binding" this festival on the Jewish people, but it seems more likely that he was officially establishing or authorizing this celebration, not imposing it on them.

9:22 *gained relief from their enemies, when their sorrow was turned into gladness.* The "relief" (or "rest") came after the resolution of the problem (cf. 2:18). This depicts a time when the bad things "were overturned" (*hapak,* as in 9:1; see note). This kind of celebration is often connected with the coming of God's salvation in eschatological texts in the prophets (Isa 35:10; 51:11; 61:3; Jer 31:13), but here it is related to the transformation of the situation in the time of Mordecai and Esther.

9:23-26a *the Jews accepted.* These verses summarize the institutionalization of the Purim festival. In certain respects, the text addresses the situation from a perspective some years after the event (cf. 9:19). As Bush (1996:487) comments, verse 23a "refers not only to the original spontaneous celebrations, but also, and principally, to the (differing) regular celebrations that they have already adopted." Acceptance implies the adoption (Bush 1996:480) of this new holiday as a custom. The institutionalization of Purim did not require the Jews in Persia to do something different from the past. It simply means that the Jewish people gladly agreed with what Mordecai said and did, so they continued in what they had already practiced for some time.

9:24 *casting lots (the lots were called* purim*).* There are two different words for "lots": one used to describe the lots used by the diviners in 3:6-7, which picked the unlucky day to execute the Jews, and then a different word for "lots" in 9:26 (it is also in the explanation in 3:7 "the lots were called *purim*"), which refers to the Jewish festival. So there is an ironic pun (Bush 1996:483) or double entendre (Jobes 1999:215) on the word "lots." The use of the term here reminds one how the evil "lots" (*goral* [TH1486, ZH1598]) cast to destroy the Jews have now ironically become the good "lots" (*purim* [TH6332, ZH7052]) that describe the festival commemorating the deliverance of the Jews from Haman's plan.

This summary of events (9:24-25) is unusually short, never mentions the role of Mordecai, and does not adequately represent all that happened; therefore, it probably is an extreme summary of Mordecai's letter. This version gives all the credit of foiling Haman's plot to the king, thus the monarchy is honored and positioned on the side of the Jews. The political reason for this spin on the news is unknown. Maybe the Jews in Persia knew of the great deeds of Mordecai and Esther but were unsure of the king's support.

9:25 But when Esther came before the king. Lit., "and when she came before the king." The NIV understands the pronoun to refer to "the plot" that came to the king's attention, while LXX has "when he [meaning Haman] came to the king." Although Esther is not mentioned by name, the third-person fem. verb form probably refers to her.

sharpened pole. This is simply "the tree" or "the pole" in Hebrew (*'ets* [TH6086, ZH6770]). Cf. notes on 2:23 and 5:14.

9:27 to all who became Jews. These could be proselytes, as NLT suggests (cf. Clines 1984b:328; Laniak 2003:264), or just those who "joined" (*nilwim* [TH3867, ZH4277]) the Jews in the celebration (8:17 uses a different term for the word "join, identify"). This is a future-oriented provision concerning those who might celebrate Purim with the Jews.

would never fail to celebrate. Using terminology similar to the Exodus, their commitment was to "not pass over" (*lo' ya'abor* [TH5674, ZH6296]), meaning "never cease" to celebrate these events. This suggests a strong commitment, almost an oath, to never forget.

9:28 remembered and kept. These instructions are reminiscent of the earlier ones found in the Pentateuch; the people were to remember and keep God's laws and feasts (Exod 13:3; 20:8). The sense again points to the hope of future celebrations (Bush 1996:484), not just to the observance of this festival in Esther's day (Fox 1991:132).

9:29-32 Queen Esther . . . wrote another letter . . . confirmed the practices of Purim. Esther is again fully introduced as the daughter of Abihail, matching the earlier introduction of Esther at the beginning of the story in 2:15. The difference is that at this point her Persian identity (Queen Esther) is merged with her Jewish identity (Jobes 1999:222). Although it seems somewhat redundant in light of Mordecai's earlier proclamation, it appears that Mordecai and Esther's letter was another effort to legitimate Purim as an official festival. It is unclear why this second letter was needed. It is also not clear why this letter that was written by both Mordecai and Esther (9:29) is later referred to as only Esther's command (9:32). Bush (1996:487) distinguishes the command of 9:32 from the second letter mentioned in 9:29, although Clines (1984b:331) and Jobes (1999:223) are probably correct to view this as a reference to the second letter.

9:32 it was all written down in the records. The title of the "book, scroll" (*seper* [TH5612, ZH6219]) that contained these things is not stated. This probably refers to the Persian royal court annals (6:1; 10:2).

COMMENTARY

Two important factors stand out in this section. First, Mordecai and Esther were aggressive in making Purim a continual Jewish holiday so that all future generations would remember how the Hebrew people were providentially delivered from near annihilation at the hand of a powerful but evil Persian man. They wanted every Jewish person in the empire to know what had happened in the courts of government. Their primary purposes seem to have been (1) to introduce people to this new festival, (2) to justify and establish this festival as a normal part of Jewish life, and (3) to explain why this festival was important. They did not address the question of whether it was legitimate to add a festival to the ones God established in Exodus 23; they just presented it as a comparable opportunity to rejoice. Writing down these events assured later readers that the details were correct and that people in faraway parts of the empire would know exactly what happened. The fact that both Mordecai and Esther sent out separate letters demonstrates how serious these leaders were about establishing this new festival. They wanted the Jewish people to remember what had happened.

Secondary reasons for promoting this festival might include (1) the desire to make it known that these two key people risked their lives to protect their people. Hopefully their example might inspire others to stand up to later threats of persecution and do everything possible to oppose evil. (2) Remembering to celebrate this festival would remind people that God was watching over and protecting his people in ways they often did not see or understand, so that others would not lose hope when days looked dark and they were being persecuted. Although these secondary purposes are left unstated, they seem to be natural implications that would inspire people when they celebrated Purim.

Another emphasis in this paragraph is that this festival is a time of joy, rejoicing, and celebration. Some other festivals were times of mourning (9:31), but this was an occasion to joyously commemorate the peace and rest they could enjoy because Haman's evil had been defeated. This festival is not described as a religious time of joyous worship for those who could travel to the Temple in Jerusalem. It was to be a time of celebration that every family and neighborhood could celebrate no matter where they lived. These factors made this festival relevant to all Jewish people, for many people throughout the Persian world faced various levels of opposition for cultural, social, or religious reasons. This celebration would give them hope in a hostile world. If God could sovereignly work out the details for Mordecai and Esther, certainly he could powerfully work out the problems in the Jews' lives.

The festival of Purim is called "the day of Mordecai" in 2 Maccabees 15:36. Josephus (*Antiquities* 11.6.13) mentions Purim as being celebrated during his lifetime (first century AD). The festival is not mentioned in the New Testament (though the unnamed festival in John 5:1 might have been Purim). Today many Jews still commemorate Purim with joyful synagogue services and the giving of presents to the poor.

◆ VII. The Greatness of Mordecai (10:1-3)

King Xerxes imposed a tribute throughout his empire, even to the distant coastlands. [2]His great achievements and the full account of the greatness of Mordecai, whom the king had promoted, are recorded in *The Book of the History of the Kings of Media and Persia.* [3]Mordecai the Jew became the prime minister, with authority next to that of King Xerxes himself. He was very great among the Jews, who held him in high esteem, because he continued to work for the good of his people and to speak up for the welfare of all their descendants.

NOTES

10:1 *Xerxes imposed a tribute.* Persian taxes on the provinces were a very heavy burden because of the free spending of the Persian government. Levenson (1997:132) suggests that this decision to tax may indicate that Mordecai had persuaded the king not to follow Haman's methods, but instead to realize that "peaceful taxation rather than plundering was the best way to fill the royal coffers." The province of Babylon supplied four months of support for the central administration, while the other provinces covered the other eight months (Baldwin 1984:115). The relevance of this event to the story about Mordecai is unclear; possibly it implies a time of stability when new taxes could be imposed and new government projects initiated.

10:2 *His great achievements.* The book ends as it began, praising the greatness and power of Xerxes, the ruler of Persia. Equally great was Mordecai, whose deeds were recorded in Persian history (though to date these documents have not been recovered by archaeologists).

10:3 *Mordecai the Jew became the prime minister. . . . He was very great among the Jews.* Mordecai did not brag like Haman did (5:11-12). Mordecai was famous because he had a high government position. He had great authority, and people gave this man high esteem. He was a righteous man who continually looked out for the good of his people.

COMMENTARY

The narrative ends with an official statement that Mordecai was permanently appointed the prime minister of Persia. His legacy is recorded with references to how greatly he was honored, the height of his political power, the extent of his approval by the people of Persia, and his deeds of kindness to others. Although one may be surprised to find no mention of Esther in this conclusion, her power and position as queen never changed. She was the instrument God used to draw attention to the evil plan of Haman, but Mordecai was the one who opposed Haman, informed Esther of Haman's plot, reversed the decree of Haman, and was transformed from one persecuted to a man in power. Of all the Jewish people, Mordecai was condemned and strongly hated by Haman, yet his destiny was reversed so that he eventually took Haman's place in the palace.

Mordecai, who had no greatness or power in the early part of the narrative, eventually became the second-in-command in Persia. Mordecai's first deeds of kindness toward the king were written down but forgotten (2:21-23; 6:1-3), but these verses indicate that his later deeds of kindness were not ignored by the people of Persia or forgotten by the king. Although the secular court annals of Persia did not survive the wars of history, Esther and Mordecai's deeds were eventually included in the Old Testament, demonstrating that God was intent on preserving the legacy of his great servants. Their boldness and courage should inspire every reader to oppose evil and serve God no matter where he has placed them. Their roles in society were important, and the things that happened to them were not mere coincidence. So also God has put believers where they are to use them to change the course of history. In faith believers can act boldly, believing that God's sovereign hand is still shaping the course of history in astounding ways that can reverse the plans of evil men.

BIBLIOGRAPHY

Baldwin, J. G.
1984 *Esther: An Introduction and Commentary.* Tyndale Old Testament Commentary. Downers Grove, IL: InterVarsity.

Beckwith, R.
1985 *The Old Testament Canon of the New Testament Church.* Grand Rapids: Eerdmans.

Berg, S.
1979 *The Book of Esther: Motifs, Themes, and Structure.* Chico, CA: Scholars Press.

Breneman, M.
1993 *Ezra, Nehemiah, Esther.* New American Commentary. Nashville: Broadman & Holman.

Brockington, L. H.
1969 *Ezra, Nehemiah, and Esther.* London: Nelson.

Bronger, H. A.
1970 Fasting in Israel and in Post-biblical Times. *Old Testament Studies* 20:1-21.

Bush, F.
1996 *Ruth/Esther.* Word Biblical Commentary 9. Dallas: Word.

Clines, D. J.
1984a *The Esther Scroll.* Sheffield: Journal for the Study of the Old Testament Press.

1984b *Ezra, Nehemiah, Esther.* New Century Bible Commentary. Grand Rapids: Eerdmans.

Cook, H. J.
1969 The A-Text of the Greek Version of the Book of Esther. *Zeitschrift für die alttestamentliche Wissenschaft* 81:369-376.

Fox, M. V.
1991 *The Redaction of the Esther Scroll.* Atlanta: Journal of Biblical Literature.

2001 *Character and Ideology in the Book of Esther.* Grand Rapids: Eerdmans.

Gaster, T. H.
1950 *Purim and Hanukkah in Custom and Tradition.* New York: Abelard-Schuman.

Gordis, R.
1976 Studies in the Esther Narrative. *Journal of Biblical Literature* 95:43-58.

1981 Religion, Wisdom and History in the Book of Esther—A New Solution to an Ancient Crux. *Journal of Biblical Literature* 100:359-388.

Greenstein, E. L.
1987 A Jewish Reading of Esther. Pp. 225-243 in *Jewish Perspectives on Ancient Israel.* Editor, J. Neusner. Philadelphia: Fortress.

Huey, B. F.
1988 Esther. Pp. 773-840 in *The Expositor's Bible Commentary*, vol. 4. Editor, F. Gaebelein. Grand Rapids: Zondervan.

Jobes, K. H.
1999 *Esther.* NIV Application Commentary. Grand Rapids: Zondervan.

Keil, C. F.
1956 *The Books of Ezra, Nehemiah, and Esther.* Biblical Commentary on the Old Testament. Grand Rapids: Eerdmans.

Laniak, T. S.
1998 *Shame and Honor in the Book of Esther.* Atlanta: Scholars Press.

2003 Esther. Pp. 169-267 in *Ezra, Nehemiah, Esther.* New International Biblical Commentary. Peabody, MA: Hendrickson.

Levenson, J. D.
1997 *Esther.* Old Testament Library. Louisville: Westminster/John Knox.

Luther, Martin
n.d. *The Table Talk of Martin Luther.* Translator, W. Hazlitt. Philadelphia: Lutheran Publication House.

McConville, J. C.
1985 *Ezra, Nehemiah, and Esther.* Daily Study Bible. Philadelphia: Westminster.

Millard, A. R.
1977 The Reliability of the Persian Names in Esther and the Reliability of the Hebrew Text. *Journal of Biblical Literature* 96:481–488.

Moore, C. A.
1971 *Esther.* Anchor Bible 7B. Garden City, NY: Doubleday.

Niditch, A.
1987 *Underdogs and Tricksters.* San Francisco: Harper.

Olmstead, A. T.
1948 *A History of the Persian Empire.* Chicago: University of Chicago Press.

Paton, L.
1908 *A Critical and Exegetical Commentary on the Book of Esther.* International Critical Commentary. Edinburgh: T&T Clark.

Pierce, R.
1992 The Politics of Esther and Mordecai. *Bulletin of Biblical Research* 2:75–89.

Sasson, J. M.
1987 Esther. Pp. 335–342 in *The Literary Guide to the Bible.* Editors, R. Alter and F. Kermode. Cambridge: Cambridge University Press.

Shea, W. H.
1976 Esther and History. *Andrews University Seminary Studies* 14:227–246.

Wenham, G. J.
1972 *Betûlāh*: A Girl of Marriageable Age. *Vetus Testamentum* 22:326–348.

Wiebe, J.
1991 Esther 4:14: Will Relief and Deliverance Arise for the Jews from Another Place? *Catholic Biblical Quarterly* 53:409–415.

Yamauchi, E.
1990 *Persia and the Bible.* Grand Rapids: Baker.

1992 Mordecai, the Persepolis Tablets, and the Susa Excavation. *Vetus Testamentum* 42:272–275.